Alexander Bain, George Grote, John Stuart Mill

Analysis of the Phenomena of the Human Mind

Volume 2

Alexander Bain, George Grote, John Stuart Mill

Analysis of the Phenomena of the Human Mind
Volume 2

ISBN/EAN: 9783337370923

Printed in Europe, USA, Canada, Australia, Japan

Cover: Foto ©Andreas Hilbeck / pixelio.de

More available books at **www.hansebooks.com**

ANALYSIS

OF THE PHENOMENA OF THE

HUMAN MIND

BY JAMES MILL

WITH NOTES ILLUSTRATIVE AND CRITICAL BY

ALEXANDER BAIN

ANDREW FINDLATER

AND

GEORGE GROTE

EDITED WITH ADDITIONAL 'NOTES BY

JOHN STUART MILL

IN TWO VOLUMES

VOL. II.

SECOND EDITION

LONDON

LONGMANS, GREEN, READER, AND DYER.

1878

CONTENTS

OF

THE SECOND VOLUME.

CHAPTER XXI.

CHAPTER XXII.

CHAPTER XXIII.

CHAPTER XXIV.

CHAPTER XXV.

ANALYSIS,

ETC.

CHAPTER XIV.

SOME NAMES WHICH REQUIRE A PARTICULAR EXPLANATION.

"Quam difficile sit inveteratas, eloquentissimorumque scriptorum authoritate confirmatas, opiniones, mentibus hominum excutere, non ignoro. Præsertim cum philosophia vera (id est accurata) orationis non modo fucum, sed etiam omnia fere ornamenta ex professo rejiciat: cumque scientiæ omnis fundamenta prima non modo speciosa non sint, sed etiam humilia, arida, et pene deformia videantur."—*Hobbes Comput. sive Logica*, cap. i. s. I.

WE have now seen that, in what we call the mental world, Consciousness, there are three grand classes of phenomena, the most familiar of all the facts with which we are acquainted,—SENSATIONS, IDEAS, and the TRAIN OF IDEAS. We have examined a number of the more complicated cases of Consciousness ; and have found that they all resolve themselves into the three simple elements, thus enumerated. We also found it necessary to shew, for what ends, and in what manner, marks were contrived of sensations and ideas, and by what combinations they were made to represent,

expeditiously, trains of those states of consciousness.
Some marks or names, however, could not be explained, till some of the more complicated states of
consciousness were unfolded ; these also are names so
important, and so peculiar in their mode of signification, that a very complete understanding of them is required.   It is to the consideration of these remarkable
cases of Naming that we now proceed.[1]

---

[1] Under the modest title of an explanation of the meaning
of several names, this chapter presents us with a series of
discussions of some of the deepest and most intricate questions
in all metaphysics.   Like Plato, the author introduces his
analysis of the most obscure among the complex general conceptions of the human mind, in the form of an enquiry into
the meaning of their names.   The title of the chapter gives a
very inadequate notion of the difficulty and importance of the
speculations contained in it, and which make it, perhaps, the
profoundest chapter of the book.   It is almost as if a treatise
on chemistry were described as an explanation of the names
air, water, potass, sulphuric acid, &c.—*Ed.*

SECTION I.

NAMES OF NAMES.

It is of great importance to distinguish this class of terms; to understand well the function which they perform, and to mark the subdivisions into which they are formed. There is not, however, such difficulty in the subject as to require great minuteness in the exposition.

As we have occasion to speak of *things;* animals, vegetables, minerals; so we have occasion to speak of the *marks,* which we are under the necessity of using, in order to record or to communicate our thoughts respecting them. We cannot record or communicate our thoughts respecting names, as man, tree, horse, to walk, to fly, to eat, to converse, without marks for them. We proceed in the case of names, as we do in other cases. We form them into classes, some more, some less, comprehensive, and give a name to each.

We have one name, so general as to include them all; Word. That is not a name of any *thing.* It is a name of the marks which we employ for discourse; and a name of them all. *John* is a word, *mountain* is a word, *to run* is a word, *above* is a word, and so on.

They are divided into classes, differently for different purposes. The grammarian, who regards chiefly the concatenation of words in sentences, divides them into *noun, adjective, pronoun, verb, adverb, preposition, conjunction ;* these words are none of them names of things. *Noun* is not a name of a "thing;" it is a name of a " class of words," as John, James, man, ox, tree, water, love, hatred ; the same is the case with adjective, verb, and so of the rest.

The philosopher makes another division of them, adapted to his purposes, which has a more particular reference to their mode of signification. Thus, he divides them into universal, and particular ; concrete, and abstract ; positive, and negative ; equivocal, and univocal ; relative, and absolute ; and so on.

It is very easy to see that the word " universal," for example, is not a name of a *thing.* Things are all individual, not general. The *name,* " man," is a " universal," because it applies to every individual of a class ; for the same reason the *name* " ox," the *name* " horse," the *name* " dog," and so on, are *universals.* The words, " genus" and " species" are synonymous with " universal ;" of course they also are names of names. Such is the word " number." " One," " two," " one hundred," " one thousand," are " numbers ;" in other words, " number" is a general name for each and all of those other names.

Beside our names for names singly, we have occasion to name combinations of names. Thus we have the name " predication." This is a name for the combination of three words, " subject," " predicate," and " copula." We have the name " sentence," which never can be less, implicitly or explicitly, than a predication, but is often more. The same is the account of the word " definition." We have the names " speech," " oration," " sermon," " conversation," all of them names for a series of sentences. We have

also names of written discourse, such as a "volume,"
a "book," a "chapter," a "section," a "paragraph."²

---

² A right understanding of the words which are names of
names, is of great importance in philosophy. The tendency
was always strong to believe that whatever receives a name
must be an entity or being, having an independent existence
of its own ; and if no real entity answering to the name could
be found, men did not for that reason suppose that none
existed, but imagined that it was something peculiarly abstruse
and mysterious, too high to be an object of sense. The meaning of all general, and especially of all abstract terms, became
in this way enveloped in a mystical haze ; and none of these
have been more generally misunderstood, or have been a more
copious source of futile and bewildering speculation, than
some of the words which are names of names. Genus, Species,
Universal, were long supposed to be designations of sublime
hyperphysical realities ; number, instead of a general name of
all numerals, was supposed to be the name, if not of a concrete
thing, at least of a single property or attribute.

This class of names was well understood and correctly
characterized by Hobbes, of whose philosophy the distinction
between names of names and of things was a cardinal point.—
Ed.

SECTION II.

RELATIVE TERMS.

The explanation of Relative Terms will run to a considerable length. The mode in which they are employed as marks is peculiar; and has suggested the belief of something very mysterious in that which is marked by them. It is therefore necessary to be minute in exhibiting the combinations of ideas of which they are the names.

One peculiarity of Relative Terms, which it is necessary for us to begin with noticing, is, that they always exist in pairs. There is no relative without its correlate, either actual or implied. Thus, we have *Father* and *Son; Husband* and *Wife; Master* and *Servant; Subject* and *King;* also *High* and *Low; Right* and *Left; Antecedent* and *Consequent.*

In these cases of relative pairs, the two names are two different words; in other cases, one word serves for both names. Of this sort are the words *Brother, Sister, Cousin, Friend, Like, Equal,* and so on. When we say that John is brother, we always mean of some one else, as James, whom we also call brother. We call Jane the sister of Ann, as we call Ann the sister of Jane. When we say that A is equal to B, we signify, by the same expression, that B is equal to A : and so on.

It is always to be remembered, that, in speaking, we are only indicating our own trains; and that of course every word is a mark of some part of a train. The parts of our trains to which we give relative names, are either simple, or complex. The simple, are either the simple sensations, or the ideas of those sensations. The complex, are either those clusters of simple ideas which we call the ideas of objects, because they correspond with clustered sensations ; or they are the clusters which the mind puts together arbitrarily for its own purposes.

If it is asked, why we give names in pairs ? The general answer immediately suggests itself ; it is because the things named present themselves in pairs ; that is, are joined by association. But as many things are joined in pairs by association, which do not receive relative names, the cause may still be inquired of the classification. What is the reason that some pairs do, while many more do not, receive relative names ? The cause is the same by which we are guided in imposing other names. As the various combinations of ideas are far too numerous for naming, and we are obliged to make a selection, we name those which we find it of most importance to have named, omitting the rest. It is a question of convenience, solved by experience. It will be seen more distinctly hereafter that relative names are one of the contrivances for epitomising ; and that they enable us to express ourselves with fewer words than we should be able to do without them.[3]

---

[3] No part of the Analysis is more valuable than the simple explanation here given of a subject which has seemed so mysterious to some of the most enlightened and penetrating philosophers, down even to the present time. The only difference between relative names and any others consist in their

I. The only, or at least the principal, occasions, for naming simple sensations, or simple ideas, in pairs, seem to be these :

1. When we take them into simultaneous view, as such and such ;

2. When we take them into simultaneous view, as antecedent and consequent.

II. The principal occasions on which we name the complex ideas, called objects, in pairs, are these four :

---

being given in pairs ; and the reason of their being given in pairs is not the existence between two things, of a mystical bond called a Relation, and supposed to have a kind of shadowy and abstract reality, but a very simple peculiarity in the concrete fact which the two names are intended to mark.

In order to make quite clear the nature of this peculiarity, it will be desirable to advert once more to the double mode of signification of concrete general names, viz. that while they denote (or are names of) objects, they connote some fact relating to those objects. The fact connoted by any name, relative or not, is always of the same nature ; it is some bodily or mental feeling, or some set of bodily or mental feelings, accompanying or produced by the object. But in the case of the ordinary names of objects, this fact concerns one object only, or rather only that one object and the sentient mind. The peculiarity in the case of relative names is, that the fact connoted concerns two objects, and cannot be understood without thinking of them both. It is a phenomenon in which two objects play a part. There is no greater mystery in a phenomenon which concerns two objects, than in a phenomenon which concerns only one. For example ; the fact connoted by the word cause, is a fact in which the thing which is the cause, is implicated along with another thing which is the effect. The facts connoted by the word parent, and also by the word son or daughter, are a long series of phenomena of which both the parent and the child are parts ; and the series of phenomena

1. When we speak of them as having an order in space ;

2. When we speak of them as having an order in time ;

3. When we speak of them as agreeing or disagreeing in quantity ;

4. As agreeing or disagreeing in quality.

III. The occasions on which we name the complex ideas of our own formation in pairs, are,

---

would not be that which the name parent expresses, unless the child formed a part of it, nor would it be that which the name son or daughter expresses, unless the parent formed a part of it. Now, when in a series of phenomena of any interest to us two objects are implicated, we naturally give names expressive of it to both the objects, and these are relative names. The two correlative names denote two different objects, the cause and the effect, or the parent and son ; but though what they denote is different, what they connote is in a certain sense the same : both names connote the same set of facts, considered as giving one name to the one object, another name to the other. This set of facts, which is connoted by both the correlative names, was called by the old logicians the ground of the relation, *fundamentum relationis.* The *fundamentum* of any relation is the facts, fully set out, which are the reason of giving to two objects two correlative names. In some cases both objects seem to receive the same name ; in the relation of likeness, both objects are said to be like ; in the relation of equality, both are said to be equal. But even here the duality holds, on a stricter examination : for the first object (A) is not said to be like, absolutely, but to be like the second object (B) ; the second is not said to be like absolutely, but to be like the first. Now though " like " is only one name, " like A" is not the same name as " like B," so that there is really, in this case also, a pair of names.

From these considerations we see that objects are said to be

1. When we speak of them as composed of the same or different simple ideas ;

2. When we speak of them as antecedent and consequent.

Whatever it may be necessary to remark, respecting relative terms, will occur in the consideration of these several cases.

I.   1.   We speak of two sensations, as *Same* or *Different, Like* or *Unlike.*

These words are Relatives of the double signification ; each individual of the pair has the same name. When we say that sensation A is the " same" with

---

related, when there is any fact, simple or complex, either apprehended by the senses or otherwise, in which they both figure.   Any objects, whether physical or mental, are related, or are in a relation, to one another, in virtue of any complex state of consciousness into which they both enter; even if it be a no more complex state of consciousness than that of merely thinking of them together.   And they are related to each other in as many different ways, or in other words, they stand in as many distinct relations to one another, as there are specifically distinct states of consciousness of which they both form parts.   As these may be innumerable, the possible relations not only of any one thing with others, but of any one thing with the same other, are infinitely numerous and various. But they may all be reduced to a certain number of general heads of classification, constituting the different kinds of Relation : each of which requires examination apart, to ascertain what, in each case, the state of consciousness, the cluster or train of sensations or thoughts, really is, in which the two objects figure, and which is connoted by the correlative names. This examination the author accordingly undertakes: and thus, under the guise of explaining names, he analyses all the principal cases which the world and the human mind present, of what are called Relations between things. — *Ed.*

sensation B, we mean that B also is the "same" with A; "different," "like," and "unlike," have the same double application.

Another ambiguity needs to be noted in the word "same." When there are *two* things, they are not the *same* thing; for "same," in the strict sense of the word, means one thing, and that only. Here it means a great degree of likeness, a sense in which, with respect to sensations and ideas, it is very frequently used.

Of two sensations, or two ideas, we, in truth, can only say, that they are like or unlike; or, that the one comes first, the other after it.

It is now necessary to attend very carefully to what happens, when we say that two sensations are like, or that they are unlike.

First of all, we have the two sensations. But what is it to have two sensations? It is merely to be conscious of a change. But to be conscious of a change in sensation, is sensation. It is an essential part of the process. Without it we should not be sentient beings. To have sensation, and not to be conscious of any change, is to have but one sensation continued. We have already seen that this is a state which seems incapable of being distinguished from that of having no sensation. At any rate, what we mean by a sentient being, is not a being with one unvaried sensation, but a being with sensations continually varied; the varying being a necessary part of the having more sensations than one; and the varying, and the being conscious of the variation, being not two things, but one and the same thing. Having *two* sensations, therefore, is not only having sensation, but the only

thing which can, in strictness, be called having sensation ; and the having two, and knowing they are two,
which are not two things, but one and the same
thing, is not only sensation, and nothing else than
sensation, but the only thing which can, in strictness,
be called sensation.   The having a new sensation, and
knowing that it is new, are not two things, but one
and the same thing.[4]

The case between sensation and sensation, resembles
that between sensation and idea.   How do I know
that an idea is not a sensation ?   Who ever thought
of asking the question ?   Is not the having an idea,

---

[4] The author is here endeavouring to express the most
fundamental fact of the consciousness—the necessity of change,
or transition from one state to another in order to our being
conscious.   He approaches very near to, without exactly touching, the inference that all consciousness, all sensation, all
knowledge must be of *doubles ;* the state passed from and the
state passed to, are equally recognised by us.   Opening the
eyes to the light, for the first time, we know a contrast,—a
present light, a past privation—but for the one we should not
have known the other.   Any single thing is unknowable by
us ; its relative opposite is a part of its very existence.

In a former page it is stated that relative names are one of
the conveniences of epitomising.   This is a narrow view to
take of them.   They are an essential part of language ; they
are demanded by the intrinsic relativity of all nameable things.
If we have a thing called " light," we have also another thing
but for which light could not be known by us, " dark."   It is
expedient to have names for both elements of the mutually
dependent couple.   And so everywhere.   Language would be
insufficient for its purposes if it did not provide the means of
expressing the correlative (called also the negative) of every
thing named.—*B.*

and the knowing it as an idea, the same thing? The
having without the knowing is repugnant. The mis-
fortune is, that the word, know, has associations linked
with it, which have nothing to do with this case, but
which intrude themselves along with the word, and
make a complexity, where otherwise there would be
none.

This is a matter which deserves the greatest attention. One of the most unfortunate cases of the illusions, which the close association of ideas with words
has produced, is created by ideas clinging to words
when they ought to be disjoined from them, and mix-
ing themselves by that means with the ideas under
consideration, when they ought to be considered wholly
distinct from them. Nothing was of more importance, than that the phenomenon, to which we are
just now directing our attention, the very first ingredient in the great mental composition, should be
accurately understood, and nothing mixed up with it
which did not truly belong to it.

There is no doubt that in one of its senses, knowledge is synonymous with sensation. If I am asked
what is my knowledge of pain? I answer, the feeling
of it, the having it. The blind man has not the
knowledge of colours ; the meaning is, he has not the
sensations : if deaf also, he is without the knowledge,
that is, the sensations, of sounds : suppose him void of
all other sensations, you suppose him void of knowledge. In many cases, however, we arrive at knowledge, by certain steps ; by something of a process.
The word, know, is most frequently applied to those
cases. When we know, by mere sensation, we say we
see, we hear, and so on ; when we know by mere ideas,

or rather ideation, if we could use such a word, we
say we conceive, we think.   The word know, therefore, being almost constantly joined with the idea of
a process, it is exceedingly difficult, when we apply it
to sensation, not to have the idea of a process at the
same time ; and thus exceedingly difficult to conceive
that sensation, and knowing, in this case, are purely
synonymous.

As the knowing I have an idea, is merely having
the idea ; as the having a sensation, and knowing I
have a sensation ; the knowing, for example, that I
have the pain of the toothache, and the having that
pain ; are not two things, but one and the same
thing ; so the having a change of sensation, and
knowing I have it, are not two things but one and
the same thing.

Having a change, I have occasion to mark that
change.   The change has taken place in a train of
feelings.   I call the first part by one name, the last
by another, and the marking of the change is effected.
Suppose that, without any organ of sense but the eye,
my first sensation is red, my next green.   The whole
process is sensation.   Yet the green is not the red.
What we call making the distinction, therefore, has
taken place, and it is involved in the sensation.

My names, green, and red, thus applied, are absolute names.   The one has no reference to the other.
Suppose that after green, I have the sensations, blue,
yellow, violet, white, black ; and that I mark them
respectively by these names.   These are still absolute names.   Each marks a particular sensation, and
does nothing more.   But, now, suppose that, after my
sensations red, green, blue, &c., I have the sensation

red again ; that I recognise it as like the sensation I had first, and that I have a desire to mark that recognition ; it remains to explain what are the steps of this process.

Having the sensation a second time needs no explanation ; it is the same thing as having it the first. But what happens in recognising that it is similar to a former sensation?

Beside the *Sensation*, in this case, there is an *Idea*. The idea of the former sensation is called up by, that is, associated with, the new sensation. As having a sensation, and a sensation, and knowing them, that is, distinguishing them, are the same thing ; and having an idea, and an idea, is knowing them ; so, having an idea and a sensation, and distinguishing the cne from the other, are the same thing. But, to know that I have the idea and the sensation, in this case, is not all ; I observe, that the sensation is like the idea. What is this observation of likeness ? Is it any thing but that distinguishing of one feeling from another, which we have recognised to be the same thing as having two feelings ? As change of sensation is sensation ; as change, from a sensation to an idea, differs from change to a sensation, in nothing but this, that the second feeling in the latter change is an idea, not a sensation ; and as the passing from one feeling to another is distinguishing ; the whole difficulty seems to be resolved ; for undoubtedly the distinguishing differences and similarities, is the same thing ; a similarity being nothing but a slight difference.[5]   As

---

[5] More properly Similarity is " agreement in difference." Difference or discrimination is one thing, one element of know-

change from red to green, and knowing the change, or from a sensation of sight, to one of any other of the senses, the most different, is all sensation; so change from one shade of red to another, is assuredly sensation. Its being a different shade consists in my feeling of it, that is, in my sensation.

Passing from red to red, red, red, through a succession of distinguishable shades, is one train of pure sensation: passing from red to green, blue, tasting, smelling, hearing, touching, is another train of pure sensation; that these are not the same trains, but different trains, consists in their being felt to be so; they would not be different, but for the feeling: and that a feeling is different, and known to be so, are not two things, but one and the same thing. Having two such trains, I want marks to distinguish them. For this purpose, I invent the words " same," " similar," and their contraries; by means of which, my object is attained. I call the parts of a train, such as the first, " same," or " similar;" those of a train like the last, " different," " dissimilar."

By these relative terms, we name the sensations in pairs. When we say, same, we mean that sensations

---

ledge or cognition; Similarity or agreement in difference is another thing, the second or completing element of knowledge. The two work together in closest intimacy, but they should neither be looked upon as the same fact, nor as merely a various shading of the same fact. Without difference there would be no similarity; but similarity is difference and something more. At their roots or first origins, the two processes lie in almost undistinguishable closeness; but in their developments they run wide apart. No fact or attribute is known, or mentally possessed, without the union of many shocks of difference with many shocks of identity, or agreement in difference.—*B*.

A, and B, are the same ; different, that A, and B, are
different ; like and unlike, the same.   By these words
we have four pairs of relative terms.

A.	B.
same	same
different	different
like	like
unlike	unlike.

The feeling is perfectly analogous in the case of the
ideas of those sensations ; and the naming is the same.
Thus the idea of red, green, and so on, and the ideas
of the different shades of red are distinguished from
one another by the ideas themselves.   To have ideas
different and ideas distinguished, are synonymous expressions ; different and distinguished, meaning exactly
the same thing.

The sensations above mentioned, and their ideas,
have the same absolute names : thus, red is at once
the name of the sensation, and the name of the idea ;
green, at once the name of the sensation and the idea ;
sweet, at once the name of the sensation and the idea.
The relative terms, it is obvious, have the same extent
of application.   Same, different, like, and unlike, are
names of pairs of ideas, as well as pairs of sensations.

It seems, therefore, to be made clear, that, in applying to the simple sensations and ideas their absolute
names, which are names of classes, as red, green,
sweet, bitter ; and also applying to them names which
denote them in pairs, as such and such ; there is
nothing whatsoever but having the sensations, having
the ideas, and making marks for them.[6]

---

[6] The author commences his survey of Relations with the
most universal of them all, Likeness and Unlikeness ; and he

2. The only other relative terms applicable to simple sensations and ideas, are those which denote them as *Antecedent* and *Consequent.*

---

examines these as subsisting between simple sensations or ideas; for whatever be the true theory of likeness or unlikeness as between the simple elements, the same, in essentials, will serve for the likenesses or unlikenesses of the wholes compounded of them.

Examining, then, what constitutes likeness between two sensations (meaning two exactly similar sensations experienced at different times); he says, that to feel the two sensations to be alike, is one and the same thing with having the two sensations. Their being alike is nothing but their being felt to be alike ; their being unlike is nothing but their being felt to be unlike. The feeling of unlikeness is merely that feeling of change, in passing from the one to the other, which makes them two, and without which we should not be conscious of them at all. The feeling of likeness, is the being reminded of the former sensation by the present, that is, having the idea of the former sensation called up by the present, and distinguishing them as sensation and idea.

It does not seem to me that this mode of describing the matter explains anything, or leaves the likenesses and unlikenesses of our simple feelings less an ultimate fact than they were before. All it amounts to is, that likeness and unlikeness are themselves only a matter of feeling : and that when we have two feelings, the feeling of their likeness or unlikeness is inextricably interwoven with the fact of having the feelings One of the conditions, under which we have feelings, is that they are like and unlike : and in the case of simple feelings, we cannot separate the likeness or unlikeness from the feelings themselves. It is by no means certain, however, that when we have two feelings in immediate succession, the feeling of their likeness is not a third feeling which follows instead of being involved in the two. This question is expressly left open by Mr. Herbert Spencer, in his " Principles

I have sensation red, sensation green. Why I
mark them red, and green, or as " different," has
already been seen. What happens in marking them

---

of Psychology;" and I am not aware that any philosopher
has conclusively resolved it. We do not get rid of any difficulty by calling the feeling of likeness the same thing with the
two feelings that are alike : we have equally to postulate likeness and unlikeness as primitive facts —as an inherent distinction among our sensations ; and whichever form of phraseology
we employ makes no difference in the ulterior developments of
psychology. It is of no practical consequence whether we say
that a phenomenon is resolved into sensations and ideas, or
into sensations, ideas, and their resemblances, since under the
one expression as under the other the resemblance must be
recognised as an indispensable element in the compound.

When we pass from resemblance between simple sensations
and ideas, to resemblance between complex wholes, the process, though not essentially different, is more complicated, for
it involves a comparison of part with part, element with element, and therefore a previous discrimination of the elements.
When we judge that an external object, compounded of a
number of attributes, is like another external object; since they
are not, usually, alike in all their attributes, we have to take
the two objects into simultaneous consideration in respect to
each of their various attributes one after another : their colour,
to observe whether that is similar; their size, whether that is
similar ; their figure, their weight, and so on. It comes at last to
a perception of likeness or unlikeness between simple sensations:
but we reduce it to this by *attending* separately to one of the
simple sensations forming the one cluster, and to one of those
forming the other cluster, and if possible adjusting our organs of
sense so as to have these two sensations in immediate juxtaposition: as when we put two objects,of which we wish to compare the
colour, side by side, so that our sense of sight may pass directly
from one of the two sensations of colour to the other. This
act of attention directed successively to single attributes, blunts

as "antecedent" and "consequent" comes next to be considered.

A sensation, the moment it ceases, is gone for ever. When I have two sensations, therefore, A, and B, one first, the other following, sensation A is gone, before sensation B exists. But though *sensation* A is gone, its *idea* is not gone. Its idea, called up by association, exists along with sensation B, or the idea of sensation B. My knowing that the idea of sensation A is the idea of sensation A, is my having the idea. Having it, and knowing it, are not two things, but one and the same thing. *Having* the idea of sensation A, that is, having the idea of the immediate antecedent of sensation B, seems, also, to be the same thing with knowing it as the idea of that antecedent. Having sensation A, and after it sensation B, is mere sensation; and having the idea of sensation A, the immediate antecedent, called up by sensation B, the immediate consequent, is knowing it for that antecedent. The links of the train are three; 1, sensation A; 2, sensation B; 3, the idea of sensation A, in a certain order with B, called up by sensation B; and after this, NAMING.

The case appears mysterious, solely, from the want of words to express it clearly; and our confirmed habit of inattention to the process. Suppose, that

our feeling of the other attributes of the objects, and enables us to feel the likeness of the single sensations almost as vividly as if we had nothing but these in our mind. Having felt this likeness, we say that the sensations are like, and that the two objects are like in respect of those sensations : and continuing the process we pronounce them to be either like or unlike in each of the other sensations which we receive from them.—*Ed.*

instead of two sensations, A, and B, we have three, A, B, and C, in immediate succession. I recognise A, as the antecedent of B ; B, as the antecedent of C. What is the process? The idea of sensation A, is associated with sensation B ; and the idea of sensation B, is associated with sensation C. But sensation C, is not associated with the idea of sensation B solely, it is associated also with the idea of sensation A. It is associated, however, differently with the one and the other. It is associated with B immediately; it is associated with A, only through the medium of B; it calls up the idea of B, by its own associating power, and the idea of B, calls up the idea of A. This second state of consciousness is different from the first. The first is that in consequence of which B receives the name " Antecedent," and C the name " Consequent." When two sensations in a train are such, that, if one exists, it has the idea of the other along with it, by its immediate exciting power, and not through any intermediate idea ; the sensation, the idea of which is thus excited, is called the antecedent, the sensation which thus excites that idea, is called the consequent.

It is evident that the terms, "antecedent," and " consequent," are not applied in consequence of sensation merely, but in consequence of sensation joined with ideas. The antecedent sensation, which is past, must be revived by the consequent sensation, which is present. It is the peculiarity of this revival which procures it the name. If revived by any other sensation, it would not have that name.

The Clock strikes three. My feelings are, three sensations of hearing, in succession. How do I know

them to be three successive sensations ? The process
in this instance does not seem to be very difficult
to trace. The clock strikes one; this is pure sensation. It strikes two; this is a sensation, joined with
the idea of the preceding sensation, and the idea of
the feeling (also sensation), called change of sensation,
or passage from one sensation to another. After two,
the clock strikes three; there is, here, sensation, and
a double association; the third stroke is sensation;
that is associated immediately with the idea of the
second, and through the idea of the second, with the
idea of the first. It is observable, that these successive associations soon cease to afford distinct ideas;
they hardly do so beyond the second stage. When
the clock strikes, we may have distinct ideas of the
strokes, as far as three, hardly farther; we must then
have recourse to NAMING, and call the strokes, four,
five, six, and so on : otherwise we should be wholly
unable to tell how often the clock had struck.

In the preceding pairs of relative terms, we have
found only one name for each pair. Thus, when we
say of A and B, that A is similar to B, we say also,
that B is similar to A. We have now an instance of
a pair of relative terms, consisting not of the same,
but of different names. If we call A antecedent, we
call B consequent. The first class were called by the
ancient logicians, synonymous, the second heterony-
mous; we may call them more intelligibly, single-
worded, and double-worded, relatives.[7]

---

[7] The next relation which the author examines is that of
succession, or Antecedent and Consequent. And here again
we have one of the universal conditions to which all our feelings or states of consciousness are subject. Whenever we have

II. Having shewn what takes place in naming simple SENSATIONS, and simple IDEAS, in pairs, both as

---

more feelings than one, we must have them either simultaneously or in succession ; and when we are conscious of having them in succession, we cannot in any way separate or isolate the succession from the feelings themselves. The author attempts to carry the analysis somewhat farther. He says that when we have two sensations in the order of antecedent and consequent, the consequent calls up the idea of the antecedent ; and that this fact, that a sensation calls up the idea of another sensation directly, and not through an intermediate idea, *constitutes* that other sensation the antecedent of the sensation which reminds us of it—is not a *consequence* of the one sensation's having preceded the other, but is literally all we mean by the one sensation's having preceded the other. There seem to be grave objections to this doctrine. In the first place, there is no law of association by which a consequent calls up the idea of its antecedent. The law of successive association is that the antecedent calls up the idea of the consequent, but not conversely ; as is seen in the difficulty of repeating backwards even a form of words with which we are very familiar. We get round from the consequent to the antecedent by an indirect process, through the medium of other ideas ; or by going back, at each step, to the beginning of the train, and repeating it downwards until we reach that particular link. When a consequent directly recalls its antecedent, it is by synchronous association, when the antecedent happens to have been so prolonged as to coexist with, instead of merely preceding, the consequent.

The next difficulty is, that although the direct recalling of the idea of a past sensation by a present, without any intermediate link, does not take place from consequent to antecedent, it does take place from like to like : a sensation recalls the idea of a past sensation resembling itself, without the intervention of any other idea. The author, however, says, that " when two sensations in a train are such that if one exists, it

such and such, and as antecedent and consequent, we
come to the second case of relative terms, that of
naming the clusters, called EXTERNAL OBJECTS, in pairs.
The principal occasions of doing so we have said are
four.

1. When we speak of them, as they exist in the
synchronous order, that is, the order in space, we use
such relative terms as the following: high, low ; east,
west ; right, left ; hind, fore ; and so on.

It is necessary to carry along with us a correct idea
of what is meant by synchronous order, that is, the
order of simultaneous, in contradistinction to that of
successive, existence. The synchronous order is much
more complex than the successive. The successive

---

has the idea of the other along with it by its immediate exciting power, and not through any intermediate idea ; the
sensation, the idea of which is thus excited, is called the antecedent, the sensation which thus excites that idea is called the
consequent." If this therefore were correct, we should give
the names of antecedent and consequent not to the sensations
which really are so, but to those which recall one another by
resemblance.

Thirdly and lastly, to explain antecedence, *i.e.* the succession
between two feelings, by saying that one of the two calls up
the idea of the other, that is to say, is followed by it, is to
explain succession by succession, and antecedence by antecedence. Every explanation of anything by states of our
consciousness, includes as part of the explanation a succession
between those states ; and it is useless attempting to analyse
that which comes out as an element in every analysis we are
able to make. Antecedence and consequence, as well as likeness and unlikeness, must be postulated as universal conditions
of Nature, inherent in all our feelings whether of external or
of internal consciousness.—*Ed.*

order is all, as it were, in one direction. The synchronous is in every possible direction. The following
seems to be the best mode of conceiving it.

Take a single particle of matter as a centre. Other
particles may be aggregated to it, in the line of every
possible radius ; and as the radii diverge, and other
lines, tending to the centre, may be continually inter-
posed, to any number, particles may be aggregated in
those numberless directions. They may also be
aggregated in those directions to a less or a greater
extent. And they may be aggregated to an equal
extent in every direction ; or to a greater extent
in some of the directions, a less extent in others.
In the first case of aggregation they compose a globe ;
in the last, any other shape.

Every one of the particles in this aggregate, has a
certain order; first with respect to the centre particle ;
next with respect to every other particle. This order
is also called, the Position of the particle. In such an
aggregate, therefore, the positions are innumerable.
It is thence observable, that position is an exceedingly
complex idea ; for the position of each of those particles is its order with respect to every one of the
other innumerable particles ; it includes, therefore,
innumerable ingredients. Hence it is not wonderful
that, while viewed in the lump, it should seem obscure and mysterious.

Of positions, thus numberless, it is a small portion
only that have names. Bulk is a name for an aggregate of particles, greater, or less. Figure is only a
modification, or case, of bulk ; it is more or fewer
particles in such and such directions.

These things being explained, it now remains to

shew, of what copies of sensations, peculiarly com bined, the complex ideas in question are composed.

The simplest case of position, or synchronous order, is that of two or more particles in one direction. Let us take the particle, conceived as the centre particle, in a preceding supposition, and let us aggregate to it a number of particles, all in the direction of a single radius, one by one. We have first the centre particle, and one other, in juxta-position. This is the simplest case of synchronous order, and this is the simplest of all positions. Let us next aggregate a second particle ; we have now the centre particle, and two more. The position of the first of the aggregated particles with respect to the centre particle is contact, or juxta-position ; that of the second is not juxta-position, but position at the distance of a particle ; the next which is aggregated, is at the distance of two ; the next of three particles, and so on, to any extent.

Particles thus aggregated, all in the direction of a single radius from the first, constitute a line of less or greater length, according to the number of aggregated particles.

Line is a word of great importance ; because it is by that, chiefly, we express ourselves concerning synchronous order ; or frame names for positions. Now it happens, that Line has a duplicity of meaning, most unfortunate, because it has confounded two meanings, which it is of the highest importance to preserve distinct.

We have already remarked the distinction between concrete, and abstract, terms ; and explained wherein the difference of their signification consists. We have also observed, that though in very many cases, the concrete term, and the abstract term, are different words, as good and goodness, true and truth, there are many others in which the concrete and abstract terms are the same ; and this is the case, unhappily, with the word Truth itself, which is used in the concrete sense, as well as the abstract. Thus we call a proposition, a Truth ; in which phrase, the word Truth, means " True Proposition ;" and in this sense we talk of eternal truths, meaning, Propositions, always true. " Property," is another word, which is sometimes concrete, sometimes abstract. Thus, a man calls his horse, his field, his house, his property. In such phrases the word is concrete. He also says, he has a property in such and such things. In these phrases, it is abstract.

Of this ambiguity, the word Line is an instance. It is applied as well to what we call a physical line, as to what we call a mathematical line. In the first case, it is a concrete, or connotative term ; in the second case, it is an abstract or non-connotative term. Let us then conceive clearly the two meanings. The purest idea of a physical line, is that which we have already formed ; the aggregate of particle after particle, in the direction of a radius. When this aggregate of particles in this order is called a line, the word, line, is connotative ; it marks or notes the *direction*, but it also marks or connotes the *particles ;* it means the particles and the direction both ; it is, in short, the *concrete* term. When it is used as the *abstract* term, the connotation is left out. It marks the direction without marking the particles.

It is here necessary to call to mind, that abstract

terms derive their meaning wholly from their concretes ; and that by themselves they have absolutely
no meaning at all.   I know a green tree, a sweet
apple, a hard stone, but greenness without something
green, hardness without something hard, are just nothing at all.

The same, in its abstract sense, is the case with
line, though we have not words by which we can convey the conception with equal clearness.   If we had
an abstract term, separate from the concrete, the
troublesome association in question would have been
less indissoluble, and less deceptive.   If we had such
a word as Lineness, or Linth, for example, we should
have much more easily seen, that our idea is the idea
of the physical line ; and that linth without a line, as
breadth without something broad, length without
something long, are just nothing at all.[8]

---

[8] This conception of a geometrical line, as the abstract, of
which a physical line is the corresponding concrete, is scarcely
satisfactory.   An abstract name is the name of an attribute, or
property, of the things of which the concrete name is predicated.   It is, no doubt, the name of some part, some one or
more, of the sensations composing the concrete group, but not
of those sensations simply and in themselves ; it is the name
of those sensations regarded as belonging to some group.
Whiteness, the abstract name, is the name of the colour white,
considered as the colour of some physical object.   Now I do
not see that a geometrical line is conceived as an attribute of
a physical object.   The attribute of objects which comes nearest
to the signification of a geometrical line, is their length : but
length does not need any name but its own ; and the author
does not seem to mean that a geometrical line is the same
thing as length.   He seems to have fallen into the mistake of
confounding an abstract with an ideal.   The line which is

What are, then, the sensations, the ideas of which, in close association, we mark by the word line ?

Though it appears to all men that they see position, length, breadth, distance, figure ; it is nevertheless true, that what appear, in this manner, to be sensations of the eye, are Ideas, called up by association. This is an important phenomenon, which throws much light upon the darker involutions of human thought.

The sensations, whence are generated our ideas of synchronous order, are from two sources ; they are partly the sensations of touch, and partly those of which we have spoken under the name of muscular sensations, the feelings involved in muscular action.[9]

---

meant in all the theorems of geometry I take to be as truly concrete as a physical line ; it denotes an object, but one purely imaginary ; a supposititious object, agreeing in all else with a physical line, but differing from it in having no breadth. The properties of this imaginary line of course agree with those of a physical line, except so far as these depend on, or are affected by, breadth. The lines, surfaces, and figures contemplated by geometry are abstract, only in the improper sense of the term, in which it is applied to whatever results from the mental process called Abstraction. They ought to be called ideal. They are physical lines, surfaces, and figures, idealized, that is, supposed hypothetically to be perfectly what they are only imperfectly, and not to be at all what they are in a very slight, and for most purposes wholly unimportant, degree.—*Ed.*

[9] In attaining the ideas of synchronous order, which is another name for Space, or the Extended World, sight is a leading instrumentality. It is by sight more than by any other sense that we get somewhat beyond the strict limits of the law of the successiveness of all our perceptions. Although we can *distinctly* see only a limited spot at one instant, we can couple

A line, we have said, is an order of particles, contiguous one to another, in the direction of a radius from one particle. Let us begin from this one particle, and trace our sensations. One particle may be an object of touch ; it may be felt, as we call it, and nothing more ; it may, at the same time, give the sensation of resistance, which we have already described as a feeling seated in the muscles, just as sound is a feeling in the ear. Resistance, is force applied to force. What we feel, is the act of the muscle. Without that, no resistance. This state of consciousness is, in reality, what we mark by the name. It is, at the same time, a state of consciousness not a little obscure ; because we habitually overlook many of the sensations of which it is composed ; because it is, in itself, very complex ; and because it is entangled with a number of extraneous associations.

We have already remarked the habit we acquire of not attending to the sensations which are seated in the muscles, of attending only to the occasions of them, and the effects of them ; that is, their antecedents, and consequents ; overlooking the intermediate sensations. In marking, therefore, or assigning our names, it seems to be rather the occasions and effects, the antecedents and consequents, than the sensations themselves, which are named. The word resistance is thus the name of a very complex

---

with this a vague perception of an adjoining superficies. This is an important sign of co-existence, as contrasted with succession, and enters with various other signs into the very complex notion of the author's synchronous order, otherwise called the Simultaneous or Co-existing in Space.—*B*.

idea.[10]   It is the name ; first, of the feelings which we
have when we say we feel resistance ; secondly, of the occasions, or antecedents, of those feelings ; and, thirdly,
of their consequents.   The feelings intermediate between the antecedents and consequents, are themselves
complex.   There are two kinds of sensations included
in them ; the sensation of touch, and the muscular
sensations ; and there is something more.   When we
move a muscle, we Will to move it.   This state of
consciousness, the Will to move it, is part of the feeling of the motion.   What that state of consciousness,
called the Will, is, we have not yet explained.   At
present we speak of it merely as an element in the
compound.   Of what elements it is itself compounded
we shall see hereafter.   In the idea of resistance, then,
there is the will to move the muscles, the sensations
in the muscles, the occasion or antecedent of those
feelings, and the effects or consequents of them.   And
there is the common complexity attending all generical
terms, that of their including all possible varieties.

These things being explained, the learner will now
be able to trace, without error, the formation of one
of the most important of all our ideas, that of resis-

---

[10] Still, when we apply an analysis to the complex facts indicated by the name, we come to a simple as well as ultimate
experience, which is correctly signified by the name Resistance.
The feeling of muscular energy expended is in all likelihood
an absolutely elementary feeling of the mind ; and the form of
this feeling that is least complicated or mixed up with other
sensibilities is what the word Resistance most usually expresses,
namely, the dead strain, that is energy without leading to movement, or causing movement in such a slight degree as not to
depart from the essential peculiarity of expended force.—B.

tance, or pressure. We touch one thing, butter, for
instance ; it yields to the finger, after a slight pressure;
that is, a certain feeling of ours. The will to move
the muscles, and the sensations in the muscles, are
both included in that feeling ; but, for shortness, we
shall speak of them, through the present exposition,
under one name, as the feelings or sensations in the
muscles. As we call the butter yellow, on account of
a feeling of sight ; odorous, on account of a feeling of
smell ; sapid, on account of a feeling of taste ; so we
call it soft, on account of a feeling in our muscles.
We touch a stone, as we touched the butter, and it
yields not, after the strongest pressure we can apply.
As we called the butter soft, on account of one muscular feeling, we call the stone hard, on account of
another. The varieties of these feelings are innumerable. Only a small portion of them have received
names. The feeling upon pressure of butter, is one
thing ; of honey, another ; of water, another ; of air,
another ; of flesh, one thing ; of bone, another. We
mark them as we can, by the terms soft, more soft,
less soft ; hard, more hard, less hard, and so on. We
have great occasion, however, for a word which shall
include all these different words. As we have " coloured" to include all the names of sensations of sight ;
" touch" all the names of sensations of touch, and so
on ; we invent the word " resisting," which includes
all the words, soft, hard, and so on, by which any of
the sensations of pressure are denoted.

Such, then, are the feelings which we are capable
of receiving from the particle with which we may suppose a line of particles to commence. These feelings,
in passing along the line, we should receive in succes-

sion from each, if the tactual sense were sufficiently fine to distinguish particles in contact from one another. It has not, however, this perfection. Even sight cannot distinguish minute intervals. If a red-hot coal is whirled rapidly round, though the coal is present at only one part of the circle at each instant, the whole is one continuous red. If the seven prismatic colours are made to pass rapidly in order before the eye, they appear not distinct colours, but one uniform white. In like manner, in passing from one to another, in a line of particles, there is no feeling of interval; there is the feeling we call continuity; that is, absence of interval.

The sensations, then, the ideas of which combined compose the idea which we mark by the word line, may thus be traced. The tactual feeling, and the feeling of resistance, derivable from every particle, attend the finger in every part of its progress along the line. What is there besides? To produce the progress of the finger, there is muscular action; that is to say, there are the feelings combined in muscular action. That we may exclude extraneous ideas as much as possible, let us suppose, that, when a person first makes himself acquainted with a line, he has the sense of touch, and the muscular sensations, without any other sense. He has one state of feeling, when the finger, which touches the line, is still; another, when it moves. He has also one state of feeling from one degree of motion, another from another. If he has one state of feeling from the finger carried along, as far as it can extend, he has another feeling when it is only carried half as far, and so on.

It is extremely difficult to speak of these feelings

precisely, or to draw by language those who are not accustomed to the minute analysis of their thoughts, to conceive them distinctly; because they are among the feelings, as we have before remarked, which we have acquired the habit of not attending to, or rather, have lost the power of attending to.

It is certain, however, that by sensation alone we become acquainted with lines; that in every different contraction of the muscles there is a difference of sensation; and that of the tactual feeling, and the feelings of the contracted muscles, all the feelings which constitute our knowledge of a line are composed.

As, after certain repetitions of a particular sensation of sight, a particular sensation of smell, a particular sensation of sight, and so on, received in a certain order, I give to the combined ideas of them, the name rose, the name apple, the name fire, and the like; in the same manner, after certain repetitions of particular tactual sensations, and particular muscular sensations, received in a certain order, I give to the combined ideas of them, the name Line. But when I have got my idea of a line, I have also got my idea of extension. For what is extension, but lines in every direction? physical lines, if real, tactual extension; mathematical lines, if mathematical, that is, abstract, extension.

It would be tedious to pursue the analysis of extension farther. And I trust it is not necessary; because the application of the same method to the remaining cases, appears completely obvious. Take plane surface for example. It is composed of all the lines which can be drawn in a particular plane; the idea of it, therefore, is derived from the tactual feeling, and the feeling of resistance, combined with the mus-

cular feelings involved in the motion of the finger in
every direction which it can receive on a plane.

Let us now take some of the words which, along
with the synchronous order, connote objects in pairs.
The names of this sort are not very numerous. High,
and low, right, and left, hind, and fore, are examples.
These, it is obvious, are names of the principal directions from the human body as a centre. The order
of objects, the most frequently interesting to human
beings, is, of course, their order with respect to their
own bodies. What is over the head, gets the name
of high ; what is below the feet, gets the name of low ;
and so on. Of the pairs which are connoted by those
words, the human body is always one. The words,
right, left, hind, fore, when they denote the object so
called, always connote the body in respect to which
they are right, left, hind, fore. We have already
noticed the cases in which the objects, thus named in
pairs, have each a separate name, as father, son ; also
those in which both have the same name, as sister,
brother. We have here another case, which deserves
also to be particularly marked, that in which only one
of them has a name. The human body, which is
always one of the objects named, when we call things
right, left, hind, fore, and so on, has no corresponding
relative name. The reason is sufficiently obvious ;
this, being always one of the pair, cannot, the other
being named, be misunderstood.

For the complete understanding of these words, it
does not appear that any thing remains to be explained. If one line, proceeding from a central particle,
be understood, every line, which can proceed from
it, is also understood. If that central point be a part

of the human body, it is plain that as the hand, passing along a line in a certain direction from that centre,
has certain muscular actions, passing along in another
direction, it has muscular actions somewhat different.
When we say muscular actions somewhat different,
we say muscular feelings somewhat different. Difference of feeling, when important, needs difference of
naming.

A particular case of association is here to be remarked; and it is one which it is important for the
learner to fix steadfastly in his memory.

We never perceive, what we call an object, except in
the synchronous order. Whatever other sensations
we receive, the sensations of the synchronous order,
are always received along with them. When we
perceive a chair, a tree, a man, a house, they are always
situated so and so, with respect to other objects. As
the sensations of positions are thus always received
with the other sensations of an object, the idea of
Position is so closely associated with the idea of the
object, that it is wholly impossible for us to have the
one idea without the other. It is one of the most
remarkable cases of indissoluble association; and is
that feeling which men describe, when they say that
the idea of space forces itself upon their understandings,
and is necessary."

---

[11] Under the head, as before, of Relative Terms, we find
here an analysis of the important and intricate complex ideas
of Extension and Position. It will be convenient to defer any
remarks on this analysis, until it can be considered in conjunction with the author's exposition of the closely allied subjects
of Motion and Space.—*Ed.*

2. We come now to the case of naming OBJECTS in pairs, on account of the Successive Order.

We have had occasion to observe that there is nothing in which human beings are so deeply interested, as the Successive Order of objects. It is the successive order upon which all their happiness and misery depends; and the synchronous order is interesting to them, chiefly on account of its connection with the successive.

When we speak of objects, it is necessary to remember, that it is sensations, not ideas, to which we are then directing our attention. All our sensations, we say, are derived from objects ; in other words, object is the name we give to the antecedents of our sensations. And, reciprocally, all our knowledge of objects is the sensations themselves. We have the sensations, and that is all. A knowledge, therefore, of the successive order of objects, is a knowledge of the successive order of our sensations ; of all the pleasures, and all the pains, and all the feelings intermediate between pleasure and pain, of which the body is susceptible.

Of successions, that is, the order of objects as antecedent and consequent, some are constant, some not constant. Thus, a stone dropped in the air always falls to the ground. This is a case of constancy of sequence. Heavy clouds drop rain, but not always. This is a case of casual sequence.[12] Human life is

---

[12] This is surely an improper use of the word Casual. Sequences cannot be exhaustively divided into invariable and casual, or (as by the author a few pages further on) into constant and fortuitous. Heavy clouds, though they do not always

deeply interested in ascertaining the constant sequences
of all the objects from which human sensations are
derived. The great business of philosophy is to find
them out ; and to record them, in the form most convenient for acquiring the knowledge of them, and for
applying it.

In the successions of objects, it very often happens,
that what appear to us to be the immediate antecedent
and consequent, are not immediately successive, but
are separated by several intermediate successions.
Thus, the falling of a spark on gunpowder, and the
explosion of the gunpowder, appear antecedent and
consequent ; but several successions in reality intervene ; various decompositions, and compositions,
in which, indeed, all the sequences cannot as yet be
traced. Most of the successions, which we are called
upon to notice and to name, are in the same situation.
We fix upon two conspicuous points in a chain of
successions, and the intermediate ones are either overlooked, or unknown.

Thus, we name Doctor and Patient, the two extremities of a pretty long succession of objects. The
Doctor is not the immediate antecedent of any change
in the patient. He is the immediate antecedent of a
certain conception, of which the consequent is, writing
a prescription ; the consequent of this, is the sending

---

drop rain, are not connected with it by mere accident, as the
passing of a waggon might be. They are connected with it
through causation : they are one of the conditions on which,
when united, rain is invariably consequent, though it is not
invariably consequent on that single condition. This distinction is essential to any system of Inductive Logic, in which it
recurs at every step.—*Ed.*

it to the apothecary; the consequent of that, is the apothecary's reading it, and so on; the whole composing a multitudinous train. Doctor and Patient, therefore, are not only two paired names of two paired objects, but names of all the successions between the one and the other. Doctor and Patient, therefore, properly speaking, are to be considered one name, though made up of two parts. Taken together, they are the name of the complex idea of a considerable train of sequences, of which a particular man is one extremity, a particular man another; just as navigation is the single-worded name of the complex idea of a very long train, of which the extremities are not particularly marked. If you say, navigation from the Thames to the Ganges, you have a many-worded name, by which the extremities of this long train are particularly marked.

The relative terms, Father and Son, are obviously included in this explanation. They are the two extremities of a train of great length and intricacy, very imperfectly understood. They also, both together, compose, as may easily be seen, but one name. Father is a word which connotes Son, and whether Son is expressed or not, the meaning of it is implied. In like manner Son connotes Father; and, stripped of that connotation, is without a meaning. Taken together, therefore, they are one name, the name of the complex idea of that train of which father is the one extremity, son the other.[13]

---

[13] It seems hardly a proper expression to say that Physician and Patient, or that Father and Son, are one name made up of two parts. When one of the parts is a name of one person

Brother and Brother are a pair of relative terms marking a still more complex idea. Two brothers are two sons of the same Father; taken together, they are, therefore, marks of all that Son, taken twice, is capable of marking. Son, as we have just seen, always implies Father; and, taken together, they are the name of a train. The relatives, therefore, brother and brother, are the compound name; two brothers, are the name of the train marked by the term, Father and Son, taken twice, the prior extremity of the train being the same in both cases, the latter different.

The above terms, Father and Son, Brother and

---

and the other part is the name of another, it is difficult to see how the two together can be but one name. Father and Son are two names, denoting different persons: but what the author had it in his mind to say, was that they connote the same series of facts, which series, as the two persons are both indispensable parts of it, gives names to them both, and is made the foundation or *fundamentum* of an attribute ascribed to each.

With the exception of this questionable use of language, which the author had recourse to because he had not left himself the precise word Connote, to express what there is of real identity in the signification of the two names; the analysis which follows of the various complicated cases of relation seems philosophically unexceptionable. The complexity of a relation consists in the complex composition of the series of facts or phenomena which the names connote, and which is the *fundamentum relationis*. The names signify that the person or thing, of which they are predicated, forms part of a group or succession of phenomena along with the other person or thing which is its correlate: and the special nature of that group or series, which may be of extreme complexity, constitutes the speciality of the relation predicated.—*Ed.*

Brother, are imposed on account of sequences which are passed. I do not at this moment recollect any relative terms imposed on account of sequences purely future. The terms, Buyer and Seller, are sometimes, indeed, used in a sense wholly future; when they mean persons having something to buy and something to sell : but they are also used in a sense wholly passed, when they signify persons who have effected purchase and sale. We have, however, many relative terms on account of trains which are partly passed and partly future. Thus, Lender and Borrower, are imposed partly on account of the passed train included in the contract of lending and borrowing ; partly on account of the future train implied in the repayment of the money. The words Debtor and Creditor are names of the same train, partly passed and partly future.

The relative terms, Husband and Wife, are of the same class ; the name of a train partly passed, to wit, that implied in entering into the nuptial contract ; and partly future, to wit, all the events expected to flow out of that contract. Master and Servant are imposed, on account of a train partly passed and partly future ; the train of entering into the compact of master and servant, and the train of acts which flow out of it. King and Subject are the name of a train similarly divided; first, the train which led to the will of obeying on the part of the people, the will of commanding on the part of the king ; secondly, the trains which grow out of these wills.

Owner and Property are relative terms, or terms which connote one another. They also are imposed on account of a train partly passed and partly future. The part which is passed is the train implied in the circumstances of the acquisition, whether inheritance, gift, labour, or purchase. The part which is future is the train implied in the use which the owner may make of the property.

Of the terms which denote objects in successive pairs, several are very general. Thus we have antecedent and consequent, which are applicable to any parts of any train. Prior and Posterior, are nearly of the same import. First and Last, are applicable to the two extremities of any train. Second, third, fourth, and so on, are applicable to the contiguous parts of any train.

We have remarked, above, that successions of objects are to be distinguished into two remarkable kinds; that of the successions which are fortuitous, and that of the successions which are constant. Names to mark the antecedent and consequent in all constant successions, which are things of such importance to us, were found of course indispensable. Cause and Effect, are the names we employ. In all constant successions, Cause is the name of the antecedent, Effect the name of the consequent. And, beside this, it has been proved by philosophers,* that these names denote absolutely nothing.

It is highly necessary to be apprized, that each of the two names, Cause and Effect, has a double meaning. They are used, sometimes in the concrete sense, sometimes in the abstract. By this ambiguity,

---

* Chiefly by Dr. Brown, of Edinburgh, in a work entitled "Inquiry into the Relation of Cause and Effect;" one of the most valuable contributions to science for which we are indebted to the last generation.—(*Author's Note.*)

ideas are confounded, which it is of the greatest importance to preserve distinct. When we say, the sun
is the Cause of light, cause is concrete; the meaning
is, that the sun always causes light. When we say
that ice is the Effect of cold air, effect is concrete;
the meaning is, that ice is effected by cold air.
"Cause," in these cases, is merely a short name for
"causing object," "Effect," a short name for "caused
object." In abstract discourse, on the other hand,
Cause and Effect are often used in the abstract sense,
in which cases Cause means the same thing as would
be meant by CAUSINGNESS; Effect, the same as would
be meant by CAUSEDNESS. They are merely the connotative or concrete terms, with the connotation dropped.

As the abstract terms have no meaning, except as
they refer to the concrete, it is in the concrete sense I
shall always use the words Cause and Effect, unless
when I give notice to the contrary.

Other terms, pairing the parts of a train, take parts
more or less distant; first and last, take the most
distant; father and son, take parts at a considerable
distance; cause and effect, on the other hand, mean
always the proximate parts. It does not, indeed,
happen, that we always apply them to the proximate parts; because the intermediate sequences are
often unknown, at other times overlooked. They are
always, however, applied to the parts regarded as
proximate. For we do not, strictly speaking, say,
that any thing is the cause of a thing, when it is only
the cause of another thing, which is the cause of that
thing; still less, when there is a series of causes and
effects, before you arrive at that which you have
marked as *the* effect, because the ultimate one. In

all the inquiries of philosophers into causes, it is the antecedent and consequent, really proximate, which is the object of their pursuit.

We have observed, in the case of the relative terms, applied to objects as successive, that the words, properly speaking, form but one name,—that of the complex idea of a train of less or greater length : thus, Doctor and Patient is a name ; Father and Son is a name ; each denoting a train of which two individuals are the principal parts.   In like manner, the relative terms Cause and Effect, taken together, are but one name, the name of a short train, that of one antecedent and one consequent, regarded as proximate, and constant.

3.   We have now shewn, in what manner the principal Relative Terms are applied, when we have to speak of OBJECTS as having order in Space, and when we have to speak of them as having order in Time. We proceed to shew in what manner they are applied, when we have to speak of objects as differing in Quantity, or differing in Quality ; and first, as differing in Quantity.

We apply the word Quantity, in a very general manner ; to things, which have the greatest diversity. Thus, we use the word quantity, when we speak of extension ; we use the word quantity, when we speak of weight ; we use it, when we speak of motion ; we use it, when we speak of heat ; we use it, in short, on almost every occasion, on which we can use the word degree.   Of course, it represents not one idea, but many ideas, some of which have the greatest diversity.

The relative terms, which we co-apply with quantity, are equal, unequal, or some particular case included under these more general terms ; as, more heavy, less heavy : more strong, less strong ; whole, part ; and so on.

When quantity is applied to extent, it may be extent either in one, or more, or every direction; it may mean either quantity in line, quantity in surface, or quantity in bulk. Accordingly, we can say, equal, or unequal, lines ; equal, or unequal, surfaces ; equal, or unequal, bulks.

Line is the simplest case ; the explanation of it will, therefore, facilitate the rest. We have already traced the sensations, which constitute our knowledge of a line. We have seen that they are certain sensations of touch, combined with the muscular sensations involved in extending the arm.

As the sensations, involved in extending the arm so far, are not the same with those which are involved in extending it farther ; and as the having different sensations, and distinguishing them, are not two things, but one and the same thing ;—as often as I have those two cases of sensation, I distinguish them from one another ; and, distinguishing them from one another, I require names to mark them. The first I mark, by the word, short; the other, by the word, long. As I call a line long, from extending my arm so far ; that is, from the sensations involved in extending it ; I call it longer from extending it farther. After experience of a number of lines, there are some which I call long, long, long, one after another, to any amount ; others which I call longer, longer, longer ; others which I call short, short, short ; and so on.

When we have perceived the sensations, on account

of which we call lines long, longer, short, shorter, we can be at no loss for the knowledge of those, on account of which we call them equal, and unequal. It is to be observed, that in applying the words long, longer, short, shorter, minute differences are not named. They cannot be named. The names would be too numerous. A general mark, however, may be invented, to shew when there is even a minute difference, and when there is not. When there is not, we call the two lines equal; when there is, we call them unequal.

We shall presently see, when we come to trace the ideas, which the class of words, called numbers, are employed to mark, what distinction of sensation it is which is marked by the words, one, and two. In the mean time, it is easy to see, that the case of sensation, when we trace one line, with the hand, and then another, is different from the case of sensation when we trace one line only, or even the same line twice; and this diversity needs marks to distinguish it. It is true, that in tracing one line, and then another, and marking the distinction, there is something more than sensation, there is also memory. But to this ingredient in the compound, after the explanation which has already been given of memory, it is not, at present, necessary particularly to advert.

When it is seen, what are the sensations which are marked by the terms longer and shorter, applied to a line, it will not be difficult to see what are the sensations, which are marked by the terms, part, and whole.

The terms, a part, and whole, imply division. Of course, the thing precedes the name. Men divided, before they named the act, or the consequences of the

act.   In the act of division, or in the results of it, no
mystery has ever been understood to reside.   It is of
importance to remark, that the word division, in its
ordinary acceptation, includes, and thence confounds,
things which very much need to be distinguished.   It
includes the will, which is the antecedent of the act;
the act itself; and the results of the act.   At present
we may leave the will aside; it will be explained
hereafter ; and, as it is not the act, but the antecedent
of the act, the consideration of it is not required for
the present purpose.

The act of dividing, like all the other acts of our
body, consists in the contraction and relaxation of
certain muscles.   These are known to us, like every
thing else, by the feelings.   The act, as act, is the
feelings ; and only when confounded with its results,
is it conceived to be any thing else.   If it be said,
that the contraction of the muscles of my arm, is
something more in me than feelings, because I see
the motion of my arm ; it is to be observed, that this
seeing, this sensation of sight, is not the act, but one
of its results ; the feelings of the act are the antecedent ; this sensation of sight one of the consequents.

In the act of dividing a line, as in the act, already
analysed, of tracing a line, there is a feeling of touch,
and there is also a muscular feeling.   There may be
more or less of cohesion in the parts of the line ; and
thence, more or less of what we call muscular force,
required to disunite them.   Of course, what we call
more or less of force, are only names for different
states of feeling.   The states of feeling which we
mark by the term, force, being antecedent, all the rest

are consequents of this antecedent. The disunion of
the parts of one line is attended with a certain muscular feeling ; I call the feeling a small force. That
of another line is attended with a muscular feeling
somewhat different ; I call it a greater force ; and so
on. This muscular feeling, however, has various accompaniments ; which are closely associated with the
idea of the act, and with its name. Thus there is the
sight of the line, there is the sight of the hands in
the act of disruption, and there is the sight of the
line after it is divided. The term division, as we
have mentioned before, includes all ; the muscular
feeling, the sight of the line before division, and the
sight of it after. I need a pair of names for the line
before division, and the line after. I call the one
whole, the other parts. Like other relative terms,
the one of these connotes the other ; whole has no
meaning, but when associated with parts ; parts have
no meaning, but when associated with whole. Taken
together ; that is, whole and parts, used as one name ;
they mark a complex idea, consisting of three principal parts ; an undivided line, the act of division,
and the consequent of that antecedent, the line after
division.

In the preceding exposition, it is actual division,
the actual making of parts, which has been spoken of.
It is observable, however, that the same language, by
which we name actual division, and actual parts, is
applied to conceived division, and conceived parts.
Thus we talk of the parts of a line, when it is not
divided, nor meant to be divided. The exposition of
this, however, is easy ; and there is obscurity only
when the double use of the terms confounds the two

cases, the division which is actual, with that which is conceived.

The division of the line may consist of one act, or of more acts than one. By the first act, it is divided into two parts; by the second into three; by the third into four, and so on. The parts of a line are so many lines. These may be equal, or unequal. But the sensations, on account of which we denominate lines equal, or unequal, have been already shewn; the equality, and inequality, therefore, of the parts of a line, need no further explanation.

When the learner conceives distinctly the sensations on account of which we apply the terms whole and parts to a line, he will not find it difficult to understand, on what account we apply them to all the modifications of extension; seeing that all these modifications are lines combined.

Thus, a plane surface is a number of straight lines, in contact, in the direction called a plane. It is of greater or less extent, according as these lines are longer or shorter from a central point; it is of one shape or another shape, according as the lines are of the same length, or of different lengths. When they are all of one length, the surface is called a circle. As they may be of different lengths in endless variety, the surface may have an endless variety of shapes, of which only a few have received names. The square is one of these names, the triangle another, the parallelogram another, and so on.

Bulk, which is the other great modification of extension, is lines from a central point in every direction. This bulk is greater or less, according as these lines are longer or shorter. The figure or shape of this

bulk is different, according as the lines are of the same
or different lengths.   If they are of the same length,
the bulk is called round, or, in one word, a sphere ;
sphere meaning exactly round bulk.   As the lines,
when they differ in length, may differ in endless ways ;
figures, or the shapes of bulk, are also endless, as our
senses abundantly testify.   Of these but a small number have received names.   In this number are the
cube, the cylinder, the cone.   We name some shapes
by referring to known objects ; thus we speak of the
shape of an egg, the shape of a pear, and so on.

It seems that nothing, therefore, is now wanting,
to shew in what manner the relative terms, expressive
of Quantity, are applied to all the modifications of
extension.

After what has been said, it will not be difficult to
ascertain the sensations on account of which we apply
the same relative terms to cases of Weight.

Weight is the name of a particular species of pressure ; pressure towards the centre of the earth.   Pressure, as we have already fully seen, is the name we
apply, when we have certain sensations in the muscles,
just as green is the name we apply when we have a
certain sensation in the eye.   As green is the name
of the sensation in the eye, pressure is the name of
the sensation in the muscles.   Pressure upwards, is
one thing ; pressure downwards, is another ; pressure
of a body, when that body is urged by another body,
is one thing ; pressure of a body, when it is not urged
by another body, is a different thing : pressure of a
body in altering the position of its parts is one thing ;
pressure, when there is no alteration of the position of
its parts, is another thing.   Of this last sort is weight,

the pressure downwards, or towards the centre of the
earth, of a body not urged by another body, and not
altering the position of its parts.

In supporting in my hand a stone, I resist a certain
pressure ; in other words, have certain muscular feelings, on account of which I call the stone heavy.   I
support other stones, and in doing so have muscular
feelings, in one case similar, in another dissimilar.   In
the case of similarity, I call two stones equal, meaning
in weight ; in the case of dissimilarity, unequal ; and
so I apply all the other relative terms by which
quantity is expressed.

It seems unnecessary to carry this analysis into
further detail.   The words equal, unequal : greater,
less ; applied to Motion, to Heat, and other modifications of sensation, have a meaning, which in following the course so fully exemplified it cannot be difficult
to ascertain.

It seems still necessary that I should say something
of the word *Quantus*, from which the word Quantity is
derived.   *Quantus* is the correlate of *Tantus*.   *Tantus*,
Quantus, are relative terms, applicable to all the objects to which we apply the terms, Great, or Little ;
they are applicable, therefore, to all the modifications
of extension, of weight, of heat ; in short, to all modifications which we can mark as degrees.

Of two lines, we call the one *tantus*, the other
quantus.   The occasions on which we do so are, when
the one is as long as the other.   *Tantus*, and *Quantus*,
then, in this case, mean the same thing as equal,
equal.   They will be found to have the same import
as equal, equal, when applied also to surface, and
bulk; and so in all other compatible cases.

E 2

What then, it may be asked, is the use of them? If it should appear that they were of no use, it would not be very surprising; considering by whom languages have been made; and that redundancy is frequent in them as well as defect. In the present case, however, a use is not wanting.

It is necessary to observe the artifice, to which we are obliged to have recourse, to name, and even to distinguish, the different modifications, not of kind but of degree, included under the word quantity. We are obliged to take some one object, with which we are familiar, and to distinguish other objects, as differing or agreeing with that object. Thus, we take some well-known line, the length of the foot, or the length of the arm, and distinguish and name all other lengths by that length; which can be divided or multiplied so as to correspond with them. In like manner, we take some well-known object as a standard weight, which we call, for example, a pound, and distinguish and name all other weights, as parts or multiples of that known weight.

Now it will be recognised, that, in applying the relative terms equal, equal, or in calling two objects equal, no one of them is marked as the standard. Both are taken on the same footing. The one is equal to the other; and the other is equal to that. But when we say that one thing is *tantus, quantus* another; or one so great, as the other is great; the first is referred to the last, the *tantus* to the *quantus*; the first is distinguished and named by the last. The *quantus* is the standard.

It is this which gives its peculiar meaning to the word Quantity, and has recommended it for that very

comprehensive and generical acceptation, in which it
is now received.

Our word Quantity, is the Latin word *Quantitas*;
and *Quantitas* is the abstract of the concrete *Quantus*.
We have no English words, corresponding to *Tantus*,
Quantus. We form an equivalent, by aid of the relative conjunctions; we say, So Great, As Great. But
these concrete terms do not furnish abstracts; we do
not say, As-greatness; in the first place, because it is
an awkward expression; and in the next place,
because the relative, "as," is not steady in its application, since we use "as great" not for *quantus* only,
but frequently also for *tantus*. As greatness, therefore, does not readily suggest the idea of the abstract
of *Quantus.*

On what account, then, is it we give to any thing
the name *Quantus?* As a standard by which to name
another thing *Tantus*. The thing called *Quantus*, is
the previously known thing, the ascertained amount,
by which we can mark and define the other amount.
Leaving out the connotation of *Quantus*, which is
some one individual body, *Quantitas* merely denotes
such and such an amount of body. *Quantitas*, if it
was kept to its original meaning, would still connote
Tantitas; just as paternity connotes filiality. But
in the case of Quantity, even this connotation is
dropped; it is used not as a *relative* abstract term,
but an *absolute* abstract term; and is employed as a
generical name for any portion of extension, any portion of weight, of heat, or any thing else, which can
be measured by a part of itself.[14]

---

[14] After analysing Position and Extension under the head
of Relative Terms, the author now, under the same head, gives

4. After tracing the sensations and ideas, which
are marked when we apply relative terms to objects,
as agreeing or disagreeing in *quantity;* we have now
to trace the sensations and ideas, which are marked,
when we apply relative terms to objects, on account of
their agreeing or disagreeing in *quality.*

First of all, the learner must take note of what he

---

the analysis of Quantity and Quality. To what he says on
the subject of Quantity it does not appear necessary to add
anything. He seems to have correctly analysed the phenomenon down to a primitive element, beyond which we have no
power to investigate. As Likeness and Unlikeness appeared
to be properties of our simple feelings, which must be postulated as ultimate, and which are inseparable from the feelings
themselves, so may this also be said of More and Less. As
some of our feelings are like, some unlike, so there is a mode
of likeness or unlikeness which we call Degree : some feelings otherwise like are unlike in degree, that is one is unlike
another in intensity, or one is unlike another in duration ; in
either case one is distinguished as more, or greater, the other
as less. And the fact of being more or less only means that
we feel them as more or less. The author says in this case, as
he had said in the other elementary cases of relation, that the
more and the less being different sensations, to trace them and
to distinguish their difference are not two things but one and
the same thing. It matters not, since there the difference still
is, unsusceptible of further analysis. The author's apparent
simplification amounts only to this, that differences of quantity, like all other differences of which we take cognizance, are
differences merely in our feelings ; they exist only as they are
felt. But (as we have already said of resemblance, and of antecedence and consequence) they must be postulated as elements. The distinction of more and less is one of the ultimate
conditions under which we have all our states of consciousness.—*Ed.*

means by *Quality.* We ascribe qualities to an object on account of our sensations. We call an object green, on account of the sensation green; hard, on account of the sensation hard; sounding, on account of the sensation sounding. The names of all qualities of objects, then, are names of sensations. Are they any thing else? Yes; they are the names of our sensations, with connotation of a supposed unknown cause of those sensations. As far, however, as our knowledge goes, they are names of sensations, and nothing else. The supposed cause is never known; the effects alone are known to us.

We ascribe qualities to objects, in two cases, which require to be distinguished: on account of the sensations which we have from them primarily; on account of those which we have from them secondarily. The first we call their sensible qualities; as green, hot, hard, sweet, scented, and so on: the second we more frequently call their powers; as the power of the loadstone to draw iron, the power of water to melt sugar. In this latter case, the sensations marked are not those which are derived from the loadstone, or from water; but those which are derived from the changes in the iron, and the sugar; of which changes, we call the loadstone, and the water, the cause. In the latter case, the train of antecedents and consequents is longer than it is in the former. When I see an object green; there is the object, the antecedent; and myself sentient of green, the consequent. When I see a loadstone draw iron, there is the following train; the loadstone, antecedent; iron drawn, first consequent; myself seeing it drawn, second consequent. When I see water melt sugar, there is the antecedent water ; sugar melting, first consequent ; myself seeing it, second consequent. What I call the powers of an object, then, are its order in re·pect to certain of my sensations, the order of antecedence, not proximate, but more or less remote.

When I say that grass is green, I trace my sensation green, no farther than to the grass. When I say, the sugar is melting, I trace my sensations (for they are several) called sugar melting, first to the sugar, and then to the water. My word green, therefore, is the notation of a sensation, and connotation of an unknown cause ; my name melting, is the notation of a compound of sensations, and connotation of two causes, an antecedent and a consequent : the first, an unknown cause in the sugar ; the second, the cause of that unknown cause, namely, the water.

In speaking of the qualities of an object, it is necessary to take notice of an inaccuracy of language ; which, not only, as Dr. Brown has well observed, lies at the bottom of many philosophical errors, but induces men to mistake the very business of the philosopher.

The term, "quality" or "qualities of an object," seems to imply, that the qualities are one thing, the object another. And this, in some indistinct way, is, no doubt, the opinion of the great majority of mankind. Yet, the absurdity of it strikes the understanding, the moment it is mentioned. The qualities of an object are the whole of the object. What is there beside the qualities ? In fact, they are convertible terms : the qualities are the object ; and the object is the qualities. But, then, what are the qualities ? Why, sensations, with the association of the object as the cause. And what is the association of the object as the cause? Why, the association of other sensations as antecedent. What, for example, are the smell, and colour, and other qualities of the rose? Is not each of the names of these qualities, that of the smell, for example, a connotative name, not only noting the sensation, of which it is properly the name, but connoting all the sensations of colour, of consistence, of figure, of position; to which, all combined by association, so as to form one complex idea, we give the specific name, rose, the more general name, vegetable, and the still more general name, object? When the smell of a rose is perceived by me, or the idea suggested to me, immediately all the other ideas included under the term rose, are suggested along with it, and their indissoluble union presupposed. But this belief of the previous indissoluble union of each of those sensations with all the other sensations, is all which I really mean when I refer each sensation to the rose as its cause.

If the learner has fully apprehended the ideas here premised, it will be easy for him to trace to the bottom the relative terms, which we apply to objects on account of their agreeing or disagreeing in *Quality*.

We say, that objects agree or disagree, on account of one quality, or more than one quality, that is, on account of single sensations, or combined sensations.

Let us first observe the case of one quality. We say, that a blade of grass is like the leaf of an oak, meaning, that in the quality of colour both are green; we say that the leaf of the rose tree, is unlike the petal of the flower, meaning in colour. By these

words, we name the objects in pairs ; first, the pair
of leaves, to each of which, we give the name, like ;
secondly, the leaf and the petal, to each of which, we
give the name, unlike. We name the first two objects,
" like," on account of the two sensations, green, and
green, one of each object ; we name the next two
objects unlike, on account of the two sensations,
green of the one, red of the other. What is done,
or rather what is felt, when we give the same, or a
different name, to each of two sensations, has been
already so fully explained, that a bare suggestion of
what has been premised, is here all that will be
required.

We have two sensations, A, B. Having two sensations, and knowing them to be two sensations, that
is, not one sensation, is having the sensations, and
nothing more.

Why do I call one sequence of sensations, green,
green ; another sequence, green, red ? Clearly on account of the sensations. No other explanation can
be given of it, nor can be required. For the same
reason for which I called the sensations of the first
sequence individually, green, green, I call them both,
like ; and for the same reason for which I called those
of the second sequence, not green, green, but green,
red, I call them, unlike.

Let us next put the case of several sensations. We
say, that one rose is like another. We have only to
take the sensations combined under the name rose,
one by one, to see that this, and the former, case, are
in reality the same. The two roses are like in colour,
like in smell, like in consistence, like in form, like in
position. The likeness of the two roses, is a likeness

not in one sensation, but in several. But the likeness of two sensations of smell, is of the same nature as the likeness of the two sensations of sight. When I call the smell, therefore, of the two roses like, it is for the same reason as I call the colour of them like, that is, the sensations. When I call the shape and consistence, and position, like, it is for the same reason still; the tactual and muscular sensations, whence the ideas are derived to which these names are annexed. In this case, however, the reason is by no means so clearly seen, first, because the sensations are complex, and secondly, because they are of that class of sensations which we habitually overlook.

The Latin words, *Talis, Qualis,* are applied to objects in the same way, on one account, as *Tantus, Quantus,* on another; and the explanation we gave of *Tantus, Quantus,* may be applied *mutatis mutandis,* to the pair of relatives we have now named. *Tantus, Quantus,* are names applied to objects on account of dimension. *Talis, Qualis,* are names applied to objects on account of all other sensations. We apply *Tantus, Quantus,* to a pair of objects when they are equal; we apply *Talis, Qualis,* to a pair of objects, when they are like.

Talis, Qualis, however, express the likeness of two objects in a manner somewhat different from the other pair of nearly equivalent relatives, "Like," and "Like." When we call two objects Like, the one is placed on the same footing as the other. No one of them is taken as the standard. When we apply, *Talis, Qualis,* the case is different. One of the objects is then the standard. The object *Qualis,* is that to which the reference is made.

This being understood, the extensive meaning which came to be given to the word Quality, may be easily explained. Quality is the Latin *Qualitas*, and *Qualitas* is the abstract of *Qualis*. The meaning of the abstract is the same with that of the concrete, the connotation being dropped. When the word *Qualis*, is applied to an object, it notes something about it in particular, but connotes the whole object. The *Qualitas* of that object, is the something noted in particular, the connotation being dropped. As *Qualis* is applied to objects, sometimes on account of one thing belonging to them, sometimes on account of another, *Qualitas* comes in turn to be applied to every thing in them, requiring at any time a separate notation. *Qualitas*, when first formed from *Qualis*, has the force of a relative, and connotes the abstract of *Talis*; but in its frequent use, in marking every thing in objects, which requires separate notation, this connotation, also, comes to be dropped; and Quality is finally used as an absolute term, the generical name of every thing in objects, for which a separate notation is required.[15]

---

[15] As in the case of Quantity, so in that of Quality, it is needless to add anything to the author's very sufficient elucidation. I merely make the usual reserves with respect to the use of the word Connotation. The concrete names which predicate qualities (for of abstract relative names the author is not yet speaking) are said by him to be the names of our sensations; green, for instance, and red. But it is the abstract names alone which are this : the names greenness, and redness. And even the abstract names signify something more than only the sensations : they are names of the sensations considered as derived from an object which produces them. The concrete name is a name not of the sensation, but of the object, of

III. It was remarked at the beginning of this investigation of relative terms or names applied in pairs, that we name in pairs—1, single sensations or ideas; 2, the clusters we call objects; 3, the complex ideas we form arbitrarily for our own purposes. Having finished the consideration of the two former cases, we shall not find occasion to speak much at length upon the last.

The clusters, formed by arbitrary association, receive names in pairs, on two occasions; either,

1. When they consist of the same or different simple ideas; or,

2. When they succeed one another in a train.

1. The ideas which we put together arbitrarily are sometimes less, sometimes more, complex, for the most part, they are exceedingly complex.

Of the less complicated kinds, are such ideas as that of the unicorn, which is a horse with one straight horn growing from the middle of its forehead; the Cyclops, a gigantic man, with a single eye in the middle of his forehead; a mermaid, of which the upper part is a woman, the lower a fish; the Brobdignagian

---

which alone it is predicable : we talk of green objects, but not of green sensations. It however connotes the quality greenness, that is, it connotes that particular sensation as produced by, or proceeding from, the object; as forming one of the group of sensations which constitutes the object. This, however. is but a difference, though a very important one, in terminology. It is strictly true, that the real meaning of the word is the sensations ; as, in all cases, the meaning of a connotative word resides in the connotation (the attributes signified by it), though it is the name of, or is predicable of, only the objects which it denotes.—*Ed.*

and Lilliputian of Swift, which are men of greatly
reduced, or greatly enlarged dimensions.

Of the more complicated kinds, are such ideas as
those which are marked by the word Science, by the
word Trade, by the word Law, by the word Religion,
by the word Faith, by the words God and Devil, by
the word Value, by the words Virtue, Honour, Vice,
Beauty, Deformity, Space, Time, and so on.

Language has not many relative terms, applicable
to ideas of this class. We speak of pairs of them as
like or unlike, same or different, greater or less ; and
except when their order in time is to be noted, we
hardly apply to them any other marks in pairs.

We say the Cyclops in Homer, and the Brobdignagian of Swift, are unlike. We do so precisely in the
same way, as we say, the rose and the lily are unlike ;
and the explanation which we have given of that
which is distinctively marked by those terms, when
applied to objects, is precisely applicable here. In
the case of objects, that which is named, is, clusters
of ideas ;[16] in the present case, that which is named, is
clusters of ideas. That one cluster has been formed
in one way, another in another, makes no difference
in annexing marks to the clusters when they are
formed.

There is as little difficulty in tracing what is marked
by the relatives, different, and same, when applied to
ideas of this class. We say, the unicorn is different

---

[16] Say rather, in the case of objects, what is named is clusters of sensations, supplemented by possibilities of sensation.
If an object is but a cluster of ideas, what is there to distinguish it from a mere thought ?—*Ed.*

from the horse; because, to the idea of the horse it adds that of a horn growing in the middle of the forehead. In the case of very complex ideas, it is much more difficult to say, with precision, what are the added and subtracted ideas, on account of which, we apply the term, different; as when we say, the courage of Ajax was different from that of Achilles; but it is not the less certain, that it is wholly on account of ideas added and subtracted, that we so denominate the courage of the two men.

Rather more explanation is needed, to shew what is peculiarly marked by the relatives equal, unequal, greater, less, when applied to the class of arbitrarily formed complex ideas.

We have already seen, that those terms are primarily applied to what we call objects, on account of their extension; objects are equal or unequal, greater or less, in extension.

We have also seen, that in marking the extension of different objects, we are under the necessity of taking some known object as a standard, and by that object naming others. Thus, we take the foot, and say that other objects are two feet, three feet, or the half or quarter of a foot, and so on.

Having become familiar with what we call degrees of extension, we are led to employ the same mode of notation, when we come to mark analogous differences in other cases of sensation. Thus, when we perceive the weight of different heavy bodies; as the terms equal, unequal, greater, less, are applied with convenience to certain cases of extension, it appears they may be applied with equal convenience, and even precision, to cases of weight. All other sensations,

having distinguishable differences, may be marked in
the same way : thus sounds are more or less loud, and
we speak of equal, or unequal, less or greater loudness
of sound ; less or greater sweetness in objects of the
palate; less or greater resistance ; less or greater pain;
less or greater pleasure.

When the terms equal, unequal, less, greater, had
been applied to simple sensations of the pleasurable
kind, and their ideas ; the transference of them to
complex ideas, of the pleasurable or painful kind, was
easy.   If the less or greater sweetness of the rose and
the woodbine, was a convenient notation, so was the
less or greater beauty of those two flowers, the less or
greater beauty of two women, the less or greater wisdom or folly, vice or virtue, of two men.

It thus appears, that, as we apply the term unlike
to our complex ideas, on account of the addition and
subtraction of ideas of *different* kinds, so we apply to
them the term unequal, on account of the addition
and subtraction of ideas of the *same* kind.   Like and
equal we apply, when we neither add, nor subtract.[17]

---

[17] In this passage the author has got as near as it is perhaps possible to get, to an analysis of the ideas of More and
Less.   We say there is *more* of something, when, to what
there already was, there has been superadded other matter of
the same kind.   And when there is no actual superadding, but
merely two independent masses of the same substance, we call
that one the greater which produces the same impression on
our senses which the other would produce if an addition were
made to it.   So with differences of intensity.   One sweet taste
is called sweeter than another because it resembles the taste
which would be produced by adding more sugar : and so forth.
In all these cases there is presupposed an original difference

2. We apply the same relative terms to successive ideas of this class, which we apply to simple ideas, or the clusters called objects, when successive. We call them antecedent and consequent, or names equivalent; as prior, posterior; first, second; or even successive, which is a name including both antecedent and consequent.

In speaking of the relative terms applied to objects as successive, we had occasion to explain the two important terms, Cause and Effect. We found that Cause and Effect, were only other names for antecedent and consequent, in a certain set of cases. We do not use the terms, Cause and Effect, as synonymous with antecedent and consequent, in those cases in which, though the objects may be antecedent and consequent to our perception, we know not whether they are parts of the same series, or parts of two different series. Within the sphere of our observation, innumerable series of events are going on ; and we are observing, first a part of one series, and then a part of another, continually. It is thus constantly happening, that those things, which are immediately antecedent and consequent to our observation, are not parts of the same series, but parts of different series ; and, of course, in those antecedents and consequents, there is no constancy ; they are accidental, as the course of each man's attention. This may be illustrated by many familiar instances. There may be

---

in the sensations produced in us by the greater mass and by the smaller : but according to the explanation now offered, the idea which guides the application of the terms is that of physical juxtaposition.—*Ed.*

immediately before me, a man playing on the violin, one series ; another man filing a saw, a second series. My attention may pass immediately from the sight of the man playing on the violin, to the sound produced by the filing of the saw. Playing on the violin, and the disagreeable sound of the file on the saw, are thus antecedent and consequent to my attention. But, as we recognise such antecedents and consequents, as parts of different series of events, we do not call them cause and effect.

There are two cases of antecedents and consequents, even when they are parts of the same series. They may be proximate ; or they may be remote ; that is, parts of the series, more or fewer, may come between them. It is only to the case of the proximate parts of the same series, that the relatives, cause and effect, are properly and strictly applied. When the series, however, is the same, the intermediate links between any two remote parts are constant. Suppose a series, A, B, C, D ; as B is the immediate consequent of A, C the immediate consequent of B, and D the immediate consequent of C ; when I know A and D as antecedent and consequent, without knowing the intermediate parts B, and C, there is little inaccuracy in naming A and D cause and effect ; because B and C are surely intermediate, and the succession of A and D, though not immediate, is constant. We accordingly do name cause and effect parts of a series thus removed from one another, in all those cases in which the intermediate parts are either unknown to us, or habitually overlooked.

The terms Cause and Effect, thus applied to Objects as antecedent and consequent, are applied also to

Thoughts as antecedent and consequent. Thus we say, that Evidence is the cause of Belief; Villany is the cause of Indignation, and so on.

Of objects, antecedent and consequent, we have observed, that innumerable series are existing at the same time; a separate series, of vegetation, for example, in every plant, of animalization in every animal, of composition and decomposition in objects without number. In the mind, however, there is but one train, not various trains at the same time; and therefore, according to the sense above applied to the terms Cause and Effect, each thought in a train is the cause of that which follows it, and each succeeding thought is the effect of that which precedes it.

But if thoughts are reciprocally Cause and Effect; that is to say, if, in trains of thought, the same antecedent is regularly followed by the same consequent, how happens it that all trains of thought are not the same? For if the ideas A, B, C, D, &c., constantly follow one another, every mind into which A may enter, goes on with B, C, D, &c., and hence all such minds should consist of the same trains, that is, should be the same.

Supposing the succession of two thoughts to have that constancy to which we apply the terms cause and effect, trains would still have that variety which we experience. Our trains consist of two distinguishable ingredients; sensations and ideas. Sensations depend upon the innumerable series of objects. They are, therefore, liable to all that variety which attends the perception of those objects. A perpetual variety in sensations produces a perpetual variety in the thoughts which are consequent upon them. The variety of sensation, is even much greater than is commonly supposed. The most active of all our sensations is the sight. But in most objects of sight there are numerous parts. Some of these are more seen, some are less seen ; some not seen at all. Of these, the parts that are more seen by one man, are less seen by another ; whence it is probable, that from an object of any complexity no two men ever receive precisely the same sensations. There is a striking exemplification of this, in the fact, so constantly observed, of the different manner in which different men are affected by the comparison of two countenances. To one man there appears a strong likeness, where another man cannot discover any. Of the minute particulars, on which the likeness depends, none, or an insufficient number, is embraced by the vision of the one, while the contrary is the case with that of the other.

The variety in the sensations, which mix in the trains of men, is one grand cause of the variety in the ideas, which make up or complete those trains. The variety in the order of those sensations is another cause. We have seen that ideas follow one another, in the order in which the sensations have followed. Thus, a man may be a kind father to his child. The sight of him to the child is habitually accompanied with agreeable sensations. The same man may be a severe master to his slaves. The sight of him to the slaves is habitually accompanied with painful sensations. A corresponding difference exists in the case of the ideas. When his image presents itself to the mind of the child, it is followed by a train of pleasurable ideas, corresponding to the plea-

surable sensations which the child has habitually enjoyed in his presence. When his image rises to the
mind of the slave, it is followed, from the contrary
cause, by ideas of the contrary description.[18]

---

[18] The author may seem to be anticipating a difficulty which
few will feel, when he asks how it happens that all trains of
thought are not the same. But what he is enquiring into is
not why this happens, but how its happening is consistent with
the doctrine he has just laid down. He is guarding against
a possible objection to his proposition, that "the succession of
two thoughts" has "that constancy to which we apply the
terms Cause and Effect." If (he says) it is by direct causation
that an idea raises up another idea with which it is associated;
and if it be the nature and the very meaning of a cause, to be
invariably followed by its effect; how is it, he asks, that any
two minds, which have once had the same idea, do not coincide
in their whole subsequent history? And how is it that the
same mind, when it gets back to an idea it has had before, does
not go on revolving in an eternal round?

Of this difficulty he gives a solution, good as far as it goes—
that it is because the train of ideas is interrupted by sensations,
which are not the same in different minds, nor in the same
mind at every repetition, and which even when they are the
same, are connected in different minds with different associations. This is true, but is not the whole truth, and a still more
complete explanation of the difficulty might have been given.
The author has overlooked a part of the laws of association, of
which he was perfectly aware, but to which he does not seem
to have been always sufficiently alive. The first point overlooked is, that one idea seldom, perhaps never, entirely fills
and engrosses the mind. We have almost always a considerable
number of ideas in the mind at once; and it must be a very
rare occurrence for any two persons, or for the same person
twice over, to have exactly the same collection of ideas present,
each in the same relative intensity. For this reason, were there

This, then, is all which seems necessary to be said
respecting the occasions on which we apply Relative

---

no other, the ideas which the mental state excites by association are almost always more or less different.

A second point overlooked is, that every sensation or idea is
far from recalling, whenever it occurs, all the ideas with which
it is associated.   It never recalls more than a portion of them,
and a portion different at different times.   The author has not,
in any part of the Analysis, laid down any law that determines
which among the many ideas associated with an idea or sensation, shall be actually called up by it in a given case.   The
selection which it makes among them depends on the truth
already stated, that we seldom or never have only one idea at
a time.   When we have several together, they all exercise their
suggesting power, and each of them aids, impedes, or modifies
the suggesting power of the others.   This important case of
Association has been treated in a masterly manner by Mr. Bain,
both in his larger treatise and in his Compendium, under the
name of Compound Association, and he lays down the following as its most general law.   " Past actions, sensations, thoughts,
" or emotions, are recalled more easily when associated either
" through contiguity or similarity, with more than one present
" object or impression." (Compendium of Psychology and Ethics,
p. 151.)   It follows that when we have several ideas in our
mind, none of which is able to call up all the ideas associated
with it, those ideas will usually have the preference which are
associated with more than one of the ideas already present.   An
idea A, coexisting in the mind with an idea B, will not select
the same idea from among those associated with it, that it
would if it occurred alone or with a different accompaniment.
If there be any one of the ideas associated with A which is also
associated with B, this will probably be one of those called up
by their joint action.   If there be any idea associated with A
which not only is not associated with B, but whose negation
is associated with B, this idea will probably be prevented from
arising.   If there are any sensations which have usually been

Terms, and to show what it is which they distinctively mark, in the trains of our sensations and ideas.

---

presented in conjunction, not with A alone or with B alone, but with the combination A B, still more likely is it that the ideas of these will be recalled when A and B are thought of together, even though A or B by themselves might in preference have recalled some other.

These considerations will be found of primary importance in explaining and accounting for the course of human thought. They enable us, for example, to understand what it is that keeps a train of thought coherent, *i.e.* that maintains it of a given quality, or directs it to a given purpose. The ideas which succeed one another in the mind of a person who is writing a treatise on some subject, or striving to persuade or conciliate a tribunal or a deliberative assembly, are suggested one by another according to the general laws of association. Yet the ideas recalled are not those which would be called up on any common occasion by the same antecedents, but are those only which connect themselves in the writer's or speaker's mind with the end which he is aiming at. The reason is, that the various ideas of the train are not solitary in his mind, but there coexists with all of them (in a greater or less degree of constancy according to the quality of the mind) the highly interesting idea of the end in view: and the presence of this idea causes each of the ideas which pass through his mind while so engaged, to suggest such of the ideas associated with them as are also associated with the idea of the end, and not to suggest those which have no association with it. The ideas all follow one another in an associated train, each calling up by association the one which immediately follows it ; but the perpetual presence or continual recurrence of the idea of the end, determines, within certain limits, which of the ideas associated with each link of the chain shall be aroused and form the next link. When we come to the author's analysis of the power of the Will over our ideas, we shall find him taking exactly this view of it.

Concerning the simultaneous existence of many ideas in the

ABSTRACT RELATIVE TERMS.

From the *Concrete relative* terms, *Abstract* terms are
formed, in the same manner as Abstract terms are

---

mind, and the manner in which they modify each other's exercise of the suggesting power, there is an able and instructive
passage in Cardaillac's Etudes Elémentaires de Philosophie,
which has been translated and quoted by Sir William Hamilton
in his Lectures, and which, being highly illustrative of the
preceding remarks, I think it useful to subjoin.

"Among psychologists, those who have written on Memory
and Reproduction with the greatest detail and precision, have
still failed in giving more than a meagre outline of these operations. They have taken account only of the notions which
suggest each other with a distinct and palpable notoriety.
They have viewed the associations only in the order in which
language is competent to express them; and as language, which
renders them still more palpable and distinct, can only express
them in a consecutive order, can only express them one after
another, they have been led to suppose that thoughts only
awaken in succession. Thus, a series of ideas mutually associated, resembles, on the doctrine of philosophers, a chain in
which every link draws up that which follows; and it is by
means of these links that intelligence labours through, in the
act of reminiscence, to the end which it proposes to attain.

"There are some, indeed, among them, who are ready to
acknowledge, that every actual circumstance is associated to
several fundamental notions, and consequently to several
chains, between which the mind may choose; they admit even
that every link is attached to several others, so that the whole
forms a kind of trellis,—a kind of network, which the mind
may traverse in every direction, but still always in a single
direction at once,—always in a succession similar to that of
speech. This manner of explaining reminiscence is founded
solely on this,—that, content to have observed all that is distinctly manifest in the phenomenon, they have paid no atten-

former from other Concrete terms.   Thus from equal,
we have equally; from unequal, unequally; from

---

tion to the under-play of the latescent activities,—paid no
attention to all that custom conceals, and conceals the more
effectually in proportion as it is more completely blended with
the natural agencies of mind.

"Thus their theory, true in itself, and setting out from a
well-established principle, the Association of Ideas, explains
in a satisfactory manner a portion of the phenomena of Reminiscence; but it is incomplete, for it is unable to account
for the prompt, easy, and varied operations of this faculty, or
for all the marvels it performs.   On the doctrine of the philosophers, we can explain how a scholar repeats, without hesitation, a lesson he has learned, for all the words are associated
in his mind according to the order in which he has studied
them; how he demonstrates a geometrical theorem, the parts of
which are connected together in the same manner; these and
similar reminiscences of simple successions present no difficulties which the common doctrine cannot resolve.   But it is
impossible, on this doctrine, to explain the rapid and certain
movement of thought, which, with a marvellous facility, passes
from one order of subjects to another, only to return again to
the first; which advances, retrogrades, deviates, and reverts,
sometimes marking all the points on its route, again clearing,
as if in play, immense intervals; which runs over, now in a
manifest order, now in a seeming irregularity, all the notions
relative to an object, often relative to several, between which
no connection could be suspected; and this without hesitation,
without uncertainty, without error, as the hand of a skilful
musician expatiates over the keys of the most complex organ.
All this is inexplicable on the meagre and contracted theory on
which the phenomena of reproduction have been thought
explained. . . . . . .

"To form a correct notion of the phenomena of Reminiscence, it is requisite that we consider under what conditions
it is determined to exertion.   In the first place it is to be noted

like, likeness; from unlike, unlikeness; from friend, friendship; and so on.

---

that, at every crisis of our existence, momentary circumstances are the causes which awaken our activity, and set our recollection at work to supply the necessaries of thought. In the second place, it is as constituting a want, (and by *want* I mean the result either of an act of desire or of volition) that the determining circumstance tends principally to awaken the thoughts with which it is associated. This being the case, we should expect, that each circumstance which constitutes a want, should suggest, likewise, the notion of the object, or objects, proper to satisfy it ; and this is what actually happens. It is, however, further to be observed, that it is not enough that the want suggests the idea of the object; for if that idea were alone, it would remain without effect, since it could not guide me in the procedure I should follow. It is necessary, at the same time, that to the idea of this object there should be associated the notion of the relation of this object to the want, of the place where I may find it, of the means by which I may procure it, and turn it to account, &c. For instance, I wish to make a quotation :—This want awakens in me the idea of the author in whom the passage is to be found which I am desirous of citing ; but this idea would be fruitless, unless there were conjoined, at the same time, the representation of the volume, of the place where I may obtain it, of the means I must employ, &c.

"Hence I infer, in the first place, that a want does not awaken an idea of its object alone, but that it awakens it accompanied with a number, more or less considerable, of accessory notions, which form, as it were, its train or attendance. This train may vary according to the nature of the want which suggests the notion of an object; but the train can never fall wholly off, and it becomes more indissolubly attached to the object, in proportion as it has been more frequently called up in attendance.

"I infer, in the second place, that this accompaniment of

After what has been said about abstract terms in general, it will not be very difficult to mark what is

accessory notions, simultaneously suggested with the principal idea, is far from being as vividly and distinctly represented in consciousness as that idea itself; and when these accessories have once been completely blended with the habits of the mind, and its reproductive agency, they at length finally disappear, becoming fused, as it were, in the consciousness of the idea to which they are attached. Experience proves this double effect of the habits of reminiscence. If we observe our operations relative to the gratification of a want, we shall perceive that we are far from having a clear consciousness of the accessory notions; the consciousness of them is, as it were, obscured, and yet we cannot doubt that they are present to the mind, for it is they that direct our procedure in all its details.

"We must, therefore, I think, admit that the thought of an object immediately suggested by a desire, is always accompanied by an escort more or less numerous of accessory thoughts, equally present to the mind, though, in general, unknown in themselves to consciousness; that these accessories are not without their influence in guiding the operations elicited by the principal notion; and it may even be added that they are so much the more calculated to exert an effect in the conduct of our procedure, in proportion as, having become more part and parcel of our habits of reproduction, the influences they exert are further withdrawn, in ordinary, from the ken of consciousness. . . . The same thing may be illustrated by what happens to us in the case of reading. Originally each word, each letter, was a separate object of consciousness. At length, the knowledge of letters and words and lines being, as it were, fused into our habits, we no longer have any distinct consciousness of them, as severally concurring to the result, of which alone we are conscious. But that each word and letter has its effect,—an effect which can at any moment become an object of consciousness,—is shewn by the following experiment. If we look over a book for the occurrence of a parti-

peculiar in the nature of this species of them. We have seen that concrete, are connotative, terms; and

---

cular name or word, we glance our eye over a page from top to bottom, and ascertain, almost in a moment, that it is or is not to be found therein. Here the mind is hardly conscious of a single word, but that of which it is in quest; but yet it is evident, that each other word and letter must have produced an obscure effect, which effect the mind was ready to discriminate and strengthen, so as to call it into clear consciousness, whenever the effect was found to be that which the letters of the word sought for could determine. But if the mind be not unaffected by the multitude of letters and words which it surveys, if it be able to ascertain whether the combination of letters constituting the word it seeks, be or be not actually among them, and all this without any distinct consciousness of all it tries and finds defective; why may we not suppose,—why are we not bound to suppose, that the mind may, in like manner, overlook its book of memory, and search among its magazines of latescent cognitions for the notions of which it is in want, awakening these into consciousness, and allowing the others to remain in their obscurity?

"A more attentive consideration of the subject will show, that we have not yet divined the faculty of Reminiscence in its whole extent. Let us make a single reflection. Continually struck by relations of every kind, continually assailed by a crowd of perceptions and sensations of every variety, and, at the same time, occupied by a complement of thoughts; we experience at once, and we are more or less distinctly conscious of, a considerable number of wants,—wants, sometimes real, sometimes factitious or imaginary,—phenomena, however, all stamped with the same characters, and all stimulating us to act with more or less energy. And as we choose among the different wants which we would satisfy, as well as among the different means of satisfying that want which we determine to prefer; and as the motives of this preference are taken either from among the principal ideas relative to each of these

that their corresponding abstracts have the same
meaning with the concretes, that which is connoted

several wants, or from among the accessory ideas which habit
has established into their necessary escorts ;—in all these cases
it is requisite, that all the circumstances should at once, and
from the moment they have taken the character of wants, produce
an effect, correspondent to that which, we have seen, is caused
by each in particular.   Hence we are compelled to conclude,
that the complement of the circumstances by which we are thus
affected, has the effect of rendering always present to us, and
consequently of placing at our disposal, an immense number of
thoughts ; some of which certainly are distinctly recognised,
being accompanied by a vivid consciousness, but the greater
number of which, although remaining latent, are not the less
effective in continually exercising their peculiar influence on
our modes of judging and acting.

" We might say, that each of these momentary circumstances
is a kind of electric shock which is communicated to a certain
portion, to a certain limited sphere, of intelligence ; and the
sum of all these circumstances is equal to so many shocks
which, given at once at so many different points, produce a
general agitation.   We may form some rude conception of this
phenomenon by an analogy.   We may compare it, in the former
case, to those concentric circles which are presented to our
observation on a smooth sheet of water, when its surface is
agitated by throwing in a pebble ; and, in the latter case, to
the same surface when agitated by a number of pebbles thrown
simultaneously at different points.

" To obtain a clearer notion of this phenomenon, I may add
some observations on the relation of our thoughts among
themselves, and with the determining circumstances of the
moment.

" 1°. Among the thoughts, notions, or ideas which belong
to the different groups attached to the principal representations
simultaneously awakened, there are some reciprocally connected
by relations proper to themselves ; so that, in this whole com-

being left out. White, for example, has a notation, and a connotation. It notes a quality, and it connotes

---

plement of coexistent activities, these tend to excite each other to higher vigour, and consequently to obtain for themselves a kind of pre-eminence in the group or particular circle of activity to which they belong.

"2°. There are thoughts associated, whether as principals or accessories, to a greater number of determining circumstances, or to circumstances which recur more frequently. Hence they present themselves oftener than the others, they enter more completely into our habits, and take, in a more absolute manner, the character of customary or habitual notions. It hence results, that they are less obtrusive, though more energetic, in their influence, enacting, as they do, a principal part in almost all our deliberations ; and exercising a stronger influence on our determinations.

"3°. Among this great crowd of thoughts, simultaneously excited, those which are connected with circumstances which more vividly affect us, assume not only the ascendant over others of the same description with themselves, but likewise predominate over all those which are dependent on circumstances of a feebler determining influence.

"From these three considerations we ought, therefore, to infer, that the thoughts connected with circumstances on which our attention is more specially concentrated, are those which prevail over the others ; for the effect of attention is to render dominant and exclusive the object on which it is directed, and during the moment of attention it is the circumstance to which we attend that necessarily obtains the ascendant.

"Thus, if we appreciate correctly the phenomena of Reproduction or Reminiscence, we shall recognise, as an incontestable fact, that our thoughts suggest each other not one by one successively, as the order to which language is astricted might lead us to infer ; but that the complement of circumstances under which we at every moment exist, awakens simultaneously a great number of thoughts ; these it calls into the presence of

something else, that which is white. The abstract whiteness marks what is *noted* by the concrete, but not what is *connoted.*

We are now to see, in what manner this applies to relative terms. I call two things like : two sensations, for example ; let us say, sensations of red. I call sensation A, like sensation B ; and, of course, sensation B, like sensation A. It is here more easy to observe distinctly what is connoted, than what is noted. What is connoted are the two sensations. They are clear and simple. What is noted is what we call their likeness. What is that ? We have remarked, that, in *having* two sensations, the *distinguishing* them one

---

the mind, either to place them at our disposal, if we find it requisite to employ them, or to make them co-operate in our deliberations by giving them, according to their nature and our habits, an influence, more or less active, on our judgments and consequent acts.

" It is also to be observed, that in this great crowd of thoughts always present to the mind, there is only a small number of which we are distinctly conscious : and that in this small number we ought to distinguish those which, being clothed in language, oral or mental, become the objects of a more fixed attention ; those which hold a closer relation to circumstances more impressive than others ; or which receive a predominant character by the more vigorous attention we bestow on them. As to the others, although not the objects of clear consciousness, they are nevertheless present to the mind, there to perform a very important part as motive principles of determination ; and the influence which they exert in this capacity is even the more powerful in proportion as it is less apparent, being more disguised by habit." (Sir William Hamilton's Lectures on Metaphysics, vol. ii. Lecture xxxii.) —*Ed.*

from another is included ; it is part of the compound
process : And that in having two sensations—red,
red, and two sensations red, green, the distinguishing
the succession red, red, from the succession red, green,
is included ; it being part of the process, which, though
in this case compound, and on that account obscure,
is not the less wholly sensation.   In the process of
sensation, then, that part which consists in distinguishing one as one, another as another, and in distinguishing one succession from another ; red, red, for
example, from red, green,—is the part which is noted
by the words like and unlike.   The thing noted is not
a distinct sensation, it is part of a process of sensation,
and a part which, being never experienced separate by
itself, it is very difficult to make a distinct subject of
attention.   Even that part of the process which consists in distinguishing, is to be distinguished into two
parts.   There is that part which consists in distinguishing the sensations from one another, as one,
and one ; and there is that part which consists in
distinguishing the two, red, and red, from the two,
red, and green.   It is this *latter part* which is *noted*
by the terms like and unlike.   What is *connoted* is all
the rest of the process.   When, therefore, we make
abstracts, from the terms like and unlike ; that is, cut
off the connotative part of their meaning, retaining
the notative only ; it is the part of the process which
consists in distinguishing, not one and one, but two
and two, which the terms distinctively mark.

We have also seen, and remarked, that having two
sensations, one after another, and knowing them to be
first one and then another, is a process of sensation
and association.   The pair of relatives, prior and pos-

terior, or antecedent and consequent, taken together,
names the whole of the process; each pair is in reality
a compound name of a complex idea, that of a certain
process, the process of having two ideas in succession,
in which process the being sensible of the successiveness is part. By all concrete relatives, something is
noted, something connoted. In the process which is
marked by the relatives prior and posterior, part is
noted, part connoted ; and the part which is noted, is
the part which it is difficult to make a separate object
of attention,—the part which consists in being sensible
of the successiveness, for which we have not a name.
By its notation and connotation, taken together, each
of the terms, prior, and posterior, is a name of something, and that something is very distinct ; prior is a
name of the first sensation and something else ; posterior is a name of the second sensation, and something
else.   It is by connotation, however, that each is the
name of its · respective sensation.   Their notative
power relates to the something else, and not to the
whole of that ; because prior and posterior, beside
connoting, each its own sensation, connote one another.   The notation and connotation, therefore, are
divided between them, in a manner which renders it
difficult to shew what belongs to each.   We have not
names adapted to the purpose.

The word prior notes something, and connotes
something.   When we make from it the abstract
term priority ; what was connoted by the concrete,
prior, is dropped ; what was noted by it is retained.
In the succession of ideas A, and B, priority is not
the name of A, it is the name of that part of the compound process, which consists in knowing A, as the

first of the two ; posteriority is not the name of B, but
of that part of the compound process, which consists
in knowing B, as the last of the two.

There is a peculiarity, however, in the abstract
terms formed from the relative concrete terms.   These
abstract terms are not, as whiteness, hardness, wholly
void of connotation.   They have a connotation of their
own.   The abstract of one relative of a pair, always
connotes the abstract of the other ; thus, priority
always connotes posteriority, and posteriority priority.

This constitutes a distinction, worth observing, between the force of the abstracts formed from the pairs
of relatives which consist of different names, as prior,
posterior; cause, effect ; father, son ; husband, wife;—
and those which consist of the same name, as equal,
equal ; like, like ; brother, brother ; friend, friend ;
and so on.   Priority and Posteriority make together
a compound name of something, of which, taken separately, each is not a name ; Causingness and Causedness, the abstracts of cause and effect, make up between them the name of something, of which each by
itself is not a name, and so of the rest.   The case is
different with such abstracts as likeness, equality,
friendship, formed from pairs which consist of the
same name.   When we call A like, and B like ; the
abstract, likeness, formed from the one, connotes
merely the abstract, likeness, formed from the other.
Thus, as priority and posteriority make a compound
name, so, likeness and likeness, make a compound
name.   But as likeness and likeness are merely a re-
duplication of the same word, likeness taken once very
often signifies the same as likeness taken twice.   Priority never signifies as much as priority and posteri-

ority taken together ; but likeness taken alone very
often signifies as much as likeness, likeness, taken
both together. Likeness has thus a sort of a double
meaning. Sometimes it signifies only what is marked
by the abstract of one of the pair, " like, like ;" sometimes it signifies what is marked by the abstracts of
both taken together. The same observation applies
to the abstracts equality, inequality ; sameness, difference ; brotherhood, sisterhood ; friendship, hos-
tility ; and so on.[19]

---

[19] The exposition here given of the meaning of abstract relative names is in substance unexceptionable ; but in language
it remains open to the criticism I have, several times, made.
Instead of saying, with the author, that the abstract name drops
the connotation of the corresponding concrete, it would, in the
language I prefer, be said to drop the denotation, and to be a
name directly denoting what the concrete name connotes,
namely, the common property or properties that it predicates :
the likeness, the unlikeness, the fact of preceding, the fact of
following, &c.

When the author says that abstract relative names differ
from other abstract names in not being wholly void of connotation, inasmuch as they connote their correlatives, priority
connoting posteriority, and posteriority priority, he deserts the
specific meaning which he has sought to attach to the word
connote, and falls back upon the loose and general sense in
which everything implied by a term is said to be connoted
by it. But in this large sense of the word (as I have more
than once remarked) it is not true that non-relative abstract
names have no connotation. Every abstract name—every
name of the character which is given by the terminations *ness*,
tion, and the like—carries with it a uniform implication that
what it is predicated of is an attribute of something else ; not
a sensation or a thought in and by itself, but a sensation or
thought regarded as one of, or as accompanying or following,
some permanent cluster of sensations or thoughts.—*Ed.*

Among the abstract terms corresponding to relative concretes, those corresponding to cause and effect, are the only ones which, on account of their importance, require to be somewhat more particularly expounded.

Cause and Effect have not abstract terms formed immediately from themselves. One of the grand causes of their obscurity is, that they are not constant in their meaning, but are sometimes used as concretes, sometimes as their own abstracts.

Cause means "something *causing ;*" effect, "something *caused.*" Causingness, therefore, is the proper abstract of cause ; and causedness, the proper abstract of effect. Of two objects, A, and B, we call the one causing, the other caused, when they are not only prior and posterior, but parts of the same series ; and, if we speak strictly, proximate parts. Of proximate parts of the same series, we call the antecedent, causing ; the consequent, caused. Causingness, and causedness, therefore, mean antecedence and consequence, and something more. The ideas are more complex. Causingness and causedness, mean, not only antecedence and consequence, but also sameness of series, and proximity of parts.

As we have seen, that priority and posteriority, taken together, form a compound name of a certain complex idea, so causingness and causedness, taken together, form the compound name of a still more complex idea. Having frequent occasion to express that idea, a separate name for it was found necessary. Accordingly, we have the term Power, which means precisely what is meant by causingness and causedness taken together. Causation has the same mean-

ing with Power, except that it connotes present time ;
Power connotes indefinite time.[20]

The connotation of *Time*, by abstract terms, is a
circumstance almost always overlooked, but of which
the observation is of the utmost importance to accuracy of thought.

When we have invented a number of marks to be
taken in pairs, as like, like; equal, equal ; antecedent,
consequent ; master, servant ; husband, wife ; father,
son ; owner, property ; author, book ; cause, effect ;
and so on ; we have occasion for a name by which to
speak of that class of names. We have invented
such a name. We call those terms " Relative
Terms."

The word " Relative," thus belongs to that class of
names, which have been called " Names of Names."
As man, tree, stone, are names of things, of those
clusters which we call objects ; as red, green, hard,
soft, are names of sensations ; as courage, wisdom,

---

[20] The term Causation, as the author observes, signifies
causingness and causedness taken together, but I do not see on
what ground he asserts that it connotes present time. To my
thinking, it is as completely aoristic as Power. Power, again,
seems to me to express, not causingness and causedness taken
together, but causingness only. Some of the older philosophers
certainly talked of passive power, but neither in the precise
language of modern philosophy nor in common speech is an
effect said to have the power of being produced, but only the
capacity or capability. The power is always conceived as belonging to the cause only. When any co-operating power is
supposed to reside in the thing said to be acted upon, it is
because some active property in that thing is counted as a con-
cause—as a part of the total cause.—*Ed.*

anger, love, are names of complex ideas arbitrarily
composed ; so adjective is the name of one class of
names, verb the name of another class of names ;
syllable, is the name of one part of a word, letter of
another ; and so, also, relative is the name of the class
of words which have this peculiarity, that they are
taken in pairs.   Thus, father and son, are relative
terms ; prior and posterior, are relative terms ; like
and like, are relative terms ; so equal, equal ; unequal, unequal; brother, brother; friend, friend; and
so on.

Relative itself corresponds with the names which it
marks, in its being one of a pair ; of that species of
pairs, which are formed by a double use of the same
word, as like, like.   When we say of father and son,
that they are relative terms, we mean that father is
relative to son, and son relative to father.

As *relative* is the name of all concrete names, taken
in pairs, such as like, like ; friend, friend ; causing,
caused ; so the abstract *relation*, formed from relative,
is the name given to all the abstract terms formed
from the concrete relatives : thus, equality, inequality,
friendship, power, are abstract terms, which we call
by a general name, relation.   As Noun is the name
of a certain class of words, so " Relation," is the name
of a certain class of words.

It is not, however, meant to be affirmed, that relative and relation, are not names which are also applied
to things.   In a certain vague, and indistinct way,
they are very frequently so applied.   This, however,
is strictly speaking, an abuse of the terms, and an
abuse which has been a great cause of confusion of
ideas.   In this way, it is said, of two brothers, that

they are relative; of father and son, that they are relative; of two objects, that they are relative in position, relative in time; we speak of the relation between
two men, when they are father and son, master and
servant; between two objects, when they are greater,
less, like, unlike, near, distant, and so on.

What, however, we really mean, when we call two
objects relative (and that is a thing which it is of
great importance to mark) is, that these objects have,
or may have, relative names. On what accounts we
give them relative names, has just been explained, and
the explanation need not be repeated. When we say
that Socrates and the Emperor Napoleon are unlike,
the men are, each, a man, distinct, separate, absolute.
We only give them a pair of related names, for the
convenience of discourse. In like manner, Charles I.
and George IV. are separate, distinct, absolute individuals. We only give them the relative names Predecessor, Successor, for the convenience of discourse, to
mark the place which they occupied in a certain series
of events. From this appears also what is meant,
when we say of two objects, that they have a relation
to one another. The meaning is, that the objects
may have relative names, and that these names may
have abstracts which we call relation. Thus we say
that two brothers have a relation to one another.
That relation is brotherhood. But brotherhood is
merely the abstract of the relative names. We say
that father and son have a relation. That relation is
fathership and sonship. These are merely the abstracts
of the two relative names. We say of two events, a
stab with a sword, and death of the person stabbed, that
they have a relation to one another. That relation is

causingness and causedness, the abstract of cause and
effect, or, in one word, power.[21]

---

[21] The application of the word Relative to Things is not
only an offence against philosophy, but against propriety of
language. The correct designation for Things which are called
by relative names, is not Relative, but Related. A Thing may,
with perfect propriety both of thought and of language, be
said to be related to another thing, or to have a relation
with it—indeed to be related to all things, and to have a prodigious variety of relations with all ; because every fact that
takes place, either in nature or in human thought, which includes or involves a plurality of Things, is the *fundamentum*
of a special relation of those Things with one another : not to
mention the relations of likeness or unlikeness, of priority or
posteriority, which exist between each Thing and all other
Things whatever. It is in this sense that it is said, with truth,
that Relations exhaust all phenomena, and that all we know,
or can know, of anything, is some of its relations to other
things or to us.—*Ed.*

SECTION III.

NUMBERS.

We have already observed, that objects exist, with respect to us, in two orders; in the synchronous order, and the successive order; and that we have great occasion for marks to represent them to us as they exist in both orders. We have also to observe, that the synchronous order, the order in which things exist together; that is, as we otherwise name it, the order of position, or the order in place; is interesting to us chiefly on account of the successive order. The order in which objects succeeds one another, that is, the order of the changes which take place, the order of events, depends almost entirely upon the synchronous order. In other words, the synchronous order is part of every successive order; it is the antecedent of every consequent; or as we otherwise express it, the cause of every effect. Thus the synchronous order, or the order in place, of the spark and the gunpowder, is the antecedent of the explosion; the synchronous order of my finger and the candle, is the antecedent or the cause of the pain which I feel.

In regard to the explosion, also, it is less or greater, according as the quantity of the gunpowder is less or greater. Of the synchronous order, therefore, one part which I am particularly interested in knowing correctly is, the amount of the things. A certain amount of gunpowder produces one set of effects, another

another: a certain amount of men produce one set of effects, another another; and so of all other things.

It is of the last importance to me not only to be able to ascertain, and know, these amounts, with accuracy, but to be able to mark them.

For ascertaining and knowing amounts, some contrivance is requisite. It is necessary to conceive some small amount, by the addition or subtraction of which, another becomes larger or smaller. This forms the instrument of ascertainment. Where one thing, taken separately, is of sufficient importance to form this instrument, it is taken. Thus, for ascertaining and knowing different amounts of men, one individual is of sufficient importance. Amounts of men are considered as increased or diminished by the addition or subtraction of individuals. A grain of gunpowder might also be taken; but it is not of sufficient importance; the quantity, taken as the instrument of measurement, must have an ascertainable influence upon the effect, for the sake of which, the ascertaining of the amount is of importance. In their simple state, men use principally the hand for their elementary ascertainments. A pinch, or as much as could be held between the finger and the thumb, was a small amount distinctly conceived, and formed the principle of measurement where small additions were important; a handful was not less distinctively conceived, and was the instrument, where only larger additions were of importance.

When one addition was made, or needed to be made, after another, and another after that, and so on, the next point of importance was to conceive exactly how often the addition was made. A few addi-

tions are distinct to sense.   Place one billiard-ball by
another, the sight of the two is distinct.   Place three
or four, it is still distinct.   Soon, however, it ceases
to be so.   Place a dozen, and you will not probably
be able to distinguish them from eleven.   You must
count them, or divide them.   If you divide them by
the eye, into two parcels, you may see that one is six
and another six ; but to benefit by this, you must
know the art of putting six and six together.

The next step, therefore, necessary in the process
of ascertaining amounts, was, to mark these additions,
one after another, in such a manner, as to make
known to what extent they had gone.   When men
were familiar with the operation of assigning names
as marks of their ideas, the course which would suggest itself to them is obvious ; they would employ a
name as the mark of each addition.   They would say,
one, for the first, two, for the second, three, for the
third, and so on.   These marks it was very useful to
make connotative, that the other important ingredient
of the process, the thing added, might be made known
at the same time.   Thus we say, one man, two men ;
one horse, two horses ; and so of all other things, the
enumeration of which we are performing.

Numbers, therefore, are not names of objects.   They
are names of a certain process ; the process of addition ; of putting one billiard-ball to another ; not
more mysterious than any other process, as walking,
writing, reading, to which names are assigned.   One,
is the name of this once performed, or of the aggregation begun ; two, the name of it once more performed ; three, of it once more performed ; and so on.
The words, however, in these concrete forms, beside

their power in noting this process, connote something else, namely, the things, whatever they are, the enumeration of which is required.

In the case of these connotative, as of other connotative marks, it was of great use to have the means of dropping the connotation ; and in this case, it would have been conducive to clearness of ideas, if the non-connotative terms had received a mark to distinguish them from the connotative. This advantage, however, the framers of numbers were not sufficiently philosophical to provide. The same names are used both as connotative, and non-connotative ; that is, both as abstract, and concrete ; and it is far from being obvious, on all occasions, in which of the two senses they are used. They are used in the connotative sense, when joined as adjectives with a substantive ; as when we say two men, three women ; but it is not so obvious that they are used in the abstract sense, when we say three and two make five ; or when we say fifty is a great number, five is a small number. Yet it must, upon consideration, appear, that in these cases they are abstract terms merely ; in place of which, the words oneness, twoness, threeness, might be substituted. Thus we might say, twoness and threeness are fiveness.[22] [23]

---

[22] The vague manner in which the author uses the phrase " to be a name of" (a vagueness common to almost all thinkers who have not precise terms expressing the two modes of signification which I call denotation and connotation, and employed for nothing else) has led him, in the present case, into a serious misuse of terms. Numbers *are*, in the strictest propriety, names of objects. *Two* is surely a name of the things which *are* two, the two balls, the two fingers, &c. The process of

It is necessary to observe, that the process, marked
by the names called numbers, though used for the

---

adding one to one which forms two is connoted, not denoted,
by the name two. Numerals, in short, are concrete, not abstract names: they denote the actual collections of things,
and connote the mental process of counting them. It is not
twoness and threeness that are fiveness : the twoness of my
two hands and the threeness of the feet of the table cannot be
added together to form another abstraction. It is two balls
added to three balls that make, in the concrete, five balls.
Numerals are a class of concrete general names predicable of
all things whatever, but connoting, in each case, the quantitative relation of the thing to some fixed standard, as previously
explained by the author.—*Ed.*

[23] Here the process of numeration generally, together with the
function of numbers carrying their separate names, are clearly
set forth ; after which we find the remark, that no distinction
is made in the name of the number, when used as an abstract
and when used as a concrete. Mr. James Mill thinks that it
would have been conducive to clearness if such distinction had
been marked by an inflexion of the name. " The names of
" numbers are used in the connotative (concrete) sense, when
" joined as adjectives with a substantive, as when we say, two
" men, three men : but it is not so obvious that they are used
" in the abstract sense, when we say three and two make five :
" or when we say fifty is a great number, five is a small num-
" ber. Yet it must upon consideration appear, that in these
" cases they are abstract terms merely : in place of which, the
" words oneness, twoness, threeness, might be substituted.
" Thus we might say, twoness and threeness are fiveness."
The last part of what is here affirmed cannot, in my judgment, be sustained. Connecting itself with one among the
many arguments between Aristotle and Plato, it lays down a
position from which both of them would have dissented. In
the last book but one (Book M) of Aristotle's " Metaphysica,"
this argument will be found set forth at length ; though with

purpose of ascertaining synchronous order, is in the mind successive; one addition follows another. Num-

---

much obscurity, which is cleared up by the lucid commentary of Bonitz. Plato distinguished two classes of numbers—the mathematical, and the ideal. The first class were the Quanta of equal and homogeneous units (One, Two, Three, &c.), any or all of which might be added so as to coalesce into one total sum. The second class were, the ideal or abstract numbers, Two *quatenus* Two, &c., represented by Dyad, Triad, Tetrad, Pentad, Dekad, &c., the characteristic property of which was, that they could not be added together nor coalesce into one sum. These were uncombinable numbers, "ἀριθμοὶ ἀσύμβλητοι —numeri inconsociabiles."—See Aristot. Metaph. M. 6. 1080. b. 12. Bonitz Comment. p. 540, 541, seq.

Plato regarded these uncombinable numbers as the highest representative specimens or coryphæi of the Platonic Ideas. In this character Aristotle reasoned against them, contending that they did nothing to remove the many objections against Plato's ideal theory. With the question thus opened, I have no present concern : all that I wish to point out is the view which Plato originated and upon which Aristotle reasoned, viz.: That these ideal or abstract numbers could not be added together, or fused into one sum total. The abstract term Twoness means Two *so far forth as two:* so also Threeness and Fiveness. You cannot truly predicate anything of Twoness which would be inconsistent with this fundamental characteristic : you cannot add it to Threeness so as to make Fiveness, nor can you subdivide Fiveness into Twoness and Threeness, without suppressing the fundamental characteristic of each. Neither of them admit of increase or diminution. In like manner, a Triangle, or every particular Triangle, may have one of its sides taken away, or two more sides added to it : on each of which suppositions it ceases to be a triangle. But if we speak of a Triangle *so far forth as Triangle,* neither of these suppositions is admissible. We may say that its three angles are equal to two right angles, but we cannot subtract

bers, therefore, in reality, name successions ; and are
easily applied to mark certain particulars of the suc-

---

from it one of its sides, nor add to it one or two other sides.
The subject of predication is so limited and specialised, that
no predicate can be allowed which would efface its characteristic feature—Triangularity.

Bonitz remarks truly that the class of numbers set forth by
Plato—the ideal or uncombinable numbers which could not
be either added or subtracted—were divested of all the useful
aptitudes and functions of numbers, and passed out of the
category of Quantity into that of Quality. The Triad was one
quality ; the Pentad was another : there was no common measure into which both could be resolved (Bonitz, Comment.
p. 540—553). *Two, three, five,* are quantifying names, de-
signating each so many numerable units : and the units counted
in each list may be added to, or subtracted from, the units
counted in the others. But when we say, Twoness or the
Dyad—Threeness or the Triad—Fiveness or the Pentad—we
then recognise a peculiar quality, founded upon each separate
variety of aggregation or quantification : so that these separate
varieties are no longer resolvable into any common measure of
constituent units. Each quality stands apart from the others,
and has its own predicates. In the view of Plato and the
Pythagoreans, the Dekad especially was invested with magnifi-
cent predicates.

I cannot therefore agree with Mr. James Mill in his opinion
that, " when we say three and two make five, we use these
numbers in the abstract sense." We clearly do not mean that
three, *so far forth as three*, and two, *so far forth as two*, make
five. But this would be what we should mean, if we used
these names of numbers in the abstract sense. What we do
mean is, that the units constituting three may be added to those
constituting two, so as to make five : and that this is equally
true, whether the units are men, horses, stones, or any other
objects. Two, three, five, &c., are general or universal terms,
capable of being joined with units of indefinite variety : but

cessive order, when the marking of those particulars
is of importance.

It is of importance, when successions take place all
of one kind ; and when consequences of importance
depend upon the less or greater length of the train.
It is then of importance, to mark the degrees of that
length, which is correctly done by the enumeration of
the links.

To take a simple and familiar instance, that of the
human steps.   They are successions all of one kind.
Consequences of importance may, and often do result
from a knowledge of the length of any particular
series of steps.   The ascertainment of an aggregate,
in this order, is made in the same way, as that which
we have traced in the synchronous order.   An element of aggregation is taken; by its successive aggre-
gations, the amount of the aggregate is correctly
conceived ; and, by a proper mark for each successive
aggregation, it is also correctly denoted.   The continued successions of day and night are all of one
kind ; and it is of the greatest importance for us to
know accurately the length of a series of those successions ; of the series between such and such events ;
between the sowing of the seed in the ground, for example, and the maturity of the crop.   This is done,
accurately, by putting a several mark upon each

---

they do not become abstract terms, until we limit them by
quátenus, καθόσον, ᾗ, *so far forth as,* &c., or by a suffix such
as *ness.*   Such abstracts would have been of little use as to
the ordinary functions of numbers ; and accordingly they have
never got footing in familiar speech, though they are occasionally employed in metaphysical discussions.—*G.*

several succession, one for the first, two for the
one after that, three for the one after that, and
so on.

If there be no mystery in one sensation after
another, or one idea after another; and, if having
them in that order and associating the idea of the
antecedent with the sensation of the consequent be to
know that they are in that order; then there is no
mystery in Numbers, for they are only marks to shew
that one is after another.

That there is no mystery in the ideas of priority
and posteriority, which are relative terms, has been
shewn under the preceding head of discourse.

The word Number itself, which is only a name
of the names, one, two, &c., nothing being a number but some one of those names, has also been
explained, when the class of words which are
distinguished as Names of Names was under consideration.

In using the terms, one, two, three, four, and so on,
the object is to ascertain with precision, the amount
of the aggregate in question. In some cases, however, it is of importance to ascertain the order of
aggregation, as well as the amount; and that, whether
a synchronous, or a successive, aggregate be the object
in view. This purpose is answered by a set of names,
called the ordinal numbers, which, applied to the units
of aggregation in the order in which they are taken,
mark precisely the order of each. Thus, when we say,
first, second, third, fourth, and so on; each of these
concrete, or connotative names, notes a certain position, if in the synchronous order; a certain link, if

in the successive; and connotes the precise object which holds that position, or forms that link.

As there is no difficulty whatsoever in tracing the ideas, which, on each occasion, receive those marks, there is no need of multiplying words in their illustration.

SECTION IV.

PRIVATIVE TERMS.

Privative terms are distinguished from other terms, by this; that other terms are marks for objects, as present or existent; privative terms are marks for objects, as not present or not existent.[24]

Thus the word Light, is the mark of a certain well-known object, as existent or present.

The word Darkness, on the contrary, is the mark of the same object, as not existent or not present. Ask any man, what he means by darkness; he says the absence of light. But the absence of light, is only another name for light absent; and light absent, is only another name for light not present. Darkness, therefore, is another name for light not present.

It thus appears, that the idea called up by the

---

[24] The author gives the name of Privative terms to all those which are more commonly known by the designation of Negative; to all which signify non-existence or absence. It is usual to reserve the term Privative for names which signify not simple absence, but the absence of something usually present, or of which the presence might have been expected. Thus *blind* is classed as a privative term, when applied to human beings. When applied to stocks and stones, which are not expected to see, it is an admitted metaphor.

This, however, being understood, there is no difficulty in following the author's exposition by means of his own language.—*Ed.*

word light, is that of a certain object associated with its presence; the idea called up by the word darkness, is that of the same object associated with its absence.

After the explanations which have been so often given, what I mean, when I speak of the idea of an object, as one thing; the idea of its presence, as another thing; ought not to be obscure. Its presence, is its existence; its absence, is its non-existence; at least, at a particular time and place. What ideas and sensations I mark by the word existent, has already been explained. The word non-existent is the mere negation of the same sensations and ideas.

We have repeatedly seen, that what we call existence, is an inference from our sensations. We have clusters of sensations; these call up the ideas of antecedents, which we call qualities; these the idea of an antecedent common to all the qualities, which we call *Substratum*; and the *Substratum*, with its qualities, we call the Object.

When we speak, then, of this *Substratum* and its qualities, as present, at a particular time and place; which is what we mean by its existence; what we affirm is this; that if there be sentient organs at such a time and place, there will be such and such sensations. When we speak of it as absent, we affirm, that though there be sentient organs at such a time and place, there will not be those sensations. These ideas, then, forming in combination a very complex idea, are what, in the respective cases, we call the presence, and the absence of an object. Any further analysis would be superfluous in this place.

A law of some importance, which has been already
explained, is, that in complex ideas there is very often
some one part, so prominent, as to throw the rest into
the shade, and confine the attention almost wholly to
itself. There is a curious exemplification of this law,
in the pair of cases before us. Thus, in the complex
idea of "the object and its presence," marked by the
word Light, the object is the prominent part, and the
presence is so habitually neglected, that it is with
some trouble it is recognised. The case is reversed in
the complex idea of "the object and its absence,"
marked by the word Darkness. In this, the absence
is the prominent part, and it so completely engrosses
the attention, that it requires reflection, to discover, that the idea of the object is necessarily combined.

There is something more in these two cases, which
it is of great importance to remember. We have two
sets of indissoluble associations, both exceedingly
numerous, the one with the idea of the object as present, the other with the idea of it as absent ; that is,
the one set with light, the other set with darkness.
Whenever we have the perception of light, we habitually have, along with it, the perception of objects ;
that is, of all sorts of colours, all sorts of shapes, all
sorts of magnitudes, all sorts of distances, and so on.
With the idea of light, then, are indissolubly associated the ideas of all sorts of objects ; of extension
in all its modifications, colour in all its modifications,
motion in all its modifications ; the word light, therefore, serves as a name, not merely of the fluid which
acts upon the eye, but of that along with its innumerable associations. Such are the perceptions and

ideas, which, when we have the perception of light, we have along with it. What are the perceptions and ideas, which, when we have not the perception of light, we have along with that state of privation ? There is, first, the want of all the perceptions, which we have along with that of light. There is, next, the disagreeable sensations we experience from not knowing what objects are approaching us, either by our motions, or by theirs ; hence the idea of dangerous objects approaching ; hence, also, the inability to perform many of the acts which are conducive either to our being, or well-being. With the idea of darkness, then, are indissolubly associated a multitude of ideas, of pain, of privation, of weakness ; all disagreeable ; with little or no mixture of any of an opposite kind. And the word darkness, therefore, stands as a name not merely of light absent, but of that along with all the accompanying sensations and ideas.

The reader will observe, and it is necessary he should well observe, that all terms might have corresponding privative terms. We have already stated, that the ordinary names of objects are names both of the object, and of its presence or existence, combined in one complex idea. Thus, rose, horse, are names of the objects as present or existent. We might have had names of them as absent or not existent. It is only, however, in a few cases, that the absence of an object is a matter of first-rate importance. It is only in those cases that it has been found requisite to have for it a particular name. The absence of light is obviously a case of the greatest importance. Consequences of the very first order, and infinite in number,

depend upon it.   An appropriate name, therefore, was
of the highest utility.

This explanation will enable us to see, without a
minute analysis, the composition of the clusters marked
by other Privative Terms.

Let us take Silence, as the next example.   Silence
is the absence of sound, either all sound, which is
sometimes its meaning ; or of some particular sound,
which at other times is its meaning.   Sound is the
name of a well-known something, as present.   Silence
is the name of the same well-known something, as
absent.   The first word, is the name of the thing, and
its presence.   The second, is the name of the thing,
and its absence.   In the case of the combination
marked by the first, namely, the thing and its presence,
the thing is the prominent part, and the presence
generally escapes attention.   In the case of the second,
the thing and its absence, the absence is the important part, and the thing is feebly, if at all,
attended to.

Ignorance is easily explained, in the same manner.
Knowledge is the name of a certain well-known something, as present or existent.   Ignorance is the name
of the same well-known something, as absent or non-
existent.

Having a sensation, or an idea, is one state of consciousness ; not having it is another state of consciousness.*   The state of consciousness called "not having"

---

* Mr. Locke recognised the fact, but gave an erroneous account of it : "I should offer this as a reason why a privative
cause might produce a positive idea ; *viz.*, that, all sensation
being produced in us, only by different degrees and modes of

it is no doubt very various; for it is any sensation or idea different from the one in question. The " Having" one sensation and another sensation, or one idea and another idea; and the " Knowing" that the one is not the other ; we have often observed to be the same thing. The great majority of names are invented, to mark sensations and ideas as " had ;" there are, however, cases, in which it is necessary to mark them as "not had." In what manner, in the more remarkable cases, this marking is performed by privative names, has now been shewn. But, beside the marks for particular cases, it was necessary to have a comprehensive or *general* mark ; which should include all cases, as well those provided with particular names, as those not so provided. " Absent" was such a word. " Absent," standing by itself, and unrestricted by connection with any other word, is a name of any thing, joined with the idea of its not being *then* and *there*. What is included in that Idea has already been shewn in explaining Belief in Existence. The mark " Absent," joined with any particular name, becomes a particular Privative Term. We have observed, that the word rose, is a mark not merely of the thing, but the thing with the idea of its presence ; we have also observed, that such Presence-affirming Terms, except

---

motion in our animal spirits, variously agitated by external objects, the abatement of any former motion, must as necessarily produce a new sensation, [for " abatement of any former motion," read, ceasing of a particular sensation ; and for " new sensation," read, new feeling, or, new state of consciousness,] as the variation or increase of it : and so introduce a new idea. B. II. ch. viii. s. 4.—(*Author's Note.*)

in remarkable cases, have not corresponding Privative, or Absence-affirming, Terms. But if we say "absent" rose, we have a Privative Term, double worded, indeed, instead of single worded, exactly corresponding to the Presence-affirming Term, rose. And, by the use of the same word, we can form Privative Terms of this description, in all cases in which they can be wanted; thus we can say, absent man, absent horse, absence of food, &c.

The word Nothing, *Nihil*, is another *generical* Privative Term. That this word has a very important marking power, every man is sensible in the use which he makes of it. But if it marks, it names; that is, names something. Yet it seems to remove every thing; that is, not to leave anything to be named.

The preceding explanations, however, have already cleared up this mystery. The word Nothing is the Privative Term which corresponds to Every Thing. Every Thing is a name of all possible objects, including their existence. Nothing is a name of all possible objects, including their non-existence.[25]

---

[25] The analysis of the facts, in all these cases, is admirable, but I still demur to the language. I object to saying, for instance, that silence is "the name of sound and its absence." It is not the name of sound, since we cannot say Sound is silence. It is the name of our state of sensation when there is no sound. The author is quite right in saying that this state of sensation recalls the idea of sound; to be conscious of silence as silence, implies that we are thinking of sound, and have the idea of it without the belief in its presence. In another of its uses, Silence is the abstract of Silent; which is a name of all things that make no sound, and of everything so

"Absent," in its unrestricted sense, above explained, comes near to this marking power of the word Nothing, but differs from it in one respect. Absent is the Privative name of all possible objects, taken one by one. Nothing is the privative name of them, taken altogether. This distinction, I presume, is sufficiently obvious, and intelligible, thus expressed ; and stands in no need of a more wordy explanation.*

We shall now take notice of the Privative Term EMPTY, which is a word of great importance.

Empty is a name applicable to all the things to which the name, full, is applicable ; in other words, to all the things which are calculated to contain other things in position, or in the synchronous order, that is, in the order of particle adjoining particle. It is necessary to mark this limitation of the word contain ; because, in another sense, a complex idea is said to contain the simple ideas of which it consists ; and a chemical compound is said to contain the simple

---

long as it makes no sound ; and which connotes the attribute of not sounding. So of all the other terms mentioned. "Nothing" is not a name of all possible objects, including their non-existence. If Nothing were a name of objects, we should be able to predicate of those objects that they are Nothing. Nothing is a name of the state of our consciousness when we are not aware of any object, or of any sensation.—*Ed.*

* The account of Privative Terms which is given by Locke, is the same with that which is presented in the text. The difference is, that Locke, who has stated the case correctly, has not attempted its analysis. He says (B. II. ch. viii.), "We have negative names, such as insipid, silence, *nihil*, &c., which words denote positive ideas ; *v.g.*, taste, sound, being ; with a signification of their absence."—(*Author's Note.*)

substances into which it can be decomposed. Empty, and Full, are names of those things only which contain, or are adapted to contain, things in position, or in the order of particle adjoining particle.

Things adapted to contain other things in position, are, themselves, a peculiar combination of positions, to which we must very attentively advert. To understand this combination, it will be necessary to remember exactly the analysis of position; of lines, surfaces, and bulks; as it has been already given in our explanation of Relative Terms.

The word "containing," applied to any thing, as when we speak of a box containing books, a cask containing liquor, a room containing furniture, generally includes the idea of limitation. That which contains, has certain boundaries within which the things contained are placed, or have their position. This idea of things having their position within another thing, is a very complex idea, the composition of which we must be at some pains to understand.

It consists, first, of the thing containing; secondly, of the things contained.

The thing containing, again, consists of two parts; first, its boundaries; and, secondly, its containing capacity within its boundaries.

Its boundaries are surfaces. How we become acquainted with surfaces; in other words, what are the sensations, the copies of which form our complex idea of surface, has been already explained. They are certain sensations of touch, and certain sensations of muscular action. This complex idea is easily distinguished into two parts; first, a certain idea of resistance; secondly, the idea of extension. The sides of a box I call resisting, and I call them extended; and I call them by both names on account of certain sensations. Let us conceive the box without a lid; each of the sides is extended and resisting. What is the top without a lid? Extended, and non-resisting. The idea of the top is that of extension without resistance; extension, in a particular direction, that of a plane surface. What is the idea of the inside of the box without its contents? That of extension in all directions without resistance. This is emptiness.

So far is plain, and not doubtful. There are still, however, some things which require explanation. What are we distinctly to understand by extension without resistance? Whenever we use the concrete extended, we mean something extended; and by that something we always mean something that resists. What do we mean when we use the abstract extension? It will be easily recollected that all this is a case of association, which has been already fully explained.

Concrete Terms are Connotative Terms; Abstract Terms are Non-connotative Terms. Concrete terms, along with a certain quality or qualities, which is their principal meaning, or notation, connote the object to which the quality belongs. Thus the concrete red, always means, that is, connotes, something red, as a rose. We have already, by sufficient examples, seen, that the Abstract, formed from the Concrete, notes precisely that which is noted by the Concrete, leaving out the connotation. Thus, take away the connotation from red, and you have redness; from hot, take away the connotation, and you have heat.

The very same is the distinction between the concrete extended, and the abstract extension. What
extended is with its connotation, extension is without
that connotation. We have then to explain, wherein
the connotation consists.

When we say extended, meaning something extended, we mean one or other of three things, a line,
a surface, or bulk. We have already explained
sufficiently in what manner we come by the ideas of
line, surface, and bulk. We have certain sensations
of touch, and of muscular action, conjoined, and the
ideas of those sensations, in conjunction, form our
ideas of line, surface, and bulk. The sensation, or
sensations, which we mark by the word resisting,
seem to be those alone which are connoted by the
word extending ; for it is most important to observe,
that what we call extending in the parts of our own
body, by the operation of its own muscles, is that
which we call extended in all other things ; and thus
the essential connotation of the concrete, extended, is,
resisting, and nothing else. In other concrete terms
the connotation is greater. Thus red, connotes a
surface, that is, something extended ; and extended
connotes resisting. And thus red connotes both extended and resisting, while extended connotes resisting
alone. It is true, that persons enjoying the faculty
of seeing cannot conceive any thing extended, without conceiving it coloured ; because in them the idea
of something extended includes, by association, the
visual, as well as the tactual, and muscular, ideas ;
and the visual being accustomed to predominate, the
tactual, and muscular, are faintly observed. This,
however, cannot be the case in persons born blind,

who have the tactual, and muscular, feelings, and not the visual at all.

Now, then, we can easily understand what extension is in all its cases. Linear extension is the idea of a line, the connotation dropped, that is, the idea of resisting, dropped ; superficial extension is the idea of a surface, the same connotation dropped ; and solid extension, or bulk, is merely the idea of bulk, the connotation, or resisting, dropped. But bulk, the connotation (*i.e.* resistance) dropped, is what ? The place for bulk : Position. But place is, what ? A portion of SPACE ; or, more correctly speaking, SPACE itself, with limitation.

We thus seem to have arrived, without any difficulty, at an exact knowledge of what is noted or marked by the word SPACE ; a phenomenon of the human mind hitherto regarded as singularly mysterious. The difficulty which has been found in explaining the term, even, by those philosophers who have approached the nearest to its meaning, seems to have arisen, from their not perceiving the mode of signification of Abstract Terms; and from the obscurity of that class of sensations, a portion of which we employ the word "extended" to mark. The word "space" is an abstract, differing from its concrete, like other abstracts, by dropping the connotation. Much of the mystery, in which the idea has seemed to be involved, is owing to this single circumstance, that the abstract term, space, has not had an appropriate concrete. We have observed, that, in all cases, abstract terms can be explained only through their concretes ; because they note or name a part of what the concrete names, leaving out the rest. If we were to make a concrete term, corresponding to the abstract term space, it must be a word equivalent to the terms "infinitely extended." From the ideas included under the name "infinitely extended," leave out resisting, and you have all that is marked by the abstract SPACE.[26]

In the idea of SPACE, the idea of Infinity is included. What the idea of Infinity is, needs therefore to be explained. When the word Infinite is not used metaphorically, as it is when we speak of the infinite perfections of God, in which case it is not a name for ideas, but for the want of them, it is applied only to Number, Extension, and Duration.

We increase numbers by adding one to one, one to two, and so on, without limit, giving a name to

---

[26] There is great originality as well as perspicacity in the explanation here given of Space, as a privative term, expressing when analysed, the absence of the feeling of resistance in the circumstances in which resistance is frequently felt, namely, after the sensations of muscular action and motion. The only part of the exposition to which I demur is the classing of Space among abstract terms. I have already objected to calling the word *line*, when used in the geometrical sense, an abstract term. I hold it to be the concrete name of an ideal object possessing length but not breadth. In like manner a Space may be said to be the concrete name of an ideal object, extended but not resisting. The sensations connoted by this concrete name, are those which accompany the motion of our limbs or of our body in all directions: and along with these sensations is connoted the absence of certain others, viz. of the muscular sensations which accompany the arrest of that motion by a resisting substance. This being the meaning of *a* Space, Space in general must be a name equally concrete. It denotes the aggregate of all Space.—*Ed.*

each aggregate.   The association of ideas which constitutes the process has been already explained.   With each number, one, two, three, four, as we go on, the idea of one more is so strongly associated, that we cannot help its existing in immediate conjunction. However high, therefore, we go in numbering, the idea of one more always forces itself upon us; and hence we say that number is infinite.   That this, literally, is not true ; that, indeed, it is a verbal contradiction, is obvious.   Number, is something numbered ; but if numbered, limited ; that is, not infinite. Number is the negation of infinite ; as black is the negation of white.   The name infinite, in this case, is, in reality, nothing but a mark for that state of consciousness, in which the idea of one more is closely associated with every succeeding number.   And Infinity, the abstract term, is the peculiar idea, without the connotation.

When we apply " infinite" to extension, we do so equally to all its three modifications, to lines, surfaces, and bulk.   How we do so is obvious.   We know no infinite line, but we know a longer, and a longer.   A line is lengthened, as number is increased, by continual additions ; a line of any length, say of an inch, is increased by the continual addition of other lengths, say of an inch.   In the process, then, by which we conceive the increase of a line, the idea of one portion more, is continually associated with the preceding length; and to what extent soever it is carried, the association of one portion more, is equally close and irresistible.   This is what we call the idea of infinite extension ; and what some people call the *necessary* idea ; which only means, that the idea of a

portion more, rises necessarily, that is, by indissoluble
association, so that we cannot help its rising. Infinite
is the concrete term, here connoting Line ; drop the
connotation, you have Infinity, the abstract.

If such be the whole of what is involved in the
idea of Infinity, in the case of a line ; call it necessary
idea, if you will ; the idea of it, in the case of
surface, and of bulk, is also explained ; for surface,
and bulk, are only lines, in such and such, or in all
directions. The idea of a portion more, adhering, by
indissoluble association, to the idea of every increase,
in any or in all directions, is the idea of "infinitely
extended," and the idea of "infinitely extended," the
connotation dropped, is the idea of Infinite Space. It
has been called a simple idea (so little has the real
nature of it been understood) ; while it is thus distinctly seen, to be one of the most complex ideas,
which the whole train of our conscious being presents.
Extreme complexity, with great closeness of association, has this effect—that every particular part in the
composition is overpowered by the multitude of all
the other parts, and no one in particular stands
marked from the rest ; but all, together, assume the
appearance of ONE. Something perfectly analogous
occurs, even in sensation. If two or three ingredients
are mixed, as wine and honey, we can distinguish the
taste of each, and say it is compound. But if a
great many are mixed, we can distinguish no one in
particular, and the taste of the whole appears a simple
peculiar taste.[27]

----

[27] This explanation of the feeling of Infinity which attaches
itself to Space, is one of the most important thoughts in the

This, indeed, is one great cause of the mistakes, which have been committed, in the examination of abstract ideas. We have shewn that they are all complex, and in the highest degree. Yet the greater number of them have always been treated as simple. Mr. Locke shewed that some of them, which he calls mixed modes, were undoubtedly compounded, as obligation, crime, &c. But they are no otherwise complex, than as power, quality, chance, fate, position, and space, are complex.

It is truly remarkable, how many of the cases of indissoluble association are all united in the idea of SPACE. First of all, with the idea of every object, the idea of *position* or *place*, is indissolubly united.

---

whole treatise; and, obvious as its truth is to a mind prepared by the previous exposition, it has great difficulty in finding entrance into other minds.

Every object is associated with some position: not always with the same position, but we have never perceived any object, and therefore never think of one, but in some position or other, relative to some other objects. As, from every position, Space extends in every direction (i.e. the unimpeded arm or body can move in any direction), and since we never were in any place which did not admit of motion in every direction from it, when such motion was not arrested by a resistance; every idea of position is irresistibly associated with extension, beyond the position: and we can conceive no end to extension, because the place which we try to conceive as its end, raises irresistibly the idea of other places beyond it. This is one of the many so-called Necessities of Thought which are necessities only in consequence of the inseparableness of an association: but which, from unwillingness to admit this explanation, men mistake for original laws of the human mind, and even regard them as the effect and proof of a corresponding necessary connexion between facts existing in Nature.—*Ed.*

Secondly, with the idea of position or place, the idea of *extension* is indissolubly united. Thirdly, with the idea of extension the idea of *infinity* is indissolubly . united. Fourthly, by the unfortunate ambiguity of the *Copula*, the idea of *existence* is indissolubly united with SPACE, as with other abstract terms. What these several ingredients, the ideas of Position, Extension, Infinity, Existence, are composed of, we have already seen. All these, forced into combination, by irresistible association, constitute the idea of SPACE.

SECTION V.

TIME.

As Space is a comprehensive word, including all Positions, or the whole of synchronous order; so Time is a comprehensive word, including all Successions, or the whole of successive order.

The difficulty of the exposition, in this case, consists not in the ideas; for they are clear and certain enough; but in finding expressions which will have even a chance of conveying to readers, who are not familiar with the analysis of mental phenomena, the ideas which it is my object to impart.

As all objects, considered as existing together, are said to exist in SPACE, so all objects considered as existing one after another, are said to exist in TIME.

Objects, however, are said to exist in Time, in two distinguishable cases; either when they are in constant flow; or, when they have, what we call, stability or duration. The constant passage of men, horses, vehicles, &c., in a busy and crowded street, is in Time; the permanence of St. Paul's, in its well-known position, is also in Time. If Time mean the succession of the objects in the one case, it must mean something else in the other. It cannot mean the succession of St. Paul's. But it may mean the idea of St. Paul's, associated with the idea of other successions.

Of TIME itself we conceive, that it is never still. It is a perpetual flow of instants, of which only one can ever be present. The very idea of Time, therefore, is an idea of successions. It consists of this, and of nothing else.

But there are no real successions, save successions of objects, that is of feelings in our minds.[28] What, then, are the successions of TIME, which are the successions of nothing? To those who have thoroughly familiarized themselves with the account which we have given of abstract terms, and who can promptly and steadily conceive the mode of their signification, we can render an answer, which will be understood at once, and will be felt to be complete and satisfactory.

We have shewn, how we form the abstracts, redness, from red ; sweetness, from sweet ; hardness, from hard ; by simply dropping the connotation of the concrete term. Thus red, always means something red ; redness, is the red without the something; so of sweetness, hardness, and so forth. When the ideas are more

---

[28] There is an unusual employment of language here, which if attention is not formally drawn to it, may embarrass the reader. By objects are commonly meant, those groups or clusters of sensations and possibilities of sensation, that compose what we call the external world. A single sensation, even external, and still less if internal, is not called an object. In a somewhat larger sense, whatever we think of, as distinguished from the thought itself and from ourselves as thinking it, is called an object ; this is the common antithesis of Object and Subject. But in this place, the author designates as objects, all things which have real existence, as distinguished from the instants of mere Time, which, as he is pointing out, have not ; and a puzzling effect is produced by his applying the name Object, in even an especial manner, to sensations : to the tickings of a watch, or the beatings of a patient's pulse.—*Ed.*

complicated, the case is still the same.   When we use
the concrete, living, it always connotes something
living ; a living man, a living quadruped, a living
bird, fish, insect, and so forth.   When we use the
abstract, life, we convey all that we convey by the
term living, except the connotation.   We say that
John is healthy, James is healthy, on account of
circumstances the idea of which forms a very complex
idea.   The concrete healthy always connotes an individual.   Use the abstract, health, you have the idea
without the connotation.

In applying this doctrine to the case of successions,
we are ill supplied with appropriate names ; and hence
the difficulty of the case, both to the teacher, and the
learner.

We have said that there are no real successions,
but successions of objects.   The tickings of my watch
are successive sounds, that is, sensations.   The beatings which are felt by the physician, in the artery of
his patient, are successive feelings or sensations of
touch.

When the different particulars of a scene in which
a man has been engaged, of a battle, for example, in
which he has commanded, pass through his mind,
there is a succession of ideas.   In all these cases of
the successions of sensations, or ideas, there is always
one present, others past, and others to come, that is,
future.   Drop the connotation of " something past,"
" something present," " something future."   You
have pastness, presentness, and futureness.   But pastness, presentness, and futureness, are TIME.   TIME can
neither be shewn, nor conceived, to be any thing else.
It is a single-worded abstract, involving the meaning

of these three several abstracts. The true meaning of these abstracts is clearly made out from their concretes. The precise idea, therefore, marked by the word TIME; if the meaning of these abstracts is sufficiently apprehended; is at last apparent. Nor is there any mysteriousness in it whatsoever, but that which has arisen from misapprehension of that grand department of Naming, which belongs to abstract terms ; and from inattention to that class of words, which are invented to supply the place, each of them singly, of several other words.

To our conclusion, that TIME is the equivalent of Pastness, Presentness, and Futureness, combined, it may be objected, that the word Time is applicable to all the three cases ; as we can say, past time, present time, and future time, all with equal propriety. This, however, is so far from being any presumption against the conclusion, that it is a clear confirmation of it ; since Time, standing by itself, marks no particular case, and, in order to do so, must have another mark applied to it to limit its signification. It is only because Time marks all the cases of pastness, presentness, and futureness, that it needs the marks past, present, or future, to confine its meaning ; present time being merely another name for presentness, future time, for futureness, and past time, for pastness. The same thing is seen in the case of all other abstracts. Redness is the name of a certain colour, in all its modifications, and to whatever object belonging. But by the addition of an appropriate mark, we confine its meaning to any particular case ; as when we say, the redness of a rose, the redness of scarlet, and so on.

The accounts, which have been rendered of Time by different philosophers, so far as they have in them any acknowledged accuracy, are, all of them, parts, and but parts, of the analysis which we have thus been presenting.   Dr. Reid says, Memory gives us the conception and belief of finite intervals of duration; and these we enlarge by our mental processes to infinity.*   We have already seen what Memory is.   It is not a faculty, as Dr. Reid supposes, which "gives" any thing; it is an idea, formed by association of the particulars of a certain train; a train of antecedents and consequents, of which the present feeling is one extremity.   Pastness is included under the term Memory.   Memory is the name of a certain whole, and Pastness is the name of a part of that whole. Memory is a connotative term; what it notes, is the antecedence and consequence of the several parts of that which forms the chain of the remembrance; what it connotes, are the feelings themselves, the objects remembered.   When what it connotes is left out, and what it notes is retained, we have the idea which is expressed by pastness.

In the chain of memory, consisting of antecedent, antecedent, antecedent, traced back to any length from the present feeling, we call that which immediately precedes the present, the nearest; the next, we call more distant; the next, more distant still; and that, between which and the present feeling the greatest number of successions intervenes, we call the most distant, also the farthest back; but the farthest back of a series of successions, is the oldest, that between

* Intellect. Powers.   Essay III. ch. v. p. 583.

which and the present time the greatest length of time
has intervened.   Greatest length of time, therefore, in
this case, is only another name for greatest number of
successions.

It has been already seen, that there is nothing in
which we are so deeply interested, as an accurate
knowledge of the antecedents and consequents, in
the midst of which we exist.   Of the different innumerable trains of antecedents and consequents which
it is important for us carefully to mark, it is observed,
that some succeed more quickly, some less.   While
the long pendulum of an eight-day clock is performing
one oscillation, the short pendulum of a table-clock
performs two or three.

What that is, to which we give the name of quickness, or slowness, in those successions; in other words,
what is the state of consciousness which we have thus
occasion to mark ; has already been seen.   Every succession, observed by us, is a case of sensation and
memory; sensation of the consequent, memory of the
antecedent.   If we have observed simultaneously the
oscillations of the two pendulums, mentioned above,
we remember two or three antecedent oscillations of
the short pendulum, before we get back to one of the
long.   It is a mere case, therefore, of the greater or
less number of antecedents in a chain of memory, expounded in a preceding chapter.

In the knowledge, so important to us, of antecedents
and consequents, it is not enough that we know what
antecedents are followed by what consequents; much
depends upon the quickness or slowness of the successions.   It is, therefore, of the highest importance that
we should have the means of marking them.

What we do is, to take some well-known case of successions, and to make that a standard, by which to ascertain the rest. We take, for example, the oscillations of a pendulum. So many of these we call a minute. So many minutes we call an hour. These minutes and hours, then, are so many oscillations, that is successions. We call them measures of time. But things are measurable only by parts of themselves; extension by extension, weight by weight, and so on. What is measure by succession, therefore, is itself nothing but succession.

Having assumed a certain case of successions as a standard, and marked it into quantities, by distinctive names, we mark or name all other successions, by the names applied to the standard case. Thus, that grand succession, on which so much of what we are interested in depends, a revolution of the earth upon its own axis, we distinguish, by the term, twenty-four hours; which we also call by the name, day; and afterwards make use of, as a standard, to mark still slower successions, such as a revolution of the moon about the earth, a revolution of the earth about the sun. In all these measurements, and expressions, of time, it is still seen, that there is nothing in reality conceived but successions.

Beside the standards, more distinctly conceived and expressed, there is always, in these estimates of time, a tacit reference to another standard, which is regarded as the unit, or minimum of time. The case here is precisely analogous to that of the unit, or minimum, of extension, which we have already observed. Our tactual, and muscular, senses are not sufficiently fine to discern objects of less than a certain magnitude.

The least which they can discern is tacitly assumed as
the unit of extension.   Nor are any of our senses fine
enough to discern successions which have more than
a certain degree of rapidity.   Thus, if the seven primitive colours are made to pass with a certain velocity before the eye, they do not appear separate, but
blended into one continuous white.   In like manner,
if sounds are made to succeed one another, at first,
slowly, afterwards, with greater and greater rapidity,
they cannot, at last, be distinguished as different
sounds, but appear as one continuous sound.   In fact,
this is probably the account of all sounds, which are
merely effects of the vibrations in the air, and therefore
pulses ; but often so quick, in succession, that no
interval is distinguishable, and the perception is that
of a continuous sound.

The close resemblance, in this respect, between sensations and ideas, is remarkable.   When sensations
are brought into close conjunction they become blended,
and appear, not several, but one.   We have seen, in a
most important case of association, that when ideas
are called up together in close conjunction, they, too,
cease to be distinguishable, and, being blended together, assume, even where there is the greatest complexity, the appearance, not of many ideas, but of
one.   Of this we have very remarkable examples, in
the two cases of SPACE, and TIME.

There is a certain succession, then, of sensations
and ideas, in which the antecedent and consequent
can be distinguished: another, in which the antecedent
and consequent, on account of quickness, cannot be
distinguished.   The quickest that can be distinguished,
is that to which, as the unit or minimum, a tacit

reference is made, in our several estimates of time.

Having thus shewn how far the account of TIME, presented by one of the most recent Philosophers of high name, goes in expounding the phenomenon, and how far it leaves it unexpounded; it will be instructive next to observe, how far the genius of the ancient Greek Philosophers carried them, in this important inquiry. It is satisfactory, that we can refer the unlearned reader to a very clear and accurate exposition of their doctrines, in a well known work in our own language, the "Hermes" of Mr. Harris; from which, for the sake of this convenience, the present account of those ancient doctrines shall be drawn.

"Time and Space," says that author,* "have this in common, that they are both of them by nature *continuous.* But in this they differ, that all the parts of Space exist *at once* and *together*, while those of Time only exist in *Transition* or Succession." This is only transcribing the common language. What remained was, to shew what are the real facts couched under this language.†

"In every given time we may assume any where a *Now* or *Instant*, and therefore, in every given *Time*, there may be assumed infinite *Nows* or *Instants*.

---

* Hermes, B. I. ch. vii.

† The expression of Ammonius, here quoted by Harris, comes nearer the fact than his own—ὁ χρόνος ὑφίσταται κατά μόνον τὸ NYN, ἐν γάρ τῷ γίνεσθαι καί φθείρεσθαι τό εἶναι ἔχει. Time subsists only in a single NOW or INSTANT, for it hath its being in beginning and ceasing to be. In other words, Time never is; all you can say of it is only this, it has been, or it is about to be.—(*Author's Note.*)

" A Now or Instant is the *Bound* of every finite *Time*. But although a *Bound*, it is not a *Part* of *Time*. If this appear strange, we may remember, that if a *Now* or *Instant*, were a *Part* of *Time*, it being essential to the character of *Parts*, that they should measure the *Whole*, it would contain within itself infinite other nows ; and this, it is evident, would be absurd and impossible."

" *The same Now* or *Instant*, may be the end of one *Time*, and the *Beginning* of another ; the first, necessarily *Past Time*, as being *previous* to *the Now* or *Instant*, which both Times include ; the other necessarily Future, as being *subsequent*. As, therefore, every Now or Instant always exists in Time, and without being Time, is *Time's Bound ;* the Bound of *Completion* to the *Past,* and the Bound of *Commencement* to the Future : from hence we may conceive its nature or end, which is *to be the Medium of Continuity between the Past and the Future, so as to render Time, through all its parts, one Intire and Perfect Whole.*"

It must be obvious to every one, who has correctly followed me through the preceding deductions, that this mysterious language, if applied to actual successions, has a distinct meaning ; if not so applied, it is jargon merely, without one idea annexed. This now, which is not *Time*, and, not being *Time*, is of course nothing else ; this nothing, then, which, though nothing is the medium of continuity between Something, namely, time past, and time future, seems to be only a mysterious name for that link which is supposed to be between every antecedent and its consequent ; which supposition of a link, or medium of continuity, we have already shewn to be a mere case of association, involving a prejudice ; the antecedent and consequent, and nothing else, being really included in a case of succession. Thus understood, however, it is a medium of continuity, forming the " *Bound of Completion*" to the previous train of successions, the "*Bound of Commencement*" to the following.

Mr. Harris proceeds to shew some of the conclusions, resulting from the account which he had thus rendered of Time. " *In the first place*," he says, " *there cannot* (strictly speaking) *be any such thing as time present.*" We will draw from this a conclusion, which Mr. Harris appears not to have seen, or does not choose to acknowledge ; That, if there be no such thing as Time present, neither can there be any such thing as Time past. For what is the past, but that which has been present ? But if there be no such thing as time present, or time past, there can be no such thing as time future. Time, therefore, is an impossibility.

Mr. Harris himself, indeed, goes a certain way toward this conclusion. " If *no Portion* of time," he says, " be the object of *any Sensation ;* further, if the Present *never* exist ; if the past be *no more ;* if the Future be not as yet ; and if these are all the parts, out of which *Time* is compounded : how strange and shadowy a Being do we find it ? How nearly approaching to a perfect non-entity ?"*

---

* It is but justice to Aristotle, to say, that he expressed the right conclusion much more distinctly than Harris thought proper to do. His mode of inferring, as translated by Harris, is as follows : That, therefore, *Time* exists not at all, or at least, has but a faint and obscure existence, one may suspect

Mr. Harris then says, " Let us try, however, since the senses fail us, if we have not faculties of higher power, to seize this fleeting Being." What then is it he does in the search of those " faculties of higher power ?" It will be seen, from the following quotation, that he merely describes a few cases of actual succession ; and says, that from them, by the help of memory, and imagination, we come by the idea of Time. But the Memory and Imagination of successions present to us nothing but the successions themselves. If then the Memory and Imagination of successions, give us the idea of Time, the idea of Time can only be some part or the whole of the idea of the successions.

" The World has been likened to a variety of Things, but it appears to resemble no one more than some moving spectacle (such as a procession or a triumph) that abounds in every part with splendid objects, some of which are still departing, as fast as others make their appearance. The Senses look on, while the sight passes, perceiving as much as is *immediately present*, which they report *with tolerable accuracy* to the Soul's superior powers. Having done this, they have done their duty, being concerned with nothing, save what is present and instantaneous. But to the *Memory*, to the *Imagination*, and above all, to

---

from hence. A part of it has been, and is no more ; a part of it is coming, and is not as yet ; and out of these is made that Time, which is without end, and ever to be assumed farther and farther. Now, that which is made up of nothing but non-entities, it should seem was incapable ever to participate of Entity.—(*Author's Note.*)

the *Intellect*, the several *Nows* or *Instants*, are not lost,
as to the *Senses*, but are presented and made objects
of *steady* comprehension, however, in their own nature,
they may be *transitory* and *passing*.

" Now it is from contemplating two or more of these
Instants under one view, together with that Interval
of Continuity, which subsists between them, that we
acquire insensibly the Idea of TIME.   For example :
The Sun rises : this I remember : *it rises again :* this
too, I remember.   These Events are not together;
there is an *Extension* between them—not however of
Space, for we may suppose the place of rising the
same, or at least, to exhibit no sensible difference.   Yet
still we recognise *some* Extension between them.   Now
what is this Extension, *but a natural day?*   And what
is that, but pure *Time?*   It is after the same manner,
by recognising two new Moons, and the Extension
between these ; two several Equinoxes, and the extension between these ; that we gain Ideas of other
Times, such as *Months* and *Years*, which are all so
many Intervals, described as above ; that is to say,
*passing Intervals of Continuity between two Instants
viewed together.*

" And thus it is THE MIND acquires the Idea of
TIME.   But this Time it must be remembered is PAST
TIME ONLY, which is always the *first Species*, that
occurs to the human Intellect.   How then do we
acquire the Idea of TIME FUTURE ?   The answer is,
we acquire it by *Anticipation*.   Should it be demanded still further, *And what is Anticipation ?*   We
answer, that, in this case, it is a kind of reasoning by
analogy from similar to similar ; from successions of
events, that are past already, to similar successions,

that are presumed hereafter. For example : I observe, as far back as my memory can carry me, how every day has been succeeded by a night ; that night, by another day ; that day, by another night ; and so downwards in order to the Day that is now. Hence, then, I *anticipate a similar succession* from the present Day, and thus gain the Idea of days and nights in *futurity*. After the same manner, by attending to the periodical returns of New and Full Moons ; of Springs, Summers, Autumns, and Winters, all of which, in Time past, I find never to have failed, I anticipate a like orderly and diversified succession, which makes Months, and Seasons, and Years, *in Time future*."

It is to be observed, that, in the above passage, Harris, beside Memory and Imagination, introduces the name of *Intellect*, as concerned in generating the idea of Time. But it will be seen that he makes no use of it, whatsoever, in giving his explanation, nor mentions any other operations than those of, memory for the past, and anticipation for the future. Indeed, it appears from a passage of his work, immediately following, that when Mr. Harris, in this inquiry, uses the word Intellect, he means nothing but Anticipation and Memory. "There is nothing," he says, " appears so clearly an object of the MIND or INTELLECT only, as *the Future* does, since we can find no place for its existence any where else. Not but the same, if we consider, is equally true of *the Past.** Here we see, that

---

* *Ibid.* He goes on to say, that, from this same doctrine, that Time exists only in the mind, some philosophers inferred,

both *the Future*, and *the Past*, are said to be objects of
the INTELLECT only.   But the future is the object of
anticipation, the past of memory ; and both memory,
and anticipation, as we have seen, are cases of association.

In the cases of succession which he adduces, as
examples, to shew, in what manner we acquire, he
says, " insensibly," the idea of time, he tells us, there
is sensation of the consequent, memory of the antecedent, and beside these, " contemplation of two or more
instants under one view, together with that Interval
of continuity, which subsists between them." But
the contemplation of two instants, one prior, another
posterior, in one view, with the interval between them,
is a circumlocution for memory. It denotes obscurely,
and imperfectly, that union, in one idea, of all the
parts of a train, to which the name memory is affixed.
From this contemplation, he says it is, " that we acquire the idea of Time."   The real meaning is thus
shewn to be, that we acquire it from memory.   Mr.
Harris, therefore, at the bottom, agrees with Dr.
Reid ; and the same observations by which we shewed

---

that if mind did not exist, neither could Time. Πότερον δὲ μὴ
οὔσης ψυχῆς εἴη ἂν ὁ χρόνος, ἀπορήσειεν ἄν τις. (*Aristot.*
Nat. Auscult. l. iv. c. 20.) Themistius, who comments the
above passage, expresses himself more positively. Εἰ τοίνυν
διχῶς λέγεται, τό τε ἀριθμητὸν, καὶ τὸ ἀριθμούμενον, τὸ μὲν, τὸ
ἀριθμητὸν δηλαδὴ, δυνάμει, τὸ δὲ, ἐνεργείᾳ, ταῦτα δὲ οὐκ ἂν
ὑποστάιη, μὴ ὄντος τοῦ ἀριθμήσοντος, μήτε δυνάμει μήτ' ἐνεργείᾳ,
—φανερὸν ὡς οὐκ ἂν ὁ χρόνος εἴη, μὴ οὔσης ψυχῆς. (*Them.*
p. 48.   Edit. Aldi.)—(*Author's Note.*)

the imperfection of Dr. Reid's account, are equally
applicable to that of Mr. Harris. The case, in
truth, is, that neither of them does any thing more
than merely state the fact, without an attempt to
explain it. That we cannot have the idea of time,
without the observation of successions ; and that
memory is joined with sense in the observation of
successions,—is the matter of fact. What TIME is,
distinct from the memory and the sensations, they
ought to have told us, but have not. They would
not have found it difficult, had they been familiar with
the distinction (of such infinite importance, in all
accurate inquiries into the human mind) between the
mode of signification of concrete words, and the mode
of signification of abstract ones ; the latter, in its
more complicated cases, of not very easy comprehension. Unfortunately, we have no concrete term,
corresponding with Time. Hence a great part of the
difficulty of conceiving distinctly the meaning of the
abstract. Time, also, is not the abstract name of any
one train, but of all trains ; as redness is not the
name of one red, but of all reds. And there is this
further complication, that the word "time" is never
applied to any train, in particular ; as time of a race,
time of a battle, and so on ; without the predominating association of that particular train, whatever it
be, minutes, hours, or days, which we are accustomed
to employ, as the measure of other successions. Without much and accurate practice, therefore, in conceiving the meaning of abstract terms, especially in the
more complex and intricate cases ; it is extremely
difficult steadily to contemplate either TIME, as the

K 2

abstract name of all successive, or SPACE, as the abstract name of all simultaneous order.*

It will be instructive, to recapitulate the indissoluble associations which are contained in the idea of Time. With every present event, is indissolubly associated the idea of an antecedent; with that antecedent, the idea of another antecedent; and so on without end. These are the ideas of Succession, and of Infinity; forced upon us by indissoluble association. The events of the present moment, are innumerable. With every one of these we associate the ideas of antecedents without end. This is the Past; an Infinity of simultaneous successions, each having antecedents, running back without end. These are successions in the concrete; successions of objects. Drop the connotation, to form the abstract, as is done in other cases; you have then successions without the objects; which is precisely the meaning of the word TIME.

As with every present event, and those infinite in number, is indissolubly associated the idea of a series of antecedents, without end, which, in the abstract, is

---

* " Multos autem in errorem ducit, quod voces generales et abstractas in disserendo utiles esse videant, nec tamen earum vim satis capiant. Partim vero à consuetudine vulgari inventæ sunt illæ ad sermonem abbreviandum, partim à philosophis ad docendum excogitatæ, non quod ad naturas rerum accommodatæ sint, quæ quidem singulares et concretæ existunt, sed quod idoneæ ad tradendas disciplinas, propterea quod faciant notiones, vel saltem propositiones, universales."—*Berkeley de Motu*, s. 7. No predecessor of Berkeley was so fully aware, as he was, of the deceptions practised on the human mind by abstract terms.—(*Author's Note.*)

TIME PAST, so with every such event, is indissolubly associated the idea of a consequent, with that the idea of another consequent, and so on, without end ; which, in the abstract, is TIME FUTURE.

The synchronous Line, or Line of *Extension*, and the successive Line, or Line of *Time*, bear a pretty close analogy.   As, in the Line of *Extension*, we have the concrete line, and the abstract line ; the concrete line being the positions with the objects ; the abstract or mathematical line, the positions without the objects ; so, in the line of *Time*, we have the concrete line, and the abstract line ; the concrete line being the successions with the objects ; the abstract line, the successions without the objects ; to which abstract line, we give the name TIME.

We have before remarked, as an important case of indissoluble association, that the idea of Position, that is, of a modification of Space, is indissolubly associated with the idea of every sensible object.   It is now to be remarked, as a not less important case, that the idea of succession or of antecedent and consequent, that is, a modification of Time, is indissolubly associated with the idea of every object.   The idea of a modification of Space, and the idea of a modification of Time, form parts of our complex idea of every object.   It is no wonder that they appear to be necessary, seeing that they force themselves upon us, by irresistible association, with the idea of every object.[29][30]

---

[29] As is shewn in the text, Time is a name for the aggregate of the successions of our feelings, apart from the feelings themselves.   I object, however, in the case of time, as I did in the

case of Space, to considering it as an abstract term. Time does not seem to me to be a name (as the author says) for the pastness, the presentness, and the futureness of our successive feelings. It is rather, I think, a collective name for our feeling of their succession—for what the author called, in a previous section, the part of the process " which consists in being sensible of their successiveness," for which part, he then said, " we have not a name." This taking notice of the successiveness of our feelings, whether we prefer to call it a part of the feelings themselves, or another feeling superadded to them, is yet something which, in the entire mass of feeling which the successive impressions give us, we are able to discriminate, and to name apart from the rest. A perception of succession between two feelings is a state of consciousness *per se*, which though we cannot think of it separately from the feelings, we can yet think of as a completed thing in itself, and not as an attribute of either or both of the two feelings. Its name, if it had one, would be a concrete name. But the entire series of these perceptions of succession has a name, Time ; which I therefore hold to be a concrete name.

However inextricably these feelings of succession are mixed up with the feelings perceived as successive, we are so perfectly able to attend to them, and make them a distinct object of thought, that we can compare them with one another, without comparing the successive feelings in any other respect. We can judge two or more successions to be of equal, or of unequal, rapidity. And if we find any series of feelings of which the successive links follow each other with uniform rapidity, such as the tickings of a clock, we can make this a standard of comparison for all other successions, and measure them as equal to one, two, three, or some other number of links of this series : whereby the aggregate Time is said to be divided into equal portions, and every event is located in some one of those portions. The succession of our sensations, therefore, however closely implicated with the sensations themselves, may be abstracted from them in thought, as completely

as any quality of a thing can be abstracted from the
thing.

The apparent infinity of Time the author, very rightly, explains in the same manner as that of Space.—*Ed.*

[30] In this section Mr. James Mill explains Time.　He tells
us that "it is a comprehensive word including all successions,
" or the whole of successive order" (p. 116)—"a perpetual flow of
" instants, of which only one can ever be present.　The very
" idea of Time is an idea of successions.　It consists of this
" and of nothing else" (pp. 116—117)—"it is the single worded
" abstract, involving the meaning of the three several abstracts,
" pastness, presentness, futureness" (p. 118).　In the line of
" Time, we have the concrete line, and the abstract line : the
" concrete line being the successions with the objects : the
" abstract line, the successions without the objects : to which
" abstract line, we give the name Time" (p. 133).

In p. 120 he gives us in a few words Dr. Reid's explanation
of Time :—and in pp. 124—130 he cites at greater length
Aristotle's explanation, as reproduced by Harris in the
Hermes.

Both Aristotle and Reid include in their meaning of Time,
not merely succession, but duration or continuity.　Mr.
James Mill includes only succession—antecedents and consequents.　He thinks that continuity is nothing else than
an illusion or prejudice, arising from extreme rapidity of
succession (pp. 123—125).

" Time and Space (says Harris, cited p. 124) have this in
" common, that they are both of them by nature continuous.
" But in this they differ—that all the parts of space exist at
" once and together ; while those of Time only exist in Transi-
" tion or Succession."　Mr. James Mill proceeds to say—
" This is only transcribing the common language.　What re-
" mained was, to show what are the real facts couched under
" this language."

Undoubtedly these facts ought to be shewn, and shewn
fully.　But I cannot think that they are shewn fully in the

present Chapter of the Analysis. On the contrary, a most important part of the case is omitted—Duration or Continuity—which Aristotle has put in the front of his exposition, and after him Read as well as Harris.

If it were true that the word Time is the abstract, having for its concrete *succeeding objects* and nothing more, we should not need the term at all. The abstract term "Succession" already answers this purpose, much more perspicuously and obviously. But Time includes something more than succession. It comprehends not merely potentiality for succeeding objects or events, but also potentiality for continuous motions or sensations: it embraces duration as well as succession.

The exposition of Aristotle is adapted to readers and debates so different from those of the present day, that it often appears strange, and even mystical, when ever so well translated. In the present case, however, we derive satisfaction from knowing, that his doctrine is, with a very small reserve, adopted by Hobbes, the most anti-mystical of all philosophers. (Hobbes' First Grounds of Philosophy—Part II., Sect. 7. 3). Aristotle has given a theory of Time at great length, perfectly clear as to its main features, though in several of its details, obscure and difficult to follow. I will add that throughout nearly the whole exposition, he keeps the abstract in close implication with the concrete: the neglect of which precaution, by many philosophers, is so justly censured by the Author of the Analysis.

Aristotle, according to a practice frequent with him, begins by enumerating various puzzles and difficulties which stand in the way of any theory (διαπορῆσαι Physic. IV. 10. p. 217. 6. 30). In doing this, here as elsewhere, he states the difficulties in a manner somewhat paradoxical. The citation of page 126, (together with note, page 127,) are all taken from this preliminary excursion, the beginning and end of which Aristotle distinctly marks (Physica IV. c. 10. p. 217 b. 30. p. 218 a. 30). He then proceeds to exposition ; and after remarking that Time is one and alike every where, amidst the greatest

diversity of events succeeding each other—he says that it is
not indeed identical with Motion, (as some theorists considered
it), but that it is nevertheless inseparable from Motion, being one
of the aspects or appurtenances of Motion. Magnitude or Body
moved—Motion—Time—all go together in Aristotle's conception. Magnitude is continuous : Motion is continuous : Time
is continuous (Physica IV. 11. p. 219. a. 12. 223. a. 10) :
Line is continuous. On the other hand, the Point is separate
and indivisible ; no two Points have any common term : a Line
is not made up of Points, but of smaller Lines ; and every
Line has Points for its bounds or limits. What the Point is
to a Line, the Now or Instant is to Time : the Instant is not
a portion of Time, but the boundary of each portion, and
the conjoining boundary between Time past and Time
future. (Physica IV. 11. p. 220. a. 5-25—VI. 3. 234.
a. 1-24).

Aristotle defines Time as the Number of Motion according
to Former and Later : i.e., Continuous Motion, considered as
numerable and successive. To take the words of Harris, from
Aristotle (cited p. 128 of the Analysis)—" It is from contem-
" plating two or more Instants under one view, together with
" that Interval of Continuity which subsists between them,
" that we acquire insensibly the Idea of Time."—" Months and
" Years are all so many Intervals described as above ; that is
" to say, passing Intervals of Continuity between two Instants
" viewed together."

Mr. James Mill hardly does justice to this exposition, when
he observes (p. 131)—" Neither Harris not Reid does any-
" thing more than merely state the fact, without an attempt to
" explain it. That we cannot have the idea of time, without
" the observation of succession ; and that memory is joined
" with sense in the observation of successions,—is the matter
" of fact. What Time is, distinct from the memory and the
" sensations, they ought to have told us, but have not."—In
this passage, the word " sensations" is evidently used by Mr.
James Mill as equivalent to " successions" or successive sensa-

tions : and the observation appears to me not well founded. I think that Aristotle *has* told us, and Harris after him, what Time is, distinct from the successive sensations.   It includes Motion and the Continuity of Motion.   These are elements of which Mr. James Mill takes no notice : and they supply the deficiency of which he complains.

It is one of the many merits of Mr. James Mill's Analysis that he has paid more attention to movements and muscular sensibility, as elements of our consciousness, than philosophers had done before him.   But in this chapter unfortunately, he has left them out, and has confined himself to successions. The explanation of Time, given in the main by Aristotle, is completed and elucidated by Professor Bain in his work on the Senses and the Intellect (chapter on the Muscular Feelings, sect. 20—23, pp. 95, 96 ; compare also p. 183, in ed. 3rd).   The feeling of continuance in our muscular exertions, of longer or shorter duration in the sweep of our limbs, is one of the primordial varieties of sensibility.   A longer expenditure of our energy affects the consciousness differently from a shorter.   In a full sweep of the arm, we are conscious of the instant of commencement as antecedent,—the interval of continued effort,—and the instant of termination as following. This is the clearest illustration of that which Aristotle and Harris describe as Time : two instants former and later, with continuous interval between them.   Motion is the most striking and obvious example of Continuity, and is therefore employed by Aristotle as the basis for his exposition of Time. The eternal and uniform motions of the celestial bodies were to him the most impressive of all phenomena ; the great standard by which all other motions were to be measured. Hobbes also takes the Line as the proper exponent of time. But though motion affords the best and amplest illustrations of Continuity, it is not motion only that is felt as continuous. The sense of continuance is felt in regard to other impressions also.   Professor Bain observes —" All impressions made on " the mind, whether those of muscular energy, or those of the " ordinary senses, are felt differently according as they endure

" for a longer or a shorter time. This is true of the higher
" emotions also. The continuance of a mental state must be
" discriminated by us from the very dawn of consciousness ;
" and hence our estimate of time is one of our earliest mental
" aptitudes. It attaches to every feeling that we possess"—
(p. 93).

We thus perceive that the sense of continuance is just as
much an original presentation to our consciousness, as the
sense of succession. This is an important fact, which has not
been sufficiently adverted to in the exposition of complex ideas
such as Time and Space. The *fundamentum* of Continual
Quantity is an immediate manifestation of our sensitive dis-
criminations not less than that of Discrete Quantity. The
complex Idea of Time embodies both.[a] Mr. James Mill in-
sists everywhere, with laudable emphasis, upon the necessity
of seeking the meaning of every abstract term in the concrete
particulars out of which it grows. But in explaining Time,
he has not set before himself *all* the concrete particulars in
their full variety and amplitude. Confining himself to Succession, and scarcely touching Continuance, he has not been
led to follow out the facts of motion in all their diversified
aspects, nor the many abstractions and generalisations which

---

[a] Aristotle's definition of Time was much discussed by his
contemporaries and successors. Both his pupils, Theophrastus
and Eudemus, accepted it: but there were many objectors, and
the earliest of them notified to us is, Straton of Lampsakus,
pupil and successor of Theophrastus. Straton objected on the
ground that the definition combined Number and Motion—Discrete Quantity and Continual Quantity—which combination he
held to be inadmissible. But this seems no valid objection.
Aristotle very properly recognises the two as distinct varieties
of Quanta—(see Categor. p. 4, b. 20) : but that is no reason
why both of them may not be combined in the same complex
idea—especially when we see that each of them has its distinct
root in different original presentations of our discriminative consciousness.

See Simplikius ad Aristot. Physic. IV. Scholia, p. 394,
b. 27—47. Brandis.

spring from comparison of motions with each other, under some one of these aspects.

In a note to this chapter of the Analysis (p. 129) attention is called by Mr. James Mill to another important doctrine cited by Harris out of Aristotle—to the relative nature of Time. Can there be any time, apart from the percipient mind? asks Aristotle—since time is the numerable element in motion, and there can be no numeration without a rational mind to number.[a] He does not affirm positively, but he speaks as conceiving number and the numbering mind to be Relatum and Correlatum, so that the former cannot exist without the latter.[b] Both Alexander of Aphrodisias and Themistius thought so likewise after him: though Boëthius and other commentators dissented from the opinion.[c] Upon this general question of relativity, Aristotle is not always consistent with himself. Though he declares explicitly, that Relata reciprocate in predication, and are implicated each with the other—and though he says that "the Soul is in a certain sense all things" (i.e. is the implied correlate of all our beliefs and disbeliefs, affirmations and negations)—yet in other places, he limits this

---

[a] Aristot. Physica. IV. 14, p. 223, a. 26.

[b] So also Hobbes' First Philosophy, Part II. 7, 3, 5 :—" Sec-" ing all men confess a year to be time, and yet do not think a " year to be the accident or affection of any body, they must " needs confess it to be, not in the things without us, but only " in the thought of the mind." (Here Hobbes goes too far, divesting time of all objective character ; instead of considering it as relative to the mind, which implies a subjective and an objective aspect combined. The next passage exhibits this.) " Time is the phantasm of before and after in motion: which " agrees with the definition of Aristotle. Time is the number " of motion according to former and latter— for that numbering " is an act of the mind. To divide Space or Time, is nothing " else but to consider one and another within the same—division " is not made by the operation of the hands, but of the mind."

[c] Themistius ad Aristot. Physic. IV. p. 337, in Spengel's edition of Themistius—partly extracted by Brandis in Scholia to Aristotle, p. 393, b. 27.

universal principle by exceptions, which some of his commentators deprecate as inadmissible."—*G*.

ª Aristot. Categor., c. 7, p. 6, a. 37, b. 28; p. 7, b. 23.
Scholia ad Categor., p. 65, b. 10—20. Brandis.

Aristot. de Animâ, III., 8, 431, b. 21, ἡ ψυχὴ τὰ ὄντα πώς
ἐςι πάντα· ἢ γὰρ αἰσθητὰ τὰ ὄντα ἢ νοητὰ, ἔςι δ' ἡ ἐπιςήμη μὲν
τὰ ἐπιςητά πως, ἡ δ' αἴσθησις τὰ αἰσθητά.

SECTION VI.

MOTION.

It is necessary to take notice of this term, because the idea which is named by it is apt to present the appearance of something mysterious, though, after the expositions with which we are now familiar, the materials of which it is compounded, will not be difficult to find.

The word Motion, is the abstract of Moving. What we have to investigate, therefore, are the sensations, on account of which, we call a body "moving;" motion being merely moving, the connotation dropped.

All motion is in a Line, either a straight line, or some other line. The idea of "moving," therefore, contains, for one ingredient, the idea of a line.

A body "moving," is a body which is successively at every point of a line. Every point of a line, as we have seen, is a particular position. A body "moving," therefore, is a body first in one position, then in another, then in another, through a certain series.

In the idea of a Body moving, then, we can enumerate the following particulars : the idea of a body, the idea of a position, the idea of a line, the idea of succession. These are all complex ideas; some of them highly complex; united into one idea, motion, they compose one of the most complex of all our ideas. The ingredients, however, being already explained, there can be no great difficulty in understanding the compound.

It is commonly said, that motion includes the idea both of Space, and of Time. As it includes the idea of Succession, it includes the idea of Time, successions in the abstract (otherwise called instants), without end, receiving the name of Time. As it includes the idea of a Line, it includes the idea of extension in one direction. As it includes the idea of Position, which is that of lines, in every direction, it includes the idea of extension in every direction ; but extension in every direction, taken abstractly, is Space.

It is important to observe, that, though we receive, and that the most frequently, information of motions by the eye, it is not from the sensations of sight, that the idea of motion is derived. It is by association of ideas alone, that we fancy we see motion, as it is thence we fancy that we see figure, and distance. The classes of sensations, from which we derive the idea of motion, and the idea of extension, are the same ; they are the muscular and tactual sensations. The man born blind, is not without the idea of motion, as he is without that of colour ; on the contrary, he has the idea probably much more precise, than we who have entangled it inextricably with the perceptions of sight.

To recur to the exposition which we have already given; we may remember, that the sensations (taking the simplest case), on account of which we apply the name Line, are partly sensations of Touch, partly sensations of Muscular Action. If we touch a line at one point with any part of our bodies, say the finger ; so long as the finger is still, we have merely the sensations, on account of which we call the line tangible. As soon as we move the finger along the line, we have the sensations and ideas, on account of which we call it extended. But these new feelings, on account of which we call the line extended, are also the feelings, on account of which we call the finger moved. The sensations, therefore, whence we derive our ideas of extension, and of motion, exist simultaneously. We have a certain compound of feelings, partly sensations, and partly ideas ; for we have already seen, that the perception of succession consists in a present sensation, associated with the idea of a past one ; and we assign to this compound, not one name, as on other occasions, but two names, after a very peculiar and remarkable manner. These two names are, Line Extended, Finger Moved. The complication of the feelings here, and of course the obscurity of them, is very remarkable ; though the naming, as in certain other cases of obscure ideas, is very distinct. We are never misled in the application of the terms, Line Extended, Finger moved ; though we may be very much puzzled to shew, of the compound of feelings which are thus named, and which, in the compound, are easily, and infallibly traced, how much is included under the one term, and how much under the other. A certain portion of the sensations in the compound is peculiar to what is called the Line, another portion is peculiar to what is called the Finger. The rest is common to both. The common part, united to what is peculiar to line, is called line extended ; the same common part, united with what is peculiar to finger, is called Finger moved.

Our ideas of extension and motion, are, no doubt,

originally derived from the action of our own bodies.
I touch something, and have the sensation of resistance. The idea of resistance is the fundamental
part in every combination to which I give the name
of object. In this case, there is the object touched,
and there is the finger touching. A certain action is
given to my finger, still touching the object. That
action involves certain feelings; these I combine both
with the object, and with the finger, and to these two
combinations I give the two names, Object Extended,
Finger Moved.

If any one shut his eyes, excluding as much as
possible, the ideas of sight, and conceiving, without
admixture, the feelings in the finger and the arm,
while the finger passes along a line, he will get some
notion of the series of antecedents and consequents,
whence the idea of Motion is derived. They are feelings, which language does not enable us to communicate by words; but it does not seem very difficult for
any man to raise the ideas of them in himself.

Let any one suppose, that the line commences
opposite to the centre of his body. He begins by
touching it at that point with the finger of his right
hand; and in this there is one state of feeling. He
gives the finger the smallest perceptible motion
towards the right: this is another state of feeling.
He gives it a further motion, the smallest perceptible,
in the same direction : this is another state of feeling ;
and so on, as far as the arm can reach. The antecedent
states are in each instance united with the present by
memory, and by the amount of the states, thus united,
the amount of the motion is computed.

Conceiving the case of a man born blind, the more

easily to exclude the illusions of association; it is obvious, that such a man can obtain the idea of another body in motion, only by accompanying it with his hand; or by associating the ideas, on account of which he calls the hand, moved, with the body in question. By frequent operations of the hand, such as that described above, he becomes familiar with the idea of the hand moved. The ideas of the sensations, on account of which, he calls it moved, are easily raised, easily form themselves into combination, and easily associate themselves with the object, Hand. The idea of Hand, and the idea of Hand moved, having become very familiar, it is an easy case of association to transfer the term *moved* to other things, as the foot moved, the body moved, the stone moved. When he has become familiar with the application of Moved, as a connotative term, to various objects, it is easy, in this, as in other cases, to drop the connotation; and then he has the abstract, MOTION.[31] [32]

---

[31] The author correctly, in my opinion, refers to our muscular sensibility (aided by Touch), the fundamental notions of Resistance, Motion, Extension, Space. He also remarks properly, that the idea of motion and the idea of extension are the same; they are merely different modes of viewing one experience. In a mutually involved series of properties such as these, the Analysis may proceed in several different arrangements, no one being apparently very decisive. The following mode is suggested as on the whole, the most consecutive.

The feeling of Resistance expresses what is probably the most fundamental state of all, the consciousness of muscular energy or expended force. Taking the case of a dead strain, or a pressure without movement, we have mere muscular energy and nothing else. We have an indivisible, unanalysable, mode of consciousness, distinct from all modes of passive sensation, and from all forms of emotion. It is a kind of consciousness remarkably constant in its character; it varies in degree, but with this peculiarity that because a man is physically weaker than usual, he does not on that account exaggerate or misrepresent the degree of his muscular expenditure; the feeling of lifting two pounds is not made the same as the feeling of lifting four pounds, although in some of the incidents of exertion, as in the organic state of exhaustion, the smaller expenditure in one state is held to be equal to the greater expenditure in another state. The consciousness of putting forth power is the most uniform, the least variable, of all our sensibilities; the same amount of actual force expended is estimated as nearly the same under all circumstances.

In being conscious of expended energy, we discriminate its degrees, within certain limits; we know when we increase or diminish the amount; and our sensibility is measured by the smallness of the difference that makes a change in our consciousness. This discrimination is the basis of our estimate of the property termed Force, Resistance, Momentum, in moving bodies. Our idea of force is a muscular idea, an idea of muscular force of a certain amount. Force may be viewed in other ways, or from other aspects, but its direct and simple estimate is muscular energy in the dead strain.

2. We are farther conscious of muscular energy as more or less enduring or continuing. Our consciousness varies according as a strain is protracted; a weight supported half a minute gives a feeling different from a weight supported a quarter of a minute.

Farther, it is important to remark that increase of continuance is not confounded with increase of force in the same time. Mechanically speaking, it is the same to us, whether we support two pounds one minute, or one pound two minutes; the energy gone out of us, the oxidation, or consumption of material, must be the same for both. But the consciousness is not the same for both; each has a character of its own, and we recognise the distinction in clear consciousness. If we confounded all modes of expended energy that are dynamically equal, we should be disqualified from attaining the ideas of motion and extension.

When energy is accompanied by *movement*, there is a new and characteristic mode of consciousness, of vital importance. Energy in the dead strain and energy with motion may be equal as regard expended force, but they are not the same to our feelings. Continuance in the one is a different fact from continuance in the other. The feeling of continuance in moving energy is the fact that we call motion ; and also the fundamental property, the starting point, with reference to Extension ; although much more is wanted to complete that cognition. Mere dead strain would not amount to extension ; and the discriminating of dead strain from moving strain is thus of essential moment. From the sense of this distinction, and the estimate of degree of continuance in movement, we begin at once the experience of motion and the ground-work of extension.

The consciousness of continuance whether of dead strain or of movement is also a consciousness of duration, but not the only mode of becoming versed in this property. All our mental states, — whether muscular feelings, sensations, emotions, thoughts, volitions,—are different as they are more or less continued, and this consciousness of difference is a consciousness of Duration or Time. Hence the usual saying that Time is a property common to the Object and to the subject. The object experiences of motion and extension are the most convenient modes of measuring time, they are the most accurate and discriminative, but they are not the only nor the chief concrete embodiments of it. We often measure time by the duration and succession of our feelings and thoughts.

3. Another mode of discrimination inhering in our muscular consciousness is the degree of movement, as slow or quick. We are differently affected according to the rapidity of our movements ; an accelerated pace in the arm, or in the whole body, sensibly alters our feelings. Farther, we do not compound this alteration with its dynamical equivalents in the

other modes—with increase in the amount of the dead strain,
in the continuance of the dead strain, or in the continuance of
movement. A characteristic mode of feeling attends this
special form of augmenting or reducing our expenditure of
force. The consequence is, a feeling of velocity or speed of
movement. But this feeling of speed is not all. We gain
another equivalent of degrees of extension ; more speed in the
same time being equal to more time with the same speed. It
is proper to remark, however, that we are premature in speaking of extension, or in regarding it as arrived at, at once by our
primary experiences of movement ; much has to be gone
through before this is fully formed or developed. Motion is
the fundamental fact, but motion is a fact of succession, and
can do nothing to suggest a group of *contemporaneous* phenomena, an outspread universe of the co-existing in time. Our
primary sensibility is a mere thread of succession, duration, or
continuance ; we have to acquire by a process of aggregation
and association, the highly artificial experience of things permanently situated in a relationship of co-existence in space or
extension.

It is at this point that Sensation comes to our aid. Passive sensation by itself is incompetent to give us the foundations of extension ; through it, we have neither resistance nor
movement, nor any fact partaking in what is essential to the
extended or object universe. Mere warmth, odour, relish,
touch, sound, colour, contain no elements of extension. The
co-operation with moving energy is what introduces us to the
object world.

How then does Sensation aid muscularity in evolving Extension ? In various ways, but chiefly thus. Our movements
are not performed in vacuo, but in conjunction with sensation.
The movements of the hand and arm, are usually conjoined
with sensations of touch. We draw the hand across a table ;
there is an arm sensibility, purely motor or energetic, which
is distinct from every mode of passive sensation. There
accompanies it, however, a series of tactile sensations, making
a united experience, active and passive. If this conjunction

were to happen but once, nothing would be thought of it farther than as a mere experience of succession. Again, in another situation the sweep of the movement ends in a contact or sensation of touch, or begins in the loss of such a contact. So far, these are mere casual conjunctions, unions of moving energy and passive sensibility. But in the course of many trials, there arise *uniform* conjunctions of movement with passive sensibility : the same movement being associated with the same tactile series, or with the same beginning or ending of tactile sensation. Take the case of the movement of the hand over the surface of our own body. A certain definite start, and definite amount of exertion brings with it a uniform tactile sensation, as in drawing the hand over the face. This uniformity generates an expectation that the same sensation will follow on the same definite energy. Many such conjunctions are formed in this manner. There is an interesting variety of the experience of such concurrences ; namely, when we *reverse* a movement, and find a series of sensations identified as the same in an inverted order. The hand passed along the side of a knife, experiences movement coupled with sensations, as often as the movement is made ; the inverted movement inverts the sensations.

The supposition, hitherto, has been confined to Touch. When we take in sight, the scope for the operation is greatly enlarged. Almost all our movements are conjoined with optical changes—sensations of colour and of visible form in a certain sequence. We speedily detect a number of uniform occurrences of movement and visible sensation. The same movement gives the same series of appearances at all times ; and an inverted movement corresponds with an inverted order. Here too we attain to a number of uniformities of coincidence, with the expectation of future occurrence. A certain movement of the eyes is accompanied with an optical series, as scanning the starry heavens ; as often as the movement is repeated from the same stand-point, the optical series is repeated ; the inverted movement gives the inverted series. We

contract an expectation, that such a coincidence will occur
in the future, and this expectation is our idea of the starry
space.

Our idea of extended things is thus completed by sensation.
It is a series of conjunctions, or associations, of movements
and sensations, in a fixed order. We do not in our idea of
space, command an entire view at one glance ; the successive
perception of points or limited portions is what we begin with,
and is the character of the mind's working even after we are
educated to the utmost. The co-existing in space, is the
mind's potentiality of finding definite sensations by means of
definite movements ; and it seems impossible to assign any
other meaning or import to the phenomena. The genesis of
the idea of space determines our mode of settling the great
question of the Perception of a material world.—*B.*

[32] It will be both useful and interesting to the inquiring
reader, if I add to the analysis of these very complex ideas by
the author of the present treatise, and to that by Mr. Bain,
the analysis given of them by the other great living master of
the Association psychology, Mr. Herbert Spencer. The following passages are from his "Principles of Psychology."
First, of Resistance :

" On raising the arm to a horizontal position and keeping it
" so, and still more on dealing similarly with the leg, a sensa-
" tion is felt, which, tolerably strong as it is at the outset, pre-
" sently becomes unbearable. If the limb be uncovered, and
" be not brought against anything, this sensation is associated
" with no other, either of touch or pressure." This is the
sensation of Muscular Tension.

" Allied to the sensation accompanying tension of the muscles,
" is that accompanying the act of contracting them—the sensa-
" tion of muscular motion. . . . While, from the muscles of a limb
" at rest, no sensation rises ; while, from the muscles of a limb in
" a state of continuous strain, there arises a continuous sensa-
" tion which remains uniform for a considerable time ; from the
" muscle of a limb in motion, there arises a sensation which is

" ever undergoing increase or decrease, or change of com-
" position.

" When we express our immediate experiences of a body by
" saying that it is *hard*, what are the experiences implied ?
" First, a sensation of pressure, of considerable intensity, is
" implied ; and if, as in most cases, this sensation of pressure
" is given to a finger voluntarily thrust against the object, then
" there is simultaneously felt a correspondingly strong sensa-
" tion of muscular tension.   But this is not all : for feelings of
" pressure and muscular tension may be given by bodies which
" we call soft, provided the compressing finger follows the
" surface as fast as it gives way.   In what then consists the
" difference between the perceptions ?   In this; that whereas
" when a soft body is pressed with increasing force, the syn-
" chronous sensations of increasing pressure and increasing
" muscular tension are accompanied by sensations of muscular
" movement ; when a hard body is pressed with increasing
" force these sensations of increasing pressure and tension are
" *not* accompanied by sensations of muscular movement.   Con-
" sidered by itself, then, the perception of softness may be de-
" fined as the establishment in consciousness of a relation of
" simultaneity between three series of sensations—a series of
" increasing sensations of pressure ; a series of increasing sen-
" sations of tension ; and a series of sensations of motion.
" And the perception of hardness is the same, with omission
" of the last series."   (pp. 212, 213.)

Of Extension ; and first, of Form or Figure :

" It is an anciently established doctrine that Form or Figure,
" which we may call the most complex mode of extension, is
" resolvable into relative magnitude of parts.   An equilateral
" triangle is one of which the three sides are alike in magni-
" tude.   An ellipse is a symmetrical closed curve, of which
" the transverse and conjugate diameters are one greater than
" the other.   A cube is a solid, having all its surfaces of the
" same magnitude, and all its angles of the same magnitude.
" A cone is a solid, successive sections of which, made at right
" angles to the axis, are circles regularly decreasing in magni-

" tude as we progress from base to apex.   Any object described
" as narrow is one whose breadth is of small magnitude when
" compared with its length.   A symmetrical figure is a figure in
" which the homologous parts on opposite sides are equal in
" magnitude.   Figures which we class as similar to each other,
" are such that the relation of magnitude between any two
" parts of the one, is equal to the relation of magnitude between
" the corresponding parts of the other.   Add to which, that an
" alteration in the form of anything, is an alteration in the
" comparative sizes of some of its parts—a change in the
" relations of magnitude subsisting between them and the other
" parts, and that by continuously altering the relative magni-
" tudes of its parts, any figure may be changed indefinitely.
" Hence, figure being wholly resolvable into relations of mag-
" nitude we may go on to analyze that out of which these rela-
" tions are formed—magnitude itself."   (pp. 224, 225.)
    Next therefore, of Magnitude :
    " What is a magnitude, considered analytically ?   The reply
" is, It consists of one or more relations of position.   When we
" conceive anything as having a certain bulk, we conceive its
" opposite limiting surfaces as more or less removed from
" each other ; that is, as related in position.   When we imagine
" a line of definite length, we imagine its termini as occupying
" points in space having some positive distance from each
" other ; that is, as related in position.   As a solid is decom-
" posable into planes ; a plane into lines ; lines into points ;
" and as adjacent points can neither be known nor conceived as
" distinct from each other, except as occupying different places
" in space—that is, as occupying not the same position, but
" relative positions—it follows that every cognition of magni-
" tude, is a cognition of one or more relations of position, which
" are presented to consciousness as like or unlike one or more
" other relations of position."   (p. 226.)
    And finally, of Position :
    " This analysis of itself brings us to the remaining space-
" attribute of body—Position.   Like magnitude, Position can-
" not be known absolutely ; but can be known only relatively.

" The notion of position is, in itself, the notion of relative
" position.   The position of a thing is inconceivable, save by
" thinking of that thing as at some distance from one or
" more other things.   The essential element of the idea will
" be best seen, on observing under what conditions only, it can
" come into existence.   Imagine a solitary point A, in in-
" finite space ; and suppose it possible for that point to be
" known by a being having no locality, what now can be predi-
" cated respecting its place ?   Absolutely nothing.   Imagine
" another point B to be added.   What can now be predicated
" respecting the two ?   Still nothing.   The points having no
" attributes save position, are not comparable in themselves ;
" and nothing can be said of their relative position, from lack of
" anything with which to compare it.   The distance between
" them may be either infinite or infinitesimal, according to the
" measure used ; and as, by the hypothesis, there exists no
" measure—as space contains nothing save these two points ;
" the distance between them is unthinkable.   But now imagine
" that a third point C is added.   Immediately it becomes pos-
" sible to frame a proposition respecting their positions.   The
" two distances, A to B, and A to C, serve as measures to each
" other.   The space between A and B may be compared with
" the space between A and C ; and the relation of position in
" which A stands to B becomes thinkable, as like or unlike the
" relation in which A stands to C.   Thus, then, it is manifest
" that position is not an attribute of body in itself, but only in
" its connection with the other contents of the universe.

   " It remains to add, that relations of position are of two
" kinds : those which subsist between subject and object ; and
" those which subsist between either different objects, or dif-
" ferent parts of the same object.   Of these the last are re-
" solvable into the first.   It needs but to remember, on the
" one hand, that in the dark a man can discover the rela-
" tive positions of two objects only by touching first one and
" then the other, and so inferring their relative positions from
" his own position towards each ; and on the other hand, that
" by vision no knowledge of their relative positions can be

" reached save through a perception of the distance of each
" from the eye; to see that ultimately all relative positions may
" be decomposed into relative positions of subject and object.

" These conclusions—that Figure is resolvable into relative
" magnitudes; that magnitude is resolvable into relative posi-
" tions; and that all relative positions may finally be reduced
" to positions of subject and object—will be fully confirmed
" on considering the process by which the space-attributes of
" body become known to a blind man. He puts out his hand
" and touching something, thereby becomes cognizant of its
" position with respect to himself. He puts out his other hand,
" and meeting no resistance above or on one side of the posi-
" tion already found, gains some negative knowledge of the
" thing's magnitude—a knowledge which three or four touches
" on different sides of it serve to render positive. And then,
" by continuing to move his hands over its surface, he acquires
" a notion of its figure. What, then, are the elements out of
" which, by synthesis, his perceptions of magnitude and
" figure are framed ? He has received nothing but simul-
" taneous and successive touches. Each touch established a
" relation of position between his centre of consciousness and
" the point touched. And all he can know respecting magni-
" tude and figure—that is, respecting the relative position of
" these points to each other—is necessarily known through the
" relative positions in which they severally stand to himself.

" Our perceptions of all the space-attributes of body being thus
" decomposable into perceptions of position like that gained
" by a single act of touch ; we have next to inquire what is
" contained in a perception of this kind. A little thought
" will make it clear that to perceive the position of anything
" touched, is really to perceive the position of that part of
" the body in which the sensation of touch is located.
" Whence it follows that our knowledge of the positions of
" objects, is built upon our knowledge of the positions of
" our members towards each other—knowledge both of their
" fixed relations, and of those temporary relations they are
" placed in by every change of muscular adjustment. That

" this knowledge is gained by a mutual exploration of the parts
" —by a bringing of each in contact with the others—by a
" moving over each other in all possible ways ; and that the
" motions involved in these explorations, are known by their
" reactions upon consciousness ; are propositions that scarcely
" need stating. But it is manifestly impossible to carry the
" analysis further without analysing our perception of motion.
" Relative position and motion are two ideas of the same expe-
" rience. We can neither conceive motion without conceiving
" relative position, nor discover relative position without motion.
" In the present, therefore, we must be content with the con-
" clusion that, whether visual or tactual, the perception of every
" statical attribute of body is resolvable into perceptions of
" relative position which are gained through motion." (pp. 226
" —229.)

In further prosecution of the analysis :

" How do we become cognizant of the relative positions of
" two points on the surface of the body ? Such two points,
" considered as coexistent, involve the germinal idea of Space.
" Such two points disclosed to consciousness by two succes-
" sive tactual sensations' proceeding from them, involve the
" germinal idea of Time. And the series of muscular sensa-
" tions by which, when self-produced, these two tactual sensa-
" tions are separated, involve the germinal idea of Motion.
" The questions to be considered then are—In what order do
" these germinal ideas arise ? and—How are they de-
" veloped ?

" . . . Taking for our subject a newly-born infant, let us
" call the two points on its body between which a relation is to
" be established, A and Z. Let us assume these points to be
" anywhere within reach of the hands—say upon the cheek.
" By the hypothesis, nothing is at present known of these
" points ; either as coexisting in Space, as giving successive
" sensations in Time, or as being brought into relation by
" Motion. If, now, the infant moves its arm in such a way as
" to touch nothing, there is a certain vague reaction upon its
' consciousness—a sensation of muscular tension. This

" sensation has the peculiarity of being indefinite in its com-
" mencement; indefinite in its termination ; and indefinite in
" all its intermediate changes. Its strength is proportionate
" to the degree of muscular contraction. Whence it follows
" that as the limb starts from a state of rest, in which there is
" no contraction ; and as it can reach a position requiring ex-
" treme contraction only by passing through positions requir-
" ing intermediate degrees of contraction ; and as the degrees
" of contraction must therefore form a series ascending by in-
" finitesimal increments from zero ; the sensations of tension
" must also form such a series. And the like must be the case
" with all subsequent movements and their accompanying
" sensations ; seeing that, be it at rest or in action, a muscle
" cannot pass from any one state to any other without going
" through all the intermediate states. Thus, then, the infant,
" on moving its arm backwards and forwards without touching
" anything, is brought to what we may distinguish as a nascent
" consciousness—a consciousness not definitely divisible into
" states; but a consciousness the variations of which pass in-
" sensibly into each other, like undulations of greater or less
" magnitude. And while the states of consciousness are thus
" incipient—thus indistinctly separated, there can be no clear
" comparison of them ; no thought, properly so called ; and
" consequently no ideas of Motion, Time, or Space, as we
" understand them. Suppose, now, that the hand touches
" something. A sudden change in consciousness is produced—
" a change that is incisive in its commencement, and, when
" the hand is removed, equally incisive in its termination. In
" the midst of the continuous feeling of muscular tension,
" vaguely rising and falling in intensity, there all at once
" occurs a distinct feeling of another kind. This feeling,
" beginning and ending abruptly, constitutes a definite state
" of consciousness ; becomes, as it were, a *mark* in conscious-
" ness. By similar experiences other such marks are pro-
" duced ; and in proportion as they are multiplied, there
" arises a possibility of comparing them, both in respect to
" their degrees and their relative positions ; while at the same

" time, the feelings of muscular tension being, as it were,
" divided out into lengths by these superposed marks, become
" similarly comparable; and so there are acquired materials
" for a simple order of thought. Observe, also, that while
" these tactual sensations may, when several things are touched
" in succession, produce successive marks in consciousness,
" separated by intervening muscular sensations, they may
" also become continually coexistent with these muscular
" sensations; as when the finger is drawn along a surface.
" And observe further, that when the surface over which the
" finger is drawn is not a foreign body, but some part of the
" subject's body, these muscular sensations, and the continuous
" tactual sensation joined with them, are accompanied by a
" series of tactual sensations proceeding from that part of the
" skin over which the finger is drawn. Thus, then, when the
" infant moves its finger along the surface of its body from A
" to Z, there are simultaneously impressed upon consciousness
" three sets of sensations—the varying series of sensations
" proceeding from the muscles in action; the series of tactual
" sensations proceeding from the points of the skin succes-
" sively touched between A and Z; and the continuous sensa-
" tion of touch from the finger-end. . . . As subsequent
" motions of the finger over the surface from A to Z always
" result in the like simultaneous sets of sensations, these, in
" course of time, become indissolubly associated. Though the
" series of tactual sensations, A to Z, being producible by a
" foreign body moving over the same surface, can be dissoci-
" ated from the others; and though, if the cheek be with-
" drawn by a movement of the head, the same motion of the
" hand, with its accompanying muscular sensations, may occur
" without any sensation of touch; yet, when these two series
" are linked by the tactual sensation proceeding from the
" finger-end, they necessarily proceed together; and become
" inseparably connected in thought. Whence it obviously re-
" sults that the series of tactual sensations A to Z, and the
" series of muscular sensations which invariably accompanies it
" when self-produced, serve as mutual equivalents; and being

" two sides of the same experience, suggest each other in con-
" sciousness.

" Due attention having been paid to this fact, let us go on
" to consider what must happen when something touches, at
" the same moment, the entire surface between A and Z. This
" surface is supplied by a series of independent nerve-fibres,
" each of which at its peripheral termination becomes fused
" into, or continuous with, the surrounding tissue ; each of
" which is affected by impressions falling within a specific area
" of the skin ; and each of which produces a separate state of
" consciousness. When the finger is drawn along this surface
" these nerve-fibres A, B, C, D . . . Z, are excited in succession;
" that is—produce successive states of consciousness. And
" when something covers, at the same moment, the whole sur-
" face between A and Z, they are excited simultaneously ; and
" produce what tends to become a single state of conscious-
" ness. Already I have endeavoured to shew in a parallel
" case, how, when impressions first known as having sequent
" positions in consciousness are afterwards simultaneously
" presented to consciousness, the sequent positions are trans-
" formed into coexistent positions, which, when consolidated by
" frequent presentations, are used in thought as equivalent to
" the sequent positions.[a] . . . As the series of tactual impres-

---

[a] " Objects laid upon the surface will come to be distinguished
" from each other by the relative lengths of the series they
" cover ; or, when broad as well as long, by the groups of series
" which they cover. . . . By habit these simultaneous excita-
" tions, from being at first known indirectly by translation into
" the serial ones, will come to be known directly, and the serial
" ones will be forgotten : just as in childhood the words of a
" new language, at first understood by means of their equiva-
" lents in the mother tongue, are presently understood by them-
" selves ; and if used to the exclusion of the mother tongue, lead
" to the ultimate loss of it." We see that " a set of [nervous]
" elements may be excited simultaneously as well as serially;
" that so, a *quasi* single state of consciousness becomes the equi-
" valent of a series of states ; that a relation between what we
" call coexistent positions thus represents a relation of successive

" sions A to Z, known as having sequent positions in con-
" sciousness, are, on the one hand, found to be equivalent to
" the accompanying series of muscular impressions; and
" on the other hand, to the simultaneous tactual impressions
" A to Z, which, as presented together, are necessarily pre-
" sented in coexistent positions ; it follows that these two
" last are found to be the equivalents of each other. A series
" of muscular sensations becomes known as equivalent to a
" series of coexistent positions ; and being habitually joined
" with it, becomes at last unthinkable without it. Thus, the
" relation of coexistent positions between the points A and Z
" (and by implication all intermediate points) is necessarily
" disclosed by a comparison of experiences : the ideas of
" Space, Time, and Motion, are evolved together. When the
" successive states of consciousness A to Z, are thought of as
" having relative positions, the notion of Time becomes
" nascent. When these states of consciousness, instead of
" occurring serially, occur simultaneously, their relative posi-
" tions, which were before sequent, necessarily become co-
" existent ; and there arises a nascent consciousness of space.
" And when these two relations of coexistent and sequent posi-
" tions are both presented to consciousness along with a series
" of sensations of muscular tension, a nascent idea of Motion
" results.

" The development of these nascent ideas, arising as it does
" from a still further accumulation and comparison of expe-
" riences, will be readily understood. What has been above
" described as taking place with respect to one relation of co-
" existent positions upon the surface of the skin—or rather, one

---

" positions, and that this symbolic relation being far briefer, is
" habitually thought of in place of that it symbolizes ; and that,
" by the continued use of such symbols, and the union of them
" with more complex ones, are generated our ideas of . . . exten-
" sion—ideas which, like those of the algebraist working out an
" equation, are wholly unlike the ideas symbolized, and which
" yet, like his, occupy the mind to the entire exclusion of the
" ideas symbolized."—(pp. 222—224.)

" linear series of such coexisting positions, is, during the
" same period, taking place, with respect to endless other such
" linear series, in all directions over the body. The like
" equivalence between a series of coexistent impressions of
" touch, a series of successive impressions of touch, and series of
" successive muscular impressions, is being established between
" every pair of points that can readily be brought into relation
" by movement of the hands. Let us glance at the chief con-
" sequences that must ultimately arise from this organization
" of experiences.

" Not only must there gradually be established a connection
" in thought between each *particular* muscular series, and the
" *particular* tactual series, both successive and simultaneous,
" with which it is associated ; and not only must there, by im-
" plication, arise a knowledge of the special muscular adjust-
" ments required to touch each special part, but, by the same
" experiences, there must be established an indissoluble connec-
" tion between muscular series in general and series of sequent
" and coexistent positions in general, seeing that this connec-
" tion is repeated in every one of the particular experiences.
" And when we consider the infinite repetition of these expe-
" riences, we shall have no difficulty in understanding how
" their components become so consolidated, that even when
" the hand is moved through empty space, it is impossible to
" become conscious of the muscular sensations, without be-
" coming conscious of the sequent and coexistent positions—
" the Time and Space, in which it has moved.

" Observe again, that as, by this continuous exploration of
" the surface of the body, each point is put in relation not
" only with points in some directions around it, but with
" points in all directions—becomes, as it were, a centre from
" which radiate lines of points known first in their serial posi-
" tions before consciousness, and afterwards in their coexistent
" positions—it follows, that when an object of some size, as
" the hand, is placed upon the skin, the impressions from all
" parts of the area covered being simultaneously presented to
" consciousness, are placed in coexistent positions before con-

" sciousness : whence results an idea of the superficial exten-
" sion of that part of the body. The idea of this extension is
" really nothing more than a simultaneous presentation of all
" the impressions proceeding from the various points it in-
" cludes, which have previously had their several relative posi-
" tions measured by means of the series of impressions
" separating them. Any one who hesitates respecting this
" conclusion, will, I think, adopt it, on critically considering
" the perception he has when placing his open hand against
" his cheek—on observing that the perception is by no means
" single, but is made up of many elements which he cannot
" think of altogether—on observing that there is always one
" particular part of the whole surface touched, of which he is
" more distinctly conscious than of any other—and on observ-
" ing that to become distinctly conscious of any other part, he
" has to traverse in thought the intervening parts ; that is, he
" has to think of the relative positions of these parts by
" vaguely recalling the series of states of consciousness which
" a motion over the skin from one to the other would involve."
(pp. 257—263).

These three different expositions of the origin of our ideas of
Motion and Extension, by three eminent thinkers, agreeing in
essentials, and differing chiefly in the comparative degrees of
development which they give to different portions of the detail,
will enable any competent reader of such a work as the present
to fill up any gaps by his own thoughts. Many pages of additional commentary might easily be written ; but they would
not add any important thought to those of which the reader is
now in possession ; and belonging rather to the polemics of
the subject than to its strictly scientific exposition, they would
jar somewhat with the purely expository character of the
present treatise.

I will only further recommend to particular attention, the
opinion of Mr. Spencer, also adopted by Mr. Bain, that our
ascribing simultaneous existence to things which excite successive sensations, is greatly owing to our being able to vary
or reverse the order of the succession. When we pass our hands

over an object, we can have the tactual and muscular sensations in many different orders, and after having them in one order, can have them in another exactly the reverse. They do not, therefore, become associated with each other in a fixed order of succession, but are called up in any order with such extreme rapidity, that the impression they leave is that of simultaneousness, and we therefore hold the parts of tangible objects to be simultaneous.—*Ed.*

SECTION VII.

IDENTITY.

There is one other term, which still requires explanation ; and that is, IDENTITY, about which there
would not have appeared any difficulty, had it not
been for Personal Identity ; which is, indeed, a complicated case, and, of course, involves the obscurity
which great complexity implies.

We have already seen, on what account we use the
marks, same, and different, when we apply them to
two simple sensations, or when we apply them to two
ideas, simple, or complex.   In these cases, the terms
are relative terms, and name the objects in pairs.

There is another case, that which now it is our
business to explain, in which the name is not applied
to two objects, but to the same object, at two different
times.   Thus it is, that I say, The bridge at Westminster, by which I crossed the Thames thirty years
ago, is the same by which I crossed it yesterday.   The
crown which was placed on the head of George IV.
at his coronation, is the same by which the kings of
England have been crowned for many centuries.   The
words which we read in the Gospel of Matthew, are
the same which were written by that evangelist.   The
words which we read in the poem called the Æneid
are the same which were written by the poet Virgil.
The church which is now at Loretto, is the same with
that which belonged to the Virgin Mary at Nazareth,
which in the month of May, in the year 1291, was

carried through the air by Angels, from Galilee to
Tersato, in Dalmatia; and again on the 10th of
December, 1294, about midnight, by what conveyance is not known, was set down in a wood in Italy,
in the district of Ricanati, about a thousand paces
from the sea.

It is evident, from the contemplation of these
instances, which might be multiplied to any extent,
that the word SAME, in this mode of applying it, is
merely the name of a certain case of Belief: a belief
which, in some of the instances, is, memory; in some,
is grounded upon testimony; in some, upon circum-
stantial evidence; and, in some, upon both testimony
and circumstances. Thus, the case of belief respecting Westminster-bridge, which I mark by the word,
same, is Memory. The cases of belief respecting the
crown of England, respecting the words of the
gospel, respecting the church of Loretto, marked
respectively by the word same, are founded on testimony, joined with circumstances.

As we have already shewn wherein Belief, in all its
cases, consists, we have implicitly afforded the exposition of Identity. From same, the concrete, comes, in
the usual way, sameness, the abstract, dropping only
the connotation of the concrete. And Identity and
Sameness are equivalent terms.

From the importance, however, which has been
attached to these words, it seems necessary to shew
to the learner, somewhat more particularly, the mode
of tracing the simple ideas composing the clusters
which they are employed to mark.

The Lily, when it produces its brilliant flower in
summer, I call the same, with the plant which began

to shew itself above the surface of the ground, in spring, from a bulb, which I had planted in a particular spot of my garden. I also called it the same, from one day to another, though changing every day in its size, and other appearances, from its germination to the present time. For what reason have I done so? On account of certain circumstances, which every body can enumerate; its rising from a certain root; the uninterrupted continuity, by means of the stalk, between the root and the other parts of the plant; its being always found in the same place, that is, in the same synchronous order with certain other things; its corresponding with other plants, the growth of which I have observed, and so on. If it had grown in a flower pot, and been transferred from one to another, the enumeration of the circumstances would have been different; the evidence of its having grown from the same root would have been drawn from other circumstances. When I say, then, that the Lily I see, with its flowers in July, is the same with the Lily just emerging from the ground in April, I only express my belief of its having sprung from a certain root, and of its having vegetated, in connexion with that root, in the way of the plants grouped in the class called Lily.

I have a male Calf, of singular beauty, produced from my cow. I observe him from day to day. From day to day I call him the Same; and I do so when he has grown a bull of the greatest size. When I do so, I merely express my belief in a certain train of antecedents and consequents, with which experience has rendered me familiar. There is a certain train of antecedents and consequents, known to me by obser-

vation, which I call the birth, growth, maturity; and,
in one word, the Life, of the animal. The birth,
growth, and maturity of one animal, is one series of
successions; the birth, growth, and maturity of
another animal, is another series of successions. When
I apply the name Same, then, to any animal, I merely
express my belief, that my present sight of the animal
is part of a particular series, of which that perception
is the last link.

The case, it will not be doubted, is perfectly analogous, when I transfer the term from one of the lower
animals to one of my fellow men. The birth, infancy,
childhood, youth, manhood, of a human being, are
names for different parts of a certain series of antecedents and consequents. This series is known to me
by experience; that is, by sensation, by memory, and
other cases of association. The life of one man is
one series. The life of another man is another series.
When I say, then, that a man is the same, I merely
express my belief in one of those series; belief
that the particular man, of the present instant, is
the last link of such and such a chain, and not of any
other.

It is, however, to be observed, that the chain, thus
believed, and the evidence upon which it is believed,
are different things; and that this evidence is different
in different cases. In the case of a person whom I
have lived with from his birth, and seen every day,
the evidence, to a great degree, is sense and memory.
Sometimes the sameness of an individual is proved
in a court of justice, by evidence, such as is applicable to any other matters of fact; by written documents, marks on the body, articles of property found

with the child, and the testimony of those whose knowledge has been uninterrupted from one time to another.

It is not to be doubted, that when I transfer the word Same, from another man to myself, all that I do is to express my belief in one of those series ; and the only difference in the case is, that it is a series of which I have evidence of a very particular kind, and of which many parts are known to me, which can be known to nobody else.

As far as memory reaches, the evidence, in regard to myself, is memory and sensation. In the case of Evidence by memory and sensation, we have observed a peculiarity, necessary to be remembered, that the Evidence, and the Belief, are not different things, but the same thing. The memory which I have of my own existence, that is, the memory of a certain train of antecedents and consequents, is the Belief of them; on account of which belief, I apply to myself the term same, in the same way as I apply it to any other of my fellow men.

But I apply the term same to myself beyond the point to which memory reaches; as far back, in short, as to other men. This is true: I believe, that a train of antecedents and consequents, corresponding to that which forms the existence of other men, has also formed my existence. Part of this train I believe, by consciousness, memory. Part, namely, that which precedes memory, I believe on other evidence. What that evidence is, it is not difficult to see. We have, in the first place, the evidence of testimony ; namely, that of all the persons who knew us from our birth, to the time to which memory extends. We have next the evidence of what happens in the existence of all other men; or that case of association which unites inseparably the idea of like antecedents with like consequents.

It may be said, however, that my belief in the Identity of other men, is a very different thing from belief in my own Identity; and that the foregoing exposition does not sufficiently account for the difference which every one remarks between them.

The foregoing exposition, when duly attended to, will be found to account completely for the difference. We have remarked, that the evidence which I have for a great part of the series, in the case of other men, and of myself, is remarkably different. In the case of other men, it consists of observation and memory; in the case of myself, it consists of consciousness and memory. In these several and respective circumstances, Observation, and Consciousness, the distinction wholly consists. The memory of a chain of facts observed, is the evidence in the one case. The memory of a chain of states of Consciousness, is the evidence in the other.

I doubt not that this, without further analysis, will be seen by many of my readers to be a complete solution of the question. It may, however, be still objected, that we resolve observation itself into states of consciousness; and, if so, that the memory of a chain of states of Consciousness, is the evidence in both cases.

This brings us to the very bottom of the matter. Every body recognises, at once, that the memory of a state of consciousness, and the memory of something observed, are two distinct things ; that the memory, for example, of one of my own sensations, and the memory of an outward fact, as of the death of my father, are specifically different : or, to take two cases still easier perhaps to distinguish ; no one will say, that the memory of one's own pain is any thing like the same state of consciousness with the memory of seeing another man in pain. In the one case, the state of consciousness remembered is the pain itself; in the other it is the sensations of sight or hearing, which indicated to me the pain of the other man, or called up the idea of his pain by association. In the one case, the memory is memory of my own sensations purely; in the other case, it is the memory of my sensations, as the evidence only of outward things.

Each of the terms, therefore, I, Thou, He, marks a particular chain of antecedents and consequents, terminating with the I, the Thou, the He, of the present moment. The I, the Thou, the He, of the present moment, is marked, by these terms, *primarily ;* the preceding links are marked, *secondarily*, that is, connoted. When I say, " I, Thou, or He, did any thing," it is the I, the Thou, the He, of the moment spoken of, that is specially noted. The rest of the chain is not particularly adverted to, except when there is particular occasion for it.

Since the I, the Thou, the He, stand for the names of three men, and equally denote the antecedents and consequents, forming what is familiarly called the thread of life, of each of those individuals ; how does it happen, that the idea, which is called up by the term I, appears to be so different, from that which is called up by the term Thou, or any term denoting the vital chain of any other man ?

In what has been already stated, is found the answer. In that chain of antecedents and consequents which I mark by the term "same man," two species of things are included ; 1. The antecedents and consequents which form the successive states of his body ; 2. The successive states of his consciousness.

In knowing the antecedents and consequents, which form the successive states of my own body and of that of another man, the mode, though in some respects different, is, in so many respects, the same, that it does not here require explanation. But the mode of knowing the successive states of my own consciousness, and of those of other men, is totally different ; and in this consists the peculiarity which appears to belong to the idea which I annex to the term I, or myself. The knowledge of my own states of consciousness is consciousness itself, for the present moment, and memory of that consciousness for all the past. Of the states of consciousness of other men, I have no direct knowledge. I draw my belief of them only from signs. These signs, too, are significant only by reference to my own states of consciousness. Certain things cognizable by my senses, are accompanied in myself by certain states of consciousness, single, or in trains. These objects of sense (sights, sounds, &c.) are closely associated with the ideas of those states of consciousness. When presented to me, therefore, as objects of sense to other men, they excite the ideas of those states of consciousness ; and hence what I call my knowledge and belief of the mental trains of other men. It is not necessary to go further in the

analysis.   It is very obvious, that two complex ideas
must be different, which are formed in these different
ways ; nor is any thing more necessary to account for
the difference between the idea annexed to the pronoun I, and that annexed to the pronoun Thou.[33]

---

[33] The author has avoided an error in the mode and order
of the enquiry, which has greatly contributed to make the explanations given by psychologists of Personal Identity, so
eminently unsatisfactory as they are.   Psychologists have
almost always begun with the most intricate part of the question.   They have set out by enquiring, what makes me the
same person to myself ? when they should first have enquired
what makes me the same person to other people ? or, what
makes another person the same person to me ?   The author of
the Analysis has done this, and he easily perceived, that what
makes me the same person to others, is precisely what makes a
house, or a mountain, the same house or mountain to them
to-day which they saw yesterday.   It is the belief of an uninterrupted continuity in the series of sensations derivable from
the house, or mountain, or man.   There is not this continuity
in the actual sensations of a single observer : he has not been
watching the mountain unintermittedly since yesterday, or
from a still more distant time.   But he believes, on such
evidence as the case affords, that if he had been watching, he
should have seen the mountain continuously and unchanged
during the whole intervening time (provided the other requi-
sites of vision were present—light to see it by, and no cloud
or mist intervening) : and he further believes that any being,
with organs like his own, who had looked in that direction at
any moment of the interval during which he himself was not
looking, would have seen it in the same manner as he sees it.
All this applies equally to a human object.   I call the man I
see to-day the same man whom I saw yesterday, for the very
reason which makes me call the house or the mountain the
same, viz., my conviction that if my organs had been in the

same position towards him all the time as they are now, and
the other conditions necessary for seeing had been present, my
perception of the man would have continued all the time without interruption.

If we now change the point of view, and ask, what makes
me always the same person to myself, we introduce, in addition
to what there was in the other case, the entire series of my
own past states of consciousness. As the author truly says,
the evidence on which I accept my own identity is that of
memory. But memory reaches only a certain way back, and
for all before that period, as well as for all subsequent to it of
which I have lost the remembrance, the belief rests on other
evidence. As an example of the errors and difficulties in which
psychologists have involved themselves by beginning with the
more complex question without having considered the simpler
one, it is worth remembering that Locke makes personal identity
consist in Consciousness, which in this case means Memory ;
and has been justly criticised by later thinkers for this doctrine,
as leading to the corollary, that whatever of my past actions I
have forgotten, I never performed—that my forgotten feelings
were not *my* feelings, but were (it must therefore be supposed)
the feelings of somebody else.   Locke, however, had seen one
part of the true state of the case ; which is, that to *myself* I am
only, properly speaking, the same person, in respect of those
facts of my past life which I remember ; but that I nevertheless
consider myself as having been, at the times of which I retain
no remembrance, the same person I now am, because I have
satisfactory evidence that I was the same to other people; that
an uninterrupted continuity in the sensations of sight and touch
caused or which could have been caused to other people,
existed between my present self and the infant who I am told
I was, and between my present self and the person who is
proved to me to have done the acts I have myself forgotten.

These considerations remove the outer veil, or husk, as it
were, which wraps up the idea of the Ego.   But after this is
removed, there remains an inner covering, which, as far as I
can perceive, is impenetrable.   My personal identity consists

in my being the same Ego who did, or who felt, some specific
fact recalled to me by memory. So be it : but what is Memory ? It is not merely having the idea of that fact recalled :
that is but thought, or conception, or imagination. It is,
having the idea recalled along with the Belief that the fact
which it is the idea of, really happened, and moreover happened
to myself. Memory, therefore, by the very fact of its being
different from Imagination, implies an Ego who formerly experienced the facts remembered, and who was the same Ego
then as now. The phenomenon of Self and that of Memory
are merely two sides of the same fact, or two different modes
of viewing the same fact. We may, as psychologists, set out
from either of them, and refer the other to it. We may, in
treating of Memory, say (as the author says) that it is the idea
of a past sensation associated with the idea of myself as having
it. Or we may say, in treating of Identity, (as the author also
says), that the meaning of Self is the memory of certain past
sensations. But it is hardly allowable to do both. At least it
must be said, that by doing so we explain neither. We only
show that the two things are essentially the same ; that my
memory of having ascended Skiddaw on a given day, and my
consciousness of being the same person who ascended Skiddaw
on that day, are two modes of stating the same fact : a fact
which psychology has as yet failed to resolve into anything
more elementary.

In analysing the complex phenomena of consciousness, we
must come to something ultimate; and we seem to have
reached two elements which have a good prima facie claim to
that title. There is, first, the common element in all cases of
Belief, namely, the difference between a fact, and the thought
of that fact : a distinction which we are able to cognize in the
past, and which then constitutes Memory, and in the future,
when it constitutes Expectation ; but in neither case can we
give any account of it except that it exists ; an inability which
is admitted in the most elementary case of the distinction,
viz. the difference between a present sensation and an idea.
Secondly, in addition to this, and setting out from the belief

in the reality of a past event, or in other words, the belief that the idea I now have was derived from a previous sensation, or combination of sensations, corresponding to it, there is the further conviction that this sensation or combination of sensations was my own ; that it happened to myself.   In other words, I am aware of a long and uninterrupted succession of past feelings going as far back as memory reaches, and terminating with the sensations I have at the present moment, all of which are connected by an inexplicable tie, that distinguishes them not only from any succession or combination in mere thought, but also from the parallel successions of feelings which I believe, on satisfactory evidence, to have happened to each of the other beings, shaped like myself, whom I perceive around me.   This succession of feelings, which I call my memory of the past, is that by which I distinguish my Self. Myself is the person who had that series of feelings, and I know nothing of myself, by direct knowledge, except that I had them.   But there is a bond of some sort among all the parts of the series, which makes me say that they were feelings of a person who was the same person throughout, and a different person from those who had any of the parallel successions of feelings ; and this bond, to me, constitutes my Ego.   Here, I think, the question must rest, until some psychologist succeeds better than any one has yet done in shewing a mode in which the analysis can be carried further.—*Ed*.

CHAPTER XV.

REFLECTION.

So much use has been made of the word REFLEC-
TION, and results of so much importance have been
referred to it, that it is necessary to shew what state
of Consciousness it denotes, in all the possible accep-
tations of it.

Mr. Locke defines it, "That notice which the
mind takes of its own operations."

When we have a sensation, we have already seen,
on various occasions, that the having the state of
consciousness, and taking notice of it, are not two
things, but one and the same thing. When we say
that one sensation is more attended to than another,
this, as we shall see hereafter, is really tantamount to
saying, that the one is more a sensation than the
other.

In like manner, when we have an idea; the having
the idea, the being conscious of the idea, knowing
the idea, observing the idea, are only different names
for the same thing. They mean the being conscious
in a particular way. But the being conscious is to
take notice of the consciousness. To be conscious,
and not to take notice, is the same thing as to be con-

scious, and not conscious. The notice is the consciousness, and the consciousness is the notice.

Thus far, therefore, it appears, with abundant evidence, that Reflection is nothing but Consciousness;
and Consciousness is the having the sensations and
ideas. But what will be objected is, that we not only
have Ideas; but we are capable of forming the idea of
that particular state of mind which exists when we
have an idea. It requires a close examination, to
discover what is really meant by the language in
which this objection is conveyed. The thing, however, to which it imperfectly points, can be made out;
though, from the imperfection of the language which
we must employ, it is not easy to explain it, with a
certainty of being understood.

When it is said, that we can not only have a particular idea, but can form an idea of that state of mind,
generally, which is called having an idea; this can
mean nothing but the distinction between the particular and the general idea. It is affirmed, that we
can not only have this idea, and that idea, but we can
have the general idea of all ideas. This is true. But
we know, by previous elucidations, what all this means.
We can have the idea not only of this man, or that man,
but we can have the idea of men in general. That is
to say, we can group all individuals of a certain description into one class, to which class we give a name,
equally applicable to every individual; which name,
accordingly, being associated equally with individuals
indefinite in number, calls up the ideas of individuals,
indefinite in number, on every application of it.

This points out a double meaning of the word
Idea; from which all the confusion of the language

about REFLECTION seems to have been derived.   The
same word, Idea, is both the *particular*, and the *general*
name.   It cannot be disputed, that so far as regards
individual Ideas, the having an idea, and knowing it,
the being in the state of consciousness, and knowing
the state of consciousness, are one and the same
thing.   And, if the being in a state of consciousness,
and knowing it, does not express all that is meant by
reflecting upon it (where reflecting is not used in
another sense, as equivalent with *remembering*), it will
remain for those who believe there is anything more,
to shew what it is.

That the general is derived from the particular,
there will be no hesitation in allowing.   The fact,
therefore, so imperfectly stated, is, that, from individual states of consciousness, we rise, by generalization, as in other cases, to the general idea which
embraces a class.   General Ideas, on account of their
complexity, are all apt to appear, to persons little
accustomed to examine them closely, more or less
mysterious.   But general ideas, not of the steady
objects of sense, but the fleeting states of consciousness, which we have so little under command, and for
the naming of which we are so ill provided with
terms, cannot fail to appear mysterious in a much
greater degree.   What we are now, therefore, contemplating is a case of generalization, which, how
certainly soever, from the common laws of the human
mind, we know that it is made, it is far from easy distinctly to conceive.   And those of my readers, who
have followed me easily in this deduction, may be
satisfied they have made no slight progress in metaphysical science.

It is evident, when all this is clearly understood, that what has been mysteriously set forth, under the name of an Idea of REFLECTION, is simply the generalization of particular states of consciousness ; which particular states of consciousness are our sensations and ideas.

There are various cases of this generalization, some more, some less, extensive.

In the same manner as we generalize the having of a single idea ; and conceive, not the having of this idea, or that idea, but the having of any idea, and all ideas ; we also generalize the having two associated ideas, and, from particulars, mount up to the general idea of the association, or train, of ideas.

It is needless to be particular in referring to the specific cases. We have seen what combination of ideas constitutes the case of memory. Individual instances of memory are generalized ; these peculiar combinations are viewed as a class ; hence the general idea, and general name of the class.

The explanation is obviously the same, in other cases, as Judgment, Reasoning, Belief, Willing. We know what is the particular case of association on which each of these names is bestowed. We know what is the state of consciousness, on each individual occasion of Judging, Reasoning, and so forth. Generalization is performed. The particular instances are viewed as composing a class. The Idea of the class is the Idea of Reflection.[34]

---

[34] To reflect on any of our feelings or mental acts is more properly identified with *attending* to the feeling, than, (as stated in the text) with merely having it. The author scarcely

recognises this as a difference.   He sometimes indeed seems to
consider attention as mental repetition; but in his chapter on
the Will, we shall find that he there identifies attending to a
feeling with merely having the feeling.   I conceive, on the
contrary, (with the great majority of psychologists) that there
is an important distinction between the two things; the ignor-
ing of which has led the author into errors.   What the distinction is, I have endeavoured to shew in my note to the
chapter on Consciousness; and the subject will return upon
us hereafter.—*Ed.*

CHAPTER XVI.

THE DISTINCTION BETWEEN THE INTELLECTUAL AND ACTIVE POWERS OF THE HUMAN MIND.

" It is the greatest triumph of philosophy to refer many, and seemingly very various, phenomena, to one, or a very few, simple principles: and the more simple and evident such a principle is, provided it be truly applicable to all the cases in question, the greater is its value and scientific beauty."—*Elements of Logic, by Dr. Whately*, p. 32.

The Phenomena of Thought have long appeared to be divisible into two great classes; which were distinguished by the names, the one of the Intellectual, the other of the Active, Powers of the Human Mind. In the phenomena which compose the first of those classes, and which we have now pretty completely surveyed, the sensations and ideas are considered merely as existing. In the phenomena which compose the second of the two classes, the sensations and ideas are to be considered as not merely existing, but also as exciting to action.[35]

---

[35] Instead of " The phenomena of *Thought*," substitute the phenomena of Mind, the Subject, or the Subject Consciousness. The use of the word " Thought" seems to justify an opinion held by Hamilton and by the German philosophers, that thought, or the cognitive function is the basis of mind,

With respect to the sensations and ideas which compose the phenomena of the first class, we have observed, that they are apt to be formed into clusters of more or less complexity ; and that they follow one another, in trains, according to certain laws.

The sensations and ideas, which compose the phenomena of the second class, are equally formed into clusters, with those composing the phenomena of the former class ; and follow one another, in trains, according to the same laws.

So far, the two classes of phenomena agree ; and so far, the analysis, which we have endeavoured to effect of the former class, is to be taken as the analysis also of the latter.   Our object, now, is, to trace to their

---

instead of being co-ordinate with the other leading functions (Feeling and Will.)   There is no evidence elsewhere that the author shares this opinion.

The defectiveness of the two-fold classification of the mind, which seems to have descended from Aristotle, and is only in the present generation supplanted by an explicitly worked-out triple division, is especially apparent in the handling of all the succeeding chapters of the present work.   The Will, or the activity of the system, is spoken of as set on indiscriminately by "sensations and ideas ;" which, as will be seen, is to mix together a number of entirely distinct processes.

There is no adequate separation of the emotional part of a Sensation, from its intellectual or knowledge-giving part.   The same confusion extends to the word "idea," which, without premonition, is employed for the memory of pleasures and pains, and for the memory of sensations of the intellectual or knowledge-giving kind.   There is, as might be expected, an insufficient treatment of the special forms of Emotion ; there being no basis laid for their exhaustive or natural classification.—*B.*

source the differences which constitute this a separate class ; to mark the subdivisions into which it can be most conveniently distributed ; and to demonstrate the simple laws, into which the whole phenomena of human life, so numerous, and apparently so diversified, may all be easily resolved.

CHAPTER XVII.

PLEASURABLE AND PAINFUL SENSATIONS.

THERE is a remarkable difference of sensations, which has been mentioned before, but which must now be more particularly attended to.

Some sensations, probably the greater number, are what we call indifferent. They are not considered as either painful, or pleasurable. There are sensations, however, and of frequent recurrence, some of which are painful, some pleasurable. The difference is, that which is felt. A man knows it, by feeling it; and this is the whole account of the phenomenon. I have one sensation, and then another, and then another. The first is of such a kind, that I care not whether it is long or short; the second is of such a kind that I would put an end to it instantly if I could; the third is of such a kind, that I like it prolonged. To distinguish those feelings, I give them names. I call the first Indifferent; the second, Painful; the third, Pleasurable; very often, for shortness, I call the second, Pain, the third, Pleasure.

We formerly shewed, that having a sensation and

knowing it, are not two things, but one and the same thing; that having two sensations and knowing them, are not two things, but one and the same thing. It is obvious, therefore, that having three sensations, an Indifferent, a Pleasurable, and a Painful, and knowing them for what they are, are not different things, but one and the same thing.

The pleasurable and painful sensations are common to all the senses. We have pleasures and pains of the eye, of the ear, of the touch, the taste, the smell, and also of many internal parts of the body, for which, though, as we shall presently see, they hold a great share in composing the springs of human action, we have not names, nor any means of accurate designation.[36]

---

[36] In the case of many pleasurable or painful sensations, it is open to question whether the pleasure or pain, especially the pleasure, is not something added to the sensation, and capable of being detached from it, rather than merely a particular aspect or quality of the sensation. It is often observable that a sensation is much less pleasurable at one time than at another, though to our consciousness it appears exactly the same sensation in all except the pleasure. This is emphatically the fact in cases of satiety, or of loss of taste for a sensation by loss of novelty. It is probable that in such cases the pleasure may depend on different nerves, or on a different action of the same nerves, from the remaining part of the sensation. However this may be, the pleasure or pain attending a sensation is (like the feelings of Likeness, Succession, &c.) capable of being mentally abstracted from the sensation, or, in other words, capable of being attended to by itself. And in any case Mr. Bain's distinction holds good, between the emotional part or property of a sensation (in which he includes the

pleasure or pain belonging to it) and its intellectual or knowledge-giving part.   It must be remembered, however, that
these are not exclusive of one another ; the knowledge-giving
part is not necessarily emotional, but the emotional part is
and must be knowledge-giving.   The pleasure or pain of the
feeling are subjects of intellectual apprehension ; they give the
knowledge of themselves and of their varieties.—*Ed.*

CHAPTER XVIII.

CAUSES OF THE PLEASURABLE AND PAINFUL SENSATIONS.

NEXT in order to the Pleasurable and Painful Sensations, it is necessary to take notice of the causes of them. We can generally trace them to certain constant antecedents; and it is evidently of the greatest importance to us to be able to do so; as it is by those means only, we can lessen the number of the painful sensations, increase the number of the pleasurable.

Of the causes of our Pleasurable and Painful Sensations, it is necessary to distinguish two classes; first, the immediate causes; secondly, the remote causes; a remote, being not, strictly speaking, the cause of the sensation, but the cause of that cause. Thus, the lash of the executioner is the immediate cause of the pain of the criminal. The sentence of the Judge, is the cause of that cause. The sound of the violin is the immediate cause of the pleasure of my ear; the performance of the musician, the cause of that sound; the money with which I have hired the musician, the cause of that performance. The money is, in this case, the cause of the cause of the cause of the sensation; or the cause, at two removes.

It is necessary to be remarked, respecting the causes of our pleasurable and painful sensations, that, they are apt to become greater objects of concern to us, to rank higher in importance, than the sensations themselves. It is a vulgar observation, with respect to money, for example, that, though useful only for obtaining pleasure, or saving from pain, it is often employed for neither purpose, but hugged as a good in itself.

The importance attached to the cause of the sensation, is a case of association easy to be traced. The pleasurable and painful sensations themselves are, specifically, not numerous. The causes of them, on the other hand, are exceedingly numerous, and diversified. Again ; the mind is not much interested in attending to the sensation. The sensation provides for itself. The mind, however, is deeply interested in attending to the cause ; that we may prevent, or remove it, if the sensation is painful ; provide, or detain it, if the sensation is pleasurable. This creates a habit of passing rapidly from the sensation, to fix our attention upon its cause.

CHAPTER XIX.

IDEAS OF THE PLEASURABLE AND PAINFUL SENSATIONS, AND OF THE CAUSES OF THEM.

WE have already seen, that all sensations are capable of being revived, without that action on the organs of sense which originally produced them; and that, when so revived, we call them ideas or copies of the sensations.

The sensations which are pleasurable and painful, are revived in the same manner as those which are indifferent; but, as the sensations which are pleasurable and painful form a class of sensations remarkably distinguished from sensations of the indifferent class, the ideas of the pleasurable and painful sensations form a class of ideas, no less remarkably distinguished from the ideas of the indifferent sensations.

It is necessary to endeavour by a particular effort to distinguish accurately from all other feelings that peculiar state of consciousness, which we call the idea of a pleasurable or painful sensation; in other words, that sensation revived, after the operation upon the senses has ceased.

This state of consciousness, like other states, is known only by having it. What it is felt to be, it is.

We can afford, therefore, no aid to the reader in distinguishing it, otherwise than by using such expressions as seem calculated to fix his attention upon it. It is his own inward, invisible state, which only he can mark for himself.

The idea of a pain or pleasure, is not a pain or pleasure. We do not say that the idea of the hand scalded is a pain, or the idea of a sweet smell is a pleasure. But this is not very satisfactory language ; for it, in reality, means little more, than that the idea of a pleasurable or painful sensation, is not a sensation. That there are some trains of ideas, however, which it is agreeable to have, others which it is disagreeable, is one among the most familiar facts of our nature. There is, therefore, a distinction among ideas, analogous to that of pleasurable and painful among sensations.

It is difficult to think of any one sensation by itself ; because each is so combined with others, that the idea of one can never present itself, but in company with more. This is peculiarly the case with sensations of the pleasurable and painful kinds : and hence the cause of the indistinctness, which seems to accompany the idea of any of those sensations, when we endeavour to take it apart, and consider what it is in itself.

An idea is the revival of a former state of feeling. The first thing which I have to consider is, what is my precise state of consciousness, when I receive a pleasurable or painful sensation.

When the sensation was present, suppose a painful one, it was a state of consciousness, so interesting to me, that it was important to find a mark for it. I called it Pain. It is a state of consciousness known to every man by his having had it, and it can be known by no other means. We call it by various names; an odious state, a disagreeable state, and so on; but these are only several modes of marking what is felt, and tell to no man anything more than his feeling has told. Except for his own knowledge of his own feeling, the words would be utterly without a meaning.

Such is the state of consciousness under the sensation. I revive the sensation.

My state of consciousness under the sensation I called a pain. My state of consciousness under the idea of the pain, I call, not a pain, but an aversion. An aversion is the idea of a pain. Whatever is included under the term idea of pain, is included precisely under the term aversion. They are not two things, but two names for the same thing.

The same explanation applies to the case of a pleasurable sensation. The state of consciousness under the sensation, that is, the sensation itself, differed from other sensations, in that it was agreeable. A name was wanted to denote this peculiarity; to mark, as a class, the sensations which possess it. The term, Pleasure, was adopted. I revive the sensation; in other words, have the idea; and as I had occasion for a name to class the sensations, I have occasion for a name to class the ideas. My state of consciousness under the sensation, I call a Pleasure: my state of consciousness under the idea, that is, the idea itself, I call a Desire. The term "Idea of a pleasure," expresses precisely the same thing as the term, Desire. It does so by the very import of the words. The idea of a pleasure, is the idea of something as good to have. But what is a desire, other than the idea of something as good to have; good to have, being really nothing but desirable to have? The terms, therefore, "idea of pleasure," and "desire," are but two names; the thing named, the state of consciousness, is one and the same.

There is an ambiguity, however, in the terms *Aversion*, and *Desire*, which contributes not a little to cast darkness upon this part of our inquiry.

They are applied to the ideas of the Causes of our Pleasurable and Painful Sensations, as well as to the ideas of those Sensations; and, of course, in a different sense. We say we have an aversion to certain kinds of food, or certain drugs; we have a desire for water to drink, for fire to warm us, and so on.

When we examine these phrases narrowly, we find that it is not literally, but by a sort of figure of speech, that the terms "Aversion," and "Desire," are applied to the Causes of Pains and Pleasures. Properly speaking, it is not to the food, or the drug, that we have the aversion, but to the disagreeable taste. The food is a substance of a certain colour, and consistence; so is the drug. There is nothing in these qualities which is offensive to us; only the taste. In like manner, it is not the water we desire, but the pleasure of drinking; not the fire we desire, but the pleasure of warmth.

The illusion is merely that of a very close association. There is no case, indeed, of association, in which the union is more intimate, than that between the idea of a pungent sensation, and its customary cause; and hence, there is no wonder that the name which properly belongs to the one, should be bestowed upon the other, or rather, that the name which belongs properly to one, should be given to the two, formed into a complex idea, in conjunction.

There is another source of perplexity, which arises from the connotative power of the terms Desire, and Aversion. They are Nouns, in the future tense ; that is, they connote futurity ; just as Verbs, in the future tense, connote futurity. Though the feeling, called the idea of a pleasurable sensation, is precisely the feeling called desirableness ; desirableness, and the idea of something pleasurable, being convertible terms, the word Desire, whenever it is applied to a particular case, carries with it a tacit reference to future time. When the idea of a sensation is present, the sensation itself is not present. The sensation has been, or is to be. It is difficult, therefore, to have the idea of a pleasurable sensation, without the association of the past, or the future. The idea of a pleasurable sensation with the association of the Past, is never called Desire. The word Desire, is commonly used to mark the idea of a pleasurable sensation, when the Future is associated with it. The idea of a pleasurable sensation, to come, is what is commonly meant by Desire. We have, however, no other name to mark the idea, when it is considered by itself, and without reference to the past, or the future. In these cases, Desire, and the idea of a pleasurable sensation ; Aversion, and the idea of a painful sensation, are convertible terms.

From this exposition, it follows, that the number of our desires is the same with that of our pleasurable sensations ; the number of our aversions, the same

with that of our painful sensations; just as the
number of our simple ideas of sight, is the same
with that of our sensations of sight; the number
of our simple ideas of sound, taste, or smell, the
same with that of our sensations of sound, taste, or
smell.[37]

---

[37] The principal doctrine of this chapter is, that Desire, and
Aversion, are nothing but the idea of a pleasurable sensation,
and the Idea of a painful sensation : which doctrine is then
qualified by saying, that a desire is the idea of a pleasure
associated with the future, an aversion the idea of a pain
associated with the future.

But according to the whole spirit of the author's speculations, and to his express affirmation in the beginning of the
next chapter, the idea of any sensation associated with the
future, constitutes the Expectation of it : and if so, it rested
with him to prove that the expectation of a pleasure, or of a
pain, is the same thing with the desire, or aversion. This is
certainly not conformable to common observation. For, on
the one hand, it is commonly understood that there may be
desire or aversion without expectation ; and on the other, expectation of a pleasure without any actual feeling of desire :
one may expect, and even look forward with satisfaction to,
the pleasure of a meal, although one is not, but only expects
to be, hungry. So perfectly is it assumed that expectation,
and desire or aversion, are not necessarily combined, that the
case in which they are combined is signified by a special pair
of names. Desire combined with expectation, is called by the
name of Hope ; Aversion combined with expectation, is known
by the name of Fear.

I believe the fact to be that desire is not Expectation, but
is more than the idea of the pleasure desired, being, in truth,
the initiatory stage of Will. In what we call Desire there is,
I think, always included a positive stimulation to action ;
either to the definite course of action which would lead to our

obtaining the pleasure, or to a general restlessness and vague seeking after it.   The stimulation may fall short of actually producing action : even when it prompts to a definite act, it may be repressed by a stronger motive, or by knowledge that the pleasure is not within present reach, nor can be brought nearer to us by any present action of our own.   Still, there is, I think, always, the sense of a tendency to action, in the direction of pursuit of the pleasure, though the tendency may be overpowered by an external or an internal restraint. So also, in aversion, there is always a tendency to action of the kind which repels or avoids the painful sensation.   But of these things more fully under the head of Will.—*Ed.*

CHAPTER XX.

THE PLEASURABLE AND PAINFUL SENSATIONS,
CONTEMPLATED AS PASSED OR AS FUTURE.

WE have considered, what the pleasurable and painful sensations are when present; what the ideas of them, considered as present, are ; and what the ideas of their causes.

Those sensations, however, together with their causes, we may contemplate, either as passed, or as future : and so contemplated, they give rise to some of the most interesting states of the human mind.

To contemplate any feeling as Passed, is to remember it ; and the explanation of Memory we need not repeat. To contemplate any feeling as Future, is merely a case of that Anticipation of the future from the passed, of which, also, we have already given the explanation.

When my finger was in the flame of the candle and burned, the painful sensation was present. The state of consciousness, however, was complex, and consisted of several ingredients ; the sight of the burning candle, the sight of my finger, the sense of a certain position or locality, namely, that of my finger and the candle, the painful sensation, and the belief that it was my sensation ; in other words, the association of that thread of consciousness in which, to me, my being consists, with the present sensation. The painful feeling was thus a feeling deeply imbedded among others.

When I remember this state of consciousness, the idea of it, which makes part of the memory, is by no means a simple idea. It is composed of the ideas of all the above-mentioned sensations, together with that of the train of consciousness, which I call myself. This last is necessary to constitute it *my* idea. This idea, thus existing as my idea, and my present idea, is associated with that part of my train or thread of consciousness which has intervened, between the present state and the remembered state ; and by this last association the idea becomes memory.

The anticipation of the Future is the same series of association ; with this difference, that, in memory, the association of the train of consciousness, which converts the idea into memory, is from consequent to antecedent, that is, backwards ; the association in the case of anticipation is from antecedent to consequent, forwards.

In anticipation, as in memory, there is, first, the complex idea, as above ; next, the passage of the mind forwards from the present state of consciousness, the antecedent, to one consequent after another, till it comes to the anticipated sensation. Suppose, that, as a punishment, a man is condemned to put his finger after two days in the flame of a candle ; wherein consists his anticipation ? The complex idea, as described above, of the painful sensation, with all its concomitant sensations and ideas, is the first part of the process. The remainder is the association with this idea of the events, one after another, which are to fill up the intermediate time, and terminate with his finger placed in the flame of the candle. The whole of this association, taken together, comprises the idea of the pain as his pain, after a train of antecedents.

The process of anticipation is so precisely the same, when the sensation is of the pleasurable kind, that I deem it unnecessary to repeat it.[38]

---

[38] This is the first place in which the author gives his analysis of Expectation ; and his theory of it is, as all theories of it must be, the exact counterpart of the same person's theory of Memory. He resolves it into the mere Idea of the expected event, accompanied by the "idea of the events, one after another," which are to begin with the present moment, and end with the expected event. But in this case, as in that of Memory, the objection recurs, that all this may exist in the case of mere Imagination. A man may conceive himself being hanged, or elevated to a throne, and may construct in his mind a series of possible or conceivable events, through which he can fancy each of these results to be brought about. If he is a man of lively imagination, this idea of the events "which are to fill up the intermediate time" may be at least as copious, as the idea of the series of coming events for a year from the present time, which according to the author's theory I have in my mind when I look forward to commencing a journey twelve months hence. Yet he neither expects to be hanged, nor to be made a king, still less both, which, to bear out the theory, it would seem that he ought.

The difference between Expectation and mere Imagination, as well as between Memory and Imagination, consists in the presence or absence of Belief ; and though this is no explanation of either phenomenon, it brings us back to one and

In contemplating a painful or pleasurable sensation as past, that is, remembering it, the mind is in general tranquil. The state is not, perhaps, a state of indifference; but it is not so far removed from it, as to call attention to itself, or require a name to mark it.

The case is different, when the sensation is contemplated as future, or anticipated. The state of consciousness is then far removed from a state of indifference. It admits of two cases. One is, when the sensation is contemplated as certainly future; the other is, when it is contemplated as not certainly future.

When a pleasurable sensation is contemplated as future, but not certainly, the state of consciousness is called Hope. When a painful sensation is contemplated as future, but not certainly, the state of consciousness is called Fear.[39]

---

the same real problem, which I have so often referred to, and which neither the author nor any other thinker has yet solved—the difference between knowing something as a Reality, and as a mere Thought; a distinction similar and parallel to that between a Sensation and an Idea.—*Ed.*

[39] The author's definitions of Hope and Fear differ from those offered in my note (p. 194). He considers these words to signify that the pleasure or the pain is contemplated as future, but without certainty. It must be admitted that the words are often applied to very faint degrees of anticipation, far short of those which in popular language would be spoken of as Expectation: but I think the terms are not inconsistent with the fullest assurance. A man is about to undergo a painful surgical operation. He has no doubt whatever about the event; he fully intends it; there are no other means, perhaps, of saving his life. Yet the feeling with which he looks for-

Again : When a pleasurable sensation is anticipated with certainty, we call the state of consciousness Joy. When a painful sensation is thus anticipated, we call it Sorrow. Neither of the two terms is good ; because not confined to this signification. Both are applied to name other things, also, which we shall presently have occasion to notice. They are, therefore, a source of confusion.

---

ward to it, and with which he contemplates the preparations for it, are such as would, I think, by the custom of language, be designated as fear. Death, again, is the most certain of all future events, yet we speak of the fear of death. It is perhaps more doubtful whether the fully assured anticipation of a desired enjoyment would receive, in ordinary parlance, the name of Hope ; yet some common phrases seem to imply that it would. We read even on tombstones "the sure hope of a joyful immortality."

A still more restricted application of the word Fear, also justified by usage, is to the case in which the feeling amounts to a disturbing passion ; and to this meaning Mr Bain, as will be seen in a future note, thinks it desirable to confine it.—*Ed.*

CHAPTER XXI.

THE CAUSES OF PLEASURABLE AND PAINFUL SENSATIONS, CONTEMPLATED AS PASSED, OR AS FUTURE.

SECTION I.

THE IMMEDIATE CAUSES OF PLEASURABLE AND PAINFUL SENSATIONS, CONTEMPLATED AS PASSED, OR AS FUTURE.

BESIDE the Sensations, the Causes of them are capable of being contemplated, both as passed, and as future.

It may be regarded as remarkable, that though the idea or thought of a disagreeable sensation, as passed, is nearly indifferent, the thought of the cause of a painful passed sensation is often a very interesting state of consciousness. This state of consciousness we sometimes call Antipathy, sometimes Hatred; though hatred, as we shall afterwards see, is more frequently the name of the Motive to which it gives birth. We have, however, but one concrete term for both of these abstracts, the verb " to hate," which, of course, performs its business ill. From this, however, it no doubt comes, that the word Hatred is often used as synonymous with Antipathy.

This is a case of association, which deserves a little attention. The idea of the cause of a painful sensation is so closely associated with that of the sensation, that the one never exists without the other. But this is not all. The anticipation of the future from the passed, is so strong an association, that, in interesting cases, it is indissoluble. The thought of the Cause of a passed painful sensation, is the idea of an antecedent and a consequent. The idea of the passed antecedent and consequent is instantly followed by that of a future antecedent and consequent; and thus the feeling partakes of the nature of the anticipation of a future painful sensation. The association may be but momentary, as it may instantly be checked by other associations. But, being momentary, it existed, and its existence is sufficient to account for the difference, which is often observable, between the state of consciousness when the sensation is remembered, and the state of consciousness when the cause of the sensation is remembered. When the sensation is remembered singly, there is not that association of a passed antecedent and consequent, which is instantly followed by that of a future antecedent and consequent of the same kind. That association takes place in the case of the remembered cause ; and hence the difference, with which every man is acquainted.[40]

---

[40] ‧The difference here brought to notice between the very slight emotion excited in most cases by the idea of a past pain, and the strong feeling excited by the idea of the cause of a past pain, will be confirmed by every one's experience ; and is rightly explained by the author, as arising from the fact that what has caused a past pain has an interest affecting the future, since it may cause future pains. It is noticeable that

The thought of the cause of a passed agreeable sensation or sensations, is also very often an interesting state of consciousness. It is called by the names both of Sympathy, and Love. Neither of the terms is confined to this signification; they are both, therefore, bad names, and a great cause of confusion of ideas; as we shall see in other instances hereafter.

The pleasurable sensations not being so pungent as the painful, it but rarely happens that the immediate cause of a single passed pleasurable sensation is an object of interest: the cause of the cessation, however, of a painful sensation is so, not unfrequently. The traveller, who was ready to perish with thirst in the desert, can never afterwards think of the well which relieved him, without emotion.

The states of consciousness which exist when we contemplate the causes of our painful and pleasurable sensations as *Future,* are easily analysed, after what has been shewn. It is a case of the anticipation of the future from the passed; with this peculiarity, that

---

the author nowhere explains why the thought of a pain as future is so much more painful, than the thought of a past pain when detached from all apprehension for the future; why the expectation of an evil is generally so much worse than the remembrance of one. This fact might have made him doubt the sufficiency of his theory of Memory and Expectation; since, according to his analysis, neither of them is anything but the idea of the pain itself, associated in each case with a series of events which may be intrinsically indifferent; and if there were no elements in the case but those which he has pointed out, no sufficient reason is apparent why there should be any inequality of painfulness between the remembrance and the expectation.—*Ed.*

the final antecedent and consequent are interesting, the one as a pleasurable or painful Feeling, the other as the cause of it.

If the anticipated sensation is painful, and contemplated as certain, the associated ideas of the cause and effect constitute a state of consciousness, which we mark by various forms of expression, but for which we have no appropriate name. We call it Hatred, we call it Aversion, we call it Horror. We call the object hateful, or disgusting, or loathsome, according to the nature of the anticipated sensation. When the sensation is contemplated as not certainly future, the state of mind is what we call Dread, in some one or other of its numerous modifications.

When the cause of a pleasure is contemplated as certainly future, such object is associated with the feeling called Joy ; when it is contemplated as not certainly future, it is associated with the feeling called Hope. What the feelings, Joy, and Hope, are, we have so recently seen, that it cannot be forgotten. In the association of the cause of a pleasure with both, the state of consciousness has no more appropriate name than that of Love. An object contemplated as a future cause of future pleasure, is an object *loved*, whether the anticipation is certain or uncertain.[41]

---

[41] A distinction should be drawn between Aversion and Fear. We may be very much averse to a thing, and yet not fear it. A courageous person is not necessarily wanting in aversions or dislikes, or in labours for warding off what is disagreeable. Anything that gives us pain, when approaching or imminent, is viewed with aversion, and stimulates efforts of counteraction, or escape ; and yet it may not inspire the state properly named Fear. The distinguishing characteristic of fear is an unhinging

excitement, a disturbance of the serenity and balance of the mind, inducing exaggerated, disproportioned or misplaced exertions. One of the causes of fear is approaching evil, but the effect does not always happen. The evil may work its proper effect upon the will, namely to prevent or evade it, without any of the perturbing accessories called being terrified or afraid.—*B.*

SECTION II.

THE REMOTE CAUSES OF PLEASURABLE AND PAINFUL SENSATIONS, CONTEMPLATED AS PAST, OR FUTURE.

Before entering into the detail of this part of the subject, one important observation is to be made; that the remote causes of our Pains and Pleasures are apt to be objects, far more deeply interesting, than those which are immediate. This at first sight appears paradoxical. It is the necessary result, however, of the general Law of our nature.

The immediate causes of our pleasurable and painful sensations have never any very extensive operation. The idea of any one is rarely associated with more than a limited number of pains or pleasures. Food, for example, the cause of the pleasures of eating; pleasures, perhaps, from the frequency with which they are repeated, and the portion of life over which they are spread, more valuable, as a class, than any other which we enjoy; has never appeared an object of sufficient interest, to make the affection with which it is regarded be thought worthy of a name. The idea of Food, though associated with pleasures which constitute so important a class, is associated with the pleasures but of one class : some of the remote causes are associated with the pleasures of almost every class. Money, for example, instrumental in procuring the causes of almost all our pleasures, and removing the causes of a large proportion of our pains, is associated with the ideas of most of the pleasurable states of our nature. The idea of an object associated with a hundred times as many pleasures as another, is of course a hundred times more interesting.

SUB-SECTION I.

Wealth, Power, and Dignity, and their Contraries, Contemplated as Causes of our Pleasures and Pains.

As among the remote causes of our pleasures and pains may be reckoned everything which in any way contributes to them, it follows that the number of such causes is exceedingly great. Of course it is only the principal cases which have been attended to, and classed under Titles. They are mostly comprehended under the following :—Wealth, Power, Dignity, as regards the pleasurable sensations ;—Poverty, Impotence, Contemptibility, as regards the painful sensations. What our states of consciousness are, when we are said to contemplate these causes of pains and pleasures, with reference to ourselves, or as causes of our own pleasures and pains, we now proceed to inquire.

One remarkable thing is first of all to be noticed : the three, above named, grand causes of our pleasures agree in this, that they all are the means of procuring for us the Services of our fellow-creatures, and themselves contribute to our pleasures in hardly any other way. It is obvious from this remark, that the grand cause of all our pleasures are the services of our fellow-creatures; since Wealth, Power, and Dignity, which appear to most people to sum up the means of human happiness, are nothing more than means of procuring those services. This is a fact of the highest possible importance, both in Morals, and in Philosophy.

That Wealth, Power, and Dignity do procure for us pleasurable sensations only by procuring for us the services of our fellow-creatures, a short illustration will suffice to shew.

Wealth enables us either to purchase directly the services of other men, as of those whom we desire to have in attendance about us; or to purchase commodities; or, it adds to our Power and Dignity. As far as it purchases the services of others directly, the truth of what we have advanced is obvious. It is hardly less obvious, that when we purchase commodities, which are the fruit of other men's labour, we, in reality, do nothing but purchase the services of those men, who, in fact, were working for us, when working at the goods which we ultimately consume. In as far as Wealth adds to Power, and Dignity, it is included under those several heads.

A man's Power means the readiness of other men to obey him. Now one man obeys another, from the prospect, either of good if he obeys, or of evil if he does not obey. Wealth is the great means of procuring obedience, through the medium of good. All hire of services, is through that medium. The power of inflicting evil, in case of disobedience, and of procuring services by fear, is what in the more peculiar sense, is meant by the term Power. It is to be observed, that the range of obedience, obtained by fear, is capable of much greater enlargement, than that which is obtained by hope. The means any man has of paying for the services of others, extends at most to some thousands; the means which some men have had of imposing their commands on other men, through fear, has extended to many millions.

Dignity is a word of much more vague signification, than Wealth, or Power. It is, therefore, much more difficult, to describe clearly its mode of operation.

Dignity, is commonly said to be that which procures us the respect of other men. But what is this respect? It is not a mere barren feeling in the mind of another man, regarded as wholly unconnected with his actions. It is regarded as a sentiment in his breast, from which actions favourable to us may proceed. It derives its whole value to us from the actions which it is likely to produce.

For the present purpose, therefore, we consider the word Dignity, as expressing all that, in, and about, a man, which is calculated to procure him the services of others, without the immediate application either of reward, or of fear.

Wealth, and Power, are the grand constituents of Dignity; and procure a man services beyond the immediate sphere, either of the good, or the evil, he can dispense. This is a remarkable case of association; and a source of very important consequences in human life.

Our proneness to sympathize with the Rich and Great, has often been taken notice of, as a remarkable phenomenon in human nature. This has been described

as a readiness to go along with them in their affections ; to desire the accomplishment of their ends ;
and to lend ourselves for the attainment of them.

I believe it will be sufficient, if I barely indicate
the mode of analysing the complicated sentiment,
which is thus described. With command over the
means of all sorts of pleasures, we associate strongly
the idea of happiness ; the idea of happiness, is an
agreeable idea ; and the idea of whatever disturbs it,
painful. The first idea is a desire ; the second, an
aversion.

Beside this ; with the Power of dispensing a great
deal of good, or evil, we associate strongly the idea of
the actual dispensation ; that is, the idea of a great
number of individuals benefited, or hurt. But no
association of good or evil to individuals is so constant and inseparable with the causes of them, as that
of good or evil to ourselves. This association takes
place in the case which we are now considering. It
may have been but momentary. It may have been
instantly overpowered by other associations, by association of the circumstances which exclude the Belief.
Still it had a momentary existence ; and, in its consequences, presents a remarkable instance of those
two very important facts, first pointed out distinctly
to the attention of philosophers by Professor Stewart ;
First, that feelings, so momentary as not to be recognised the moment after they have passed, may not
only have existed, but have given its whole character
to some important phenomenon of the human mind ;
and, Secondly, that there is no conception, that is,
idea, without the momentary belief of the existence

of its object.[42] The momentary conception and belief of good or evil to ourselves, in the association constituting the idea of a man of wealth and power, has a great share in the character which that association bears.

The Power of doing good or evil, though the foundation of our idea of Dignity, is not the only ingredient in it; the Disposition to make use of it enters for a great share. The disposition to make use of it only for evil, if carried to a certain pitch, would

---

[42] This is the place where the author most clearly enunciates the doctrine which is the indispensable basis of his theory of Belief, viz. that there is no idea "without the momentary belief of the existence of its object." This opinion, as the author observes, is maintained also by Dugald Stewart; but I have never seen any positive evidence in its favour. All which has been established is, that the belief *may* have momentarily existed, although immediately afterwards forgotten, and replaced by disbelief. But no proof of this momentary existence has been given, except that it is supposed that what is not believed to be real cannot cause strong emotion (terror, for instance), nor prompt to outward action. Yet nothing can be more certain than that a mere idea can exercise direct power over our nerves of motion, and through them, over the muscles; as the author shows by examples further on. It is true that, as Mr. Bain has pointed out, this power of an idea over the active energies is the only germ of belief which exists originally, and the foundation of the power of Belief in after life; but it is not the less true that the power of Belief as it exists in after life, stands broadly distinguished from the power of the Fixed Idea, and that this last may operate not only without, but in defiance of, a positive Belief. That a contrary belief has momentarily intervened is a mere conjecture, which can neither be refuted nor proved.—*Ed.*

sink the idea of dignity, and leave dread and abhor-
rence in its place.

Beside the disposition to make a good use of wealth
and power, which is virtue ; Knowledge, and Wisdom
enter as an important ingredient in Dignity.   In the
possessor of wealth and power, they are necessary to
give effect to his good disposition ; in all men they
are an instrument of power; and they are intimately
associated, in well-educated minds, with the idea of
the great benefits to mankind, which have been, and
will be, derived from them.   In such minds, they,
therefore, inspire a very lively sympathy.

I do not think it necessary to lengthen this exposition, by offering any analysis of the corresponding
causes of pain,—Poverty, Weakness, and Contemptibility.   The reader, after what he has learned, will,
without difficulty, perform it for himself.

What we have now to consider, is the affection or
state of mind, which is formed, when we contemplate
each of those causes, first, as the past cause of past
sensations, and secondly, as the future cause of future
sensations.

We are singularly ill-provided with names, to mark
those several states of our consciousness.   It is very
obvious, that we ought to have two names for each
cause ; for example, one, to mark the state of mind,
when Wealth is contemplated as the *past* cause, of *past*
sensations, and one to mark the state of mind, when
it is contemplated as the *future* cause of *future* sensations.   We have but one name for both.   We call by
the single name, " Love of Wealth," both the pleasurable state when we associate with the idea of our past
wealth the past pleasures we have derived from it, and

when we anticipate the future, and associate with the idea of future wealth, the idea of the pleasures to be derived from it. There is no wonder that the two states should be confounded; and that the love of wealth should be a vague, indefinite term.

The imperfection of our language is the same in regard to the two other causes of our pleasures. The Love of Power, and the Love of Dignity, are names for both states of mind, both the contemplation of the past, and the contemplation of the future. The indistinctness of our language here, too, prevents the distinctness of our ideas.

The word Hatred, renders the same service in regard to the causes of evil. Hatred of poverty, is the name for both states of mind, both that in which the future, and that in which the past, is the object of contemplation. Hatred of imbecility, hatred of contemptibility, are not common expressions, but we have for the states in question no other names.

It is to be observed, that Wealth, Power, and Dignity, derive a great portion of their efficacy, from their comparative amount; that is, from their being possessed in greater quantity than most other people possess them. In contemplating them with the satisfaction with which powerful causes of pleasure are contemplated, we seldom fail to include the comparison. And the state of consciousness, formed by the contemplation and comparison taken together, is called Pride.

We are said to be proud of our Wealth, proud of our Power, proud of our Dignity; and also, of any of the ingredients of which our power or dignity is composed ; of our knowledge, of our eloquence, of our family, of our personal beauty.

Of course the name has a very different meaning in each of these applications ; a difference, however, which in ordinary minds, the use of the same term, almost completely confounds.

It is obvious, that, in the contemplation of our own Wealth, Power, and Dignity, as greater, we include the contemplation of another man's Wealth, Power, and Dignity, as less. As the state of consciousness, thus formed, is called Pride when the reference is to ourselves, it is called Contempt when the reference is to others.

When the case is reversed, and a man contemplates his Wealth, Power, and Dignity as less than those of other men, the state of consciousness is called Humility. As towards the other member of the comparison, the men who possess the greater amount of those advantages, it has the name of Respect, or Admiration.

SUB-SECTION II.

Our Fellow-Creatures contemplated as Causes of our Pleasures and Pains.

Wealth, Power, and Dignity, being the origin of such powerful affections as we find them to be, though the causes of Pleasure to us only by being the causes of the actions of our Fellow-creatures ; it would be wonderful, if our Fellow-creatures themselves, the

more immediate causes of those actions, should not be
the origin of affections.

This is not the case.   Our Fellow-creatures are the
origin of affections of the greatest influence in human
life ; to the examination of which it is now our business to proceed.   It is, in the first place, however, to
be observed, that Wealth, Power, and Dignity, afford
perhaps the most remarkable of all examples of that
extraordinary case of association, where the means to
an end, means valuable to us solely on account of their
end, not only engross more of our attention than the
end itself, but actually supplant it in our affections.
What the associating process is by which this effect is
produced, we need not stay to inquire.   That it is
produced, to a remarkable degree, in the case of
Wealth, Power, and Dignity, is familiar to every
man's observation.   How few men seem to be at all
concerned about their fellow-creatures !   How completely are the lives of most men absorbed, in the pur-
suits of wealth, and ambition !   With how many men
does the love of Family, of Friend, of Country, of
Mankind, appear completely impotent, when opposed
to their love of Wealth, or of Power !   This is an
effect of misguided association, which requires the
greatest attention in Education, and Morals.

We contemplate our Fellow-creatures as causes of
our Pleasures, either Individually, or in Groups.   We
shall consider the several cases, which have attracted
sufficient attention to be distinguished by names: 1st,
That of Friendship ; 2dly, That of Kindness ; 3dly,
That of Family ; 4thly, That of Country ; 5thly,
That of Party ; and 6thly, That of Mankind.

1.—*Friendship.*

In what manner the associations are formed constituting that feeling towards another man which we call friendship, it seems not very difficult to trace. The states of circumstances in which the Feeling originates are very numerous.   But they are all, without exception, of one kind.   They are all states of circumstances, in which a greater proportion than usual of our own pleasures, come to be associated with the idea of the Individual.   It often originates in companionship, between men who for some time have indulged their Tastes, and prosecuted their pleasures in company.   It is perfectly obvious how the idea of such men will occur to one another, not simply as the idea of a man, but so enveloped by the trains of pleasurable ideas associated with the man, that the idea of him is upon the whole a highly pleasurable idea.   When to this is added, the expectation of future pleasures, not merely the continuation of the companionship, but services of importance ; when the wisdom of the man promises light and guidance from his counsels ; when his fidelity makes it safe to trust him ; when his benevolence towards us makes us count upon his services, whenever they are required, and his reputation and influence in the world are such as to give weight to his endeavours, there is a sufficient accumulation of pleasurable ideas with that of the individual to account for the affection denominated Friendship.

2.—*Kindness.*

There is nothing which more instantly associates with itself the ideas of our own Pleasures, and Pains, than the idea of the Pleasures and Pains of another of our Fellow-creatures. The expositions already afforded sufficiently indicate the source of this association, which exerts a powerful and salutary influence in human Life.

The idea of a man enjoying a train of pleasures, or happiness, is felt by every body to be a pleasurable idea. The idea of a man under a train of sufferings or pains, is equally felt to be a painful idea. This can arise from nothing but the association of our own pleasures with the first idea, and of our own pains with the second. We never feel any pains and pleasures but our own. The fact, indeed, is, that our very idea of the pains or pleasures of another man is only the idea of our own pains, or our own pleasures, associated with the idea of another man. This is one not of the least important, and curious, of all cases of association, and instantly shews how powerfully associated trains of ideas of our pains and pleasures must be with a feeling so compounded.[43]

---

[43] That the pleasures or pains of another person can only be pleasurable or painful to us through the association of our own pleasures or pains with them, is true in one sense, which is probably that intended by the author, but not true in another, against which he has not sufficiently guarded his mode of expression. It is evident, that the only pleasures or pains of which we have direct experience being those felt by ourselves, it is from them that our very notions of pleasure and pain are derived. It is also obvious that the pleasure or pain with which we contemplate the pleasure or pain felt by somebody else, is itself a pleasure or pain of our own. But if it be meant that in such cases the pleasure or pain is consciously referred to self, I take this to be a mistake. By the acts or other

The Pleasurable association composed of the ideas of a man and his pleasures, and the painful association composed of the ideas of a man and his pains, are both Affections, which have so much of the same tendency that they are included under one name, Kindness ; though the latter affection has a name appropriate to itself, Compassion.

3.—*Family.*

The Group, which consists of a Father, Mother, and Children, is called a Family. The associations which each member of this group has of his pains and pleasures, with the pains and pleasures of the other members, constitute some of the most interesting states of human consciousness.

The affection of the husband and wife is, in its origin, that of two persons of different sex, and need

---

signs exhibited by another person, the idea of a pleasure (which is a pleasurable idea) or the idea of a pain (which is a painful idea) are recalled, sometimes with considerable intensity, but in association with the other person as feeling them, not with one's self as feeling them. The idea of one's Self is, no doubt, closely associated with all our experiences, pleasurable, painful, or indifferent; but this association does not necessarily act in all cases because it exists in all cases. If the mind, when pleasurably or painfully affected by the evidences of pleasure or pain in another person, goes off on a different thread of association, as for instance, to the idea of the means of giving the pleasure or relieving the pain, or even if it dismisses the subject and relapses into the ordinary course of its thoughts, the association with its own self may be, at the time, defeated, or reduced to something so evanescent that we cannot tell whether it was momentarily present or not. —*Ed.*

not be further analysed. To this source of pleasurable association is added, when the union is happy, all those other associations, just enumerated, which constitute the affection of Friendship. To this another addition is made by the union of interests; or that necessity, under which both are placed, of receiving pain and pleasure from the same causes. As, in too many instances, these pleasurable associations are extinguished, by the generation of others of an opposite description; in other cases, they are carried to such a height, as to afford an exemplification of that remarkable state of mind, in which a greater value is set upon the means, than upon the end. Persons have been found, the one of whom could not endure to live without the other.

The Parental affection requires to be somewhat more minutely analysed.

First of all, there can be no doubt, that all that power of exciting trains of ideas of our own pains and pleasures, which belongs to the pains and pleasures of any of our fellow-creatures, is possessed by the pains and pleasures of a man's child.

In the next place, it is well known that the pains and pleasures of another person affect us; that is, associate with themselves the ideas of our own pains and pleasures, with more or less intensity, according to the attention which we bestow upon his pains or pleasures. A parent is commonly either led or impelled to bestow an unusual degree of attention upon the pains and pleasures of his child; and hence a habit is contracted of sympathizing with him, as it is commonly, and not insignificantly named; in other words, a facility of associating the ideas of his own pains and pleasures, with those of the child.

Again, a man looks upon his child as a cause to him of future pains or pleasures, much more certain, than any other person. The father regards the son somewhat in the light of another self, a great proportion of the effects of whose acts, whether good or evil, will redound to himself. An object regarded as a great future cause to us of future pains or pleasures, we call an object of intense interest; in other words, a train of interesting ideas, that is, of ideas of pains or pleasures, is associated with it.

The vivacity and simplicity of the expressions of the pains and pleasures of children, in their looks, and tones, and attitudes, as well as words, give them a peculiar power of exciting sympathy, that is, of associating with them trains of the analogous feelings of ourselves. The frequency with which a parent is called upon to attend to those expressions in his child, gives him a habit of forming the associations to which they lead.

The perfect dependence of the child upon the parent is a source of deep interest. The whole of its pleasures being the fruit of his acts, he more easily associates with them the trains of his own pleasures, than with those of any person not so connected with him. His acts, too, being required to save it from the worst of pains, and from destruction, the idea of its pains, arising from any relaxation of his care, calls up, in strong association, both the analogous pains of himself, and also the opposite pleasurable feelings arising from the continuance of the acts by which the pleasures of the child are produced. And to all these sources of association is added, that which is always agreeable, the train making up the ideas of our own power; no case of power being so perfect as that of the parent over his helpless offspring.

Another important source of agreeable association is yet to be mentioned. Man becomes fond (it is a matter of daily observation) of that on which he has frequently conferred benefits. This is a fact of considerable importance in human nature; for, under the little care which hitherto has been bestowed in generating, by education, the associations on which Beneficence depends, a considerable part of the beneficence existing in the world has been produced by this cause. It is also a case of association, which strongly illustrates the fact, that pleasures, produced by our own acts, have a peculiar power in associating with them trains of the ideas of our own pleasures. Not only a Fellow-creature, but even one of the lower animals, by having been the object of repeated acts of kindness, becomes an object of affection. Trains of our own pleasures are so often united with the idea of such an object of our kindness, that the idea of the object becomes at last an idea made up of the original idea of the individual and of trains of our own pleasures : a compound idea, made up, in great part, of pleasurable ideas; that is, an Affection.

That the whole of the parental affection is derived from these and similar associations, is proved by some decisive facts.

Whenever it happens that a man is placed in circumstances which produce those associations, he feels the parental affection, without parentage. Facts of this description are so frequent, and so notorious, that it is hardly necessary to produce an instance of them. How else does it happen, that a man who does not suspect the infidelity of his wife, rears as his own, and without any difference of affection, the offspring of the man who has injured him? Cases, for the credit of our nature, are not wanting, and when education is better, they will be less rare, in which a family of orphans is taken under the protection of a man of virtue. By acting towards them the part of a parent, he never fails to acquire for them the affection of a parent.

There are equally notorious and decisive facts to prove, that whenever the parent is placed in circumstances which either wholly, or to a great degree, prevent the formation of the associations with the child to which we ascribe the parental affection, there is a corresponding want of the affection. The case of illegitimate children is pregnant with evidence to this point. In the great majority of cases of this description, no affection exists. The parent may feel the obligation of maintaining the child, because public opinion, or perhaps the law, requires it : but this is the extent of the bond.

The circumstances of Families, in the two opposite states, of great poverty, and great opulence, are unfavourable to the formation of those associations of which the parental affection consists.

In cases of extreme poverty, which alone are the cases here understood ; because, in the more moderate cases of poverty, the parental affection exists in considerable strength ; the circumstances which lead to the formation of agreeable associations with the child, are either wanting, or counteracted by circumstances

of an opposite tendency. The parent has little tho
means of bestowing pleasures on his child ; he has
not the means of saving it from an almost constant
series of pains. The means which he employs in
saving the child from pains, are taken from the means
of saving himself from pains. Constantly occupied
in the labours which yield him a scanty means of subsistence, he spends but little time in the company of
his child, and has therefore little opportunity of attending to the engaging expressions of its pains and
pleasures. It is needless to carry the enumeration of
particulars farther. The circumstances which tend to
generate agreeable associations with the child are few.
The circumstances which tend to generate painful
associations with it are many.

In Families of great opulence, the attention of the
parent, averted either by the calls of pleasure, or the
avocations which his position in society creates, is but
little bestowed upon his children. Where the pains
and pleasures of others are not attended to, no association with those pains and pleasures exists ; where
there is not a habit of forming the associations, the
Affection does not exist.

The mode in which the child of the man of opulence is maintained and educated, proceeds so remotely
from the acts of the parent, that the agreeable associations, which we have with our own acts of beneficence, are, in the case of such a parent, very imperfectly formed.

The man of opulence naturally regards his children
as part of his state ; as the inheritors of his fortune ;
or as belonging to the same line of ancestors with
himself ; and with both those constituents of his

dignity he has many agreeable associations. But
these are an imperfect substitute for the habits of
agreeable association which are generated in more
favourable circumstances.

Hitherto, we have considered only the parental
affection of the Father. The parental affection of
the Mother differs from that of the Father in the
associations which she forms with her child in her
own peculiar situations of gestation and nursing.
That these are such as to create intense associations
every one will admit. Every movement of the child
during the period of gestation is to her a sensation.
Every thought of it is connected with that flood of
hopes and fears attached to the awful hour, never
absent from her thoughts, which, through a series of
cruel pains, will either stretch her a lifeless corpse, or
render her a rejoicing mother. As a nurse, the child
is to her a source, both of agreeable sensations, and
agreeable ideas. On the sensations we need not
dilate. They are known only to those who have experienced them. But it is not possible to conceive a
case more calculated to associate strongly the ideas of
our own pleasures, with the ideas of the pleasures we
bestow, than that of the mother, when she presses
her infant to her bosom, and communicates to him the
means of life, and the only pleasures he is capable of
enjoying, not only by her own acts, but from her own
substance ; and when she perceives how soon in the
mind of the child, the idea of herself is associated
with the existence of all his pleasures, and the removal
of all his pains ; in other words, how quickly she
becomes not only the object of his affections, but the
one and only object.

Having explained at so much length the grand case of the Domestic Affections, we may pass over the rest with a very cursory notice.

Even the Filial affection has in it nothing peculiar. In the child, the idea of his parent, as a being with power almost unlimited over him, creates the associations which constitute reverence, and respect; and the perpetual use of that power on the part of the parent to give him pleasures, or the command of pleasures, to remove from him pains, or give him the means of removing them, naturally creates the associations which constitute affection.

The affection which exists among Brothers and Sisters, has in it most of the ingredients which go to the formation of Friendship. There is first of all Companionship; the habit of enjoying pleasures, in common, and also of suffering pains: hence a great readiness in sympathizing with one another; that is, in associating trains of their own pains and pleasures, with the pains and pleasures of one another. There is next, when the Education is good, a constant reciprocation, to the extent of their power, of beneficent acts. And lastly there is their common relation to the grand source of all their pleasures, the Parent.

When the affections of the domestic class exist in perfection (in such a state of Education and Morals as ours this rarely can happen), they afford so constant a succession of agreeable trains, that they form, perhaps, the most valuable portion of human happiness. Acts of beneficence to larger masses of mankind, afford still more interesting trains to those who perform them. But they are the small number. The happiness of the Domestic affections is open to all.

4.—*Country.*

The word country is the name of an idea of great complexity. In that idea are included all the multitudes of persons, and all the multitudes of things, and all the multitudes of positions, in a certain portion of the Globe of the Earth. Nor are these present existences alone included in that idea : the HISTORY of the country is included, that is, the whole series of prior existences ; and not the PAST HISTORY only, but the FUTURE HISTORY also, or series of future existences, as far as our power of anticipation reaches. This is a remarkable example of the power of association, to unite ideas without number in such closeness, that their individuality is unperceived, and the cluster, however large, resembles a single uncompounded idea.

This cluster is not wholly made up of indifferent ideas. There is included in it the sources of all our pleasures, and almost all the objects with which we have been accustomed to associate trains of agreeable ideas. The plains, the mountains, the valleys, the rivers, with which we have formed agreeable associations, are all there ; the individual objects with which we have formed similar associations, the trees, the houses ; the house, for example, in which we were born, the tree under which we have sat to enjoy the affections of our parents, or indulge our sympathies with other objects of our love, the paths in which we have strayed, the fields through which we have roamed, the riches wherewith we have seen them periodically clothed, the labours of those fields, the labourers, their manners, appearance, and character,

the flocks and herds, the cities and towns, with all
their inhabitants, and all their operations, the wonderful proceedings of the manufacturers, the arrival and
departure of ships, loaded with the precious commodities of the different regions of the Earth.

To these sources of Interest is to be added, all that
portion of our fellow-creatures with whom we have
been accustomed to associate our Pains and Pleasures.
Here are our Parents, our Brothers and Sisters, our
Sons and Daughters. Here are the men, and here
the women, who have engaged our affections. Here
are our Benefactors, here are our Instructors, here are
the manners which alone from habit are agreeable to
us. And here are the Institutions from which we
have derived Protection, and to which, in their usual
state of imperfection, we are apt to lend a reverence,
such is the strength of the association, far beyond the
measure of their worth.

Sufficient sources have now been pointed out, to
shew whence it is that the Idea of country, as it
involves a great number of agreeable associations,
becomes, or more properly speaking is, an Affection.

5.—*Party; Class.*

That which constitutes a Party, or class, is always
some community of Interest : in other words, some
thing or things, to be obtained, secured, or augmented, by the common endeavours of the class, and
operating as a cause of pleasure to all of them.

The People, that is, the Mass of the community,
are sometimes called a class ; but that is only to distinguish them, like the term Lower Orders, from the

Aristocratical class. In the proper meaning of the term class, it is not applicable to the People. No interest is in common to them, which is not in common to the rest of the community. There is nothing which can operate as a cause of benefit to them exclusively. Whatever operates as a cause of benefit to them in common, operates equally as a cause of benefit to every part of the community, saving and excepting those who are in possession of some mischievous power over a portion, greater or less, of the community. It may no doubt very easily happen, that what is a benefit to the rest of the community, is an evil to the possessors of such power; as what is an evil, and the greatest of all Evils, to the Community, is a Benefit to them.

There is no Love of Class, therefore, but in a Privileged Order. The Patricians, in ancient Rome, were a Class of this sort. And in modern Europe there are two such classes: the Nobility, in each Country: and the Incorporated Clergy; calling themselves the Church, in Catholic countries, the Established Church, in Non-catholic countries.

The associations which the members of a governing class have with one another, individually, as fathers, sons, companions, friends, are not here to be taken into account. The associations connected with the privileges which constitute any body of men a class, are alone concerned in forming the states of mind which we now are explaining.

Such privileges consist of Wealth, Power, Dignity, one, or all, conferred by Legislative act: that is, not the result of natural acquisition, but of a sort of force, or compulsion, put upon other people.

We need not again enter into an explanation of the agreable associations which every man has with his own Wealth, Power, and Dignity, and with the causes, either of their existence, or of their increase, or of their security. When these causes to one man, are causes also to a circle of other men, the whole Body has both individually and collectively the associations with those causes, which constitute Affection.

6.—Mankind.

The word Mankind is the name of another of those remarkable associations, by which countless ideas are so combined, that their individuality is sunk, and the aggregate is, to appearance, one idea.

The Idea Mankind, like the Idea Country, is not made up wholly of indifferent ideas. It has in it all the trains of pleasurable ideas which we associate, either with individuals, or with subdivisions, of the whole mass.

We have interesting associations with the idea of a man, as a man. The idea of his pains, and his pleasures, call up, unavoidably, trains of the ideas of our own pains and pleasures. The Idea of a man, therefore, naturally includes, the love of his pleasures, hatred of his pains.

From our earliest Infancy, we have had experience of nothing more constantly than this; that a great proportion of our pleasures proceeded from a certain disposition towards us, on the part of those of our fellow-creatures who were near us; and a great proportion of our Pains from a certain other disposition on their part. Those Dispositions, taken in the most general sense, are Kindness, which we have already explained; and its opposite, Unkindness. We have, therefore, very intense associations of Pleasure, with the idea of the Disposition towards us, called Kindness, in other men ; and very intense associations of Pain with that of the Disposition in them called Unkindness towards us.

In our Idea of each individual man, therefore, is included not only the Love of his Pleasures and Aversion to his Pains ; but, in addition to this, the Love of his Disposition of Kindness towards us, and Aversion to his Disposition of Unkindness towards us.

Now, as our complex Idea of Mankind, is made up of the aggregate of the ideas of Individuals, including the interesting trains called Love of their Pleasures, Hatred of their Pains ; Love of their Kindness, Aversion to their Unkindness; the generation of the affection, called Love of Mankind, is, for our present purpose, sufficiently shewn." "

SUB-SECTION III.

The Objects called Sublime and Beautiful, and their Contraries, contemplated as Causes of our Pleasures and Pains.

These objects have received much of the attention of Philosophers ; and great progress has been made in

---

⁴⁴ As carrying out the principle of association, in the domain of the Feelings, the foregoing chapters, from XIX. onwards, are unexceptionable and cogent. As furnishing the complete

analysing the associations which form the complicated
feelings, ranged under the name of Emotions of the
Sublime and Beautiful.

account of the Benevolent and Malevolent Affections, and of
the Sympathies or disinterested impulses, they are defective.
Indeed, the whole subject of the Emotions is placed by the
author upon a too narrow basis.   Any theory that looks solely
to the circumstance of pleasure and pain, (important as that
is) fails to grapple with all the facts.   For example, there is
no account rendered of the very familiar emotion of Wonder.

That the Emotions are all compounded of elements of Sense
(in the widest comprehension, that is, with Muscularity included) may be maintained on good grounds.   Nevertheless,
in order to a satisfactory analysis of even the commoner
emotions, such as Tenderness, there is wanted a more exhaustive detail of the pleasures and pains of sense than is furnished
in the present work.

A few remarks on the generic example of the Tender Feeling, on which the author has expended the greatest part of his
illustration, will show the method to be pursued.   It is a case
where certain primary sensibilities, correctly ranked under Sensation, together with the associating principle, seem to account
for the whole of the phenomenon.   In such a case as Wonder,
the explanation involves an additional element.

The pleasures of Tender Feeling, or Love and the Affections,
are no doubt, as remarked in the text, in a considerable part
associations with other pleasures, such as nourishment.   An
animal and a child would contract a pleasurable association
with the person that brings them their food, or ministers to
their bodily wants.   Still, there is something different from
this in Tenderness or Love.   The fact essential to the state is
the gratification from the acts of caressing, fondling, and
embracing ; a pleasure that has its independent sources in the
human and animal sensibilities, and does not need the association with being fed and cared for, although enhanced and
stimulated by that association.   Even apart from the powerful

It does not belong to the present purpose to go into the details of this subject, which, for obvious reasons, have been pursued to great length.   It is necessary,

---

element of sexuality, there is a great mass of pleasurable animal feeling awakened in the loving embrace of two individuals of the warm-blooded species. We may instance, among these, the pleasures of Touch in the soft warm contact ; the muscular pleasures co-operating ; the organic feelings connected with secretions stimulated in the act, of which the lachrymal is the prominent but not the solitary case ; the peculiar sensibility of the pharynx, which is probably the sign of a less acute but more extended influence in the alimentary canal generally ; to all which, is to be added, in women, the genial secretion of the breasts, going on incessantly, although more profuse in nursing mothers. The coalition of these tactile, muscular, and organic sensibilities, is the pleasure of love by itself, or as it might be felt between two living sentient creatures, in no other way the givers or receivers of benefits. Nor does this exhaust the circle.   The eye, and the ear, and even the smell, may be also included.   The visible aspects of living beings are often highly agreeable from the first, and become so to a farther extent by association with the tactile and organic pleasures.   Similarly, the ear may be charmed with the sounds emitted by another human being or animal, and may also form associations with the still more potent pleasures above named.   Once more, the odour of one animal may be intrinsically sweet to another animal ; while here too, associations may be added.

The pleasure of Tender feeling must therefore be pronounced to have an independent standing in the sentient framework, although susceptible of being analysed into the primary pleasures of the senses, together with the influence of association. All the affections derive the chief part of their strength from this complex source.   For, although the acts of fondling and caressing are not universally practised between every two persons that have a mutual affection, or are so only in the very

however, for that purpose, to shew, into what general laws the phenomena are capable of being resolved.

The feelings which are marked under the name of

limited form of the shake of the hand, yet there is an echo of these, and a stimulus to the organic accompaniments, in the sight of each other, in the sounds of the voice, and in the more intellectual forms of indicating attachment. It can be proved that the two higher senses enter deeply into the tender emotion, (as they do into the Beautiful). The well-known Dr. Kitto, who was stone-deaf, in describing his experience, states that, as regarded his pleasures, the loss that affected him most was his inability to hear the voices of his children. It is evident that the same remark, as to the mutilation of an organ of tender feeling, is applicable to the blind. The pathos of the lines in Paradise Lost contains this implication.—B.

[45] The two preceding subsections are almost perfect as expositions and exemplifications of the mode in which, by the natural course of life, we acquire attachments to persons, things, and positions, which are the causes or habitual concomitants of pleasurable sensations to us, or of relief from pains : in other words, those persons, things, and positions become in themselves pleasant to us by association ; and, through the multitude and variety of the pleasurable ideas associated with them, become pleasures of greater constancy and even intensity, and altogether more valuable to us, than any of the primitive pleasures of our constitution. This portion of the laws of human nature is the more important to psychology, as they show how it is possible that the moral sentiments, the feelings of duty, and of moral approbation and disapprobation, may be no original elements of our nature, and may yet be capable of being not only more intense and powerful than any of the elements out of which they may have been formed, but may also, in their maturity, be perfectly disinterested : nothing more being necessary for this, than that the acquired pleasure and pain should have become as independent of the native elements from which they are formed, as the love of wealth

Emotions of the Sublime and Beautiful, are so much alike, that the distinction of them into two species is somewhat arbitrary.   Though the Romans did apply

and of power not only often but generally become, of the bodily pleasures, and relief from bodily pains, for the sake of which, and of which alone, power and wealth must have been originally valued.   No one thinks it necessary to suppose an original and inherent love of money or of power ; yet these are the objects of two of the strongest, most general, and most persistent passions of human nature ; passions which often have quite as little reference to pleasure or pain, beyond the mere consciousness of possession, and are in that sense of the word quite as disinterested, as the moral feelings of the most virtuous human being.

The author, then, has furnished a most satisfactory and most valuable explanation of certain of the laws of our affections and passions, and has traced the origin and generation of a great number of them.   But it must be remarked of the whole exposition, that it accounts truly, but only partially, for this part of human nature.   It affords a sufficient theory of what we may call the mental, or intellectual element of the feelings in question.   But it does not furnish, nor does the author anywhere furnish, any theory of what may be called the animal element in them.   Yet this is no unimportant ingredient in the emotional and active part of human nature : and it is one greatly demanding analysis.   Let us take the case of any of the passions : and as one of the simplest as well as one of the most powerful of them, let us take the emotion of Fear. The author gives no account of Fear but that it is the idea of a painful sensation, associated with the idea of its being (more or less uncertainly) future.   Undoubtedly these elements are present in it ; but do they account for the peculiar emotional character of the passion, and for its physiological effect, such as pallor, trembling, faltering of the voice, coldness of the skin, loss of control over the secretions, and general depression of the vital powers ? The case would be simpler if these great

the word *sublimis*, and its abstract, *sublimitas*, in a
certain rhetorical way, to objects of Taste, their word
Pulchrum, properly denoted all that is expressed by

disturbances of the animal functions by the expectation of a
pain were the same in kind as the smaller modifications produced by the mere idea. This, however, is by no means the
case; Ideas do produce effects on the animal economy, but not
those particular effects. The idea of a pain, if it acts on the
bodily functions at all, has an action the same in kind (though
much less in degree) as the pain itself would have. But the
passion of fear has a totally different action. Suppose the
fear to be that of a flogging. The flogging itself, if it produced
any physical demonstrations, would produce cries, shrinkings,
possibly muscular struggles, and might by its remoter effects
disturb the action of the brain or of the circulation; and if
the fear of a flogging produced these same effects, in a mitigated
degree, the power of fear might be merely the power of the
idea of the pain. But none of these are at all like the characteristic symptoms of fear: while those characteristic symptoms are much the same whatever be the particular pain
apprehended, and whether it be a bodily or a purely mental pain,
provided it be sufficiently intense and sufficiently proximate.
No one has ever accounted for this remarkable difference, and
the author of the Analysis does not even mention it. The
explanation of it is one of those problems, partly psychological
and partly physiological, which our knowledge of the laws of
animal sensibility does not yet enable us to resolve. In whatever manner the phenomena are produced, they are a case of
the quasi-chemistry of the nervous functions, whereby the
junction of certain elements generates a compound whose
properties are very different from the sum of the properties of
the elements themselves.

This is the point which the author's explanations of the
emotional part of human nature do not reach, and, it may even
be said, do not attempt to reach. Until, however, it is reached,
there is no guarantee for the completeness of his analysis of

our Sublime and Beautiful, taken together.   The
Greek word, καλόν, also clearly included every thing
which we rank under the name of Sublime.   Longinus,
indeed, who lived at a very late and degenerate period
of Grecian literature, wrote a treatise to which he gave
the affected Title, Πέρι Ὑψοῦς, or " About Height ;"
and as that has been a very popular treatise in modern
times, it is not improbable, that the use of the word
Sublime, which has become so prevalent in the discourse
of the moderns, derives its origin from no higher source.

Mr. Alison, who wrote a very pleasing, and, to a
certain degree, a Philosophical Book, on the Emotions
of Taste, has shewn by an abundance of well-chosen
illustrations, that it is not the immediate sensations,
received by us from the objects of Taste, which constitute them a cause of our pleasures.   The immediate
sensations are commonly indifferent, or approaching
the indifferent.   It is only when they introduce, by
association, a train of pleasurable ideas, that the feelings called the pleasures of Taste, are ever enjoyed.

I believe that I may assume this as an established

---

even the mental element in the passions : for when the effect
exhibits so much which has not, in the known properties of the
assigned cause, anything to account for it, there is always room
for a doubt whether some part of the cause has not been left
out of the reckoning.   This doubt, however, does not seriously
affect the most important of the author's analyses, viz. those
which, without resolving the emotions themselves into anything more elementary, expound their transfer by association
from their natural objects to others ; with the great increase of
intensity and persistency which so often accompanies the
transfer, and which is in general quite sufficiently accounted
for by the causes to which the author refers it. —*Ed.*

fact in our nature ; and I shall only adduce as much
of the evidence as may teach those of my readers, to
whom these inquiries may be new, the mode in which
the truth of the proposition becomes apparent. I also
think it useful to avail myself, not only of the illustrations, but as much as possible of the words, of Mr.
Alison, as exhibiting the clear conviction of the wonderful effects of association, in one instance, on the
part of a writer, who seems to have had no idea of its
affording an equally satisfactory solution of the other
complex phenomena of mind.

What are called the external objects of Taste, are
mostly objects of Hearing, objects of Sight, or objects
of that Muscular Sense, from which we derive the idea
of extension.

That the feelings we have by these senses are
generically distinct from the emotions of Sublimity
and Beauty, might, I imagine, be trusted to an appeal
to each man's consciousness. There are innumerable
cases, however, which may be regarded as decisive
experiments upon the subject.

Of the sounds which can be adduced as Sublime or
Beautiful, there is, perhaps, not one, which is not often
heard in circumstances, wherein no tendency to Emotion is felt. The circumstances in which the Emotion
is felt, and those in which it is not felt, are those in
which a train of pleasurable ideas is, or is not, introduced by association.

" All sounds," says Mr. Alison, " are in general
SUBLIME, which are associated with Ideas of great
Power or Might : the Noise of a Torrent,—the Fall
of a Cataract,—the Uproar of a Tempest,—the Explosion of Gunpowder,—the Dashing of the Waves, &c.

" All sounds, in the same manner, are sublime, which are associated with Ideas of Majesty, or Solemnity, or deep Melancholy, or any other strong Emotion : the Sound of the Trumpet, and all other warlike instruments,—the Note of the Organ,—the Sound of the Curfew,—the Tolling of the Passing bell, &c.

" There is a great variety of sounds also, that occur in the scenes of Nature, which are productive of the Emotion of BEAUTY : the Sound of a Waterfall,—the Murmuring of a Rivulet,—the Whispering of the Wind,—the Sheepfold-bell,—the sound of the Curfew, &c.

" That the Notes or Cries of some Animals, are Sublime, every one knows : the Roar of the Lion, the Growling of Bears, the Howling of Wolves, the Scream of the Eagle, &c. In all those cases, those are the notes of animals remarkable for their strength, and formidable for their ferocity. It would seem very natural, therefore, that the sublimity of such sounds should arise from the qualities of which they are expressive.

" The Bleating of a Lamb, is beautiful in a fine day in spring : the Lowing of a Cow at a distance, amid the scenery of a pastoral landscape in summer. The Call of a Goat among rocks is strikingly beautiful, as expressing wildness and independence. The Hum of the Beetle is beautiful in a fine summer evening, as appearing to suit the stillness and repose of that pleasing season. The Twitter of the Swallow is beautiful in the morning, and seems to be expressive of the cheerfulness of that time."

This enumeration of cases, which is only a selection from those of Mr. Alison, is far more than

sufficient for the purpose, as indeed it is one defect
of his book that his propositions are overlaid with
evidence.

That these sounds, as sensations, do not constitute
the pleasures enjoyed, he demonstrates, by shewing
that on many occasions, on which the sensations
exist as perfectly as on any other occasion, no pleasure
is felt. He also shews, that when the pleasures
are felt, a train of pleasurable ideas is introduced by
association.

" The sound of Thunder, he says, is perhaps of all
others in Nature, the most Sublime." Yet the rolling
of stones from a cart, produces a sound so exactly
the same, that it is often mistaken for thunder.
While the mistake lasts, the feeling of sublimity
lasts. When the mistake is corrected, it instantly
vanishes ; that is, the association is dissolved.

" There is scarcely in nature," says Mr. Alison, " a
more trifling sound than the buzz of Flies ; yet, I
believe, there is no man of common Taste, who, in
the deep silence of a summer's noon, has not found
something strikingly sublime, in this inconsiderable
sound. The falling of a drop of water, produces in
general a very insignificant and unexpressive sound ;
yet sometimes in Vaults, and in large Cathedrals, a
single drop is heard to fall, at distant intervals, from
the roof ; than which, I know not if there is a single
sound more strikingly sublime."

Mr. Alison further remarks, that to those who have
no trains of pleasurable ideas associated with sounds,
" or who consider them simply as sounds, they have
no beauty. It is long before children shew any
sensibility to the beauty of sounds. To the greater

number of the sounds which we denominate beautiful,
the common people, in the same manner, are altogether
indifferent.   To the peasant, the Curfew is only the
mark of the hour of the evening,—the Sheep-bell, the
sign of the neighbourhood of the flock,—the sound of
a Cascade, the sign of the falling of water, &c.   Give
him the associations which men of cultivated imagination have with such sounds, and he will infallibly
feel their beauty."

Mr. Alison shews, that when the notes or cries of
animals are stripped of certain associations, they are
unproductive of Emotions of sublimity or beauty.
" There is not one of these sounds," he says, " which
may not be imitated in some manner or other; and
which, while we are ignorant of the deception, does
not produce the same Emotion with the real sound :
when we are undeceived, however, we are conscious
of no other Emotion, but that, perhaps, of simple
pain from its loudness.   The howl of the Wolf is
little distinguished from the howl of the Dog, either
in its tone or in its strength, but there is no comparison between their sublimity.   Few, if any, of the
sounds felt as sublime are so loud as the most common of
all sounds, the lowing of a Cow ; yet this is the very
reverse of sublimity.   Imagine this sound, on the
contrary, expressive of Fierceness and Strength, and
there can be no doubt, that it would become sublime.
The scream of the Eagle is simply disagreeable, when
the bird is either tamed or confined ; it is Sublime,
only when it is heard amid Rocks and Deserts, and
when it is expressive to us, of Liberty and Independence, and savage Majesty.   The noise of the Rattle-
snake (that most dangerous animal of all his tribe)

is very little different from the noise of a child's play-
thing ; yet who will deny its sublimity ? The growl
of the Tiger, resembles the purring of a Cat ; the one
is sublime, the other insignificant."

Mr. Alison, with great propriety, adds, " Upon the
principle of the absolute and independent Sublimity
or Beauty of Sounds, it is very difficult to account for
the different sounds which have been mentioned as
productive of these Emotions. There is certainly no
resemblance, as sounds, between the noise of Thunder,
and the hissing of a Serpent,—between the growling
of a Tiger, and the explosion of Gunpowder,—between the scream of an Eagle, and the shouting of a
multitude ; yet all of these are sublime. In the
same manner, there is as little resemblance, between
the tinkling of the Sheepfold-bell, and the murmuring
of the Breeze; between the hum of the Beetle and
the song of the Lark ; between the twitter of the
Swallow, and the sound of the Curfew; yet all of
these are beautiful. Upon the principle of association, they are all perfectly accountable."

I shall not follow Mr. Alison in his illustrations
of the beauty and sublimity felt in the tones of the
human voice, or in the composition of sounds, called
Music; because I have no doubt but it will be allowed
that they derive the whole of what is called their
expression,—in other words, their power of pleasing,
—from the associations connected with them.[46] I

---

[46] What the author thinks himself dispensed from either
proving or illustrating because he has no doubt that it will be
allowed, is, on the contrary, one of the most disputable parts
of his theory. That very much of the pleasure afforded by

shall also produce a very few specimens of the illustrations which he adduces to show that what is called the Beauty and Sublimity of objects of sight, is derived wholly from association.

The following observations are general, and very instructive.

" The greatest part of colours are connected with a kind of established Imagery in our minds, and are considered as expressive of many very pleasing and affecting Qualities.

" These Associations may perhaps be included in the following Enumeration : 1st, Such as arise from

---

Music is the effect of its expression, i.e. of the associations connected with sound, most people will admit : but it can scarcely be doubted that there is also an element of direct physical and sensual pleasure. In the first place, the quality of some single sounds is physically agreeable, as that of others is disagreeable. Next, the concord or harmony of pleasant sounds adds a further element of purely physical enjoyment. And thirdly, certain successions of sounds, constituting melody or tune, are delightful, as it seems to me, to the mere sense. With these pleasures those of the associated ideas and feelings are intimately blended, but may, to a certain extent, be discriminated by a critical ear. It is possible to say, of different composers, that one (as Beethoven) excels most in that part of the effect of music which depends on expression, and another (as Mozart) in the physical part.

That the full physical pleasure of tune is often not experienced at the first hearing, is a consequence of the fact, that the pleasure depends on succession, and therefore on the coexistence of each note with the remembrance of a sufficient number of the previous notes to constitute melody : a remembrance which, of course, is not possessed in perfection, until after a number of repetitions proportioned to the complexity and to the unfamiliar character of the combination.—*Ed.*

the nature of the objects thus permanently coloured :
2ndly, Such as arise from some analogy between certain Colours, and certain Dispositions of mind : and,
3rdly, Such as arise from accidental connexions,
whether national or particular.

" 1.   When we have been accustomed to see any
object capable of exciting Emotion, distinguished by
some fixed or permanent colour, we are apt to extend
to the Colour the Qualities of the object thus
coloured, and to feel from it, when separated, some
degree of the same emotion which is properly excited
by the object itself.   Instances of this kind are within
every person's observation.   White, as it is the colour
of Day, is expressive to us of the cheerfulness or
gaiety which the return of day brings.   Black, as the
colour of Darkness, is expressive of gloom and melancholy.   The colour of the heavens, in serene weather,
is Blue : Blue, is therefore expressive to us of somewhat of the same pleasing and temperate character.
Green, is the colour of the Earth, in Spring : it is,
consequently, expressive to us of some of those delightful Images which we associate with that season.
The expressions of those colours, which are the signs
of particular passions in the Human countenance,
and which, from this connexion, derive their effect,
every one is acquainted with.

" 2.   There are many colours which derive expression from some analogy we discover between them
and certain affections of the Human Mind.   Soft or
Strong, Mild or Bold, Gay or Gloomy, Cheerful or
Solemn, &c., are terms, in all languages, applied to
colours ; terms obviously metaphorical, and the use of
which indicates their connexion with particular quali-

ties of Mind. In the same manner, different degrees
or shades of the same colour have similar characters,
as Strong, or Temperate, or Gentle, &c. In consequence of this Association,—which is, in truth, so
strong, that it is to be found in all mankind,—such
colours derive a character from this resemblance, and
produce in our mind some faint degree of the same
Emotion, which the qualities they express are fitted
to produce.

" 3. Many colours acquire character from accidental
Association. Purple, for instance, has acquired a
character of Dignity, from its accidental connexion
with the Dress of Kings. The colours of Ermine
have a similar character, from the same cause. The
colours, in every country, which distinguish the Dress
of Magistrates, &c., acquire dignity in the same
manner. Every person will, in the same manner, probably, recollect the particular colours which are
pleasing to him, from their having been worn by
people whom he loved, or from some other accidental
association."

That it is not from the sensation, but from those
trains of associated Ideas, that the feeling of Beauty
in colours, whenever we have it, is derived, he demonstrates, by adducing some well-chosen instances to
shew that the sensation may exist as well without the
association as with it; and that, as often as it is
unaccompanied with the association, it is unaccompanied with any feeling of Beauty. When it has the
association, Beauty is felt : when it has not the association, Beauty is not felt. The association, therefore,
is the cause of the Beauty.

" Black," says Mr. Alison, " is to us an unpleasant
colour, because it is the colour appropriated to mourning. In Venice and Spain, it is agreeable, because it
is the colour which distinguishes the dress of the
Great. White is beautiful to us, in a supreme
degree, as emblematical both of Innocence and Cheerfulness. In China, on the other hand, it is the
colour appropriated to Mourning, and, consequently,
very far from being generally beautiful.

" The common colours of the indifferent things
which surround us,—of the Earth, of Stone, of Wood,
&c.,—have no kind of Beauty. The things themselves are so indifferent to us, that they excite no
kind of emotion ; and, of consequence, their colours
produce no greater emotion as the signs of such
qualities, than the qualities themselves. The colours,
in the same manner, which distinguish the ordinary
Dress of the Common People, are never considered as
beautiful. It is the colours only of the Dress of the
Great, of the Opulent, or of Distinguished Profes-
sions, which are ever considered in this light.

" No new colour is ever beautiful, until we have
acquired some pleasing associations with it. This is
peculiarly observable in the article of Dress ; and
indeed it is the best instance of it, because no other
circumstance intervenes by which the experiment
can be influenced. Every man must have observed,
that, in the great variety of new colours, which
the caprice of Fashion is perpetually introducing,
no new colour appears at first sight as beautiful.
A few weeks, even a few days alter our opinion ; as
soon as it is generally adopted by those who lead

the public Taste, and has become in consequence the mark of Rank and Elegance, it immediately becomes beautiful.

" When the particular associations we have with such colours, are destroyed, their beauty is destroyed at the same time.

" The different machines, instruments, &c., which minister to the convenience of Life, have, in general, from the materials of which they are composed, or from the uses to which they are applied, a fixed and determinate colour. This colour becomes accordingly in some degree beautiful, from its being the sign of such qualities ; change the accustomed colour of such objects, and every man feels a kind of disappointment. This is so strong, that, even if a colour more generally beautiful is substituted, yet still our dissatisfaction is the same ; and the new colour, instead of being beautiful, becomes the reverse. Rose-colour, for instance, is a more beautiful colour than that of Mahogany : yet, if any man were to paint his doors and windows with Rose-colour, he would certainly not add to their beauty. The colour of a polished steel grate is agreeable, but is not in itself very beautiful. Suppose it painted green, or violet, or crimson, all of them colours much more beautiful, and the beauty of it is altogether destroyed. Instances of this kind are innumerable."[47]

---

[47] The elements contributed by association are certainly more predominant in the pleasure of colours than in that of musical sounds ; yet I am convinced that there is a direct element of physical pleasure in colours, anterior to association. My own memory recals to me the intense and mysterious

Mr. Alison produces a very long train of illustrations to show that the Beauty of Forms is not the mere sensation of Form, but consists, as in the case of sounds and colours, in the train of pleasurable ideas associated with the sensation. Mr. Alison is less happy, and more tedious, in the illustration of this than the preceding parts of his subject. We shall make little use of his proofs ; because we can arrive, by a short process, at a very satisfactory conclusion.

Mr. Alison seems not to have been aware of the

---

delight which in early childhood I had in the colours of certain flowers ; a delight far exceeding any I am now capable of receiving from colour of any description, with all its acquired associations. And this was the case at far too early an age, and with habits of observation far too little developed, to make any of the subtler combinations of form and proportion a source of much pleasure to me. This last pleasure was acquired very gradually, and did not, until after the commencement of manhood, attain any considerable height. The examples quoted from Alison do not prove that there is no original beauty in colours, but only that the feeling of it is capable, as no one doubts that it is capable, of being overpowered by extraneous associations.

Whether there is any similar organic basis of the pleasure derived from form, so far at least as this depends on proportion, I would not undertake to decide.

The susceptibility to the physical pleasures produced by colours and musical sounds, (and by forms if any part of the pleasure they afford is physical); is probably extremely different in different organisations. In natures in which any one of these susceptibilities is originally faint, more will depend on association. The extreme sensibility of this part of our constitution to small and unobvious influences, makes it certain that the sources of the feelings of beauty and deformity must be, to a material extent, different in different individuals.—*Ed.*

origin of our ideas of Form ; and thence in expounding them has found many difficulties which do not in reality belong to the subject. He supposes that Form is altogether a sensation of sight. In a former part of this Inquiry, we ascertained the sensations : we saw that Form, in all its cases, is merely a modification of extension ; that it is made known to us, by those feelings, which accompany the motion of certain of our members, as that of a finger, or a hand. Those feelings are in no danger of being confounded with the emotion of Beauty. They are feelings so completely indifferent, that in most of the associations into which the ideas of them enter as essential ingredients they are overlooked, and the very existence of them is commonly unknown.

If the sensation is no cause of the Pleasure derived from Forms, it will not be questioned that association is the cause.

Forms are either Animate or Inanimate. The associations with the Animate only differ from those with the Inanimate, in holding some additional ingredients. Some Forms affect us, by their magnitude, naturally associated with the idea of Power ; some, by the uses to which they are applied, as the more powerful instruments of war; some, by the extent of their duration, with which we have obvious associations ; some, by the splendour or magnificence, with the ideas of which they are associated,—the Throne, the Diadem, the Triumphal Car.

The natural movements of the arm, from its turning in its socket as round a centre, are all waving ; circles, or portions of circles, running into one another. All other movements are forced upon it, and the effect of constraint. Hence the beauty of waving lines, because associated with the agreeable ideas of Ease, and absence of Restraint.

As nothing is more agreeable to us than to trace the operation of design, of successful contrivance, some Forms affect us strongly by the idea of their Fitness, of their adaptation to an End.

Others affect us not only by the idea of their adaptation to an end, but by the value which we attach to the end. In this case it is by their utility that they are said to please us.

We associate with the idea of certain states of the Human Body, or at least of the Bodies of Animals in general, certain inward Dispositions; with great strength we associate great Wilfulness, and little regard of others; with frailness, we associate Delicacy, the ideas of gentleness, compliance, and regard for others. The forms of inanimate objects sometimes bear such an analogy to the Delicate and Frail in human Forms, that the ideas associated with the animate, are called up by the inanimate, and produce the emotion of Beauty.

This emotion, however, is altogether prevented, when the more potent idea of Fitness intervenes. Any thing analogous to the slender form, which is so exquisitely beautiful in the more elegant grasses, would be a real deformity in the-oak.

More than one of those sources of agreeable association are often united in the same subject, and increase the emotion produced by it.

Mr. Alison goes on to the exposition of the associations which constitute the Beauty of Motion, and the Beauty of the Human Form and Countenance.

But after what has been said, these associations are not difficult to trace ; and I have already carried the illustration of this subject farther than I should have done, if I had not regarded this case of Association as affording most important aid toward the developement of all the more mysterious phenomena of the Human Mind.

We have here a class of Pleasures ; the Feeling of Beauty, the Feeling of Sublimity ; exercising a great influence over all cultivated minds. These Feelings, when taken as objects of general contemplation, appear perfectly simple. To such a degree have they assumed the appearance of simple and original feelings of our nature, even to Philosophers of eminence, that a particular sense has been supposed necessary to account for their existence. Yet all this apparent simplicity is only an exemplification of that association, by which a multitude of ideas are so intimately, and instantaneously blended together, that they appear to be not many ideas, but one idea.

Of this highly important fact, we have had occasion to take notice of various leading cases, before. In the present case, however, there is a peculiarity ; which it has in common with the various cases called Affection, which we have recently been engaged in considering. In the cases which occurred for examination, in the earlier part of this Inquiry, where we found long trains of Ideas so blended together, by association, as to appear not many ideas, but one ; that of Motion, that of Space, that of Time, that of Personal Identity ; the ideas associated were those of *indifferent* sensations. The ideas, on the other hand, which are associated under the terms

Beauty and Sublimity, are ideas of *pleasurable* sensations. The difference is that which is testified by every man's consciousness.

That there should be a remarkable difference between a train composed of ideas of the indifferent class, and a train composed of ideas of the pleasurable class, can be easily supposed. It is necessary further to observe, that between two trains, both of the pleasurable class, there are such important differences, as to have suggested the use of marking them by different names. Thus, even in the class which we have been now considering, one train is composed of pleasurable ideas, of such a kind, that we call it sublime ; another, of pleasurable ideas of such a kind, that we call it Beautiful. From the train of ideas associated with the form of the statue called the Venus de Medicis, we call it beautiful. We have a train of ideas, also pleasurable, associated with the bust of Socrates. But this is a train not reckoned to belong to the class either of the beautiful or the sublime ; it is a train including all the grand associations connected with the ideas of intellectual, and moral, worth.

A particular description of the sort of ideas which constitute each of the more remarkable cases of our pleasurable trains (that they are of one kind in one train, of another kind in another train,—of one kind, for example, in the trains called Sublimity, another in the trains called Beauty, another in the trains for which we have no better name than moral approbation, no one can doubt) would be highly necessary in a detailed account of Human Nature. It is not necessary for the Analysis which is the object of this

Work ; and would engage us in too tedious an exposition.[48]

---

[48] The objection commonly made to the psychological analyses which resolve Beauty into association, is that they confound the Beautiful with the merely agreeable. This objection is urged, for example, by Coleridge, in his Biographia Literaria. He admits, with every one else, that things not in themselves agreeable, are often made agreeable by association ; that is, the pleasantness which belongs to the ideas with which they are associated, adheres to themselves : but this cannot, it is asserted, be the cause of their producing the particular emotion to which we attach the name of Beauty ; because, as no feeling of beauty belongs to the ideas that are supposed to generate the emotion, no such feeling can be transferred from them to what they are associated with.

Any one who has studied the Analysis up to this point, is aware of the inconclusiveness of this last argument. That a complex feeling generated out of a number of single ones, should be as unlike to any of those from which it is generated, as the sensation of white is unlike the sensations of the seven prismatic colours, is no unexampled or rare fact in our sensitive nature.

But it will also, I think, be found, in the case of our feelings of Beauty, and still more, of Sublimity, that the theory which refers their origin mainly to association, is not only not contradictory to facts, but is not even paradoxical. For if our perceptions of beauty and sublimity are of a more imposing character than the feelings ordinarily excited in us by the contemplation of objects, it will be found that the associations which form those impressions are themselves of a peculiarly imposing nature. This is apparent even from Alison ; and if the author of the Analysis had written later, he might have referred to a deeper thinker than Alison, and a more valuable because an unconscious witness to the truth of the Association theory. Mr. Ruskin, with profounder and more thoughtful views respecting the beauties both of Nature and of Art than any

psychologist I could name, undertakes, in the second volume
of "Modern Painters," to investigate the conditions of Beauty.
The result he brings out is, that every thing which gives us
the emotion of the Beautiful, is expressive and emblematic of
one or other of certain lofty or lovely ideas, which are, in his
apprehension, embodied in the universe, and correspond to the
various perfections of its Creator.   He holds these ideas to be,
Infinity, Unity, Repose, Symmetry, Purity, Moderation, and
Adaptation to Ends.   And he is, in my judgment, to a very
considerable degree successful in making out his case.   Mr.
Ruskin, it is true, never thinks of inferring that our feelings
of Beauty are the actual consequence of our having those
elevating or cheering ideas recalled to us through manifold
channels of association.   He deems the emotion to be arbitrarily attached to these ideas by a pre-established harmony.
But the evidence which he adduces goes far to prove the other
point.   If he succeeds, as I think he does, in showing that the
things which excite the emotions of beauty or sublimity are
always things which have a natural association with certain
highly impressive and affecting ideas (whether the catalogue
which he has made of those ideas is correct and complete or
not), we need no other mode of accounting for the peculiar
character of the emotions, than by the actual, though vague
and confused, recal of the ideas.   It cannot be deemed surprising that a state of consciousness made up of reminiscences
of such ideas as Mr. Ruskin specifies, and of the grand and
interesting objects and thoughts connected with ideas like
those, must be of a more elevated character, and must stir our
nature to a greater depth, than those associations of commonplace and every-day pleasures, which often combine with them
as parts of the mass of pleasurable feeling set up in us by the
objects of Nature and Art.   In a windy country, a screen of
trees so placed as to be a barrier against the prevailing winds,
excites ideas of warmth, comfort, and shelter, which belong to
the "agreeable," as distinguished by Coleridge from the Beautiful; and these enter largely into the pleasurable feeling with
which we contemplate the trees, without contributing to give

them the peculiar character distinctive of æsthetic feelings. But besides these there are other elements, constituting the beauty, properly speaking, of the trees, which appeal to other, and what we are accustomed, not without meaning, to call higher, parts of our nature ; which give a stronger stimulus and a deeper delight to the imagination, because the ideas they call up are such as in themselves act on the imagination with greater force.

As is observed by the author of the Analysis, the exposition in detail of the associations which enter into our various feelings of the sublime and beautiful, would require the examination of the subject on a scale not suited to the character nor proportioned to the dimensions of this Treatise. Of all our feelings, our acquired pleasures and pains, especiallly our pleasures, are the most complex ; resulting from the whole of our nature and of our past lives, and involving, consequently, a greater multitude and variety of associations than almost any other phenomena of the mind. And among our various pleasures, the æsthetic are without doubt the most complex. It may also be remarked, and is a considerable confirmation of the association theory, that the feelings of beauty or sublimity with which different people are affected by the contemplation of the same object, are evidently as different, as the pleasurable associations of different persons with the same object are likely to be. But there are some ingredients which are universally, or almost universally, present, when the emotions have their characteristic peculiarity ; and to which they seem to be mainly indebted for the extraordinary power with which they act on the minds which have the greatest susceptibility to them. These ingredients are probably more numerous and various than is commonly suspected ; but some of the most important and powerful of them are undoubtedly pointed to, and illustrated with great force, in the discussion which I have mentioned, by Mr. Ruskin ; to whose work I willingly refer the psychological student, as a copious source of at least far-reaching suggestions, and often of much more.

Supposing that all Beauty had been successfully analysed

into a lively suggestion of one or more of the ideas to which
it is referred by Mr. Ruskin, the question would still remain
for psychologists, why the suggestion of those ideas is so impressive and so delightful. But this question may, in general,
be answered with little difficulty. It is no mystery, for example, why anything which suggests vividly the idea of infinity,
that is, of magnitude or power without limit, acquires an
otherwise strange impressiveness to the feelings and imagination. The remaining ideas in Mr. Ruskin's list (at least if we
except those which, like Moderation, are chiefly ancillary to
the others, by excluding what would jar with their effect) all
represent to us some valuable or delightful attribute, in a completeness and perfection of which our experience presents us
with no example, and which therefore stimulates the active
power of the imagination to rise above known reality, into a
more attractive or a more majestic world. This does not
happen with what we call our lower pleasures. To them there
is a fixed limit at which they stop: or if, in any particular
case, they do acquire, by association, a power of stirring up
ideas greater than themselves, and stimulate the imagination
to enlarge its conceptions to the dimensions of those ideas,
we then feel that the lower pleasure has, exceptionally, risen
into the region of the æsthetic, and has superadded to itself
an element of pleasure of a character and quality not belonging
to its own nature.—*Ed.*

CHAPTER XXII.

MOTIVES.

SECTION I.

PLEASURABLE OR PAINFUL STATES, CONTEMPLATED AS CONSEQUENTS OF OUR OWN ACTS.

In contemplating pains and pleasures as future ; in other words, anticipating them, or believing in their future existence ; we observe, that, in certain cases, they are independent of our actions ; in other cases, that they are consequent upon something which may be done, or left undone by us.

Thus, in certain cases, we foresee that a painful sensation or sensations will be given us, but that something may be done by us which will prevent it : Again, that a pleasurable sensation, or sensations will be given us, but not unless something be done by us, of which the sensations are the consequence.

It is necessary that those two cases, a pain to be prevented, and a pleasure to be obtained, by our own actions, should be distinguished from one another ; but as they both rank under the title of a good, and, as it will shorten our phraseology to name them together, we shall speak of the removal of pain, in the present section, at least, under the denomination of a pleasure.

We have seen what is the state of consciousness, produced by the contemplation of a pleasurable sensation as future; that it is called Joy, if the pleasure is contemplated as certainly future, in other words, believed; that it is called Hope, if the sensation is contemplated as not certainly future, that is, if the anticipation does not amount to belief.

We have also seen what is our state of consciousness, when we contemplate the cause of a future pleasure, and the pleasure, together. It is a mixture of Love, and Joy; Love as regards the cause; Joy as regards the sensation.

The association which constitutes those States of Mind (AFFECTIONS, as they are commonly called) it is hardly necessary to repeat. The anticipation of a future sensation, is merely the association, the result of prior sensations, of a certain number of antecedents and consequents. I anticipate, for example, the pleasing sensation of light, at a certain hour to-morrow morning. The meaning is, that with my sensations of the present moment, are associated those of the next; with those of the next those of the following; and so on, till sleep; after sleep, waking, and then the anticipated sensation.

When the cause is contemplated along with the sensation, the association which constitutes the process of anticipation is the same, till we arrive at the link which immediately precedes the sensation. Thus, if instead of the pleasurable sensation of light, the pleasure of breakfast, is my anticipation of to-morrow morning ; in that case, the idea of the pleasure of eating is associated with the idea of the food, not as with an ordinary antecedent, but that peculiar antecedent which is called a cause.

When the idea of the Pleasure is associated with an action of our own as its cause; that is, contemplated as the consequent of a certain action of ours, and incapable of otherwise existing; or when the cause of a Pleasure is contemplated as the consequent of an action of ours, and not capable of otherwise existing ; a peculiar state of mind is generated which, as it is a tendency to action, is properly denominated MOTIVE.

The word MOTIVE is by no means steadily applied to its proper object.   The pleasure, for example, which is the consequent of the act, is apt to be regarded as alone the impelling principle, and properly entitled to the name of *Motive*.   It is obvious, however, that the idea of the pleasure does not constitute the motive to action without the idea of the action as the cause : that it is the association, therefore, to which alone the name belongs.

As every pleasure is worth having ; for otherwise it would not be a pleasure ; the idea of every pleasure associated with that of an action of ours as the cause, is a motive ; that is, leads to the action.   But every motive does not produce the action.   The reason is, the existence of other motives which prevent it.   A man is tempted to commit adultery with the wife of his friend ; the composition of the motive obvious. He does not obey the motive.   Why ?   He obeys other motives which are stronger.   Though pleasures are associated with the immoral act, pains are asso-

ciated with it also ; the pains of the injured husband ;
the pains of the injured wife ; the moral indignation
of mankind ; the future reproaches of his own mind.
Some men obey the first, rather than the second
motive. The reason is obvious. In them, the association of the act with the pleasure, is, from habit,
unduly strong; the association of the act with the
pains, is, from want of habit, unduly weak. This is a
case of bad Education ; and one highly unfortunate,
for the value of the pleasures in question is infinitely
outweighed by the value of the pains. The business
of a good education is to make the associations and
the values correspond.

In the preceding paragraph, I have spoken of the
abstaining from an act, as an act. Though this
language is not rigidly correct, yet as it will lead to
no confusion, and will often permit the use of abridged
expressions, I shall not scruple, as often as I find
occasion, to adopt it.

In the cases adduced above, of one man who obeys
the motive to commit a crime, of another who obeys
the motive to abstain from it, we have an example of
an important fact ; that, among the different classes of
motives, there are men who are more easily and
strongly operated upon by some, others by others.
We have also seen, that this is entirely owing to
habits of association. This facility of being acted
upon, by motives of a particular description, is that
which we call DISPOSITION. And it is necessary to
take notice of the name and its meaning here ; because
we shall find that many of the names of *Motives* are
names also of the corresponding *Dispositions ;* and we
should not, therefore, be able to exhibit distinctly the

marking power of such names, without an accurate conception of what it is which, in this mode of using them, they are employed to mark.

Each of the senses affords sensations, which, associated with the act which is its proper antecedent, may be considered as forming a class of motives.

In most of its cases, this association, taking place uniformly and habitually, is, like the motion of the eyelids, unnoticed, and not provided with a name.

Two cases, however; one, the pleasures of the palate; the other, those of sex ; act so important a part in human life, that the motives they constitute by association with their antecedents, have not been left without names ; though very defective ones have been applied to them.

Thus, for the motive of Eating, we have the name Gluttony : but gluttony is applied to it only when it is unduly strong. In like manner, we have the name Lust for the motive of sex ; but that, too, only when the motive is unduly strong, or in some other respect faulty.

We have here an instance of that confusion of names which was noticed above ; the same word employed as the mark of two different things ; first, the Motive ; secondly, the readiness to be acted upon, and strongly acted upon, by it. The name Gluttony is not only the name of a certain *Motive;* it is also the name of the corresponding *Disposition;* a readiness to obey that motive. The name Lust is not only the name of the *Motive;* but also of the *Disposition*, or a readiness to obey the motive.

Drunkenness is a name used in the same way exactly as the preceding two. It is the name of a motive, only in the case of excess. And it is a name with a double meaning, being applied both to the Motive, and the Disposition.

For these several motives, in the cases which are not considered as in excess, we have none but circumlocutory names; as, love of eating; love of drinking; love of sex. It is to be observed, also, that the circumlocutory names have the same double meaning, as the preceding single name; they are the names both of the *Motive*, and the *Disposition*.

The motives, arising from the pleasures of the palate, and from the pleasures of sex, are sometimes spoken of as two species of one genus. To this the name *Sensuality* is applied. The fact, however, rather is, that the cases of excess, named Gluttony, Drunkenness, Lust, are considered as the species of a certain genus. Sensuality is rather a generical name of the cases of excess, than of those of moderation.

Sensuality has the same duplicity of meaning, with all the other names, just enumerated; it is the name, both of the *Motive*, and of the *Disposition*.

Temperance, and *Intemperance*, are names of Dispositions, which have a reference to pleasures generally.

We have seen, from a previous illustration, that when the motive resulting from the association of a pleasure is not obeyed, it is owing to the association of a pain. When the association of the pain resulting from any act so balances that of the pleasure, that when the value of the pain exceeds that of the pleasure, the pleasure never prevails,—the Disposition called *Temperance* exists ; that is, an equal facility of associating with any act both its pleasures and its pains.

When the association in the two cases is not in this manner equally balanced ; that is, when the association of the pleasures is an overmatch for the pains, the Disposition called *Intemperance* exists.[49]

---

[49] A Motive is that which influences the will ; and the Will is a subject we have not yet arrived at the consideration of. Meanwhile, it is here shewn that a motive to an act consists in the association of pleasure with the act ; that a motive to abstain from an act, is the association of pain with it ; and we are prepared to admit the truth deduced therefrom, that the one or the other motive will prevail, according as the pleasurable or the painful association is the more powerful. What makes the one or the other more powerful, is (conformably to the general laws of association) partly the intensity of the pleasurable or painful ideas in themselves, and partly the frequency of repetition of their past conjunction with the act, either in experience or in thought. In the latter of these two consists the efficacy of education in giving a good or a bad direction to the active powers.

In further elucidation of Motives, I cite the following passages from the First Appendix to the author's " Fragment on Mackintosh" (pp. 389, 390) :—

" A motive is something which moves—moves to what ? To " action. But all action, as Aristotle says, (and all mankind " agree with him) is for an end. Actions are essentially means. " The question, then, is, what is the end of action ? Actions, " taken in detail, have ends in detail. But actions, taken in " classes, have ends which may be taken in classes. Thus the " ends of the actions which are subservient to the pleasures of " sense, are combined in a class, to which, in abstract, we give " the name sensuality. The class of actions which tend to the

' increase of power, have a class of ends to which we give the
" name ambition, and so on.   When we put all these classes
" together, and make a *genus* ; that is, actions in general ; can
" we in like manner make a genus of the ends ; and name ends
" in general ?

    " If we could find what the several classes of ends ; sensu-
" ality for example ; ambition ; avarice ; glory ; sociality, &c. ;
" have in common, we could.

    " Now, they have certainly this in common, that they are all
" agreeable to the agents.   A man acts for the sake of some-
" thing agreeable to him, either proximately or remotely.   But
" agreeable to, and pleasant to ; agreeableness, and pleasant-
" ness, are only different names for the same thing ; the plea-
" santness of a thing is the pleasure it gives.   So that pleasure,
" in a general way, or speaking generically ; that is, in a way to
" include all the species of pleasures, and also the abatement
" of pains ; is the end of action.

    " A motive is that which moves to action.   But that which
" moves to action is the end of the action, that which is sought
" by it ; that for the sake of which it is performed.   Now that,
" generically speaking, is the pleasure of the agent.   Motive,
" then, taken generically is pleasure.   The pleasure may be in
" company or connection with things infinite in variety.   But
" these are the accessaries ; the essence, is the pleasure.   Thus,
" in one case, the pleasure may be connected with the form,
" and other qualities of a particular woman ; in another, with a
" certain arrangement of colours in a picture ; in another, with
" the circumstances of some fellow-creature.   But in all these
" cases, what is generical, that is the essence, is the pleasure,
" or relief from pain.

    " A motive, then, is the idea of a pleasure ; a particular
" motive, is the idea of a particular pleasure ; and these are
" infinite in variety.

    " Another question is, in what circumstances does the idea
" of a pleasure become a motive ?   For it is evident, that it
" does not so in all.   It is only necessary here to illustrate,
" not to resolve the question.   First, the pleasure must be

" regarded as attainable. No man wills an act, which he
" knows he cannot perform, or which he knows cannot effect
" the end.   In the next place, the idea of the particular plea-
" sure must be more present to the mind, than any other of
" equal potency.   That which makes the idea of one pleasure
" more potent than another; or that which makes one idea
" more present to the mind than another, is the proximate
" cause of the motive, and a remote cause of the volition.   The
" cause of that superior potency, or of that presence to the
" mind, is a cause of the volition, still more remote, and so
" on."—*Ed.*

SECTION II.

CAUSES OF OUR PLEASURABLE AND PAINFUL STATES, CONTEMPLATED AS THE CONSEQUENTS OF OUR OWN ACTS.

The motives which are formed by the association of our actions, not with our pleasures immediately, but the causes of them, are much more numerous than those which are formed by the association of them with the pleasures themselves; and give birth to a much greater number of actions.

The cause of this we have already explained, and need not explain it again.

The causes of our Pleasures, including as well the remote as the proximate, are so numerous, that it is necessary to speak of them in classes.

We have surveyed them under the following Heads; Wealth, Power, Dignity, our Fellow-creatures, the objects called Sublime and Beautiful; and having fully explained the associations by which they become AFFECTIONS, we have now only to shew, by what additament these Affections are converted into MOTIVES.

It is not difficult to trace the course of association. The idea of the pleasure carries us to the idea of the cause; the idea of that cause, to the idea of its cause; and so on till we arrive at that action of ours which is the commencing cause, and gives birth to all the rest. This association forms a complex state of consciousness, which receives the name of MOTIVE.

It is also to be observed, that when a grand cause of pleasures has been associated with a great many pleasures, and a great many times, the association acquires a peculiar character and strength. The idea of the cause, as cause, is so lost among the innumerable ideas of the pleasures combined with it, that it seems to become the idea of pleasure itself. An instance commonly adduced to illustrate the important class of associations to which this belongs, is that of *Money;* and a remarkable instance it is. Many are the instances in which the association of pleasures with money constitutes so vehement an affection that it is an overmatch for all others.

In those cases the association which constitutes the motive seems to consist of a single link. The money is the passion; the idea of the action which is to add to it, or prevent its diminution, associated with the passion, constitutes the Motive.

The Motive which leads to the acquisition of wealth, great as is the part which it plays in human life, has no appropriate name. Avarice, Rapacity, like the words Gluttony, and Lust, are only names for cases of excess. It is observable, however, that they have the above-noticed duplicity of meaning; that they are names both of the Motive, and of the Disposition.

We have noticed three states of consciousness into which the idea of a cause of our pleasures enters as a main ingredient: 1. The mere contemplation of it as a cause, past or future; which is called the AFFECTION: 2. The association of an act of ours, as the cause of the cause; which is called the MOTIVE: 3. A readiness to obey this motive, which is called the DISPOSITION.

We have seen, that in regard to Wealth, we had no other name for the first of those states of Consciousness, or the AFFECTION, than the term "Love of Wealth." It is here of importance to observe, that for the MOTIVE also, or the second of those states, unless in its cases of excess, we have no other name than the name of the affection. We call the *Motive* also, "love of wealth." Nor have we any other name for the *Disposition.* This, therefore, is a case of great confusion. We have but one name for the *Affection*, for the *Motive*, and for the *Disposition.* They are states of consciousness, therefore, perpetually confounded.

Power, as a cause of pleasure, is rather a less distinct and definite idea, than Wealth. The associations formed with it partake of this indistinctness. The *Motive* which is formed by association of the idea of Power, with that of an act of ours, which is to add to it, is a more vague idea than that formed of the idea of Wealth associated with the ideas of the acts which are to add to it. Our present purpose, however, does not require a minute analysis. The acts by which, in the different degrees in which it is possessed, men are commonly enabled to add to their power, are vulgarly known. Power, like wealth, becomes itself a sort of primary affection. The association with it of acts of ours as causes of its increase, constitutes the state of mind called the Motive.

This Motive receives the name of Ambition; and that name is so applied pretty generally; though its original and more appropriate application seems to be, to great acquisitions of power, or additions made to great acquisitions.

The same duplicity of meaning, which we have so often remarked, meets us here. In whatever sense Ambition is the name of the *Motive*, it is also a name of the *Disposition*.

The term "Love of Power," which we have found to be the name of the *Affection*, is also applied to the two other states of mind, the *Motive*, and the *Disposition*. The three, therefore, *Affection*, *Motive*, *Disposition*, are commonly confounded.

Dignity is a more vague term than even Power; including a still greater number of undefined particulars. But to understand sufficiently the three states of mind which it contributes to form, no further enumeration of those particulars is necessary. The idea of Dignity, as cause, associated with the idea of pleasures as effect, constitutes the state of mind called *Affection*. The state of mind called affection associated with the idea of an act of ours as cause of the cause, is the state of mind called the *Motive*. And a facility of being acted upon by the motive, is the *Disposition*.

We have only one name, "Love of Dignity," for all the three.

We have seen that the value of Wealth, Power, and Dignity, is greatly enhanced, by their comparative amount; that is, the degree in which they are possessed by us, compared with the degree in which they are possessed by others.

We have seen in what manner this comparison generates certain affections, which have received the

names of Pride, on the one hand, Contempt, on the
other; Humility, on the one hand, Respect, Admira
tion, on the other.   We have now to shew in what
manner this comparison generates both *Motives*, and
Dispositions.

As it is not only of value to me to have more
Wealth, Power, and Dignity ; but of additional value
to have more than other men ; the surpassing of other
men becomes, thus, a cause of Pleasure ; and hence
the idea of this surpassing, associated with the ideas
of my own acts, as the cause, becomes a *Motive.*

We may endeavour to surpass other men, by either
of two ways ; by adding to our own Wealth, Power,
Dignity ; or, by abstracting from theirs.

When only the acts which add to our advantages
enter into the Motive, it is called Emulation.   When
those which abstract from the advantages of another
enter into it, it is called Envy.

Emulation is sometimes the name of the *Disposition*,
as well as of the *Motive.*   Ambition, however, is very
often used as the name of the *Disposition* corresponding to the *Motive*, Emulation.

Envy. is the name both of the *Disposition* and the
Motive.   It has the appearance also of being the name
of the corresponding *Affection ;* or of the state of consciousness arising from the comparison of another
man's greater, with our own less advantages.   This,
however, is only Humility.   It is never Envy, but
when the *Motive* to reduce them is felt.   It may be a
Motive without effect, being counteracted by other
motives.   And it is this state in which it assumes the
appearance of an *Affection.*

In these instances, the same end is attainable by

two sets of means ; the one virtuous ; the other vicious.
The man who takes the virtuous course, that is, obeys
the virtuous motive, is the man who has formed the
habit of associating his idea of the good to be derived
from surpassing others, with the acts which lead to
the increase of his own advantages.   The man who
takes the vicious course, is the man who has formed
the habit of associating with his idea of the benefit
of surpassing others, the acts, by which their advantages are diminished.

This a case of the greatest importance, in Education, and Ethics.

We now come to the explanation of that important
class of Motives which arise from the contemplation
of our FELLOW-CREATURES, as the cause of our Pleasures, and Pains.

With respect to our Fellow-creatures, a distinction
must be carefully observed.   They are sources to us
of Pleasure or Pain, in two ways ; either by their
STATES ; or, by their ACTIONS.   Their ACTIONS give
birth to a set of Associations of the greatest importance, which remain to be considered under a Head
by themselves.   What the *Affections* are, which are
generated by the association of our pains and pleasures, with the STATES of our Fellow-creatures, taken
individually, or in groups, we have recently examined.
We have now only to shew, and for this a few words
will suffice, what are the *Motives*, generated by the
association of acts of ours with those STATES ; acts
contemplated as causes of such alterations in the
States as render them to a greater or less degree
causes of our pleasures or pains.

1. What the state of my *Friend* is, as respects both

his outward circumstances and his inward disposition, which renders him, more or less, a source, to me, of pleasure on the one hand, or pain on the other, it is not necessary, after what has been said, any further to illustrate. When alterations can be effected in that state by my actions, of a kind to render my Friend more a cause of Pleasure to me, or less a cause of Pain, the association takes place of my pleasures as effect with such alterations as cause of those pleasures, and with my own acts, as cause of those alterations.

The MOTIVE, therefore, exists. And when a facility of forming this association, in other words, a readiness of obeying the MOTIVE, is contracted, the DISPOSITION exists.

It is important to observe, that the word, *Friendship*, has all that equivocation, or variety of meaning, which we have detected in other words expressing our states of mind towards the causes of our pleasures or pains. It is, at once, the name of the AFFECTION, the name of the MOTIVE, and the name of the DISPOSITION.

2. We have seen what the State of any one of our fellow-creatures is, which so associates with it the ideas of our own pains and pleasures, as to make him an object of *Kindness*. It is easy to see in what manner the ideas of our own acts are so joined to those associations, as to constitute *Motives*. When the idea of additions to the pleasures of a man, calls up the idea of additions to our pleasures; the idea of a diminution of his pains, the idea of a diminution of our pains ; and when to this is added the idea of our own acts as cause of those additions and diminutions, the association exists which we call MOTIVE.

The motive, which we are now considering, though in most men, owing to a bad education, in which so important an association has been neglected, it is too feeble, not to give way to any of the stronger propensities of our nature, is, nevertheless, from the constancy of its action, a powerful agent in human life, and the cause of no small portion of all the happiness which exists in the world.

A readiness to be acted upon by this MOTIVE; a main object of good Education; constitutes the DISPOSITION.

The AFFECTION, the MOTIVE, the DISPOSITION, have all but one name. Each is denominated *Kindness*. When the more immediate effect is the removal of pain, we use the term *Compassion;* which is, in like manner, a name of the affection, the motive, and the disposition.

3. The State of the group, denominated a Family, is a copious source of pain, or pleasure, to the members of it. We have explained, above, the associations which constitute the Family *Affections*. The formation of the *Motives* it is now easy to trace.

To take the principal case, that of the Parent; The pleasurable associations which he has with the pleasures, and removal of the pains, of his child, joined with the idea of his own acts, as cause of those pleasures and removals, constitute a MOTIVE, the importance of which we daily observe. Notwithstanding the defects of the parental associations, under such a state of Education and Morals as ours, no other source of generosity in Human Nature produces uniformly so large a portion of its proper effects.

It is not necessary to explain in what manner the affections, either of the child towards the parent, or of brothers and sisters towards each other, become motives. That such motives often exist, and in great strength ; and that no small portion of human happiness is derived from them, is matter of experience.

We have no appropriate name for either the AFFECTION, or the MOTIVE, or the DISPOSITION, in the case, either of the Parent toward the child, or of the child toward the Parent, or of the children among themselves. We are under the necessity of forming circumlocutory names, by aid of the general term Love. We say the Love of Family ; the Love of a Parent toward his offspring ; the Love to one another of brothers and sisters. And these are names, at once, of the AFFECTION, the MOTIVE, and the DISPOSITION. So imperfectly have some of the most interesting and important of our states of consciousness been distinguished.

4. The idea of our *Country* is associated, as in some sort their cause, with a great portion of all the pleasures which we enjoy. And the difference of the states, in which it may be placed, makes a prodigious difference in the amount of pleasures, which we derive from it. When actions of ours, therefore, can influence the state of our country, we associate the idea of those acts as causes, with the pleasurable results as effects, and hence the MOTIVE exists.

To individuals of the great body of the people, wholly in most countries deprived of power, their country can seldom present itself in the light of a motive, because with few acts of theirs as cause, can they associate a benefit to their country as the Effect. Their exertions in repelling from it the invasion of a destructive enemy, or freeing it from the power of a mischievous government, are the principal exceptions to this general rule.

The way in which the idea of Country becomes a *Motive* to a man whose actions are more widely operative, may thus be conceived. In the prosperity of his country, is included a portion of his own prosperity, and of that of all the individuals who are objects of his affection. Such actions of his, therefore, as are calculated to add to the prosperity of his country, are associated with all the agreeable trains, which additions to the prosperity of himself, and of all those with whom he has any sympathies, imply.

There are cases, though rare, in which this motive has existed in extraordinary force; in which men have been found capable of sacrificing every thing for their country. This happens most readily in times of great excitement; that is, when public opinion holds out a great reward; and when the object rather is, to ward off some great calamity, than to obtain an accession of good. [50]

---

[50] It is too limited a view of the effect of "times of great excitement" in intensifying the patriotic feelings, to identify it with the influence of a more than usual reward held out by public opinion. That fact often contributes its share, but there are other causes fully as effectual. In times of excitement, the idea of Country, the ideas of all the interests involved in it, and of the manner in which those interests will be affected by our action or by our forbearance to act, exist in the mind in greater intensity, and are recalled with far greater frequency, than in ordinary times. Moreover, the fact that a feeling is shared by all or many of those with whom we are in frequent intercourse, strengthens, by an obvious consequence, all the associations, both of resemblance and of contiguity,

It is important to observe, that this motive tends different ways, according to the different positions of the individual. Where the inhabitants of a country are divided into classes, a Ruling Class, and a Subject Class, the members of the Ruling Class have hardly any sympathies, except with one another; in other words, have agreeable associations with the pleasures, and removal of the pains, of hardly any persons, but those who belong to the same class. In this class are contained, their Parents, their Brothers and Sisters, their Sons and Daughters, their Companions, whether Male or Female, and their Friends: the manners of this class, are to them the only agreeable manners; the morals of this class the only virtue. It hence appears, that the principal part of the associations, which make the idea of country an AFFECTION, are, in their case, connected exclusively with the good of their own class. When their own acts, as causes, are associated with accessions to this good, as effects, the *Motive* created is that of benefit to the class. Patriotism, in their case, means, literally, 1st, Affection for their own class; 2ndly, The Motive to benefit that class; and 3rdly, A readiness to obey that Motive.

It is to be observed, that Patriotism is the only

which give that feeling its force. This is the well-known influence of sympathy, so strikingly evinced by the vehement feelings of a crowd. To these might be added another influence, belonging rather to physiology than to psychology. When the nervous system has been highly strung up by the influence of any strong feeling, it seems to become more acutely sensible to feeling of any sort, those feelings excepted which jar with, and are counteracted by, the prevailing tone of the system.—*Ed.*

T 2

name provided for all the three states of the agreeable trains connected with the idea of country, the AFFECTION, the MOTIVE, and the DISPOSITION,—and that it is commonly used in a laudatory sense; to mark an unusual degree of the Affection, the Motive, or the Disposition.

It follows, from what has been said, that there can be no real Patriotism, no pointing of the *Affection*, the *Motive*, and *Disposition*, steadily to the good of the whole, without preference of any particular part; except, either in men of elevated minds and affections, in whom the larger associations, generated by a good Education, control the narrow associations, growing out of a particular position; or, in men whose position is such as to give them pleasurable associations chiefly with individuals of the general mass, whose good has this happy quality, that it is always identified with that of the community at large.

5. The group, called a *Party*, or *Class*, generates associations, which have produced great, we may say terrible, effects, in human life; and which thence deserve a great degree of attention. The associations, of which the AFFECTION consists, and by which the interest of the class comes to be identified, as it were, with the interest of the individual, have been already pointed out. From this the generation of the MOTIVE is easily traced.

When the interests of the class are contemplated as capable, either of receiving increase, or of being preserved from diminution, by the acts of the class, collectively, or individually; that is, when the increase, or the preservation from diminution, is associated, as effect, with acts of the class, collectively, or individually, as cause, the MOTIVE exists.

When a readiness to obey this MOTIVE; that is, a facility of forming the associations which constitute the MOTIVE, exists, the corresponding DISPOSITION exists.

There are no appropriate names for these states of consciousness. We make, by the usual forced service of the word Love, a name for necessary occasions. A nobleman says, he has a Love for his Order; and that term, Love of his Order, is the name for all the three states, the AFFECTION, the MOTIVE, and the DISPOSITION.

The Clergy have invented a name for their own case. It is Love of the Church. This means, the love of the interests of the class; of the Wealth, Power, and Dignity, of the Clergy. The term Love of the Church has the usual variety of meaning. It is the name not only of the AFFECTION, but also of the MOTIVE, and the DISPOSITION.

It is moreover a name well contrived for the purposes of the class; because it is calculated to keep the real character of the associations out of sight.

6. The aggregate, included under the comprehensive term *Mankind,* is in so many ways associated with our pains and pleasures, that the interest of each individual appears, in some degree, bound up in the interest of the race. Any act of ours, then, by which the interest of the race can be promoted, is associated in our minds with our own interest; and becomes a MOTIVE. A readiness to act upon this MOTIVE, is the DISPOSITION : and the AFFECTION, the

MOTIVE, and the DISPOSITION, have but one name, Love of Mankind.

This motive operates feebly, and is easily overruled by other motives, in the great majority of men. A very general idea, such as that of *Mankind,* is an indistinct idea ; and no strong association is formed with it, except by the means of Education. In the common run of men, the narrow sympathies, alone, act with any considerable force. Such men can sympathize with this individual, and the other individual, with their own Family, or their own class. But to sympathize with mankind at large, or even with the body of the people in their own country, exceeds the bounds of their contracted affections.

Large Classes, which cannot be the object of our Senses, become steady subjects of contemplation, only through the medium of General Terms. Applied, in comprehensive, and important Propositions, General Terms call forth associations of the most interesting nature; and to men, who are in the habit of so applying them, become the source of an affection, powerful enough to control every other propensity of their nature. It is only by a Philosophical Education, that men are early trained to the use of General Terms, and comprehensive Propositions; and have the means of forming those associations, on which the most ennobling of all the states of Human Consciousness depends.[51]

---

[51] This Section is devoted to an exposition of the manner in which facts which are not pleasures or pains, but causes of pleasures or of pains, become so closely associated in thought

with the pains and pleasures of which they are causes, as not only to become themselves pleasurable or painful, but to become also, by their association with acts of our own by which they may be brought about, motives of the greatest strength. The value of a due understanding of this fact, both for the purposes of psychological science and for those of practical education, is evidently very great : and the author, to whose mind the bearings of speculative philosophy on the practical interests of the human race were ever present, has not failed to make some ethical and political applications of the psychological truth which he has here so excellently illustrated.—*Ed.*

CHAPTER XXIII.

THE ACTS OF OUR FELLOW-CREATURES, WHICH ARE CAUSES OF OUR PAINS AND PLEASURES, CONTEMPLATED AS CONSEQUENTS OF OUR OWN ACTS.

WE are now in a condition to explain the Phenomena, which have been classed under the titles of Moral Sense, Moral Faculty, Sense of Right and Wrong, Moral Affection, Love of Virtue, and so on, which are all names of similar import.

We have already remarked, that, of all the Causes of our Pleasures and Pains, none are to be compared in point of magnitude, with the actions of ourselves, and our Fellow-creatures. From this class of causes, a far greater amount of Pleasures and Pains proceed, than from all other causes taken together. It follows, that these causes are objects of intense affection to us ; either favourable, if they are the cause of Pleasure ; or unfavourable, if they are the cause of Pain.

The actions from which men derive advantage have all been classed under four Titles ; Prudence, Fortitude, Justice, Beneficence.

We apply the names Prudent, Brave, Just, Bene-

ficent, both to our own acts, and to the acts of other
men.

When those names are applied to our own acts, the
first two, Prudent and Brave, express acts which are
useful to *ourselves*, in the first instance ; the latter
two, Just, and Beneficent, express acts, which are
useful to *others,* in the first instance.

When we apply the same names, not to our own
acts, but to the acts of other men, the first two,
Prudent and Brave, express acts which are useful to
them in the first instance ; the latter two, Just and
Beneficent, express acts which are useful to others,
in the first instance.

It is further to be remarked, that those acts of
ours, which are primarily useful to ourselves, are
secondarily useful to others ; and those which are
primarily useful to others, are secondarily useful to
ourselves. Thus, it is by our own Prudence and
Fortitude, that we are best enabled to do acts of
Justice and Beneficence to others. And it is by acts
of Justice and Beneficence to others, that we best
dispose them to do similar acts to us.

Again, in the case of other men, the acts which are
primarily useful to themselves, their Prudence, their
Fortitude, are secondarily useful to others, as by
them they are the better enabled to be always just
and beneficent ; and the acts by which they are
primarily useful to others, their Justice, their Beneficence, are secondarily useful to themselves, as dis-
posing others the more to be just and beneficent
toward them.

We have two sets of associations, therefore, with
the acts which are thus named ; one set of associations

with them, when they are considered as our own
acts ; another set of associations with them, when
they are considered as the acts of other men.

1. When they are considered as our own acts ; in
other words, when we consider our own Prudence,
Bravery, Justice, and Beneficence, we have associations with them of the following kind. With our
own acts of Prudence and Bravery, we associate good
to ourselves ; that is, either Pleasure, or the cause of
Pleasure, as the immediate consequent. Acts of
PRUDENCE, for example, are divided into two sorts ;
the sort productive of good, and the sort preventive of evil. All acts which add to our Wealth,
Power, and Dignity, or any one of them, so far as
they produce this effect without counterbalancing
evil, may be called acts of Prudence. Thus, incessant Labour, by all those to whom it is necessary for
subsistence, or for reputation, is a course of Prudence.
Prudence, however, in its common acceptation, is
more employed to denote the acts by which we avoid
evils, than those by which we obtain good ; those by
which we reject present pleasures when followed by
pains which overbalance them, and by which we
endure present pains when they prevent the following
of greater pains, or secure the following of pleasures
which overbalance them.

It thus appears, that, for the most perfect performance of acts of prudence, the greatest measure of
knowledge is required. It is the choice made, among
all the innumerable acts within our power, of those,
the consequences of which, when the pleasurable and
painful are balanced against one another, constitute
the greatest amount of good. To this is requisite a

knowledge of all the train of consequences, which
each act can produce; that is, a knowledge of the
qualities of almost every thing, animate and inanimate, with which we are surrounded; and a judgment,
constantly upon the alert, to draw correct conclusions
from what we know.

When we perform acts of COURAGE or FORTITUDE,
the chance of Evil, that is, danger, is incurred for the
sake of a preponderant good. If the good were not
something more than a balance for the chance of Evil,
the consequences of the act would not be a balance of
good, but of evil. It would, therefore, be an immoral, not a moral, act; and would have no title to
the name of Courage.[52]

Knowledge is, therefore, as necessary to the exercise of this virtue as to that of Prudence. Courage,
in fact, is but a species of the acts of Prudence: a
class selected for distinction by a particular name;
that class, in which evils, of great magnitude, or
rather of a particular description, are to be hazarded,
for the sake of a preponderant good. But how is the

---

[52] The virtue of Prudence might apparently have included
Courage or Fortitude; we cannot be said to be prudent, if we
are unable to face a certain amount of evil or danger, for the
sake of a greater good. Doubtless, however, the author felt
that Prudence does not suggest the full scope of so eminent a
quality as Courage. The reasons of this are interesting to
explore.

Of various considerations that might be adduced, by far the
most pertinent is the following. Courage, as a virtue esteemed
and extolled in all ages, involves a certain amount of self-
sacrifice. If it were limited to the control of the state of fear,
so as to enable one never to fail in the pursuit of one's own

amount of the good, or of the evil, to be ascertained, but by that power of tracing the consequences of acts, for which the greatest knowledge, and the most accurate judgment, are required ?

When, with the ideas of our acts of Prudence, and acts of Courage, past, and future, have been associated, sufficiently often, the classes of benefits which are the consequences of them, the Ideas of those acts are no longer SIMPLE IDEAS, INDIFFERENT IDEAS ; they are PLEASURABLE IDEAS ; that is, AFFECTIONS.

The MOTIVE, in this case, presents a peculiarity, which requires attention. In the case of the Love of Wealth, Power, or Dignity, the Love of Individuals, the Love of Family, and all other causes of our Pleasures, we have uniformly found the *Affection* to be one thing, the *Motive* another. The *Affection* consisted of the association of the idea of the object as Cause, with that of our Pleasures as Effect. The *Motive* consisted of the association of the idea of the object, as cause, with that of our pleasures, as effect, and the idea of an act of ours, as cause of that cause. When it is an act of our own, however, which is the cause of our Pleasure, there is no act of ours to be associated as cause of that cause. The

---

interest, by giving way to unreasonable alarms, it would be respected as a manifestation of strength, but it would not receive the warm admiration that we usually bestow upon courageous men. The nobility of courage is its devotedness. The courageous soldier is not he that maintains a post of *apparent* danger unmoved, knowing there is no real danger ; which would be the prudent man's courage. Something very different is exacted in return for the epithet "a brave man."
—*B*.

ideas of the act, and its consequences, are the Motive. The MOTIVE, therefore, and the AFFECTION, are in this case the same.

The next two classes of acts are those to which the names, Justice, and Beneficence, have been applied. Taken together, they are the names of all those acts of a man, by which he does good to others. Out of these, the name Justice selects a particular class, and all the rest are Beneficence.

Men, in society, have found it essential, for mutual benefit, that the powers of Individuals, over the general causes of good, should be fixed by certain rules; that is, Laws. Acts done in conformity with those rules are called Just Acts; and, when duly considered, they are seen to include the main portion of acts of beneficence in general; of those acts of ours, the immediate object of which is the good of others. To the performance of a certain portion of the acts of Justice, our Fellow-creatures compel us, by annexing penalties to the non-performance of them. A large portion, however, remain to be performed without compulsion.

Our Beneficent acts are either causes of pleasure to others immediately, or causes of the causes of their pleasures. The act of him who gives a cup of water to the thirsty traveller in the Desert, may be said to be cause of the pleasure of the Traveller. The act of him who instructs the Traveller, before he proceeds on his journey, where in the Desert water is to be found, is the cause of the cause of his Pleasure. To speak generally, all acts of ours, by which increase is imparted to the Wealth, Power, and Dignity of another person, and to the favourable disposition of other persons towards him ; or by which diminution of those advantages is prevented, are acts of Beneficence towards him.

It is easy to trace in what manner the ideas of those acts become *Affections*. In the first place, we have associations of pleasure with all the pleasurable feelings of a Fellow-creature. We have associations of pleasure, therefore, with those acts of ours which yield him pleasure. In the second place, those are the acts which procure to us one of the most highly valued of all the sources of our pleasures, the favourable Disposition of our Fellow-men. With our acts of Justice and Beneficence, therefore, we have associations of all the pleasures which the favourable disposition of other men towards us is calculated to produce. By those associations, the Idea of our own beneficent acts is no longer an INDIFFERENT IDEA ; it becomes a PLEASURABLE IDEA, that is, an AFFECTION.[53]

---

[53] The affirmations in this paragraph require to be tested in the detail, in order to find out their limitations.

That " we have associations of pleasure with all the pleasurable feelings of a Fellow-creature " is true in a great many instances. By the law of association, the signs of happiness tend to suggest the happy feelings themselves, and even to induce these to some extent upon the beholder. The sight of happy beings is a positive contribution to our own happiness ; the obverse fact being equally well marked. We are delighted with the playful gambols of animals, and of children, and with the pleased expression of our fellow-creatures generally. On this ground, we have an interest in conferring happiness upon all our associates, and upon every one whose signs of pleasure and of displeasure come under our notice. Hence, in the absence of other motives, we are disposed to be the authors of pleasure, rather than of pain, wherever we go. Our first im-

Pleasurable ideas, as effects, associated with acts of our own as the cause, constitute the MOTIVE, as well as the AFFECTION. The reason of this, we have just stated, and need not repeat.

We have now seen by what associations both AF-FECTION, and MOTIVE are created, in the case of our own acts of Prudence, Fortitude, Justice, and Bene-ficence. The DISPOSITION, as in all other cases, con-sists in a facility, from habit, of performing the asso-ciations; in other words, a readiness of obeying the Motive.

In each of the cases, the Affection, the Motive, and the Disposition, have the same name. Thus, Prudence is the name of the Affection, and Motive, and also of the Disposition, to acts of Prudence ; so is Fortitude, Justice, and Beneficence, each in regard to its own class of acts.

Beside the four specific names, Prudence, Fortitude,

---

pulse towards a stranger would always be, from this considera-tion, to confer some benefit or perform some agreeable act. From this origin, there flows a considerable fraction of the generosity and the courtesy of human beings.

But the tendency is thwarted, and often extinguished, by other powerful impulses of the mind. There are two principal counteractives,—Rivalry in interests generally, and the Love of Power.

If the expression of pleasure manifested by any sentient being, is procured at our expense, we fail to realise the happy feelings ; we are, on the contrary, pained and embittered by the display. Now this is a fact of very frequent occurrence in all conditions of human beings; and, to the extent of its occurrence, it mars the strength and purity of the association.

The Love of Power works in the same direction. It not only reconciles the mind to displays of pain, but it may render

Justice, and Beneficence, we have a Generical Name, which includes them all. VIRTUE is the name of Prudence, Fortitude, Justice, and Beneficence, all taken together. It is also, like the name of each of the species included under it, at once the name of the Affection, the Motive, and the Disposition. The man who has the Disposition toward all the four, Prudence, Fortitude, Justice, Beneficence, in full strength; that is, who has acquired, from habit, the facility of asso-

---

these a delight and luxury. Being an emotion little checked in ordinary human beings, it provides a considerable share of gratification, through the infliction of pain. This, therefore, is a second interference with the law that would connect the signs of happiness with a thrill of pleasure in the beholder. One can easily suppose, and one frequently finds, the emotion of power in such a pitch of development as to make the pleasure of seeing happy beings the exception, and not the rule.

So much for the first of the two motives in the text. The second,—the procuring of reciprocal benefits by benefits conferred,—is everything that a motive can be. We are all our lives engaged in working out good for ourselves, and if, by doing good to others, we obtain a corresponding measure of our own advantage, we employ that instrumentality. But then the prospect must be clear; the instrument must be a promising one. Now there are some situations wherein we have a reasonable security of a return. When there is a legal guarantee, as in bargains, and in covenanted services, we are (as a rule) ready to fulfil our own share. Also, in very little things, such as the courtesies of civilised society, we contribute our part willingly; we are nearly sure of a full return for the trifling nature of the service. But there are multitudes of cases where (as we suppose) there would be no adequate return, or no return at all; all of which interfere with the growth of the association between benefits conferred and pleasure to ourselves.

It is not necessary, in order to the pleasure of benevolence,

ciating with those acts the pleasures which result from them, in other words, a habit of obeying the motives, is perfectly virtuous.

It requires the most perfect education to create those associations adequately, in other words, to give the motives such power within us, that, when counteracted by other motives, they may always prevail. Under the present imperfect state of education, it is rather by their constant action, than their force, that they produce the very considerable effects, of which we see that they are the causes. In few men, are they a

---

that the return should be either in kind, or in flattery. If we can only obtain *love* for our benefits, we think them well bestowed. A great many benefits are conferred with no other view; and the appreciation of the extent of this motive is necessary to do justice to the author's theory of the derivation of Benevolence from Prudence.

It does not admit of question, that if all the services that each person is disposed to bestow, were fairly requited in kind, in praise, or in love, the motive to seek the good of others would have an overpowering strength of association, such as the author assigns to it. The finishing stroke, in all cases of strong and unremitted association,—the transfer to the means of the feeling originally due to the end, and even the sinking of the end out of view,—would be a sure result of the operation. But so partial, as human beings are now constituted, is the operation of the principle ; so seldom are people satisfied, that they have the full equivalent of benefits imparted ;—that, unless in select instances, there is as much of mistrust as of confidence and hope, in the reciprocation of services of any great magnitude. Of course, people will differ greatly in their estimate of this fact ; but on no reasonable and candid calculation, is the association strong enough to account for the intensity and diffusion of disinterested impulses as actually found among mankind.—*B.*

match for any of the more potent motives; and, in
most men, they give way, habitually, whenever they
are opposed by any other motive even of moderate
strength.   There are so many occasions, however, in
every part of our lives, for acts of virtue, when other
motives do not intervene, that we may still ascribe to
the motives of virtue, feeble as they generally are, a
large portion of the happiness which we observe in
the world.

2. Having considered the associations which each
of us has with the ideas of his own acts of Prudence,
Fortitude, Justice, and Beneficence, it remains that
we consider the associations which each of us has with
other men's acts of Prudence, Fortitude, Justice, and
Beneficence.

We have already observed, that the Prudence of
other men is primarily useful to themselves, secondarily
useful to others.   A man who is to a certain degree
imprudent, deprives himself of the power of being
useful either to himself or to others.   As we have
agreeable associations with acts which produce pleasure to others, so we have agreeable associations with
the cause of such acts, the power of producing them;
and, of course, disagreeable associations with the acts
which deprive a man of the means of doing good to
others, and warding off evil from himself.   It is not
necessary to enter into a more minute analysis to
show in what manner our Idea of another man's Prudence becomes a Pleasurable Idea, in other words, an
AFFECTION.

We next proceed to the case of Fortitude, Courage.
We have seen that Fortitude is the name of that class
of acts, in which a good is aimed at by the risk of a

great evil. There is a grand class of cases in which
the good aimed at is not the peculiar good of the Individual or Individuals by whom the act, or series of
acts, is performed, but a good common to others, to a
whole People; as, for example, when another hostile
People is encountered and overcome. Of course, in
such a case, we have a strong association of our own
pleasures, or exemption from pains, with other men's
courage, whether we are sharing with them in the
danger, or exempted from it by their acts. This
association is such as to constitute, and we know by
experience does constitute, a very strong AFFECTION.
Even when the good sought by the act of courage is
only the good of the individual, we have a sufficient
association with it of pleasurable ideas to constitute it
an AFFECTION. We have, first of all, an agreeable
association with the balance of good which the act is
calculated to produce to the actor. And next we have
a very powerful association of pleasure with the state
of mind in which the Idea of a great evil is controlled
by the Idea of a greater good. When the motive
exists to do us good in a man who has such a mind,
he will not be deterred by the prospect of an inadequate evil. When we encounter danger in company
with such a man, we shall not be exposed to greater
danger by his deserting us.

As other men's acts of Justice and Beneficence are
directly beneficial to them who are the objects of them,
it is impossible that every man should not have pleasurable associations, first with the acts of Justice and
Beneficence of the men, whose sphere of action extends
to himself, and then with the acts of Justice and
Beneficence of all men. And as the benefits which

spring from such actions are very great, the AFFECTION, generated by association of the Ideas of those Benefits, is proportionally strong.

Of all the MOTIVES, competent to our nature, those belonging to this class are by far the most important. As there is nothing in which I am so deeply interested, as that the acts of men, which regard myself imme- diately, should be acts of Justice and Beneficence, and those which regard themselves immediately, should be acts of Prudence and Fortitude, it follows, that I have an interest, proportionally deep, in all those acts of my own, which operate as causes of those acts in other people.

Of acts of other men, which are useful to us, a great number can be bought by wealth, or commanded by power, or elicited by dignity. The mode of the operation of those causes has already been explained, and the motives into the composition of which they enter, form a different class. The acts of beneficence, of justice, of fortitude, and of prudence, performed by other men in our behalf, are, to a vast extent, such as can neither be bought, nor commanded. What means have we of increasing to the utmost, the number of those acts ; diminishing to the utmost, the number of those of an opposite tendency ?

Those means are of two sorts : 1st, Similar actions on our part ; 2dly, The manifestation on our part, of the disposition to perform similar actions.

1. It is interesting here to observe, by what a potent call we are summoned to Virtue. Of all that we enjoy, more is derived from those acts of other men, on which we bestow the name VIRTUE, than from any other cause. Our own virtue is the principal

cause why other men reciprocate the acts of virtue
toward us.   With the idea of our own acts of virtue,
there are naturally associated the ideas of all the
immense advantages we derive from the virtuous acts
of our Fellow-creatures.   When this association is
formed in due strength, which it is the main business
of a good education to effect, the motive of virtue
becomes paramount in the human breast.

2. We strongly act upon other men, when we
manifest on our parts, a disposition to perform acts in
their favour, in consequence of the acts performed by
them in favour of others.   This disposition we manifest, when we praise those acts ; or, as we otherwise
phrase it, when we declare our approbation, or admiration, of them.

It is to be observed, that all our names for those
acts ;—Prudence, Fortitude, Justice, Beneficence, Virtue ; are names of Praise. They are names, not merely
of the acts, but of the acts associated with the ideas of
the benefits resulting from them ; and further associated with the idea of those acts of ours, which are
the causes of such acts ; acts of similar utility on our
part to the Authors of the acts which are useful
to us.

Praise, also, is extensive in its operation.   The *acts*
of any individual can afford a retribution for the
virtuous acts of a very small number of men.   His
Praise can extend to all men ; and its effects are most
important.   Not only does it indicate the affection of
him who is the author of it, toward him who is the
object ; but it points out him who is the object of it,
to all other men, as the proper object of a similar
affection in them.   This indication has some tendency

to propagate the favourable affection or disposition towards the object of the applause ; but it has a much greater tendency to propagate the praise ; and when praise is sounded from many lips, that is, when a disposition is expressed by many persons favourable to the man who has been the author of the applauded acts, a number of acts in his favour are the natural consequence.

That we have pleasurable associations of great potency, with this manifestation of the favourable disposition of others towards us, is matter of common and constant experience.   It is called, in its more remarkable states, the LOVE OF FAME, and is known to operate as one of the most powerful motives in our nature.   One of its cases is a remarkable exemplification of that high degree of association, which has been already explained, and to which we have frequently had occasion to advert, in explaining other phenomena ; the degree which constitutes belief, and which gives to that belief, even when momentary, and instantly overruled by other associations, a powerful effect on our actions.

Not only that Praise of us, which is diffused in our lives, and from which agreeable consequences may arise to us, is delightful, by the associated ideas of the pleasures resulting from it ; but that Praise, which we are never to hear, which will be diffused only when we are dead, and from which no actual effects can ever accrue to us, is often an object of intense affection, and acts as one of the most powerful motives in our nature.

The habit which we form, in the case of immediate praise, of associating the idea of the praise with the

idea of pleasurable consequences to ourselves, is so
strong, that the idea of pleasurable consequences to
ourselves becomes altogether inseparable from the idea
of our Praise. It is one of those cases in which the
one Idea never can exist without the other. The
belief, thus engendered, is of course encountered immediately by other belief, that we shall be incapable
of profiting by any consequences, which posthumous
fame can produce : as the fear, that is, the belief of
ghosts, in a man passing through a churchyard at
midnight, may be immediately encountered by his
settled, habitual belief that ghosts have no existence ;
and yet his terror, not only remains for a time, but is
constantly renewed, as often as he is placed in circumstances with which he has been accustomed to
associate the existence of ghosts.[54]

---

[54] The case here put, that of the desire of posthumous fame,
affords no real support to the author's doctrines, that a high
degree of association constitutes belief, and that belief is always
present when we are determined to action. The case is merely one
of many others, in which something not originally pleasurable
(the praise and admiration of our fellow-creatures) has become
so closely associated with pleasure as to be at last pleasurable
in itself. When it has become a pleasure in itself, it is desired
for itself, and not for its consequences ; and the most confirmed
knowledge that it can produce no ulterior pleasurable consequences to ourselves will not interfere with the pleasure given by
the mere consciousness of possessing it, nor hinder that pleasure
from becoming, by its association with the acts which produce it,
a powerful motive. It is a frequent mode of talking, to speak of
the desire of posthumous fame in a kind of pitying way, as
grounded on a delusion ; as a desire which implies a certain
infirmity of the understanding. Those who thus speak must be
prepared to apply the same disparaging phrases to the interest

The operation of Dispraise is similar, to prevent the performance of acts contrary to Justice, Beneficence, Fortitude, and Prudence. Dispraise is the manifestation of a Disposition, unfavourable to the object of it, a disposition to abstain from acts useful to him, not to abstain from acts hurtful to him. It is not necessary to point out the associations formed in this case. It is a matter of common and constant experience, that we have associations of painful consequences, with the idea of the unfavourable disposition of our fellow-creatures, associations which constitute some of the most painful feelings of our nature. This it is, which is commonly expressed by the terms loss of reputation, loss of character, disgrace, infamy. In some instances, the Association rises to that remarkable case, which we have had frequent occasions of observing; when the means become a more important object than the end, the cause, than the effect. It not unfrequently happens, that the idea of the unfavourable sentiments of mankind, becomes more intolerable than all the consequences which could result from

---

taken in the welfare of others after our own death; for in that case also, no beneficial consequences to ourselves personally can ever follow from the realization of the object of our desire. But there is nothing at variance with reason in the associations which make us value for themselves, things which we at first cared for only as means to other ends; associations to which we are indebted for nearly the whole both of our virtues, and of our enjoyments. That he who acts with a view to posthumous fame has a belief, however momentary, that this fame will produce to him some extraneous good, or that he shall be conscious of it after he is dead, I shall not admit without better evidence than I have ever seen or heard of.—*Ed.*

them ; and men make their escape from life, in order
to escape from the tormenting idea of certain consequences, which, at most, would only diminish the
advantages of living.[65] Nor is the Idea of posthumous
Disgrace, less operative than that of posthumous
Fame, and from the same species of association.　In
men, in whom the associations which constitute the
pain of disgrace are strong ; though not sufficiently
strong to restrain them from deeds which incur the
execration of mankind, the thought of what they have
done is agonizing.　Along with it, constantly rises up,
before them, the idea of the condemnatory countenance,
the condemnatory sentiment, the retributive acts, of
every human being the idea of whom is presented to
them.　They are never at rest.　The Idea of the horrid
Deed or Deeds becomes associated with almost every
point of their consciousness.　At every moment, it
rises up in their minds, and along with it the over-

---

[65] They do not seek death to escape from the idea of any
consequences of the unfavourable sentiments of mankind. The
mere fact of having incurred those unfavourable sentiments
has become, by the adhesive force of association, so painful in
itself, that death is sometimes preferred to it.　There is often
no thought of the consequences that may arise from the unfavourable sentiments; and when consequences are thought of,
they are usually rather those which are mere demonstrations
of feeling, and owe their painfulness to the sentiment of which
they are demonstrations, than those which directly grate upon
our senses or are injurious to our interests.　It is true that a
vague conception of the many unpleasant consequences liable
to arise from the evil opinion of others, was the crude matter
out of which the horror of the thing itself was primitively
formed : but, once formed, it loses its connexion with its
original source.—*Ed.*

whelming train of ideas, with which it is connected. In its more awful cases, this state of mind is called Remorse; and is generally regarded as the most perfect state of suffering to which a human Being is exposed.

The same considerations account for that remarkable phenomenon of our nature, eloquently described, but not explained, by Adam Smith, that, in minds happily trained, the love of Praiseworthiness, the dread of Blameworthiness, is a stronger feeling, than the love of actual Praise, the Dread of actual Blame. It is one of those cases, in which, by the power of the association, the secondary feeling becomes more powerful than the primary. In all men, the idea of praise, as consequent, is associated with the idea of certain acts of theirs, as antecedent; the idea of blame, as consequent, with the idea of certain acts of theirs, as antecedent. This association constitutes what we call the feeling, or notion, or sentiment, or idea (for it goes by all those names), of Praiseworthiness, and Blameworthiness.[56] The anticipation, in the one case, is delightful; in the other painful. The association

---

[56] This paragraph, unexplained, might give the idea that the author regarded praiseworthiness and blameworthiness as having the meaning not of deserving praise or blame, but merely of being likely to obtain it. But what he meant is, that the idea of *deserving* praise is but a more complex form of the association between our own or another person's acts or character, and the idea of praise. To deserve praise, is, in the great majority of the cases which occur in life, the principal mode of obtaining it; though the praise is seldom accurately proportioned to the desert. And the same may be said of blame. A powerful association is thus, if circumstances are favourable, generated between deserving praise and obtaining

exists in different men, in all possible degrees of strength. In some men it exists in so great a degree of strength, that not only, the pleasure of immediate praise, the pain of immediate blame, but every other feeling of their nature, is subdued by it.

The case is perfectly analogous to that of the love of posthumous praise, the dread of posthumous blame, and is a still more important principle of action, as it has reference, not to what is, or to what shall be, but to what ought to be, the sentiments of mankind.

Such, then, are the AFFECTIONS which we bear toward the just, the beneficent, the courageous, the prudent acts of other men, and the contrary; that is, such are the associations we have with them of pleasurable or painful consequences. Such also are the MOTIVES; that is, the feelings generated by the association of certain acts of ours, as cause, with the virtuous acts of other men, as their effects.

Of those MOTIVES, that which involves the acts of praising and blaming, is in constant and strong opera-

---

it; and hence between deserving praise, and all the pleasurable influences on our lives, of other people's good opinion. And this association may become sufficiently strong to overcome the direct motive of obtaining praise, where it is to be obtained by other means than desert; the rather, as the desire of undeserved praise is greatly counteracted by the thought that people would not bestow the praise if they knew all. That what has now been stated was really the author's meaning, is proved by his going on to say, that praiseworthiness and blameworthiness, as motives to action, have reference "not to what is, or to what shall be, but to what ought to be, the sentiments of mankind."—*Ed.*

tion.   It is from the great use made of those acts in
the Education of children, and even in the rude
management of them in the nursery, that praise and
blame acquire the influence in most cases, the ascendancy in some, which they are seen to exercise over
us.   It is this sensibility to praise and blame, in other
words, the associations we have with them, which
gives its effect to what is called POPULAR OPINION, or
the POPULAR SANCTION, and, when the acts of Justice,
Beneficence, Fortitude, and Prudence of other men
are the objects of it, the MORAL SANCTION ; *Popular
Opinion*, being a phrase which expresses the Praise or
Blame which the people bestow ; and the *Sanction*
being the good or evil consequences which men are
accustomed to associate with that praise or blame.

In the present state of Education, the Praise and
Blame of most men are very erroneously bestowed,
with great precipitation, commonly in excess upon
small occasions, with little regard to its justice ; blame
being very often inflicted where applause is due, and
applause lavished where blame ought to be bestowed.
When Education is good, no point of morality will be
reckoned of more importance than the distribution of
Praise and Blame ; no act will be considered more immoral than the misapplication of them.   They are
the great instruments we possess for ensuring moral
acts on the part of our Fellow-creatures ; and when
we squander away, or prostitute those great causes of
virtue, and thereby deprive them of a great part of
their useful tendency, we do what in us lies to lessen
the quantity of Virtue, and thence of Felicity, in the
world.

The MOTIVES, which are generated by the associa-

tion of our own acts of Justice and Beneficence as
cause with other men's acts of Justice and Beneficence as effects, are subject, unhappily, to strong
counteraction ; because it rarely happens that we can
perform acts of Justice and Beneficence without more
or less of sacrifice to ourselves.   The association, at
the same time, is strong, in all men.   All men have
the daily experience, that their own acts of Justice,
and Beneficence, dispose other men to be Beneficent
to them ; their own acts of injustice and malevolence,
dispose other men to bring evil (which in this case
they call punishment) upon them ; and to abstain
from doing them good.   This experience is of course
followed by the usual association between cause and
effect.   The man who does acts of Justice and Beneficence, anticipates the favourable disposition of mankind, as their natural effect ; and this association is
his belief, or conviction, or sense (he calls it by all
those names), of deserving the favourable sentiments
of mankind.   The man, on the other hand, who performs acts which are unjust and hurtful to others,
anticipates the unfavourable and hostile sentiments of
mankind, as the natural consequents of his acts ; in
other words, has the belief, or conviction, or sense
(for the association in this case also has these various
names), of deserving, not well, but ill, at the hands of
other men.

There are no men, however vicious, in whom those
associations do not produce constant and numerous
effects.   When they have not been happily cultivated,
and when the counteracting associations, of which we
just now made mention, have been allowed to acquire
a mischievous strength, acts in opposition to them

are, occasionally, but, even in the worst men, no more than occasionally, produced.

This anticipation of the hostile, or benevolent sentiments of mankind, as the natural effects of actions of a certain description on our part, is the foundation of that remarkable association of which we had very recently occasion to make mention, the association which Dr. Smith has called the love of Praiseworthiness, and which is sometimes found to be much more powerful than the love of actual Praise.

The DISPOSITION which corresponds to those MOTIVES, or the facility of forming the associations which constitute them, is the result of habit in this as in all other cases.

The AFFECTION, in this case, has the name of *Moral approbation* and *Disapprobation.* The same is the only name we have for the MOTIVE. It is also the only name we have for the DISPOSITION. The terms Moral Sense ; Sense of Right and Wrong ; Love of Virtue, and Hatred of Vice, are sometimes used as synonymous terms ; but they are not equally appropriate. Virtue, as we have seen, is a name which is given to each of the three, the Affection, the Motive, the Disposition ; Morality is a name which is applied with similar latitude.[57] [58]

---

[57] The foregoing analysis of the Moral Sentiment proceeds upon a number of unquestionable psychological data. That we have a strong personal interest in the virtues of Prudence, Fortitude, Justice and Beneficence, in the manner stated, is most certain ; and that this personal interest will incline us to practise those virtues ourselves, and to encourage them in

others, is also certain. The only doubt is, as to whether the motives to rectitude of action are exhausted in this analysis.

The sufficiency of an analysis is less easily tested in mental phenomena, than in physical phenomena. The chief reason is that, in the mind, we cannot make exact numerical estimates ; and, therefore, cannot show, by casting up a sum, that the assigned constituents of a compound exactly amount to the total. The several constituents put down may be actually present, without our being sure whether they are the whole. Hence the Deductive verification, so valuable in physical science, does not carry with it the same precision, in mental science.

To evade this source of uncertainty we are thrown back upon the Experimental Canons, or the Four Methods. We know by these, that if an analysis is good, there must be present in each instance of the phenomenon the causes assigned, one or more ; and should one exist in a low degree, or be entirely wanting, the others must have a compensating intensity. If, on the other hand, the whole of the causes have not been assigned, there will, almost inevitably, occur instances, either without the causes stated, or with these in an obviously insufficient amount.

The following facts and considerations render doubtful the completeness of the author's explanation of the Moral Sentiment.

The affirmation in the text is that not merely the self-regarding virtue—Prudence, but also the two great social virtues—Justice and Beneficence, are developed from associations with our own personal interest. In other words, they grow up exactly by the same course as the virtue of Prudence ; they are strong as that happens to be strong, and weak as that happens to be weak ; the most prudent man being the most just and beneficent man. This inference can be avoided only by drawing some distinction between the interested associations entering into prudence, and the interested associations entering into justice and beneficence ; but no such distinction is drawn in the foregoing chapter, at least in such a way 'as to meet the difficulty thus suggested.

Now, on an appeal to the facts, we find that the virtue of prudence is not uniformly concomitant with the virtues of justice and beneficence ; that, on the contrary, except in the more highly cultivated moral natures, they are frequently manifested in the inverse proportion. A human being, by cherishing interested associations, does not as a matter of course attain to either justice or beneficence. Even the most far-sighted prudence, as regards self, would not develop the whole virtue of justice, nor the whole virtue of beneficence. On the other hand, beneficence is often abundant and pronounced in cases where interested associations with self have been very slightly cultivated.

The illustration of this generic discrepancy, between the author's theory and the more obvious facts, might be extended. There is, however, another mode of proceeding, perhaps more decisive ; that is, to show that the mind contains sources of the moral sentiment besides the associations with self-interest.

It does not appear easy, at first sight, to establish the existence of purely disinterested impulses in our mental constitution ; the admixture of self being so seldom unequivocally absent from human conduct. Still, if these impulses do exist, there will probably be found instances where they are manifested in convincing isolation.

Perhaps the desired isolation is most readily afforded in some of the familiar forms of Pity. There are instances, no doubt, where pity may have a selfish motive, as when we compassionate the sufferings of parents, friends, and benefactors. But, in other instances, it arises not only without any selfish bearing, but in opposition to powerful associations of interest. The pity that we often extend to enemies and to criminals is a case in point. Even when the punishment of wrong-doers is bound up with our strongest interests, the spectacle of their sufferings often moves us to remit the punishment necessary for our own protection. Now, with beings made up of purely interested considerations, the *argumentum ad misericordiam,* under those circumstances, would be void of effect.

Another example is furnished by those acts of lavish generosity and charity that perhaps ruin the giver, and do harm to the recipient. If one's moral education were exclusively conducted through the building up of associations with self, by what class of associating links is this impulse generated?

It is no less difficult to account for the actions of men wholly devoted to philanthropy, like Howard. So very small is the result to self from the labours and sacrifices of such men, that we are unable to account for their motives without assuming an independent source of disinterested affections. The difficulty is greatly increased in the case of minds little cultivated, as in the heroic devotion of the common soldier.

Observation of children reveals a specific power in the spectacle of misery or suffering to awaken pity and generous sympathies. The effective impulse to sympathy has little to do with a prudential education, or with the following out of self-interest in its associations with the welfare of others. The patriotic orator never trusts wholly to interested motives; he does not omit these; but he expects much from the lively description of suffering and misery to people generally; and if the picture comes home to the experience of his hearers, they will be moved by it, on account of each other, as well as on account of their separate selves.

From such facts as these, it is admissible to lay down, as a general law, that the sight of misery in others prompts us, irrespective of our own interest, to enter into, and to relieve, that misery. This is the essential fact of Sympathy.

The principle thus announced is not an ultimate law of the mind. It may be brought under a still higher law, of which some notice will be taken afterwards (see note on the Will, chap. XXIV.), namely, the tendency of every idea to act itself out, to become an actuality, not with a view to bring pleasure or to ward off pain—which is the proper description of the will— but from an independent prompting of the mind that often makes us throw away pleasure and embrace pain. The full exposition of this principle would add greatly to the evidence for pure disinterested impulses, by showing that the fact described operates in a much wider sphere than the moral sentiment.

On a survey of the different theories of the mental origin of Benevolent impulses, we may reduce them under the following heads.

1. They have been ascribed to direct and immediate self-interest, either from the return of benefits in kind, or from the pleasure of praise and flattery.   This is substantially the position of Mandeville.

2. It is said we are so constituted that the sight of misery is a pain to us; and that we work to rid ourselves of that pain, as we should work to assuage thirst, to banish toothache, or to escape reproach.   This view was held by Hobbes. It is forcibly brought in in the following anecdote recorded of him by Aubrey (Lives II. p. 623).

"One time, I remember, goeing in the Strand, a poor and infirme old man begged his almes; he beholding him with eies of pitty and compassion, putt his hand in his pocket, and gave him 6d.; Sayd a divine [Dr. Jaspar Mayne] that stood by, 'Would you have done this, if it had not been Christ's Command?' 'Yea,' sayd he: 'Why?' quoth the other; 'Because,' sayd he, 'I was in paine to consider the miserable condition of the old man; and now my almes, giving him some relief, doth also ease me.'"

There is a certain amount of truth in this statement; and taking the fact by itself, we might find some difficulty in drawing the line between a volition moved by our own pain, and the acting out of the idea of pain in favour of the sufferer. The best reply, perhaps, is to compare the *amount* of pain incurred and of pleasure remitted or sacrificed by the sympathiser, with the utmost value fairly ascribable to his own mental pain. The pain of misery witnessed is frequent and habitual, and although it has a certain depressing effect upon the mind, yet we should generally bear it much more easily than the pains of self-sacrifice it often incites us to.

3. We may be endowed with a positive susceptibility to pleasure from acts of kindness to others; so that in doing good, we are still moved in exact proportion to our own gratification. This expresses very nearly Bentham's view of Disinterestedness; which, however, equally with the foregoing, comes short of the facts. Supposing some such pleasure to exist, no one could show that in degree it fully corresponds to the effects prompted by benevolent impulse.

4. *Habits* of acting in favour of others may be formed to such an extent, that our virtuous actions, begun under our own pleasures and pains, may at last cease to have any reference to those pleasures and pains. Here, also, the appeal is to an undeniable fact of our mental constitution. Actions that begin as proper voluntary actions—on the spur of pleasure and pain—often pass into a mechanical routine, and are persisted in even when they thwart our pleasures. Any one placed for a number of years in a position of danger, and habituated to troublesome precautions, is almost sure to keep up the same routine, after the occasion has ceased ; mothers are liable to this unreasonable continuance of solicitude about their children. The application of the fact to moral education is of great moment. If the young are initiated betimes into a regard to the feelings and interests of others, they will grow up with a sort of mechanical unquestioning tendency towards the same line of conduct.

These are the four different modes of stating the origin of disinterested conduct, apart from the assumption of a source of purely disinterested impulses in the constitution of the mind. Such a source has been indicated above, in what may be called the power of the "fixed idea," having its seat in the region of the intellect, and operating to thwart the proper voluntary impulses, which are instigated by our pleasures and pains.—*B*.

I.

[58] It had been pointed out, in a preceding chapter, that Wealth, Power, Dignity, and many other things which are not

in their own nature pleasures, but only causes of pleasures
and of exemption from pains, become so closely associated
with the pleasures of which they are causes, and their absence
or loss becomes so closely associated with the pains to which
it exposes us, that the things become objects of love and
desire, and their absence an object of hatred and aversion, for
their own sake, without reference to their consequences. By
virtue of the same law of association, it is pointed out in the
present chapter that human actions, both our own and those
of other people, standing so high as they do among the causes
both of pleasure and of pain to us (sometimes by their direct
operation, and sometimes through the sentiments they give
birth to in other persons towards ourselves) tend naturally to
become inclosed in a web of associated ideas of pleasures or of
pains at a very early period of life, in such sort that the ideas
of acts beneficial to ourselves and to others become pleasurable
in themselves, and the ideas of acts hurtful to ourselves and to
others become painful in themselves: and both kinds of acts
become objects of a feeling, the former of love, the latter of
aversion, which having, in our minds, become independent of
any pleasures or pains actually expected to result to ourselves
from the acts, may be truly said to be disinterested. It is no
less obvious that acts which are not really beneficial, or not
really hurtful, but which, through some false opinion prevailing among mankind, or some extraneous agency operating
on their sentiments, incur their praise or blame, may and often
do come to be objects of a quite similar disinterested love or
hatred, exactly as if they deserved it. This disinterested love
and hatred of actions, generated by the association of praise
or blame with them, constitute, in the author's opinion, the
feelings of moral approbation and disapprobation, which the
majority of psychologists have thought it necessary to refer to
an original and ultimate principle of our nature. Mr. Bain,
in the preceding note, makes in this theory a correction, to
which the author himself would probably not have objected,
namely, that the mere idea of a pain or pleasure, by whomsoever
felt, is intrinsically painful or pleasurable, and when raised in

the mind with intensity is capable of becoming a stimulus to
action, independent, not merely of expected consequences to
ourselves, but of any reference whatever to Self; so that care
for others is, in an admissible sense, as much an ultimate fact
of our nature, as care for ourselves; though one which greatly
needs strengthening by the concurrent force of the manifold
associations insisted on in the author's text.   Though this of
Mr. Bain is rather an account of disinterested Sympathy, than
of the moral feeling, it is undoubtedly true that the *foundation*
of the moral feeling is the adoption of the pleasures and pains
of others as our own : whether this takes place by the natural
force of sympathy, or by the association which has grown up in
our mind between our own good or evil and theirs. The moral
feeling rests upon this identification of the feelings of others
with our own, but is not the same thing with it. To constitute
the moral feeling, not only must the good of others have
become in itself a pleasure to us, and their suffering a pain,
but this pleasure or pain must be associated with our own acts
as producing it, and must in this manner have become a motive, prompting us to the one sort of acts, and restraining us
from the other sort.   And this is, in brief, the author's theory
of the Moral Sentiments.

The exhaustive treatment of this subject would require a
length and abundance of discussion disproportioned to the com-
pass and purposes of a treatise like the present, which was
intended to expound what the author believed to be the real
mode of formation of our complex states of consciousness, but
not to say all that may and ought to be said in refutation of
other views of the subject. There are, however, some important
parts of the author's own theory, which are not stated in this
work, but in a subsequent one, of a highly polemical character,
the "Fragment on Mackintosh :" and it may be both instructive and interesting to the reader to find the statement here.
I therefore subjoin the passages containing it.

"Nature makes no classes.   Nature makes individuals.
"Classes are made by men ; and rarely with such marks as
"determine certainly what is to be included in them.

" Men make classifications, as they do everything else, for
" some end. Now, for what end was it that men, out of their
" innumerable acts, selected a class, to which they gave the
" name of moral, and another class, to which they gave the
" name of immoral ? What was the motive of this act ? What
" its final cause ?

" Assuredly the answer to this question is the first step,
" though Sir James saw it not, towards the solution of his
" two questions, comprehending the whole of ethical science ;
" first, what makes an act to be moral ? and secondly, what are
" the sentiments with which we regard it ?

" We may also be assured, that it was some very obvious
" interest which recommended this classification ; for it was
" performed, in a certain rough way, in the very rudest states
" of society.

" Farther, we may easily see how, even in very rude states,
" men were led to it, by little less than necessity. Every day
" of their lives they had experience of acts, some of which
" were agreeable, or the cause of what was agreeable, to them ;
" others disagreeable, or the cause of what was disagreeable
" to them, in all possible degrees.

" They had no stronger interest than to obtain the repetition
" of the one sort, and to prevent the repetition of the other.

" The acts in which they were thus interested were of two
" sorts ; first, those to which the actor was led by a natural
" interest of his own ; secondly, those to which the actor was
" not led by any interest of his own. About the first sort
" there was not occasion for any particular concern. They
" were pretty sure to take place, without any stimulus from
" without. The second sort, on the contrary, were not likely
" to take place, unless an interest was artificially created, suffi-
" ciently strong to induce the actor to perform them.

" And here we clearly perceive the origin of that important
" case of classification . . . . . the classification of acts as
" moral and immoral. The acts, which it was important to
" other men that each individual should perform, but in which
" the individual had not a sufficient interest to secure the per-

" formance of them, were constituted one class.   The acts,
" which it was important to other men that each individual
" should abstain from, but in regard to which he had not a per-
" sonal interest sufficiently strong to secure his abstaining
" from them, were constituted another class.   The first class
" were distinguished by the name moral acts; the second by
" the name immoral.

" The interest which men had in securing the performance
" of the one set of acts, the non-performance of the other, led
" them by a sort of necessity to think of the means.   They had
" to create an interest, which the actor would not otherwise
" have, in the performance of the one sort, the non-performance
" of the other.   And in proceeding to this end, they could not
" easily miss their way.   They had two powers applicable to
" the purpose.   They had a certain quantity of good at their
" disposal; and they had a certain quantity of evil.   If they
" could apply the good in such a manner as to afford a motive
" both for the performance and non-performance which they
" desired, or the evil, in such a manner as to afford a motive
" against the performance and non-performance which they
" wished to prevent, their end was attained.

" And this is the scheme which they adopted; and which,
" in every situation, they have invariably pursued.   The whole
" business of the moral sentiments, moral approbation, and
" disapprobation, has this for its object, the distribution of
" the good and evil we have at command, for the production
" of acts of the useful sort, the prevention of acts of the
" contrary sort.   Can there be a nobler object ?

" But though men have been thus always right in their
" general aim, their proceedings have been cruelly defective in
" the detail ; witness the consequence,—the paucity of good
" acts, the frequency of bad acts, which there is in the world.

" A portion of acts having been thus classed into good and
" bad ; and the utility having been perceived of creating mo-
" tives to incite to the one, and restrain from the other, a sub-
" classification was introduced.   One portion of these acts
" was such, that the good and evil available for their production

"and prevention, could be applied by the community in its
"conjunct capacity.   Another portion was such, that the good
"and evil available could be applied only by individuals in
"their individual capacity.   The first portion was placed
"under the control of what is called law ; the other remained
"under the control of the moral sentiments ; that is, the dis-
"tribution of good and evil, made by individuals in their
"individual capacity.

   "No sooner was the class made, than the rule followed.
"Moral acts are to be performed ; immoral acts are to be ab-
"stained from.

   "Beside this the general rule, there was needed, for more
"precise direction, particular rules.

   "We must remember the fundamental condition, that all
"rules of action must be preceded by a corresponding classifi-
"cation of actions.   All moral rules, comprehend in the
"great moral rule, must relate to a class of actions compre-
"hended within the grand class, constituted and marked by
"the term moral.   This is the case with grand classes in
"general.   They are subdivided into minor classes, each of
"the minor classes being a portion of the larger.   Thus, the
"grand class of acts called moral has been divided into certain
"convenient portions, or sub-classes, and marked by particular
"names, Just, Beneficent, Brave, Prudent, Temperate ; to
"each of which classes belongs its appropriate rule that
"men should be just, that they should be beneficent, and so
"on . . . . .

   "In the performance of our duties two sets of cases may
"be distinguished.   There is one set in which a direct estimate
"of the good of the particular act is inevitable ; and the man
"acts immorally who acts without making it.   There are
"other cases in which it is not necessary.

   "The first are those, which have in them so much of sin-
"gularity, as to prevent their coming within the limits of any
"established class.   In such cases a man has but one guide ;
"he must consider the consequences, or act not as a moral, or
"rational agent at all.

"The second are cases of such ordinary and frequent oc-
"currence as to be distinguished into classes. And everybody
"knows . . . that when a class of acts are performed regularly
"and frequently, they are at last performed by habit; in other
"words, the idea of the act and the performance of it follow
"so easily and speedily that they seem to cohere, and to be
"but one operation. It is only necessary to recall some of the
"more familiar instances, to see the mode of this formation.
"In playing on a musical instrument, every note, at first, is
"found by an effort. Afterwards, the proper choice is made
"so rapidly as to appear as if made by a mechanical process
"in which the mind has no concern. The same is the case
"with moral acts. When they have been performed with fre-
"quency and uniformity, for a sufficient length of time, a
"habit is generated . . . . .

"When a man acts from habit, he does not act without
"reflection. He only acts with a very rapid reflection. In no
"class of acts does a man begin to act by habit. He begins
"without habit; and acquires the habit by frequency of acting.
"The consideration, on which the act is founded, and the act
"itself, form a sequence. And it is obvious from the familiar
"cases of music and of speaking, that it is a sequence at first
"not very easily performed. By every repetition, however, it
"becomes easier. The consideration occurs with less effort;
"the action follows with less effort; they take place with
"greater and greater rapidity, till they seem blended. To say,
"that this is acting without reflection, is only ignorance, for it
"is thus seen to be a case of acting by reflection so easily and
"rapidly, that the reflection and the act cannot be distin-
"guished from one another . . . . . .

"Since moral acts are not performed at first by habit, but
"each upon the consideration which recommends it; upon
"what considerations, we may be asked, do moral acts begin to
"be performed ?

"The question has two meanings, and it is necessary to
"reply to both. It may be asked, upon what consideration
"the men of our own age and country, for example, at first

" and before a habit is formed, perform moral acts ? Or, it may
" be asked, upon what consideration did men originally per-
" form moral acts ?

" To the first of these questions every one can reply from
" his own memory and observation. We perform moral acts
" at first, from authority. Our parents tell us that we ought
" to do this, ought not to do that. They are anxious that we
" should obey their precepts. They have two sets of influ-
" ences, with which to work upon us ; praise and blame ;
" reward and punishment. All the acts which they say we
" ought to do, are praised in the highest degree, all those
" which they say we ought not to do, are blamed in the highest
" degree. In this manner, the ideas of praise and blame
" become associated with certain classes of acts, at a very
" early age, so closely, that they cannot easily be disjoined.
" No sooner does the idea of the act occur than the idea of
" praise springs up along with it, and clings to it. And
" generally these associations exert a predominant influence
" during the whole of life.

" Our parents not only praise certain kinds of acts, blame
" other kinds ; but they praise us when we perform those of
" the one sort, blame us when we perform those of the other.
" In this manner other associations are formed. The idea of
" ourselves performing certain acts is associated with the idea
" of our being praised, performing certain other acts with the
" idea of our being blamed, so closely that the ideas become at
" last indissoluble. In this association consist the very im-
" portant complex ideas of praise-worthiness, and blame-
" worthiness. An act which is praiseworthy, is an act with
" the idea of which the idea of praise is indissolubly joined ;
" an agent who is praiseworthy is an agent with the idea of
" whom the idea of praise is indissolubly joined. And in the
" converse case, that of blame-worthiness, the formation of the
" idea is similar.

" Many powerful circumstances come in aid of these im-
" portant associations, at an early age. We find, that not
" only our parents act in this manner, but all other parents·

" We find that grown people act in this manner, not only
" towards children, but towards one another. The associations,
" therefore, are unbroken, general, and all comprehending.

" Our parents administer not only praise and blame, to
" induce us to perform acts of one sort, abstain from acts of
" another sort, but also rewards and punishments. They do
" so directly ; and, further, they forward all our inclinations in
" the one case, baulk them in the other. So does everybody
" else. We find our comforts excessively abridged by other
" people, when we act in one way, enlarged when we act in
" another way. Hence another most important class of asso-
" ciations ; that of an increase of well-being from the good-
" will of our fellow-creatures, if we perform acts of one sort, of
" an increase of misery from their ill-will, if we perform those
" of another sort.

" In this manner it is that men, born in the social state,
" acquire the habits of moral acting, and certain affections
" connected with it, before they are capable of reflecting upon
" the grounds which recommend the acts either to praise or
" blame. Nearly at this point the greater part of them remain,
" continuing to perform moral acts and to abstain from the
" contrary, chiefly from the habits they have acquired, and the
" authority upon which they originally acted ; though it is not
" possible that any man should come to the years and blessing
" of reason, without perceiving, at least in an indistinct and
" general way, the advantage which mankind derive from their
" acting towards one another in one way, rather than another.

" We come now to the second question, viz. what are the
" considerations upon which men orginally performed moral
" acts ? The answer to this question is substantially contained
" in the explanation already given of the classification of acts
" as moral and immoral.

" When men began to mark the distinction between acts,
" and were prompted to praise one class, blame another,
" they did so, either because the one sort benefited, the other
" hurt them ; or for some other reason. If for the first reason,
" the case is perfectly intelligible. The men had a motive

" which they understood, and which was adequate to the end.
" If it was not on account of utility that men classed some
" acts as moral, others as immoral, on what other account
" was it?

" To this question, an answer, consisting of anything but
" words, has never been returned.

" It has been said, that there is a beauty, and a deformity,
" in moral and immoral acts, which recommended them to the
" distinctions they have met with.

" It is obvious to reply to this hypothesis, that the mind of
" a savage, that is, a mind in the state in which the minds of
" all men were, when they began to classify their acts, was not
" likely to be much affected by the ideal something called the
" beauty of acts.   To receive pain or pleasure from an act, to
" obtain, or be deprived of, the means of enjoyment by an act ;
" to like the acts and the actors, whence the good proceeded,
" dislike those whence the evil proceeded; all these were things
" which they understood.

" But we must endeavour to get a little nearer to the bottom
" of this affair.

" In truth, the term beauty, as applied to acts, is just as
" unintelligible to the philosopher, as to the savage.   Is the
" beauty of an act one thing ; the morality of it another ?   Or
" are they two names for the same thing ?   If they are two
" things, what is the beauty, distinct from the morality ?   If
" they are the same thing, what is the use of the name mora-
" lity ?   It only tends to confusion.

" But this is not all.   The beautiful is that which excites
" in us the emotion of beauty, a state of mind with which we
" are acquainted by experience.   This state of mind has been
" successfully analysed, and shewn to consist of a train of
" pleasurable ideas, awakened in us by the beautiful object.

" But is it in this way only that we are concerned in moral
" acts?   Do we value them for nothing, but as we value a pic-
" ture, or a piece of music, for the pleasure of looking at them,
" or hearing them ?   Everybody knows the contrary.   Acts
" are objects of importance to us, on account of their conse-

" quences, and nothing else. This constitutes a radical dis-
" tinction between them and the things called beautiful. Acts
" are hurtful or beneficial, moral or immoral, virtuous or
" vicious. But it is only an abuse of language, to call them
" beautiful or ugly.

" That it is jargon, the slightest reflection is sufficient to
" evince ; for what is the beauty of an act, detached from its
" consequences ? We shall be told, perhaps, that the beauty
" of an act was never supposed to be detached from its conse-
" quences. The beauty consists in the consequences. I am
" contented with the answer. But observe to what it binds
" you. The consequences of acts are the good or evil they do.
" According to you, therefore, the beauty of acts is either the
" utility of them, or it is nothing at all ;—a beautiful ground
" on which to dispute with us, that acts are classed as moral,
" not on account of their utility, but on account of their beauty.

" It will be easily seen, from what has been said, that they
" who ascribe the classification of acts, as moral, and immoral,
" to a certain taste, an agreeable or disagreeable sentiment
" which they excite (among whom are included the Scottish
" professors Hutcheson, and Brown, and David Hume himself,
" though on his part with wonderful inconsistency)—hold the
" same theory with those who say, that beauty is the source of
" the classification of moral acts. Things are classed as beau-
" tiful, or deformed, on account of a certain taste, or inward
" sentiment. If acts are classed in the same way, on account
" of a certain taste or inward sentiment, they deserve to be
" classed under the names beautiful, and deformed ; otherwise
" not.

" I hope it is not necessary for me to go minutely into the
" exposure of the other varieties of jargon, by which it has
" been endeavoured to account for the classification of acts, as
" moral and immoral. ' Fitness' is one of them. Acts are
" approved on account of their fitness. When fitness is hunted
" down, it is brought to bay exactly at the place where beauty
" was. Fitness is either the goodness of the consequences, or
" it is nothing at all.

"The same is the case with 'Right Reason,' or 'Moral
" Reason.' An act according to moral reason, is an act,
" the consequences of which are good. Moral reason, there-
" fore, is another name, and not a bad name, for the principle
" of utility." [a]

The following passage from another part of the same work,
is also very much to the purpose.

"The terms moral and immoral were applied by men,
" primarily, not to their own acts, but the acts of other men.
" Those acts, the effects of which they observed to be benefi-
" cial, they desired should be performed. To make them be
" performed, they, among other things they did, affixed to
" them marks of their applause ; they called them, good,
" moral, well-deserving ; and behaved accordingly.

"Such is the source of the moral approbation we bestow on
" the acts of other men. The source of that which we bestow
" on our own is twofold. First, every man's beneficial acts,
" like those of every other man, form part of that system of
" beneficial acting, in which he, in common with all other
" men, finds his account. Secondly, he strongly associates
" with his own beneficial acts, both that approbation of other
" men, which is of so much importance to him, and that ap-
" probation which he bestows on other men's beneficial acts.

" It is also easy to shew what takes place in the mind of a
" man, before he performs an act, which he morally approves
" or condemns.

" What is called the approbation of an act not yet per-
" formed, is only the idea of future approbation : and it is not
" excited by the act itself ; it is excited by the idea of the act.
" The idea of approbation or disapprobation is excited by the
" idea of an act, because the approbation would be excited by
" the act itself. But what excites moral approbation or dis-
" approbation of an act, is neither the act itself, nor the
" motive of the act ; but the consequences of the act, good
" or evil, and their being within the intention of the agent.

---

[a] Fragment on Mackintosh, pp. 247—265.

" Let us put a case. A man with a starving wife and family
" is detected wiring a hare on my premises. What happens?
" I call up the idea of sending him to prison. I call up the
" ideas of the consequences of that act, the misery of the
" helpless creatures whom his labour supported ; their
" agonizing feelings, their corporal wants, their hunger, cold,
" their destitution of hope, their despair : I call up the ideas of
" the man himself in jail, the sinking of heart which attends
" incarceration ; the dreadful thought of his family deprived
" of his support; his association with vicious characters; the
" natural consequences,—his future profligacy, the consequent
" profligacy of his ill-fated children, and hence the permanent
" wretchedness and ruin of them all. I next have the idea
" of my own intending all these consequences. And only
" then am I in a condition to perform, as Sir James says,
" the 'operation of conscience.' I perform it. But in this
" case, it is, to use another of his expressions, 'defeated.'
" Notwithstanding the moral disapprobation, which the idea
" of such intended consequences excites in me, I perform the
" act.

" Here, at all events, any one may see, that conscience, and
" the motive of the act, are not the same, but opposed to one
" another. The motive of the act, is the pleasure of having
" hares ; not in itself a thing anywise bad. The only thing
" bad is the producing so much misery to others, for securing
" that pleasure to myself.

" The state of the case, then, is manifest. The act of which
" I have the idea, has two sets of consequences; one set
" pleasurable, another hurtful. I feel an aversion to pro-
" duce the hurtful consequences. I feel a desire to produce
" the pleasurable. The one prevails over the other. . . . . .

" . . . Nothing in an act is voluntary but the consequences
" that are intended. The idea of good consequences intended,
" is the pleasurable feeling of moral approbation ; the idea of
" bad consequences intended is the painful feeling of moral
" disapprobation. The very term voluntary, therefore, ap-
" plied to an act which produces good or evil consequences,

" expresses the antecedence of moral approbation or dis-
" approbation."ᵃ

I will quote one short passage more, in correction of the
very vulgar error, that to analyse our disinterested affections
and resolve them into associations with the ideas of our own
elementary pleasures and pains, is to deny their reality.

" Sir James must mean, if he means anything, that to trace
" up the motive affections of human nature to pain and plea-
" sure, is to make personal advantage the only motive. This
" is to affirm, that he who analyses any of the complicated
" phenomena of human nature, and points out the circum-
" stances of their formation, puts an end to them.

" Sir James was totally ignorant of this part of human
" nature. Gratitude remains gratitude, resentment remains
" resentment, generosity generosity in the mind of him who
" feels them, after analysis, the same as before. The man
" who can trace them to their elements does not cease to feel
" them, as much as the man who never thought about the
" matter. And whatever effects they produce, as motives, in
" the mind of the man who never thought about the matter,
" they produce equally, in the minds of those who have
" analysed them the most minutely.

" They are constituent parts of human nature. How we are
" actuated, when we feel them, is matter of experience, which
" every one knows within himself. Their action is what it is,
" whether they are simple or compound. Does a complex
" motive cease to be a motive whenever it is discovered to be
" complex? The analysis of the active principles leaves the
" nature of them untouched. To be able to assert, that a
" philosopher, who finds some of the active principles of
" human nature to be compound and traces them to their
" origin, does on that account exclude them from human
" nature, and deny their efficiency as constituent parts of that
" nature, discovers a total incapacity of thinking upon these
" subjects. When Newton discovered that a white ray of

ᵃ Fragment on Mackintosh, pp. 375—378.

"light is not simple but compound, did he for that reason
"exclude it from the denomination of light, and deny that
"it produced its effects, with respect to our perception, as if
"it were of the same nature with the elementary rays of which
"it is composed?"[a]

II.

The reluctance of many persons to receive as correct this
analysis of the sentiments of moral approbation and disapprobation, though a reluctance founded more on feeling than
on reasoning, is accustomed to justify itself intellectually, by
alleging the total unlikeness of those states of mind to the
elementary one, from which, according to the theory, they
are compounded. But this is no more than what is observed
in every similar case. When a complex feeling is generated
out of elements very numerous and various, and in a corresponding degree indeterminate and vague, but so blended
together by a close association, the effect of a long series of
experiences, as to have become inseparable, the resulting feeling
always seems not only very unlike any one of the elements
composing it, but very unlike the sum of those elements.
The pleasure of acquiring, or of consciously possessing, a
sum of money (supposed not to be desired for application to
some specific purpose,) is a feeling, to our consciousness, very
different from the pleasure of protection against hunger and
cold, the pleasure of ease and rest from labour, the pleasure of
receiving consideration from our fellow-creatures, and the
other miscellaneous pleasures, the association with which is
admitted to be the real and only source of the pleasure of
possessing money. In the case, then, of the moral sentiments,
we have, on the one hand, a *vera causa* or set of causes,
having a positive tendency to generate a sentiment of love for
certain actions, and of aversion for certain others; and on the
other hand, those sentiments of love and aversion, actually
produced. This coincidence between the sentiments and a

---

[a] Fragment on Mackintosh, pp. 51, 52.

power adequate to produce them, goes far towards proving
causation. That the sentiments are not obviously like the
causes, is no reason for postulating the existence of another
cause, in the shape of an original principle of our nature.

In a case, however, of so great interest and importance, a
rigid adherence to the canons of inductive proof must be insisted on. Those who dispute the theory are entitled to
demand that it shall conform strictly to the general law of
cause and effect, which is, that the effect shall occur with the
cause, shall not occur without the cause, and shall bear some
proportion to the cause. Unless it can be shewn that when
the effect is not produced, the cause is either absent, or
counteracted by some more powerful agency ; and unless, when
there is any marked difference in the effect, a difference can
be shewn in the cause, sufficient to account for it ; the
theory must give way, or at least, cannot be considered as
proved.

The principal case in which the effect is absent, notwithstanding the apparent presence of the cause assigned for it, is
anticipated by the author, and provided for after his manner,
in the first of the passages quoted from the Fragment on
Mackintosh. There are actions (he observes) as beneficial as
any others, which yet do not excite the moral sentiment of
approbation ; but it is because the spontaneous motives to
those beneficial acts are in general sufficient : as to eat when we
are hungry, or to do a service for which we are to be amply
paid. There are, again, actions of a very hurtful character,
but such that the spontaneous motives for abstaining from
them may be relied on, without any artificial addition : such,
in general, are acts destructive of one's own life or property.
But even in these cases the hurtful acts may become objects
of moral reprobation, when, in any particular case, the natural
deterrents prove insufficient for preventing them.

The author seems to think that the difference here pointed
out, is explained by the fact that the moral sentiment is in
the one case needed, in the other not needed, for producing
the useful or averting the hurtful act ; that, in short, we are

made to have the feeling, by a foresight that our having it will
operate usefully on the conduct of our fellow-creatures. I
cannot accept this explanation. It seems to me to explain
everything about the moral feelings, except the feelings themselves. It explains praise and blame, because these may be
administered with the express design of influencing conduct.
It explains reward and punishment, and every other distinction which we make in our behaviour between what we desire
to encourage, and what we are anxious to check. But these
things we might do from a deliberate policy, without having
any moral feeling in our minds at all. When there is a moral
feeling in our minds, our praise or blame is usually the simple
expression of that feeling, rather than an instrument pur-
posely employed for an end. We may give expression to the
feeling without really having it, in the belief that our praise
or blame will have a salutary effect; but no anticipation of
salutary effects from our feeling will ever avail to give us the
feeling itself: except indeed, what may be said of every other
mental feeling—that we may talk ourselves into it; that the
habitual use of the modes of speech that are associated with
it, has some tendency to call up the feeling in the speaker himself, and a great tendency to engender it in other people.

I apprehend, however, that there is another, and more
adequate reason why the feeling of moral approbation is
usually absent in the case of actions (or forbearances) for
which there are sufficient motives without it. These actions
are done, and are seen to be done, by everybody alike. The
pleasant associations derived from their usefulness merge,
therefore, in our feelings towards human life and towards our
fellow-creatures generally, and do not give rise to any special
association of pleasure with given individuals. But when we
find that a certain person does beneficial acts which the
general experience of life did not warrant us in counting upon
—acts which would not have been done by everybody, or
even by most people, in his place; we associate the pleasure
which the benefit gives us, with the character and disposition
of that individual, and with the act, conceived as proceeding

from that specially beneficent disposition. And obversely, if a person acts in a manner from which we suffer, but which is such as we should expect from most other people in a parallel case, the associations which his acts create in our minds are associations with human life, or with mankind in general; but if the acts, besides being of a hurtful kind, betoken a disposition in the agent, more hurtful than we are accustomed to look for in average men, we associate the injury with that very man, and with that very disposition, and have the feeling of moral disapprobation and repugnance.

There is, as already intimated, another condition which those who hold the Association theory of the moral sentiments are bound to fulfil. The class of feelings called moral embraces several varieties, materially different in their character. Wherever this difference manifests itself, the theory must be required to shew that there is a corresponding difference in the antecedents. If pleasurable or painful associations are the generating cause, those associations must differ in some proportion to the difference which exists in what they generate.

The principal case in point is the case of what is called Duty, or Obligation. It will probably be admitted that beneficial acts, when done because they are beneficial, excite in us favourable sentiments towards the agent, for which the utility or beneficial tendency of the actions is sufficient to account. But it is only some, not all, of these beneficial acts, that we regard as duties; as acts which the agent, or we ourselves if we are the persons concerned, are bound to do. This feeling of duty or obligation, it is contended, is a very different state of mind from mere liking for the action and good will to the agent. The association theory may account for the two last, but not for the former.

I have examined this question in the concluding chapter of a short treatise entitled "Utilitarianism." The subject of the chapter is "the connexion between Justice and Utility." I have there endeavoured to shew what the association is, which exists in the case of what we regard as a duty, but does not exist in the case of what we merely regard as useful, and which gives to the feeling in the former case the strength, the gravity, and pungency, which in the other case it has not.

I believe that the element in the association, which gives this distinguishing character to the feeling, and which constitutes the difference of the antecedents in the two cases, is the idea of Punishment. I mean the association with punishment, not the expectation of it.

No case can be pointed out in which we consider anything as a duty, and any act or omission as immoral or wrong, without regarding the person who commits the wrong and violates the duty as a fit object of punishment. We think that the general good requires that he should be punished, if not by the law, by the displeasure and ill offices of his fellow-creatures : we at any rate feel indignant with him, that is, it would give us pleasure that he should suffer for his misconduct, even if there are preponderant reasons of another kind against inflicting the suffering. This feeling of indignation, or resentment, is, I conceive, a case of the animal impulse (I call it animal because it is common to us with the other animals) to defend our own life or possessions, or the persons whom we care for, against actual or threatened attack. All conduct which we class as wrong or criminal is, or we suppose it to be, an attack upon some vital interest of ourselves or of those we care for, (a category which may include the public, or the whole human race): conduct which, if allowed to be repeated, would destroy or impair the security and comfort of our lives. We are prompted to defend these paramount interests by repelling the attack, and guarding against its renewal ; and our earliest experience gives us a feeling, which acts with the rapidity of an instinct, that the most direct and efficacious protection is retaliation. We are therefore prompted to retaliate by inflicting pain on the person who has inflicted or tried to inflict it upon ourselves. We endeavour, as far as possible, that our social institutions shall render us this service. We are gratified when, by that or other means, the pain is inflicted, and dissatisfied if from any cause it is not. This

strong association of the idea of punishment, and the desire
for its infliction, with the idea of the act which has hurt us, is
not in itself a moral sentiment ; but it appears to me to be the
element which is present when we have the feelings of obligation and of injury, and which mainly distinguishes them from
simple distaste or dislike for any thing in the conduct of another
that is disagreeable to us; that distinguishes, for instance,
our feeling towards the person who steals our goods, from our
feeling towards him who offends our senses by smoking
tobacco.   This impulse to self-defence by the retaliatory
infliction of pain, only becomes a moral sentiment, when it is
united with a conviction that the infliction of punishment in
such a case is conformable to the general good, and when the
impulse is not allowed to carry us beyond the point at which
that conviction ends.   For further illustration I must refer to
the little Treatise already mentioned.—*Ed.*

CHAPTER XXIV.

THE WILL.

WE have now considered the class of sensations, called Pleasurable, and Painful. We have also considered the Ideas of those sensations, or that revival of them which is capable of taking place, when the outward action upon the senses is removed. The Idea of the pleasurable sensation, and the Desire of it ; the Idea of the painful sensation, and the Aversion to it ; are respectively names for one and the same state of consciousness.

We have also considered the Ideas of the Causes of our Pleasurable and Painful sensations. We have found that those Ideas are never Ideas of the Causes separately ; but Ideas both of the causes and of their effects, inseparably joined by association. They are not, therefore, indifferent Ideas ; they are always either pleasurable or painful ; being complex Ideas, to a great degree composed of the Ideas of pleasurable and painful sensations.

As the simple Idea of a pleasurable or painful sensation, is a DESIRE or an AVERSION ; so the complex Idea, composed of the Ideas of a Cause of pleasurable or painful sensations, and its effects, is called an AFFEC-

TION ; which receives different names, according as it is modified by different circumstances ; of time, for example, past or future ; and if future, certainly or uncertainly, future.

We next observed, that our own acts were very often the cause of the causes of our pleasures, and of the prevention of our pains. The Idea of an action of our own, as cause, strongly associated with the Idea of a pleasure as its effect, we found to be a state of mind peculiarly important ; because it excites to action. In what manner this state of mind gives birth to action, is the question which we now have to resolve.

The object of the Inquiry is, to find out, what that peculiar state of mind or consciousness is, by which action is preceded. From all men it receives the same name. It is called the Will, by every body ; and by every body this Will is understood to be a state of mind or consciousness ; but how formed, or wherein consisting, is variously and vehemently disputed.

Much of the confusion of Ideas which has darkened this controversy arose from the misconception, so long universal, respecting the Idea of a Cause. The will was invariably, and justly, assumed as the cause of the action ; but unhappily there was always assumed as a part of the Idea of this cause, an item, which is found to be altogether imaginary. In the sequence of events called Cause and Effect, men were not contented with the Cause and the Effect ; they imagined a third thing, called Force or Power, which was not the cause, but something emanating from the cause, and the true and immediate cause of the

Effect. This illusion has been minutely examined, as we have already remarked, by a late Philosopher; by whom it has been proved, beyond the reach of contradiction, that the power of any cause is nothing different from the cause. A cause, and the power of a cause, are not two things, but two names for the same thing. With the Idea of Cause is always united the Idea of Effect. It is one of the cases of inseparable conjunction. The Idea of the Cause as existing, is irresistibly followed by the Idea of the Effect as existing. Not only does the one Idea always follow the other; but it is not in our power to prevent their following. Now the Idea of any thing as existing, when that idea forces itself upon us, and cannot be resisted, is that which we call Belief. In all this, however, there is nothing but the idea of an Antecedent and a Consequent, and a fixed order of Association. Our object, therefore, in this Inquiry will be completely attained if we discover which is the real state of mind which immediately precedes an action.

The actions of a human being may be divided into two sorts: I. Those which are called the actions of his Body; II. Those which are called the actions of his mind. We shall endeavour to ascertain what are the antecedents of both, and shall begin with the Body.

I. The actions of the Body are all of one sort. They consist essentially of that action of certain fibres, which is called contraction. The object of this part of our Inquiry, therefore, is to ascertain what are the states of mind which immediately precede a fibrous contraction.

We can show that muscular or fibrous contractions follow, 1st, Sensations; 2dly, Ideas: and we can also shew, that in a vast proportion of those cases, the sequence is invariable; in other words, that the Sensation, or Idea, is the cause of the contraction.

1. It is no part of our present business to adduce what has been discovered by physiologists in tracing the physical antecedents of a contracting muscle. The mental antecedent is the object of our inquiry; and whether a physical link, or more than one physical link, intervenes between it and the contraction, alters not the question as to the state of the mental cause; nor the fact as to the ultimate effect. Facts are abundant, to prove, that the nerves are the immediate instrument of contraction; and also that the effect produced by the mental state is first upon the nerves, and only through the nerves upon the muscle. A paralytic limb, is a limb, the movement of which is not consequent upon that mental state which is usually followed by such a movement. But a paralytic limb is only a limb, the nerves of which are deprived of their usual power by a disorder in that part of the brain in which they originate.

Innumerable facts are capable of being adduced, to prove that sensation is a cause of muscular action. There is, however, little necessity to be tedious with the proof; because there will be little difficulty in assenting to the proposition.

The distinction, which we formerly drew, between those sensations which we have by what is called the external senses, in other words, on the surface of our body, and those (numerous, not individually only, but also in their species or kinds), which we have in the internal parts of our bodies, it is here peculiarly necessary to remember, and strongly to remark. The muscles themselves are internal parts of the body. The feelings in the muscles are one species of those internal sensations. And, in general, as it is easy to conceive, the internal sensations are a leading cause of such actions as take place in the internal organs of the Body.[59]

Some of the external cases are remarkably familiar and precise. A pungent odour enters the nostrils; first, a certain sensation follows, and immediately after, the violent action of a great number of muscles, called Sneezing. In drinking, a drop of water sometimes enters the larynx; it produces a certain sensation, immediately followed by the action of certain muscles, from which we have the very painful feeling of suffocation. There is a very remarkable exemplification of the same law, in the case of the sensation

---

[59] The actions which take place in the interior of the body are not always, nor perhaps even generally, produced by sensations. A large portion of them are not preceded by any sensation of which we are aware, and have been ascertained to depend on nerves not terminating in the brain, which is the seat of sensation, but stopping at the spinal cord. These actions are inferred to be the results of a mere physicial stimulus, operating either upon the local nerves, or upon the spinal ganglions with which those nerves communicate, and not attended with any consciousness.

Many of the instances which the author goes on to enumerate, of muscular action excited by sensation, are, in all probability, cases of this description. The muscular action is directly excited by the physical irritation of the nerves, and any sensation which accompanies it is not its cause, but a simultaneous effect.—*Ed.*

of light.   The Pupil of the Eye contracts or dilates, according as a greater or less degree of light falls upon the retina.   The eyelids are in perpetual motion in consequence of sensations to which we do not attend.   The painful sensation pervading the body, when we plunge into cold water, produces so much action in the muscles, that we sob and respire in a convulsive manner.   The lachrymal glands are moved to action, by certain effluvia, as those of onions, by smoke, and various gases, and even by certain states of the air, so as to shed tears abundantly.   The action of food is similar upon the salivary glands ; and of heat and cold upon the skin, the one opening, the other contracting its pores.

In respect to a great number of the contractions of muscles, which take place in consequence of impressions on the surface of our bodies, the evidence is not so precise ; because, though contractions are originally performed by sensation, they are afterwards and more habitually performed by Ideas.   We shall be able, therefore, to speak of them more instructively, when more familiar with the sequence consisting of Ideas antecedent, and the contraction of muscles consequent.

The action of the internal organs in consequence of internal sensations, is proved by many familiar, as well as by many interesting phenomena.   The action of coughing, than which none more familiar, is the highest evidence.   The sensation here, is not one of those which are neglected and obscure.   A violent action of the muscles is its immediate consequence.   Hiccup is also produced by a sensation in the stomach ; and affords evidence definite and decisive.   Vomiting is another very instructive case.   We

know that it is the ultimate effect of something which
produces disagreeable sensations in the stomach. The
sensation, indeed, in this case, is not so well distinguished from others, nor so precisely known, as in
the case of coughing. We know, however, its general
character, and we know well the violent contraction
of muscles, which is the consequence of it. In connexion with this, we may notice the peculiar sensations in the *Uterus*, which produce the muscular
actions of Parturition; some of the most violent
belonging to the human frame. The sensations,
which are the cause of cramps, are commonly obscure.
It is the Effect which engages all our attention.
There is no doubt, however, that it is by an internal
sensation, that this very painful effect is produced.
A greater proportion of those painful muscular actions
called spasms, are the effect of sensations; though
Ideas, also, appear to be concerned in the production
of those which become frequent. One very remarkable case, which is named the Locked Jaw, is often
the result of a pain produced by an external wound.

Not any of our bodily functions is more important
than Respiration. It is a very extensive action of
muscles habitually performed by sensation merely.
The sensations, however, escape our attention to such
a degree, that we lose the power of attending to
them. And it is only by the effort we are capable of
to stop Respiration, when a painful sensation after a
time renders the action of the muscles irresistible,
that we get a sort of conjectural knowledge of what
the ordinary sensation is.

There are some most important cases of the action
of our internal organs, in consequence of sensation, in

which, from the habitual neglect of that which never calls for our attention, both cause and effect, to our ordinary perception, are alike unknown. That the heart is a part of the body endowed with sensation, is abundantly known, as often as, by a departure from its habitual state, it becomes the seat of sensations other than the habitual sensations, to which, from habit of inattention to them, we have lost the power of attending. The blood cannot flow into the heart, without a sensation of the heart. The contraction of the heart is the consequence of that sensation; thence the circulation of the blood; thence respiration, and all the trains, both of sensations, and of actions, which constitute the general working of the human machine. In truth, the actions of the alimentary canal, necessary to keep up the supply of the blood and the actions of the circulating system, which impart their action to most of the assimilating and secreting organs of the human body, all taking place in sensitive parts, all, of course, attended by sensation, and all produced by sensation, constitute a system of internal sensations, numerous beyond what it is easy to conceive,—some pleasurable, some painful,—and of all possible modifications of pain and pleasure; but to which, singly, the habit of inattention is so complete, that it amounts to inability of attending to them.

When they are very extensively of a pleasurable, or very extensively of a painful kind, they produce a general state, which often calls our attention; but for which, as it is a vague, indeterminate feeling, we have only vague, indeterminate names: we call it a

state of comfort or discomfort ; of cheerfulness, or
gloom ; high spirits, or low spirits ; and so on.   The
incessant motion of the blood, in so many sensitive
tubes, in every part of the body, constitutes a system
of sensations pervading the whole frame ; as the contact of the air produces a system of sensations, pervading every part of the surface of our bodies, but to
which our habit of inattention is so complete, that we
are equally incapable of attending to them as we are
of attending to the sensations produced in our arteries
and veins, by the motion of the blood, and in the
secreting and absorbing vessels when excited to
action.*

We are rather more attentive, perhaps, to the
general states produced by the extensive diffusion of
pleasurable or painful sensations in the alimentary
canal, than in the channels of the blood, and perhaps
we sometimes confound them.   To some of the
feelings in the upper part of the canal we attend
sufficiently to distinguish them ; the feeling called
nausea, for example, in its numerous modifications.
To those in the other parts, unless they amount to
acute pain, we never attend, till they are so extensively diffused, as to constitute a state, to which we
assign the terms, Comfort, Discomfort, or some other

---

* " Is there not reason to suspect, that our unconsciousness,
in health, of the Impressions made on our organs by the fluids
which they contain, depends on our being accustomed to the
sensations which they incessantly excite ; so that there remains
but a confused perception which in time disappears."—*Elements
of Physiology*, by A. Richerand, translated by James Copeland,
M.D., 4th ed., p. 21.—(*Author's Note.*)

of the vague names, by which a state made up of an
indefinite number of painful or pleasurable sensations
is usually denominated.   Yet we know that actions
of great importance are the result of those unnoticed
sensations ; the secretion of the gastric juice ; the
secretion of the bile ; the separation of the nutritive
from the innutritive part of the food ; the operation
of the lacteal and lymphatic vessels, and that extraordinary motion called the peristaltic, which aids in
carrying on the contents of the bowels to the place of
their discharge.   It is probable, that the pleasurable
states of the alimentary canal are commonly joined,
or synchronous, with pleasurable states of the channels
of the blood ; and the painful states, the same.   That
the healthy, or unhealthy state of the one, accompanies that of the other, we know.   And that certain
diseased states of the circulating system, are accompanied with that general state of feeling, called discomfort, or wretchedness, which implies the wide
diffusion of painful sensations throughout the system,
is but too well known to all who have experienced
any modification of the febrile state ; nor can it be
doubted, that the joyous state of perfect health, in
which we feel delight in our being, and our whole
frame seems to be a source of pleasure to us, is in a
great degree produced by the innumerable unnoticed
and unnoticeable sensations, produced by the motion
and contact of the blood, in every part of our frame.

   We seem authorized, therefore, by the fullest Evidence, to assume that Sensation, is the mental cause,
whatever the physical links, of a great proportion of
the muscular contractions of our frame ; and that

among those so produced are found some of the most constant, the most remarkable, and the most important, of that grand class of corporeal phenomena.

2. To prove that Ideas, as well as Sensations, are the cause of muscular actions, it is necessary to make choice of cases, in which the Idea is in no danger of being confounded with that state of mind called the Will. And hardly any case will answer this condition, except some of those which are held to be involuntary, for the Idea itself never can be very clearly distinguished from the Will.

The Winking of the Eyelids, when a person moves his hand rapidly close to the eyes of another person, is a familiar case of an action of the muscles, which we cannot prevent. The idea is that of pain, from the contact of the hand with the eye. A sudden sensation of pain in the eye makes the eyelid close. This is the case, already examined, of contraction by sensation. When this has been performed a number of times, the idea of pain in the eye, and the idea of the contraction of the muscles, that is, of the sensations contained in the contraction of the muscles, become associated together, so strongly, that the one can never exist without the other. The next step of the process is, that the contraction follows upon the Idea, in the same manner as it followed upon the sensation. This is not a matter of conjecture, it is matter of fact. It is an experienced event. We do not undertake to say, what physical links are between the Idea and the contraction, any more than between the sensation and the contraction. The Idea is the last part of the mental operation. And as the Idea and the sensation are feelings so nearly alike, there is no difficulty in believing that like effects proceed from like causes.[60]

The origin of the sensation, and the origin of the Idea seem to be different. The sensation originates in the extremity of the nerves at some particular part of the body. Something, we know not what, happens at the extremity of those nerves; something, we know not what, is conveyed along the nerves to the brain; and then sensation exists. From the brain, in its state of sensation, something, we know not what, is conveyed along the nerves to the contracting muscle, and the contraction takes place. Also, from the Brain, in its state of Ideation, if I may here, for the sake of the analogy with sensation, use a word of my own coining, something is conveyed along the nerves to the contracting muscle, and the contraction takes place. The sensation does not originate in the Brain; the Idea does. But if the state of the Brain when it has a sensation, and when it has the idea of that sensation, be, as we may natu-

---

[60] The act of winking or wincing under the threat of a blow on the eyes is a good example of strong, and even indissoluble association. Any one making the experiment with an infant will find that there is no original tendency to perform the act. It is an association generated under the impressiveness of an acute pain, mingled with terror; a state of things under which an indelible mental connexion will be established in a very small number of repetitions. As a dog that has once suffered from a burnt cinder will dread for ever any commotion or stirring of the fire, so one smart in the eye will be associated with the cause in an indissoluble bond; and the mere sight of anything in motion towards the face will induce the preventive volition.—B.

rally suppose, very nearly the same; and if the state of the Brain is a necessary link in the chain of antecedents and consequents which terminates in the contracted muscle, the effect is so far accounted for.

Yawning is a familiar case of contraction, produced by sensation. We yawn without intending it; we know that we yawn in consequence of an antecedent state of feeling, of which, from never attending to it particularly, we have no distinct Idea; but which we recognise sufficiently as the antecedent of the act. This act, however, we also know is frequently the effect of Ideas. If we see another person yawn, it rarely happens that we do not yawn along with him. The act of yawning is so strongly associated with the idea of the feelings which precede it, that the sight of the act by another person calls up in us strongly the idea of the precedent feelings. The Idea exists, and as the contraction was the effect of the sensation, so is it also of the Idea.

The same is the account to be rendered of the infectious power of convulsions. In assemblies of men and women, especially under such a state of excitement (religious enthusiasm, for instance) as implies the strong association of certain trains of Ideas, if one person is attacked with convulsions, it commonly happens that others are attacked, and frequently great numbers. That this is a case of Ideas is certain; because nothing is conveyed to the spectators from a person convulsed, but the sight of the person; and the sight can do nothing but excite associated Ideas. The associated Ideas exist: the convulsions follow.

Laughter is a curious phenomenon of human nature. The analysis of it is not here required. It

will be easily recognised as a remarkable instance of
the production of muscular action by Ideas. We
laugh, either when certain ideas are suggested to us
by others, or when they proceed from our own associations. In either case, the Ideas exist ; the Laughter
follows.

Sobbing and weeping, in grief, afford a similar
instance. What we call grief, is the existence of
certain trains of Ideas. The Ideas exist : the weeping follows.

The swallowing of the saliva affords a good experiment. If a friend assures you that you cannot
refrain, for the space of a minute, from this act, and
you are tempted to try, you are almost sure to fail.
By the attention fixed on the act, the ideas of the
feelings, which precede the act, are so strongly called
up by association, that the act follows of course.[61]

There are many acts of familiar occurrence to shew,
that those actions of our organs which are the most

---

[61] This is a pure example of the " fixed idea," or of the tendency to work out into full actuality whatever is strongly
presented in idea. The case also shows this power *in conflict*
with the Will ; we are supposed to be trying hard to prevent
the act (which is volition), and yet there is, in the intense
possession of an idea, a power greater than the will. The fact
of being strongly excited to avoid swallowing the saliva,
increases the force of the idea of swallowing it, and makes
that idea almost omnipotent to work itself out. The
same baffling of the will, the making it recoil upon itself,
is shown in our attempt to forget or banish a painful idea.
The more intensely we will to forget the idea, the more do we
stamp it on the mind, through the excitement engendered by
the volition.—*B*.

habitually produced by sensations, are capable of being strongly modified by Ideas. The effect of Fear, for example, on the action of the heart, is known to be very remarkable. So it is on the action of the bowels, of the kidneys, and of the skin. One of its effects is perspiration ; another, paleness : another, cold.*

The cases which we have just adduced, of yawning, and contagious convulsions, may be regarded as belonging to an extensive class ; which obtains the general name of Imitation. There is more or less of a propensity to Imitation in all men, that is, to perform the act which we see another man performing. In most children the propensity is very strong ; and

---

* The operation of Ideas on the internal parts of the body is so familiar, that we meet everywhere with pleasant stories of it. Zachary Gray, in one of his notes on Butler's Hudibras, alluding to the story of the countryman, who, receiving a prescription from the doctor, and being told by him to take that, swallowed the paper, asks, "And why might not this operate upon a strong imagination, as well as the ugly parson, the very sight of whom in a morning (Oldham's Remains) would work beyond Jalap or Rhubarb ; and a Doctor prescribed him to one of his patients as a remedy against costiveness : Or what is mentioned by Dr. Daniel Turner (De Morbis Cutaneis), that the bare imagination of a purging potion has wrought such an alteration in sundry persons, as to bring on several stools like those they call physical ; and he mentions a young gentleman, his patient, who having occasion to take many vomits, had such an antipathy to them, that ever after he would vomit as strongly by the force of imagination, by the bare sight of the emetic bolus, as most could do by medicine. The application of a clyster-pipe, without the clyster, has had the same effect upon others."—(*Author's Note.*)

to it they owe much of the celerity with which they make certain acquirements; to that of imitating sounds, for example, the celerity with which they learn to speak. The propensity to imitate musical sounds so adheres to persons of a musical ear, even in mature age, that they can scarcely forbear humming every tune which they hear. Children learn to stutter and to squint, from imitation of their companions. We know how universally it happens that young persons acquire the manner and the air of those with whom they habitually live. These are cases not only of action, but of habits of action, produced by the agency of Ideas. It requires only cases of strong association to produce analogous effects, at all periods of life. "When we see a stroke," says Mr. Smith, "aimed and just ready to fall upon the leg or arm of another person, we naturally shrink and draw back our own leg, or our own arm. The mob, when they are gazing at a dancer on the slack rope, naturally writhe and twist, and balance their own bodies as they see him do. Persons of delicate fibres and a weak constitution of body, complain, that in looking on the sores and ulcers which are exposed by beggars in the streets, they are apt to feel an itching or uneasy sensation in the correspondent part of their own bodies. Men of the most robust make, observe, that in looking upon sore eyes, they often feel a very sensible soreness in their own." There are few persons who do not put on a cheerful countenance, upon the sight of the cheerful countenances of their friends; still fewer whose countenance is not made sorrowful by sight of the sorrowful countenances of their friends. It is well known, that Tears are contagious; and upon this some well-known rules for the countenance both of the orator and the actor are prescribed. It is not necessary further to accumulate instances of this description ; nor further to enter into the analysis of them, than to remark, that the action, the idea of which is conveyed to us by what we thus hear or see, calls up, by association, the idea of the feelings which precede the action. The Idea of the feelings exists, and the action follows.

There is a case of the action of the muscles which requires particular attention ; that in which we *learn* to make use of them ; in which we acquire what we call command over them only by degrees. There is more or less, probably, of this process in all the sorts of muscular action which are not performed originally by sensation ; and the process seems to be longer or shorter according as the number of muscles, which must act together in order to the production of the effect, is greater or less. We know how slowly the child acquires the power of so balancing his body as to hold it erect. To this Effect the action of a great number of muscles is required. Yet, before the age at which reflection begins, the power is so completely acquired, that the mental process escapes our attention. To be erect, seems the posture into which our body puts itself of its own accord. There are circum-stances, however, in which we become distinctly con-scious of the powerful effort, which is required for that purpose, though, from its being habitual, we are in ordinary circumstances wholly insensible of it. If we allow sleep to come upon us, while we are in an erect posture, so far, that the ideas which maintain the muscular action begin to give way, we have im-

mediately the sensation of falling, and a strong
perception of the effort required to keep the body
erect.

We observe how slowly the child learns to perform, with the requisite precision, the contractions on
which the operation of walking depends. And every
man can remember the difficulty with which he has
learned to perform any new combination of contractions. Whoever has learned to dance, knows how
imperfectly, till after a multitude of repetitions, he
performed the simplest steps. Whoever has been
drilled, as they call it; that is, trained to perform
with the firelock the acts required of the soldier,
knows with what difficulty, each of them, however
simple, was originally performed.

There is another very familiar instance, that of
learning to write. Most men can remember, when
they began this process, how imperfectly the hand
obeyed them; and how awkwardly they made even
the simple strokes. Every man can make the experiment with his left hand. After the habit of performing with the right hand is completely attained,
he is almost unable to form a letter with the left. The
cases of this incapacity of the left hand to perform the
acts which we perform habitually with the right are
innumerable; and afford decisive illustration of the
great fact which is now the subject of our attention.
To perform the contractions of a number of muscles,
the contractions of all of which must be combined in
the action, the idea whereon each of the contractions
depends must previously exist, and in the requisite
order. That is to say, a certain association of Ideas
must be performed. But we know, that no new

association of Ideas is easily or steadily performed. This is the effect of Repetition. As soon as the association of the ideas is completely established by repetition, the process, both bodily and mental, goes on with ease; and where the habit is great, with so much ease, as even to escape attention. The process of learning to play on a musical instrument is slow and difficult. By habit the associations become so close, that an expert performer can execute the most difficult pieces, and carry on another and even an intricate process of thought at the same time.

How slowly, and with how much difficulty do children acquire command over the organs of speech? And how totally without effort on our part in after life does the sound appear immediately to cling to the Idea of the word? Yet, in learning the new sounds of a foreign language we become abundantly sensible of the difficulty, sometimes altogether insurmountable, of performing the precise combination of contractions which a particular sound requires.

It seems to be established, therefore, by an ample induction, that muscular actions follow ideas, as invariable antecedent and consequent, in other words, as cause and effect; that whenever we have obtained a command over the ideas, we have also obtained a command over the motions; and that we cannot perform associate contractions of several muscles, till we have established by repetition, the ready association of the Ideas.

I believe that nothing more need be said for the establishing of these truths. I shall adduce a few more instances, chiefly with the view to familiarize my readers with the mode of applying to this in-

teresting class of facts, the principles with which they
are now fully acquainted.

There is no part of the body with the use of which
we are so perfectly familiar as the hand.   There are
no actions, of the sort at least to which we are attentive, the repetition of which is so incessant.   Of
course, the associations of the ideas corresponding to
the associate contractions of the muscles which produce the various movements or actions of the hand,
are formed in the most perfect manner ; and we never
have the Ideas, as antecedent, without the movement
as consequent.   This inseparable connexion between
the Ideas, and the contractions, which we call the
Power of the Will, is gradually formed.   At first the
hand of the infant is moved by sensations.   If the
inside of the hand is touched, so at least as to make
the sensation considerable, the fingers bend ; and perform more or less of the act of grasping.   Here is a
train of events.   First, the sensation of touch, from
the application of the external object ; next, an influence from the seat of the sensation in the brain,
transmitted along the nerves of certain muscles ; then
the contraction of the muscles, with the various
sensations which the action upon those organs, and
the action excited in them, imply.   When the sensation has been often repeated, in conjunction with its
effect, the Idea of the sensation becomes familiar and
distinct ; and capable of producing many of the
effects which the sensation itself produces.   It is also
closely associated with the idea of the motion, and
all its accompanying sensations as the effect ; and the
chain of antecedents and consequents proceeds in uninterrupted order.

As similar instances of motions, at first produced by sensations, afterwards by ideas, we may adduce the remarkable cases of the sphincters of the bladder and *anus.* At first, children perform their evacuations, as they sneeze and cough, when the sensations excite them. Afterwards, they learn, but by slow degrees, to bring them under the command of ideas. There is no case, however, which affords more decisive evidence of the power of ideas over the actions of particular parts, than those which are called Amatory ; because the effects, which are produced by the Ideas, cannot be produced by the will.

There is another set of cases, which deserve attention ; those in which the ideas which are followed by the action of certain muscles, acquire associations with other sensations or Ideas which call them up, and thence give action to the muscles, upon very inconvenient occasions. A woman who has accustomed herself to scream out, upon every sudden idea of the slightest danger, cannot abstain from screaming. The awkward motions, for which some, even eminent, men have been remarkable, Dr. Johnson, for instance, are completely explained by this principle. The ideas, whence the motions proceed, have become associated, in ways which can seldom be traced, with sensations, or ideas of frequent recurrence. And hence are the motions frequently produced.

There are equally remarkable cases, in which the associations, necessary to produce the idea on which the muscular actions depend, are prevented by other associations more powerful. Men admitted to the presence of a great personage have found themselves wholly unable to articulate a word. The Ideas of

Power and Dignity, with all their associates of terror and of hope, were called up in such irresistible association by the presence of him who was clothed with them; that the ideas necessary to the articulation of words were excluded, and the power of speaking was lost.

We have now established, by an ample Induction, that the action of muscles follows, as an effect its cause; first, upon sensations; secondly, upon Ideas. The language which Professor Stewart has applied to a similar case, is perfectly applicable here. " It may, indeed, be said, that these observations only prove the possibility, that our muscular contractions may be all performed by sensations and Ideas. But, if this be admitted, nothing more can well be required; for, surely, if these phenomena are clearly explicable, from the known and acknowledged laws of the human mind, it would be unphilosophical to devise a new principle, on purpose to account for them."*

I believe, indeed, that this conclusion is not at variance with the common belief upon the subject. It appears to me to be not inconsistent with the language of the advocates for what is called the Freedom of the Will, to admit, that the action of the muscle takes place in consequence of the Idea; and that our power of willing consists in the power of calling into existence the appropriate Idea; that the power of the will is not immediate over the muscle, but over the Idea.

The following observations of Dr. Reid, though not remarkable for their precision, seem fully to justify this Inference.

---

* Elements of the Philosophy of the Human Mind. Chap. ii.

" *First*, every act of will must have an object. He
that wills, must will something; and that which he
wills is called the object of his volition. As a man
cannot think without thinking of something, nor remember without remembering something, so neither
can he will without willing something. Every act of
will, therefore, must have an object; and the person
who wills must have some conception, more or less
distinct of what he wills.

" A *second* observation is, that the immediate object
of will must be some action of our own."

There are two assertions here which demand our
attention; 1, that what is willed is an action of our
own; 2, that to such will a conception, that is, an
Idea, more or less distinct, of this action of ours, is
indispensable.

He adduces some particulars, in illustration, which
impart something more of precision to his meaning.

" A healthy child, some hours after its birth, feels
the sensation of hunger, and, if applied to the breast,
sucks and swallows its food very perfectly. We have
no reason to think, that before it ever sucked, it has
any conception of that complex operation, or how it is
performed. It cannot, therefore, with propriety, be
said that it wills to suck." It appears, from this
example, that the muscular actions, which are performed by Sensation, Dr. Reid distinguishes from
those, which he calls voluntary; that he denominates
voluntary, those only which are performed by Ideas.
It also appears fully, from the example, that the Idea
of the action willed, which he considers the foundation of volition, must, in all cases, be subsequent to
the performance of the act by Sensation; in other

words, that the idea cannot exist but in consequence of the sensation.

What has yet been advanced, however, is not a full explanation of the subject. For, after it is admitted that the motion of the muscles is, in all cases, the immediate effect of the appropriate Idea, there is still one class which all men agree to call involuntary; another which many contend are voluntary. It now remains that we inquire wherein the difference consists.

There is one point which is established by the mere statement, and which goes a certain way towards the solution of the question. Since the action of the muscles follows upon the existence of the Idea, whatever calls up the Idea produces the action. The Question, then, may be resolved into these two: In what manner is the Idea called up in cases called involuntary? In what manner is it called up in those called voluntary?

In the cases called not voluntary, I doubt not, it will be easily admitted, that the Idea is raised in the way of ordinary association, by a preceding Sensation, or Idea. In the yawning which proceeds from the sight of another person yawning, the idea is called up by a Sensation. In the laughter which is excited either by ideas suggested to us from without, or ideas which spring up in our associated trains, the idea which is proximate to the muscular action is, of course, called up by an Idea.

There appears no circumstance by which the cases called voluntary are distinguished from the involuntary, except that in the voluntary there exists a Desire. Shedding tears at the hearing of a tragic story, we do not desire to weep: laughing at the recital of a comic story, we do not desire to laugh."² But, when we elevate the arm to ward off a blow, we desire to lift the arm; when we turn the head to look at some attractive object, we desire to move the head. I believe that no case of voluntary action can be mentioned, in which it would not be an appropriate expression, to call the action desired.

We have already examined the meaning of the word Desire. We have seen that it is applied to pleasurable sensations; to exemption from painful sensations; and to the causes of them. We have also seen, and to the present purpose this is a point of great importance, that when the word desire is applied to the cause of a sensation, or of an exemption from a sensation, it is employed in a figurative, or metaphorical, not in a direct sense. Few of our actions can be called pleasurable sensations; or exemption from painful; in propriety of language perhaps none. Our actions are causes of those two classes of events; and on that account are called, but only in a metaphorical sense, objects of desire.

In a voluntary action, then, we recognise two Ideas; first, the idea of the sensation or exemption, which two, for shortness, we shall call by one name, Pleasure; secondly, the idea of an action of our own as the cause of the pleasure. It is also easy to see how the Idea of a pleasure should excite the Idea of the action which is the cause of it; and how, when the Idea exists, the action should follow.

---

⁶² These are emotional and not volitional manifestations. They are the natural signs, expression, or embodiment of a feeling, as feeling, and apart from the power to move the will, which is a separate fact.—B.

We have seen, that the idea of a pleasure, as effect, associated with the Idea of an act of our own, as its cause, is one of the cases of motive. In the preceding paragraph it seems also to be one of the cases of will. It may then be asked, if the will is, or is not, any thing different from the motive?

The course pursued by the mind in devising and executing a train of means for the accomplishment of an end, has been often described. The End; that is, the advantage or pleasure desired; is the first thing in the contemplation of the mind; the step nearest to the end in the process of attainment, is the second; the step immediately preceding that is the third; and so on, to the step at which the process of execution must begin. Thus, suppose the pleasure of living in a handsome house is the end; the apartments, and furniture, and accommodations of such a mansion is the nearest step; the one immediately preceding that is the building and furnishing it; the one preceding that, the employing an architect and upholsterer; the one preceding that, the finding the money. Such is the order in which the mind proceeds from the primary conception of the End through the requisite series of means. The order of execution is directly the reverse. It begins where the other ends, and ends where the other begins. If the person we have supposed proceeds to the execution of his plan, his first step is, to find the money, his next to provide the architect, and so on from step to step, till he places himself in the pleasurable situation he originally contemplated.

There is this double operation in what we may call the formation and execution of motives. The first association starts from the pleasure. The idea of the

pleasure is associated with its immediate cause, that
cause with its cause, and so on, till it reaches that act
of ours which is the opposite end of the train. The
process may stop here, and in that case the motive
does not excite to action. If it excites to action, the
process is exactly reversed. In the first process of
association, the pleasure was the first link in the chain,
the action the last ; in the second process, the action
is the first, the pleasure the last. When the first process only is performed, the association is called MOTIVE.
When the second is performed it is called WILL.

A difficulty, however, presents itself. The first
process terminates in an Idea of the action. The
second process commences with an idea of the action.
The Idea of the action is thus excited twice. But
the first time it is not followed by the action ; the
second time it is. How is this to be reconciled with
the supposed constancy of connexion between the
muscular action and the Idea which produces it?
The difficulty is solved by observing, that the phrase,
" Idea of the action," has two meanings. There are
two Ideas, very different from one another, to both of
which we give the name, " Idea of the action." Of
these Ideas, one is the outward appearance of the
action, and is always a very obvious Idea. The other
is the copy of those internal sensations which originally called the muscles into action, to which, from
habit of not attending to them, we have lost the power
of attending. This last is by no means an obvious
Idea. And the mind passes from it so quickly, intent
upon the action which is its result, that it is almost
always swallowed up in the mass of association. It
constitutes, in fact, one of the most remarkable in-

stances of that class of links in a chain, which, how important soever to the existence of the chain, are passed over so rapidly, that the existence of them is hardly ever recognised.

This last Idea alone, is that upon which the contraction of the muscle is consequent. In the process of association which we call the motive, as described above, the first of the two above-mentioned ideas of the action, that of its outward appearance, is the idea excited. If the association stops there, the motive is inoperative; if the association does not stop there, but the idea of the outward appearance of the action, calls up that other, the idea of the internal feelings of the action, the motive is then operative, and we are said TO WILL.

If we are asked, how an Idea, as that of the outward appearance of an act, should at one time excite an idea, as that of the internal feelings of the act, at another time not excite it, we can only refer to the laws of association, as far as they have been ascertained. We know there are certain cases of association, so strong, that the one Idea never exists without calling up the other. We know there are other cases in which an Idea sometimes does, and sometimes does not, call up such or such an Idea. Sometimes it is easy to trace the cause of this variety; sometimes difficult.[63]

---

[63] This analysis of the power of the Will over muscular action is substantially that of Hartley, though more clearly and forcibly stated, and more amply illustrated. In the field of mental philosophy this is the point at which Hartley approached nearest to the most advanced thoughts of his suc-

II. But even when it is admitted that all muscular contraction is the effect of association, in the
way which we have described, there are other pheno-

cessors, and left least for them to do beyond the task of
commentators and defenders.

The doctrine of Hartley on the Will may be summed up in
the following propositions.   1. All our voluntary movements
were originally automatic : meaning by automatic, involuntary,
and excited directly by sensations.   2. When a sensation has
the power of exciting a given muscular action, the idea of
that sensation, if sufficiently vivid, will excite it likewise.   3.
The idea of the sensation which excites an automatic action
of the muscles, persists during the action, and becomes associated with it by contiguity, in such a manner as to be itself,
in its turn, excited by any vividly recalled idea of the muscular
act.   4. The following is what takes place in voluntary
motion.   The idea of the end we desire, excites by association
the idea of the muscular act which would procure it for us.
The idea of this muscular act excites, by association, the idea
of the sensation which originally excited the same muscular
action automatically.   And lastly, the idea of this sensation
excites the action, as the sensation itself would have done.
5. These associations being formed gradually, and progres-
sively strengthened by repetition, this gives us the explanation of the gradual and slow process whereby we gain what is
called command of our muscles ; i.e. the process by which the
actions, originally produced automatically by sensations, come
to be produced, and at last, to be easily and rapidly produced,
by the ideas of the different pleasurable ends to which those
muscular actions are the means.   6. In this chain of association, as is so often the case in chains of association, the links
which are no otherwise interesting to us than by introducing
other links, gradually drop out of consciousness, being, after
many repetitions, either forgotten as soon as felt, or altogether
thrown out ; the latter being the supposition which Hartley
apparently favours.   The link that consists in the idea of the

mena to be accounted for. We may still be reasonably
called upon to explain the power which the mind appears to possess over its associations. There is a

---

internal sensations which excited the muscular action when it
was still automatic, being the least interesting part of the
whole series, is probably the first which we cease to be aware
of. When the succession of the ideas has become, by frequent
repetition, extremely prompt, rapid, and certain, another link
tends to disappear, namely, the ideas of the muscular feelings
that accompany the act. A practised player, for example, on
a keyed instrument, becomes less and less conscious of the
motions of his fingers, until there at last remains nothing in
his consciousness to shew that the muscular acts do not arise
without any intermediate links, from the purpose, i.e. the idea
in his mind, which made him begin playing. At this stage
the muscular motion, which, from automatic, had become
voluntary, has become, from voluntary, what, in Hartley's
phraseology, is called secondarily automatic; and it seems to
be his opinion that the ideas which have disappeared from consciousness, or at all events from memory, have not been (as
maintained by Stewart) called up, and immediately afterwards
forgotten, but have ceased to be called up; being, as it were,
leapt over by the rapidity with which the succeeding links rush
into consciousness

This theory, as we have seen, is adopted, and more fully
worked out, by the author of the Analysis. He proves, by
many examples, that sensations excite muscular actions; that
ideas excite muscular actions; and that, when a sensation has
power to excite a particular muscular action, the idea of the
sensation tends to do the same. It is true that many, if not
most, of what he presents as instances of muscular action
excited by sensations, are cases in which both the sensation
and the muscular action are probably joint effects of a physical
cause, a stimulus acting on the nerves. This misapprehension
by the author reaches its extreme point when he declares
traumatic tetanus to be produced not by the wound but by

distinction in the trains of the mind which is observed
by every body. Some trains, as those in dreams, in
delirium, in frenzy, are supposed to proceed according

the pain of the wound ; and cramps to be produced by sensations, instead of merely producing them. But the error is
quite immaterial to the theory of the Will; the two suppositions being equivalent, as a foundation for the power which
the idea of the muscular sensation acquires over the muscular
action. Whether the sensation is the cause of the automatic
action, or its effect, or a joint effect of the cause which produces
it—on all these hypotheses the sensation and the action are
conjoined in such a manner, as to form so close an association
by contiguity that the idea of the sensation becomes capable
of exciting the action. This being conceded, it follows, by the
ordinary laws of association, that whatever recals the idea of
the sensation, tends, through the idea, to produce the action.

Now, there is nothing so closely associated with the
idea of the muscular sensation, as the idea of the muscular
act itself, such as it appears to outward observation. Whatever, therefore, calls up strongly the idea of the act, is likely
to call up the idea of the accompanying muscular sensation, and so produce the act. But the idea of the act is
called up strongly by anything which makes us desire to perform it ; that is, by an association between it as a means, and
any coveted pleasure as an end. The act is thus produced by
our desire of the end ; that is (according to the author's theory
of desire) by our idea of the end, when pleasurable ; which, if
an end, it must be. The pleasurable association may be
carried over from the ultimate end to the idea of the muscular
act, through any number of intermediate links, consisting of
the successive operations, probably in themselves indifferent,
by which the end has to be compassed ; but this transfer is
strictly conformable to the laws of association. When the
pleasurable association has reached the muscular act itself,
and has caused it to be desired, the series of effects terminates
in the production of the act. What has now been described

to the established laws of association without any direction from the mind. Other trains; a piece of reasoning, for example; any process of thought, directed to an end ; are considered as wholly under the guidance of the mind. The guidance of the mind is but another name for the will. And thus it is inferred that the will is not association, but something which controuls association.

We now proceed to the solution of this difficulty. It can be supposed that the will controuls association, in only one of two ways ; either, by calling up an Idea, independently of association ; or, by making an Idea call up, not the Idea which would follow it spontaneously, but some other Idea.

The first supposition, that an Idea can be called up by the will, is relinquished by the common consent of philosophers.

We cannot will without willing something ; and in willing we must have an Idea of the thing willed. If we will an Idea, therefore, we must have the Idea. The Idea does not remain to be called up. It is called up already. To say that we will to have an Idea, when we already have it, is a mere absurdity.[64]

---

is, in the opinion of the author, the whole of what takes place in any voluntary action of the muscles. At the close of the chapter we shall consider whether there is any part of the facts, for which this theory does not sufficiently account.—*Ed.*

[64] What we have in mind when we will to remember anything, is of course not the thing to be remembered, but some collateral, or something to determine our search for it. We will to remember an opinion found in a certain book. We have not in our mind the actual opinion sought ; what we have in mind is the book, and portion of the book, and the

The second supposition is, that will can prevent an Idea from calling up one idea, make it call up another; prevent its calling up the Idea which would have followed it spontaneously, make it call up the Idea which the mind is in quest of.

The first question is, how the will, or the mind willing, can prevent an Idea from calling up another. We know that this is wholly impossible in all those cases in which the association is strong. We cannot think of colour without thinking of extension; we cannot think of the word bread without thinking of its meaning. It can be supposed that we have such power in those cases only in which an Idea has not an inseparable association with the idea in question, but only such an association with it as it has with many others. But how is it that we can hinder an idea which has those associations, from calling up any of the ideas with which it is associated? How can we foresee which of those ideas it will call up? And, if we do foresee that it will call up the idea which we desire to avoid, it follows that the Idea is already in our mind. There seems, therefore, the same incongruity in the supposition that the will can directly prevent, as that it can directly produce, an idea.

If the mind, then, possesses any power over its trains, it seems to be confined to its power of making

---

subject that the opinion refers to; and we desiderate the filling up of the blank in our present ideas. We will to remember the Greek name of the god, called by the Romans, Bacchus. We have in mind the name Bacchus, and the knowledge that the Greeks had a different name for the god; we have not in our mind that name; and we put forth an effort of recollection to arrive at it.—*B.*

an idea call up other ideas than those which it would spontaneously excite.   And if it possesses this power, it possesses that also of excluding ideas which would otherwise exist; since a new train of associations must take its origin from the state of consciousness thus produced.   It is, therefore, in this, if in any thing, that the power of willing consists.

We are, however, immediately encountered by the question, If the mind cannot will an Idea, what power does it possess of introducing any idea into a train, but such as comes of its own accord?   If it has the idea, it is in the train already.   If it has it not, what can it do in order to obtain it?   There is the existing train; but how can that be made any thing but what it is; or have any associations but those which are already established?

In cases where language is too imperfect to ensure the conveyance of definite ideas, there is an advantage in particular instances.   There are two familiar processes, which are commonly adduced as examples of the power which the mind exercises over its trains. The one is, the endeavour to recollect something we do not remember.   The other is, the process of attention.

When anything is remembered, the idea of the thing is always in the mind along with certain associations.   In recollection, therefore, the object is attained by the excitement of this idea.   Sometimes the effort which we make is successful; sometimes it is not.   We are said to will to recollect; but this is obviously an improper expression.   To recollect is to call up an Idea.   But this, as we have seen already, is not within the province of will.   When it is said that we will to recollect, the meaning only is, that we desire to recollect.

But it is also to be inquired, what here is the meaning of the word Desire. We have seen that it is a term applied to Pleasure, or the Cause of Pleasure. The idea, in this instance, which the mind is in quest of, is desired. But why desired? As Pleasure; or the Cause of Pleasure? As Cause, we may reply, in all instances. The idea is wanted for some purpose or end. In that End the pleasure is involved.

The End is thus a pleasurable, that is, an interesting, Idea. But it is in the character of interesting ideas, to dwell in the mind. The meaning is, that they are easily called up by other ideas; and, thus, that there is a perpetual recurrence of them. A young man in love, is said to be engrossed with the idea of his mistress. No sooner has her idea suggested another idea, that is, given place to it, than her idea is again suggested by another, and so on, continually. The man, who is to be executed to-morrow, can think of nothing but the terrible event which is approaching. It can be banished, hardly for an instant. Every thing serves to recall it; and along with it a rush of ideas of the most painful description. There is no law of association more remarkable than that of the rapidity with which pleasurable and painful ideas call up trains of great complexity, and the facility with which they themselves are excited by almost every idea which enters the mind.

When we endeavour, therefore, to recollect any thing, the pleasurable idea, the purpose or end, predominates in the mind, and gives birth to those associations, which are called the effort of recollection. The idea sought after, is sought as a means to this end. Till that idea is recalled, the Idea of the end, that is, an unsatisfied desire, exists, and calls up one circumstance after another, more or less connected with the Idea which is sought after. If these circumstances do not recall the idea; the feeling of unsatisfied desire still continues. The feeling of unsatisfied desire, accompanying successive cases of association, constitutes the feeling to which we give the name of effort of recollection. And the Idea of the End, perpetually calling up the idea of the absence of what is wanted, as the means to that end, and hence calling up in close association every circumstance connected with that unknown something, constitutes the feeling which we call casting about, for the unknown Idea. I believe that this is a full, though summary account of the mental process, or succession of ideas, which takes place when we endeavour to recall a forgotten idea.

The other process, through which the mind is supposed to influence its trains, is Attention. We seem to have the power of attending, or not attending to any object; by which is meant, that we can Will to attend to it, or not to attend. By attending to an object, we give it the opportunity of exciting all the ideas with which it is associated. By not attending to it we deprive it of more or less of that opportunity. And if the will has this power over every idea in a train, it has thence a power, which may be called unlimited, over the train.

What remains, therefore, to complete this inquiry, is, to point out the real process, on which the name

ATTENTION is in this manner bestowed. The exposition has been substantially given by preceding writers. But it is desirable, if it be in our power, to set forth the several steps of the process a little more distinctly than has hitherto been done.

At first sight, the objects of attention seem to be infinite. When traced to their sources, however, it is found, that they are of two species only. We attend to Sensations; we attend to Ideas; and there is no other object of our attention.

For the present purpose, it is peculiarly necessary to bear in mind the important distinction we have already noticed, between the class of indifferent sensations, and the class of pleasurable or painful, which we may call, by one name, interesting, sensations. Uninteresting sensations are never, for their own sakes, an object of attention. If ever they become objects of attention, it is when they are considered as causes, or signs, of interesting sensations.

A painful or a pleasurable sensation is a peculiar state of mind. A man knows it, only by having it; and it is impossible that by words he can convey his feeling to others. The effort, however, to convey the idea of it, has given occasion to various forms of expression, all of which are greatly imperfect. The state of mind under a pleasurable or painful sensation is such, that we say, the sensation engrosses the mind; but this really means no more than that it is a painful or pleasurable sensation; and that such a sensation is a state of mind very different from an indifferent sensation. The phrase, engrossing the mind, is sometimes exchanged for the word Attention. A pleasurable or painful sensation is said to fix the

Attention of the Mind. But if any man tries to satisfy himself what it is to have a painful sensation, and what it is to attend to it, he will find little means of distinguishing them. Having a pleasurable or painful sensation, and attending to it, seem not to be two things, but one and the same thing. The feeling a pain is attending to it; and attending to it is feeling it. The feeling is not one thing, the attention another; the feeling and the attention are the same thing.

An objector may appeal to certain cases, in which one sensation of the pleasurable or painful kind seems to be swallowed up, as it were, by another. Thus, in the agony of the gout, or toothache, the uneasiness of some local cutaneous inflammation is hardly perceived. The case here is that of two uneasy sensations, one slight, the other intense. According to the supposition, that attention is but a name given to the having of an interesting sensation, what ought to happen in this case is that precisely which does happen. The stronger sensation is, the stronger attention. And that the feebler sensation merges itself in the stronger, and is lost in it, is matter of common and obvious experience. Thus we are every instant, as long as we are awake, shutting and opening our eyelids. We are, therefore, alternately in light and darkness. But as the light is the stronger sensation of the two, we have the sensation of light without interruption. Thus, too, if a stick ignited at one end is rapidly turned round in a circle, though it is obvious that the ignited object is at only one part of the circle at a time, and all the other parts are in darkness, the circle, nevertheless, assumes the appearance of being wholly ignited. There is not a more striking exemplification of this law than what is exhibited by the comparison of our sleeping and waking thoughts. In dreams, when our trains are composed of Ideas, unmixed with sensations, the Ideas have so much vividness as to be taken for sensations.[65] In our waking trains, sensations and ideas are mixed together; but as each sensation introduces many ideas, however numerous the sensations may be, the ideas are many times more numerous. Yet such is the effect of the more vivid to obscure the less vivid feeling, that our day does not appear a day of ideas, but a day of sensations.

There are cases in which the effect which is thus produced by a stronger sensation with respect to a weaker, or by sensations with respect to ideas, is also produced by one idea with respect to another. Innumerable cases can be adduced to prove, and,

---

[65] The author makes frequent reference to dreams, but it may be doubted whether he has seized the explanation of that obscure phenomenon. It is an approximately correct statement of one circumstance of dreams, that the Ideas are unmixed with sensations; in a sound slumber, we are inaccessible to the sensations of the five senses. We are not equally fortified against the organic sensations, as those of digestion and other functions. The sensations absent are a very important class, as regards objective or outward reality; and it is probably their absence, as competitors on this ground, that allows the ideas to swell out into an unnatural and illusory prominence, as if they alone were the full reality. This is a more probable account of the illusion, than the circumstance given in the text, "the greater vividness" of the monopolising Ideas, although that too is a fact, and may tend in the same direction.—*B.*

indeed, it forms one of the great features of what we call the intellectual nature of man, that Ideas, by their accumulation, are capable of acquiring a power, superior to that of sensations, both as pleasure and as pain. The pleasures of Taste, the pleasures of Intellectual exertion, the pleasures of Virtue, acquire when duly cultivated, a power of controlling the solicitations of appetite, and are esteemed a more valuable constituent of happiness than all that sense can immediately bestow.

On the power of ideas, as the stronger feelings, to swallow up sensations, in the same manner as stronger sensations swallow up the weaker, some decisive experiments have been made. The wretches who, nearly a century ago, were made tools of in France, under the title of *convulsionnaires*, to carry on the purposes of Fanaticism, were so placed under the dominion of certain ideas, being persons of weak intellects and strong imagination, and operated upon, by men skilled in the ways of perverting feeble understandings, that the ideas became feelings far more potent than the sensations; and when the bodies of the frenzied creatures were subjected to operations calculated to produce the most intense sufferings, they denied that they felt any thing, and by the whole of their demeanour confirmed, as far as it could confirm, the truth of their asseverations. That men in the ardour of battle receive wounds of a serious nature, without being aware of them, till after a considerable lapse of time, is testified upon unsuspicious evidence.

These instances, therefore, it is manifest, form no objection to our conclusion, that the attending to an

interesting sensation, and the having the sensation,
are but two names for the same thing.

We have now to consider, what it is, to attend to
an indifferent sensation. The force of the word indifferent implies, that an indifferent sensation is not
an object of attention on its own account. If it
were an object of attention on its own account, it
would not be indifferent. If it is regarded, however,
as the cause, or the sign, of an interesting sensation,
we are already acquainted with the process which
takes place. The idea of the interesting sensation is
immediately associated with it; the state of consciousness then is not an indifferent sensation merely;
it is a sensation and an idea in union. The idea besides is an interesting idea, that of a pain or pleasure.

The union of an interesting idea, with an indifferent sensation, makes a compound state of consciousness which, as a whole, is interesting. As the
having an interesting sensation, and the attending to
it, are but two names for the same thing; the having
a sensation rendered interesting by association, and
the attending to it, cannot be regarded as two different
things. In the first case, attention is merely a sensation of a particular kind; in the second, it is merely
an association of a particular kind.

We have now to shew what takes place, when the
attention, to use the common language, is not directed
to Sensations but Ideas.

Ideas are, like sensations, of two kinds. They are
either interesting, or not interesting. We need not
repeat what has been so often said respecting the
origin and composition of those two classes of Ideas,
and the cause of their difference.

An indifferent idea, like an indifferent sensation, is, in itself, not an object of attention. If it were an object of attention, it would not be indifferent; in other words, it would be interesting. In fact, it is in the very import of the word attention, that the object of it is interesting. And if an object is interesting it must be so, either in itself, or by association.

As we found that the having an interesting sensation, and the attending to that sensation, were not two distinguishable states of consciousness, but one and the same state of consciousness, let us now observe, as carefully as we can, whether the having an interesting idea is a state of consciousness, which can be distinguished from attending to it, or whether they are not merely two names for the same thing. When the young man, in love, has the idea of the woman, who is the object of his affections, is not attention merely another word for the peculiar nature of the Idea? In like manner in the mind of the man, who is to be executed to-morrow, the idea of the terrible event before him, is an idea in the very essence of which attention is involved. Attention is but another name for the interesting character of the idea.

If there are any cases to which an objector's appeal can be made, they will be found, upon examination, to resemble those which we considered in the case of sensation, and which we found to be nothing more than instances of the prevalence of a stronger feeling over a weaker; stronger, either by its nature, or the peculiar circumstances of the moment. We shall not, therefore, stay to propound and explain them.

It only remains to expound the case in which an indifferent Idea becomes interesting by association. It cannot do so in any other way, than those in which it appeared that an indifferent sensation becomes interesting. It may be considered as the cause, or the sign, of some interesting state of consciousness. When that which is interesting becomes associated with that which is uninteresting, so as to form one compound state of consciousness, the whole is interesting. An idea, in itself indifferent, associated with interesting ideas, becomes part of a new compound which, as a whole, is interesting : and an interesting idea existing, and an interesting idea attended to, are only two names for the same thing.

In the case of Ideas, then, as in the case of sensations, attention to an interesting Idea, is merely having it ; attention to an indifferent idea, is merely associating with it some idea that is interesting.

As far then, as ATTENTION gives us power over the trains of our ideas, it is not Will which gives it to us, but the occurrence of interesting sensations, or ideas.

There is not any of the phenomena, which are usually appealed to as the great manifestations of the power of the mind over its trains, which this mode of exposition does not satisfactorily account for. We may take as a sufficient exemplification of them all, the composition of a Discourse upon any important topic. The operation of the mind upon such an occasion seems to consist in a perpetual selection ; that is, in the exercise of an uninterrupted power over the trains of association. There is no doubt that it consists of that peculiar class of associations, to which we give the names, of selection, and power.

In composing a Discourse, a man has some end in view. It is for the attainment of this end, that the Discourse is undertaken. If every thing in the discourse tends to the accomplishment of the end, the Discourse is said to be coherent, appropriate, consistent. If there are many things in it which have no tendency, or but little tendency, to the accomplishment of the end, the discourse is said to be rambling, and incoherent.

This is a case, the exposition of which corresponds very much with that which we have already explained; the endeavour to recollect a forgotten Idea. In that case, the existence of an interesting idea calls up a variety of circumstances, that is, a variety of ideas; and it very often happens, that the idea which is sought for, is called up among them.

In this case, what the seeker has occasion for, is a single Idea; a single idea accomplishes the end he has in view. In the case of the composer of a discourse a great many ideas are wanted. His end cannot be attained by one or a few. But his proceeding is precisely of the same kind in regard to his many Ideas, as that of the man who desires to recollect in regard to his single Idea. He knows there are a number of ideas, connected with the end he has in view, which he can employ for his purpose, provided he can call them up. How they are called up, after the practice we have had in those solutions, requires but little explanation. The end in view is an interesting Idea. It is, at the time, the prevalent Idea.

It is that by which the man is stimulated to action. This idea calls up by association many ideas and trains of Ideas. Of these a large proportion pass, and are not made use of. Others are detained and employed. This detaining and employing is all that needs to be explained. It is the same sort of result as the recognition of the forgotten Idea, in the case of recollection.

The forgotten Idea is an Idea associated, as cause, with the end to be obtained by it, as its effect. The same is the case with the ideas which the composer of a discourse selects out of the multitudes, which the continual suggestions of the interesting Idea by which he is actuated, that of his end, bring before him. The greater number are not associated with the idea of his end as cause and effect. Some among them are. These immediately suggest the use to be made of them; and thence, by the regular chains of association, the operations take place.

It is from these explanations, also, easy to see what constitutes the difference between the man who composes a coherent, and the man who composes a rambling discourse. In the man who composes the coherent discourse, the main Idea, that of the end in view, predominates, and controls the association, in every part of the process. It is not only the grand suggesting principle, which sets trains of the ideas connected with itself in motion; but it is the grand selecting principle. As ideas rise in the train, this interesting and predominating idea stands ready to be associated as effect with every idea in the train which can operate as cause; it so associates itself with no other; and therefore no wrong selection is made.

If, however, it does not thus predominate in the mind
of the composer of the discourse, as his exclusive end;
if it gives way at every turn to some other end; as
the idea of applause from some lively jest, from some
gaudy description, from some florid thought, the
selection is made so far upon other principles, and the
object of the discourse is forgotten.[66]

---

[66] The account here given of Attention, though full of instructive matter, I cannot consider to be at all adequate. When
it is said that a sensation, by reason of its highly pleasurable
or painful character, engrosses the mind, more is meant than
merely that it is a highly pleasurable or painful sensation.
The expression means, first, that when a sensation is highly
pleasurable or painful, it tends, more or less strongly, to exclude from consciousness all other sensations less pleasurable
or painful than itself, and to prevent the rising up of any ideas
but those which itself recals by its associations. This portion
of the facts of the case is noticed by the author, though not
sufficiently prominent in his theory. But there is another
portion, altogether untouched by him. Through this power
which the sensation has, of excluding other sensations and
ideas, it tends to prolong its own existence; to make us continue conscious of it, from the absence of other feelings which
if they were present would either prevent us from feeling it, or
would make us feel it less intensely; which is called diverting
our attention from it. This is what we mean when we say
that a pleasurable or painful idea tends to fix the attention.
We mean, that it is not easy to have, simultaneously with it,
any other sensation or idea; except the ideas called up by
itself, and which in turn recal it by association, and so
keep it present to the mind. Becoming thus a nearly exclusive object of consciousness, it is both felt with greater intensity, and acquires greater power of calling up, by association,
other ideas. There is an increase both in the multitude, the
intensity, and the distinctness of the ideas it suggests; as is

I cannot deem it necessary, after the training which
we now have had, to give these expositions in more

always the case when the suggesting sensation or idea is increased in intensity. In this manner a sensation which gets
possession of our consciousness because it is already intense,
becomes, by the fact of having taken possession, still more
intense, and obtains still greater control over the subsequent
train of our thoughts. And these also are precisely the effects
which take place when, the sensation not being so pleasurable
or painful as to produce them of itself, or in other words to
fix the attention, we fix it voluntarily. All this is as true of
Ideas as of Sensations. If a thought is highly painful, or
pleasurable, it tends to exclude all thoughts which have no
connexion with it, and which if aroused would tend to expel
it—to make us (as we say) forget the pain or the pleasure.
By thus obtaining exclusive possession of the mind, the pleasurable or painful thought is made more intense, more painful
or pleasurable; and, as is the nature of pains and pleasures,
acquires, in consequence, a greater power of calling up whatever
ideas are associated with it. All this is expressed by saying
that it fixes the attention. And ideas which are not of themselves so painful or pleasurable as to fix the attention, may
have it fixed on them by a voluntary act. In other words,
the will has power over the attention.

But how is this act of will excited, and in what does it consist? On this point the author's analysis is conclusive, and
admirable. The act, like other voluntary acts, is excited by
a motive; by the desire of some end, that is, of something
pleasurable; (including in the word pleasurable, as the author
does, exemption from pain). What happens is, that, the idea
on which we are said to fix our attention not being of itself
sufficiently pleasurable to fix it spontaneously, we form an
association between it and another pleasurable idea, and the
result then is that the attention is fixed. This is the true
account of all that we do when we fix our attention voluntarily; there is no other possible means of fixing it. It thus

minute detail.   But it seems to be proper to notice,
in a few words, the explanation which they afford of

---

appears, that the fixing of attention by an act of will depends
on the same law, as the fixing it by the natural pleasantness or painfulness of the idea.   Of itself the idea is not
pleasant or painful, or not sufficiently so to fix the attention ;
but if it were considerably more pleasant or painful than it is,
it would do so.   It becomes considerably more pleasurable by
being associated with the motive—that is, by a fresh association of pleasure with it—and the attention is fixed.   This
explanation seems complete.

It may be said, however, by an objector, that this accounts
only for the case in which the voluntary attention flows easy
and unimpeded, almost as if it were spontaneous ; when the
mere perception that the idea is connected with our purpose—
with the pleasurable end which suggested the train of thought,
at once and without difficulty produces that exclusive occupa-
tion of the mind with it, which is called fixing the attention.
But it often happens that the mere perception of its connexion
with our purpose is not sufficient : the mind still wanders from
the thought : and there is then required a supplementary
force of will, in aid of association ; an effort, which expends
energy, and is often both painful and exhausting.

Let us examine, then, what takes place in this case.   The
association of the thought with the pleasurable end in view, is
sufficient to influence the attention, but not sufficient to command it.   The will, therefore, has to be called in, to heighten
the effect.   But in this case, as in every case, the will is called
into action by a motive.   The motive, like all other motives,
is a desire.   The desire must be either the same desire which
was already felt, but made more effectual than before, or
another desire superadded to the first.   The former case pre-
supposes the latter : for the desire which was not sufficient to
fix the attention firmly on that which is the means to its
fulfilment, cannot be sufficient to call forth the voluntary effort
necessary for fixing it : some other desire must come to its

the phenomena which are usually named the power or
want of power over the trains of the ideas — in a still

assistance. What, then, is this other desire? The question
is not difficult. The present is one of the complex cases, in
which we desire a different state of our own desires. By supposition, we do not care enough for the immediate end, that is
the idea of it is not sufficiently pleasurable, or the idea of its
frustration sufficiently painful, to exert the force of association required. But we are dissatisfied with this infirmity
of our desires: we wish that we cared more for the end : we
think that it would be better for us if either this particular
end, or our ends generally, had greater command over our
thoughts and actions than they have. There is thus called up,
by our sense of the insufficiency of our attention in the particular case, the idea of another desirable end—greater vigour
and certainty in our mental operations. That idea superadds
itself to the idea of the immediate end, and this reinforcement
of the associating power at last suffices to fix the attention. Or
(which is the same thing in effect) the painful idea is called
up, of being unable to fix our attention, and being in consequence thwarted generally in our designs ; and this pain
operates, in the same manner as a pleasure, in fixing our
attention upon the thought which, if duly attended to, will
relieve us from the oppressive consciousness.

It will be asked, whence come the sense of laborious effort,
and the subsequent feeling of fatigue, which are experienced
when the attention does not fix itself spontaneously, but is
fixed with more or less difficulty by a voluntary act? I conceive them to be consequences of the prolongation of the state
designated by the author, in the text, as a state of unsatisfied
desire. That state, whatever view the psychologist takes of it,
is a condition of the brain and nerves, having physiological
consequences of great importance, and drawing largely on that
stock of what we call nervous energy, any unusual expenditure
or deficiency of which produces the feeling of exhaustion. The
waste of energy, and the subsequent exhaustion, are greatest

more important instance than the composition of a
discourse, that of the conduct of life.   Some men are
distinguished for a steady direction of their actions,
through the course of their lives, to some general end,
or ends.   One man attaches himself to the cultivation
of his mind ; another, to the accumulation of wealth ;
another, to the acquisition of fame.   There are other
men whose lives appear to be a perpetual fluctuation.
They either shift from one great end to another perpetually; or, in their trains, the great ends appear to
have no ascendancy over the little.   There are men
who seem to have a different end of their actions,
every day they rise from their beds.   The men, in
whose minds the great purposes of life seem to have
no greater ascendancy than the minor objects, are
called frivolous men.   It sometimes happens, that a

---

when the desire seems continually on the point of obtaining
its gratification, but the gratification constantly eludes it.
And this is what actually happens in the case supposed.   The
attention continually fastens on the idea which we desire to
attend to, but, from the insufficient strength of the pleasurable
or painful association, again deserts it; and the incessant
alternation of hope and disappointment produces, as in other
cases, the nervous disturbance which we call the sense of effort,
and which is physiologically followed by the sensations of nervous exhaustion.   It is probable that whatever is not muscular
in the feeling which we call a sense of effort, is the physical
effect produced by a more than usual expenditure of nervous
force : which, reduced to its elements, means a more than
usually rapid disintegration and waste of nervous substance.

Let me here remark, that the recognition, by the author of
the Analysis, of a peculiar state of consciousness called a state
of unsatisfied desire, conflicts with his doctrine that desire is
nothing but the idea of the desired pleasure as future.   In

man who chooses a frivolous end is steady in the pursuit of it. The common case, however, is, that no one frivolous end acquires a steady ascendancy; and the man is in a state of perpetual fluctuation.

The solution of these phenomena is obvious. When the idea of any of the great purposes of life exists habitually in controlling strength, it performs the same function in regard to the selection of actions, which the Idea of the end or purpose of the Discourse performs in regard to ideas, in the case of the man who is composing it. Out of the whole number of ideas, which present themselves to him, the idea of his End associates itself with those which can operate as causes of its attainment; and this association is followed by all the other associations which produce the employment of the Ideas. In like manner, when

---

what sense is it possible to speak of an unsatisfied idea? If even we insert the omitted element of Belief, and resolve desire not into the mere idea, but into the expectation of a pleasure; though we might rationally speak of an unsatisfied expectation, it would only mean an expectation not fulfilled, in other words, an expectation of pleasure not followed by the pleasure; an expectation followed by a mere negation. How a pleasant idea, followed, not by a pain, but by nothing at all, is converted into a pain, the pain of unsatisfied desire, remains to be explained: and the author has not pointed out any associations which account for it. If it be said that the expectation is perpetually renewed and perpetually disappointed, this is true, but does not account for more than a continual alternation between a pleasant idea and no idea at all. That an element of pain should enter into unsatisfied desire, is a fact not explained by the author's theory; and it stands as evidence that there is in a desire something inherently distinct from either an idea or an expectation.—*Ed.*

the great purposes of life are established into predominating ideas, they associate themselves strongly
with the ideas of those actions which contribute to
their attainment ; and those associations are followed
by all the other associations, which produce their
adoption.

The interpretation which belongs to the phrases,
when we hear of men who have, and men who have
not, their ideas and actions under command, is, that
the one set of men have certain leading ideas, called
purposes, so established, as to maintain a control over
both their Ideas and their actions ; the other set have
not ideas so formed as to exercise this ascendancy.
That man may be justly said to have the greatest
command over his ideas, whose associations with the
grand sources of felicity are the most numerous and
strong.   When the grand sources of felicity are
formed into the leading and governing ideas, each in
its due and relative strength, Education has then performed its most perfect work ; and thus the individual
becomes, to the greatest degree, the source of utility
to others, and of happiness to himself.

In regard, then, to that state of mind which precedes action, we seem to have ascertained the following indisputable facts : That actions are, in some instances, preceded by mere sensations ; that, in other
instances, they are preceded by ideas ; that, in all
cases in which the action is said to be Willed, it is
desired, as a means to an end ; or, in more accurate
language, is associated, as cause, with pleasure as
effect : that the idea of the outward appearance of the
action, thus excited by association, excites, in the
same way, the idea of the internal feelings, which are

the immediate antecedent of the action, and then the
action takes place; that whatever power we may
possess over the actions of our muscles, must be
derived from our power over our associations; and
that this power over our associations, when fully
analysed, means nothing more than the power of
certain interesting Ideas, originating in interesting
sensations, and formed into strength by association.[67][68]

---

[67] The analysis contained in this chapter affords, as it appears
to me, a sufficient theory of the manner in which all that we
denominate voluntary, whether it be a bodily action or a
modification of our mental state, comes to be produced by a
motive, i.e. by the association of an idea of pleasure or of exemption from pain with the act or the mental modification.
But there is still an unexplained residuum which has not yet
been brought to account. There are some bodily movements
the consequence of which is not pleasure, but pain. Painful
states of consciousness, no less than pleasurable ones, tend to
form strong associations with their causes or concomitants.
The idea, therefore, of a pain, will, no less than that of a pleasure, become associated with the muscular action that would
produce it, and with the muscular sensations that accompany
the action; and, as a matter of fact, we know that it does so.
Why, then, is the result not merely different, but contrary?
Why is it that the muscular action excited by association with
a pleasure, is action towards the pleasure, while that excited
by association with a pain is away from the pain? As far as
depends on the law of association, it might seem that the
action, in both cases, would be towards the fact with which the
action is associated. There are some remarkable phenomena
in which this really happens. There are cases in which a vivid
imagination of a painful fact, seems really to produce the
action which realizes the fact. Persons looking over a precipice
are said to be sometimes seized with a strong impulse to throw

themselves down.   Persons who have extreme horror of a
crime, if circumstances make the idea of committing it vividly
present to their mind, have been known, from the mere intensity of their horror, to commit the crime without any
assignable motive ; and have been unable to give any account
of why they committed it, except that the thought struck them,
that the devil tempted them, and the like.   This is the case of
what is sometimes called a fixed idea ; which has a sort of
fascinating influence, and makes people seek what they fear or
detest, instead of shunning it.   Why is not this extremely
exceptional case the common one ?   Why does the association
of pain with an act, usually excite not to that act, but to the
acts which tend to prevent the realization of the dreaded
evil ?

It seems, that as the author has had to admit as an ultimate
fact, the distinction between those of our sensations which we
call pleasures and those which we call pains, considered as
states of our passive sensibility, so also he would be compelled
to admit, as a fact unreached by his explanations, a difference
between the two in their relation to our active faculty ; an
attraction in the one case, and a repulsion in the other.   That
is, he must admit that the association of a pleasurable or painful idea (at all events when accompanied by a feeling of expectation) with a muscular act, has a specific tendency to
excite the act when the idea is that of a pleasure, but, when it
is the idea of a pain, has a specific tendency to prevent that
act, and to excite the acts that are associated with the negation of the pain.   This is precisely what we mean when we
say that pleasure is desired, that pain is an object of aversion,
and the absence of pain an object of desire.   These facts are
of course admitted by the author : and he admits them even as
ultimate : but, with his characteristic dislike to multiply
the number of ultimate facts, he merges them in the admitted
ultimate fact of the difference between pleasure and pain.   It
is chiefly in cases of this sort—in leading him to identify two
ultimate facts with one another, that his love of simplification,
in itself a feeling highly worthy of a philosopher, seems to

mislead him. Even if we consent to admit that the desire of
a pleasure is one and the same thing with the idea of a pleasure, and aversion to a pain the same thing with the idea of a
pain—it remains true that the difference which we passively
feel, between the consciousness of a pleasure and that of a pain,
is one fact, and our being stirred to seek the one and avoid
the other is another fact; and it is just this second fact that
distinguishes a mere idea of something as future, from a
desire or aversion. It is this conscious or unconscious
reference to action, which distinguishes the desire of a pleasure
from the idea of it. Desire, in short, is the initiatory stage of
volition. The author might indeed say, that this seeking of
the sensation is involved in the very fact of conceiving it as
pleasant; but this, when looked into, only means that the two
things are inseparable; not that they are, or that they can
ever be thought of, as identical; as one and the same thing.

It appears, then, that there is a law of voluntary action, the
most important one of all, which the author's explanations do
not attempt to reach. Yet there is no necessity for accepting
that law as ultimate. A theory resolving it into laws still
more fundamental, has been propounded by Mr. Bain in his
writings, and a masterly statement of it will be found in the
succeeding note. If, as I expect, this theory makes good its
footing, Mr. Bain will be the first psychologist who has succeeded in effecting a complete and correct analysis of the
Will.

In the same note will be found an analysis of the case of an
idée fixe—the most striking case of which, is that of a terrific
idea, exceptionally drawing the active power into the direction
which leads towards the dreaded catastrophe, instead of, as
usual, into the opposite direction. This peculiar case obliges
us to acknowledge the coexistence of two different modes in
which action may be excited. There is the normal agency of
the ideas of a pleasure and a pain, the one determining an
action towards the pleasure, the other an action away from the
pain; and there is the general power of an extremely strong
association of any kind, to make the action follow the idea.

The reason why the determination of action towards a pain by the idea of the pain is only exceptional, is, that in order to produce it, the general power of a strong association to excite action towards the fact which it recals, has to overcome the specific tendency of a painful association to repel action from that fact. But the intensity of the painful idea may be so great, and the association of the act with it so strong, as to overpower this repulsive force by a greater attractive force : and it is then that we find the painful idea operating on action in a mode contrary to the specific property which is characteristic of it, and which it usually obeys.

It has been suggested, that the intensity with which the mind sometimes fixes upon a frightful idea, may operate by paralysing for the time being the usual voluntary efforts to avoid pain, and so allowing the natural impulse to act on a predominant idea to come into play.—*Ed.*

[68] This chapter is a remarkably searching discussion of the Will, not as a metaphysical puzzle, but as a leading function of the mind. It is greatly superior to any previous handling of the subject.

Of the facts brought forward in illustration of voluntary movement, some are more properly referable to other parts of the mental system.

First. Such actions as sneezing, coughing, contraction of the pupil of the eye, hiccup, parturition, lock-jaw, respiration, the movements of the heart, the peristaltic movements of the intestines,—all which are stated to be movements prompted by sensation,—are nearly, if not altogether, involuntary. They are more usually termed Reflex Actions. In a certain number, sensation is present, but is not essential ; as in coughing, sneezing, parturition. In others, for example, the movements of the heart and the intestines, there is no sensation ; the assumption made in the text, that the blood cannot flow into the heart without being accompanied with sensation, is incorrect.

These actions are interesting to study in connexion with the will, but rather in the way of contrast than of similarity.

There is probably a deep community in the foundations of the two classes of movements; but, in their more obvious aspect, and for all psychological purposes, they are opposed. It is common to apply to the Reflex class the name "involuntary."

Secondly. The movements in yawning, laughter, sobbing; the altered action of the heart, the bowels, the kidneys, the skin, in Fear,—are allied with sensations or feelings; but they are not correctly classed with the Will; in fact, some of them are performed through involuntary muscles. A different view must be taken of these effects. They are the inseparable physical accompaniments of feeling; the physical side or counterpart of the mental fact; in their absence the feeling itself would not exist. Fear would not be fear, if the emotional state were not attended with a series of physical effects, partly of movement, partly of altered secretions. These physical accompaniments supply the appearances known to all men as the *expression* of feeling; which although to a great degree made up of movements, is totally distinct from the voluntary promptings of the feelings. The smile that accompanies a pleasure tasted is one thing: the activity inspired to prolong the enjoyment is another thing. The two kinds of movement are frequently mingled; thus, in acute pains, the cries and contortions of feature are the embodiment of the feeling: the gestures and movements of the body, may be partly expression, but are also attempts to obtain relief. Expression in its purity is well seen in a shock of surprise; a state which being often entirely neutral as regards pleasure or pain, has no voluntary prompting whatsoever. Every feeling has a certain definite physical embodiment with much or with little outward display; this belongs to the feeling as such; it is a phenomenon of feeling or emotion, and not of volition.

Thirdly. The operation of Ideas, in such instances as involuntary imitation, contagious convulsions, the influence of the imagination,—is a genuine source of actions, but is yet to be distinguished from the Will. When the idea of a certain medicine produces the very same effect as the medicine actually applied, when a person yawning makes the beholder yawn, or when, standing on the brink of a precipice, one is tempted to jump down,—there is no intervention of the will properly so called ; on the contrary, there may be a conflict between the influence of the idea and the true volitional promptings. The characteristic feature of the voluntary activity is to follow pleasure and to retreat from pain ; some of the tendencies growing out of an idea are in the direction of pain.

This, in many respects remarkable, phenomenon is better assigned to the Intellectual part of our nature, although it has consequences on our actions. When a sensation passes into an idea, it still retains, in a diminished form, many of its characteristic properties. The sensation of a savoury morsel in the mouth is accompanied with a gush of saliva ; the corresponding idea in any way aroused, as when just commencing to eat, induces the very same flow, expressed by the phrase "the mouth watering." The mode of interpreting the phenomenon is the announcement of a pregnant law of the mind (two-sided like the mind itself), that the idea is embodied in the same tracks as the sensation, although commonly in a weaker form. There is a standing mental determination, whereby all ideas tend to work themselves out into full actuality ; a power that the will and other influences are constantly employed in checking. The sight of a person yawning gives the idea of the act ; and the idea, unless counteracted, brings forth the reality. The sight of a precipice gives very forcibly the idea of something falling headlong down, and that idea possesses the mind of the spectator so strongly that but for a restraining volition, he would act it out in his own person.

By far the most interesting application of the law is to explain the workings of Sympathy, in the form of purely beneficent disinterested impulses. Allusion has already been made to the law, in this peculiar aspect, in a former note (Chap. XXIII. p. 302).

These three great classes of phenomena being withdrawn from the region of the Will, the remaining facts mentioned in the text can be viewed in a clearer light.

1 It is justly stated that the Will is an extensive and

laborious *acquisition*, pursued, especially at the commencement, in the midst of considerable difficulties.

2. In the mature will, the immediate antecedent of a voluntary act is an *idea* of the thing to be done. This is true, but not the precise, nor the whole truth.

3. The author's mode of viewing the influence of Attention points to the really fundamental and typical fact of the Will. He says, Attention is merely another name for the engrossing effect of a pleasurable or a painful sensation. " Having a pleasurable or painful sensation, and attending to it, seem not to be two things, but one and the same thing." That is to say, there is a power in pleasure as such, and in pain as such, to stimulate action or movement with reference to the pleasure or the pain. This is the nearest approach that is made in the text to a statement of the law of voluntary action.

The law has been differently expressed. Locke said, the will moves to the greatest uneasiness, which is no doubt the fact. Still, by a wider induction, we obtain a more comprehensive, as well as more accurate, generalization.

If we observe one of the most familiar instances of voluntary action—the process of eating, for example, we find that what happens is as follows:—The contact of the food with the tongue and palate stimulates, by an immediate impulse, all the movements of mastication and swallowing (in its first stage), and the further movements for placing more food in the mouth. We find that the intensity of the stimulation is in proportion to the degree of the pleasurable excitement, being highest at the commencement, and sinking gradually in the approach to satiety. There is no fact that can be produced more exactly typifying the primary action of the will. A tasted pleasure, everywhere, at all times, from the beginning to the close of life, is an immediate inducement to activity. Coming out of a chilling atmosphere into a place of genial warmth, our energy is at once aroused to follow the cue. The striking up of a band attracts and detains all listeners susceptible to the charm. There is, in such instances, no intermediate process of reflection, deliberation, or resolution; a

simple, an indivisible, link unites a burst of pleasure and a
burst of activity following up the pleasure.

Reverting to the first example, the act of eating, we may
detect another phase of the voluntary sequences. Suppose a
morsel, admitted in good faith, to disclose a very bad taste,
say the taste of soot; what is the immediate, unreflecting, re-
sponse? The *first* effect is a collapse and suspension of all
the masticating movements. From the earliest infancy, this
consequence would be shown. There commonly succeeds, and
often with great rapidity, a *second* effect, which we shall consider under another head—the energetic discharge of the
morsel from the mouth; but long before children are capable
of the second act, they fall into the first—the suspension of
the activity at the time.

On extending our survey to the analogous cases, we are
enabled to announce this also, as a typical situation of the
Will, namely :—That, as pleasure furthers activity in its own
direction, pain arrests activity in its own direction. Turning
a street corner, we encounter suddenly a bitter wintry blast;
we feel at once an arrest upon our movements. An ill odour,
a painful contact, a grating noise, a disagreeable spectacle,
have all the same immediate efficacy. The proper, the direct
consequent of an incursion of pain, is suspended activity. Not
only is this second law conformable to observation, it is the
implication, the obverse, of the previous law connecting
pleasure with increased activity.

The apparent exceptions to the second law need to be adverted to. The most obvious is the exciting effect of a smarting sensation, as the stroke of a whip. A light, smarting,
pungent, stimulus, amounting to pain, quickens the general
activity of the system for the time; while a more severe blow
operates according to the general principle, and suspends
activity. To quicken an animal's pace, the light smart is often
the best application; to arrest an access of action, there must
be greater severity. The excitement of an acute smart is due
not to the pain of it, but to the mere shock imparted to the
nerves; if a similar intensity of nervous shock were also a

cause of pleasure, the stimulating effect would be far greater, and more prolonged; for the element of pain, in the case of the painful smart, destroys the activity in the second stage, when the nervous excitement has subsided. Any one walking at a certain pace, and suddenly jolted, is momentarily awakened to a higher pitch of nervous excitement; but goes on, after the shock, at a slackened pace. An acute smart has thus a twofold efficacy; it is both a temporary stimulant of activity, and a cause of reduced energy on the whole, according to the second law of the Will.

Another apparent exception is the vehemence manifested in escaping from pain; a mode of activity almost indistinguishably mixed up with the writhings and contortions of a creature under suffering, in other words, with the physical embodiments of the state of pain. The sudden excitement just adverted to also enters into the complex effect; being brought out at the first moment of the infliction, and at every new twinge in fitful modes of suffering. This energetic activity for escape is a distinct aspect of voluntary power. It is Locke's typical form of the Will, but is here regarded as secondary or circuitous, and not as the primitive situation.

Thirdly. We must now then consider expressly the influence of pain in stimulating action for alleviation or escape, as when we draw back from anything that pains or offends us. To call the pain the direct stimulant in this situation, would be to connect pain and pleasure equally with the exaltation of our energies; which would be a contradiction, or else would tend to show that there is no casual connexion between pleasure or pain and our active exertions. The real motive force of pain, however, is not the state of suffering, but the *relief*; and relief from pain is another form of pleasure. That pleasure stimulates, that pain depresses, that alleviation of pain stimulates, are all one and the same phenomenon—statements of the same law.

There are two stages in the operation of pain. The first is, when under a present pain, something happens to give us relief; in which case, we experience on the instant, a burst of physical elation, exactly as from a sudden access of pleasure. In exposure to a cold wind, we have the depression accompanying a massive pain; in coming gradually under shelter, we feel buoyed and elated, our movements are quickened, and we follow the lead with growing energy. Every one has experienced the stimulus of success, and the damping effect of failure; although, practically viewed, the success should dispense with the newborn energy, and the failure should bring about an increase of exertion. It takes a mind of unusual strength, to resist these natural tendencies.

In the second stage, pain is found acting as a stimulant, without present alleviation, and therefore without the benefit of the law of pleasure. How is this? The answer is, that the *idea* of the relief is the operative circumstance. The pedestrian exposed to a freezing wind is urged to an accelerated pace, by the secondary or derived impulse, growing out of the idea or anticipation of relief through a certain amount of exertion. That this idea is the real source of the new strength, is attested by the known facts and circumstances of the situation. A sufferer, having no idea, prospect, or hope of alleviation, flags and succumbs, in accordance with the proper tendency of pain; the stimulation of the active powers does not follow the degree of the misery, but the openings of a better lot. What was noted above as the strength of mind that induces a successful man to refrain from pushing on still farther, and an unsuccessful man to struggle the more, means the firm possession of an *idea*, to oppose the power of the present,—under success, an idea of moderation, and, under misery, an idea of relief to supply the active spur that the situation restrains. We call a man strong-minded, if he resists the pressure of the actual in favour of an ideal. This is the highest manifestation of energy of will. It owes its merit, and even its meaning, to the fact that a present pleasure inflames and a present pain quenches the activities; and that, to counterwork these tendencies, there must be a strong conception of ideal pain in the one case, and of ideal pleasure in the other; which is the same law of the mind in another form. We cannot remain quiescent under a vivid and growing pleasure, unless by the prospect of pain in the distance ; nor do we rouse up under pain without some idea of relief, that is, pleasure in the distance.

No general law of the mind is more thoroughly confirmed by the experience of human actions than the principle now stated in its three several aspects. There is, as has been seen, something to be accounted for, in the lively stimulus under acute smarts ; there is, also, an obverse of this fact, in certain forms of pleasure (as gentle warmth) which are lulling and soporific ; but these are the consequence of another law of the mind, in some degree complicating the phenomena, without disproving the main law of the Will.

Possibly, this principle, wide as it is, may be subsumed under a still wider :—namely, a principle connecting pleasure with nutrition, or the supply of vital power and stimulus, and, by implication, pain with the abatement or loss of vital energy ; from which the law of the will would be a consequence. The attempt to resolve it so is highly interesting ; but, in the psychological explanation of the will, we may be satisfied, for the present, to start from the less imposing, but well-grounded generality now given. At the same time, it will be found that, having once caught a glimpse of the higher law, we cannot avoid occasionally falling into the language suggested by it ; so suitable does it often appear to the expression of the facts.

With regard to one great aspect of voluntary action,—our being moved *to* pleasure and *from* pain, the law is the full and precise summary. The element of the will remaining unexplained, is the *selection* of the proper movements in each case ; as when we start up and walk in the direction of a pleasing sound. The rendering an account of this selective adaptation is the theory of the growth or development of the will.

In the delicate and difficult enquiry as to the manner of first attaining the voluntary command of the movements, the law of the will, just expounded, must still be referred to. But taken by itself, that law does not explain the beginnings of the will. It accounts for the keeping up of a movement

bringing pleasure, and the dropping of a movement bringing
pain, but it does not account for the ability to single out, and
set a-going, movements calculated to enhance pleasure and
subdue pain, actual or distant.   There is not, within its com-
pass, any specifying or selective faculty.

The complete explanation of the Will demands a reference
to two other laws of the mind.   The first is the Spontaneous
beginning of Movements; the second, the Retentive or Asso-
ciative process constituting the basis of all our acquisitions.

By the Spontaneity of Movement is meant the tendency of
human beings, and of animals generally, to begin acting
without the express stimulus of sensation from without, and
by virtue of the fund of power residing in the active organs
themselves.   By means of nourishment, the animal is disposed
to pass into movement, from the mere abundance of the motor
energy in the nerve centres and in the muscles.   A large proportion of the activity of the more active creatures,—as the
human species (especially the young), quadrupeds, birds,
fishes, and insects,—is due to the presence of an active ma-
chinery provided with superabundance of motive power.
Apart from the stimulus of sensation, from the wants and the
pleasures of the animal, there is a necessity for the active
organs to put forth their activity.   The energy is greatly
heightened,—often doubled or tripled, by the stimulation of
the senses, and, after a certain education, by the influence of
ideas; but it is far from remaining in abeyance till operated
upon by stimulants from without or from within.

Besides summing up a large amount of the activity familiar
to us in the life of human beings, and of animals, this Spontaneity has a special importance as a starting-point for the
will.   We have seen that the difficulty unprovided for by the
law of pleasure and pain, is the singling out, or commencing,
of the suitable movements.   The utmost that the law can
ensure is to retain or continue them, when once commenced.
Now, the tendency to spontaneous action applies to all the
voluntary members—locomotive organs, trunk, head, jaw,

tongue, mouth, eyes, voice, &c. There is, at the outset, no
rule or order for the spontaneous outburst, except the physical
condition of each organ, including the nervous connexions.
The animal, in its exuberant phase, after nourishment and
rest, may become active at any point; it may run, gesticulate,
chew, gaze, cry out; or having expended itself in any one
direction, it may fall into other regions of activity where the
force is still abundant.

One or two instances must here suffice to indicate the process of attaining the selective faculty of the will, through
Spontaneity, joined with the law of pleasure and pain. In the
maturity of the will, we have the power of following with the
eyes a moving object, partly by revolving the eye-balls, and
partly by turning the head. An infant has no such power.
The manner of arriving at it is open to observation, and is
typical of the less obvious cases. Suppose the child to have
its gaze fixed upon a light, or some other appearance of a
stimulating kind. The physical effect of the stimulus, always
conjoined with the mental effect, is an increase of energy (by
the primary law of the will), which would manifest itself in
quickening and retaining the child's gaze; there is displayed
a more energetic strain of the attention than had existed when
the eyes found nothing to impart a special charm. Suppose
next that the light is withdrawn, by being moved to one side.
The loss of the stimulus instantly works as a depression; the
heightened strain of attention collapses. Still, the child is
not reduced to absolute quiescence; it has an internal fund of
energy, independent of casual stimulations; the flowing out of
this energy consists in a series of movements for the most part
at random. It may happen, that one of these chance movements is a rotation of the eyes, or of the head, in the exact
direction of the pleasing object, and therefore tending to
recover the illumination. Instantly, there is a burst of heightened energy, according to the law of pleasure; and the movement accidentally commenced is persistently stimulated so long
as the pleasure of the spectacle grows or continues. The con-
currence is fortuitous; the prolongation of it is not fortuitous,

but follows the law of the will—the abiding by whatever move-ment is giving pleasure.

The completing step is due to the Retentive or plastic power of the mind. An association is begun between the optical effect of a light retreating from the full gaze to the right or to the left, and the muscular movements that enable the eye to follow it. After a certain number of similar chance coincidences, this bond of association is rendered firm enough to ensure the movement at once when the sensation is present ; and one of the many thousand links constituting the mature will is thereby forged. The very same course of proceeding is followed in a host of other instances.

The beginnings of Imitation are also highly illustrative of the process. There is no trace of imitative power during the first months of infancy. The rise and progress of the power may be visibly discerned by any observer ; and perhaps the best example for the purpose is Speech. In the beginnings of this extensive acquirement, the basis is most obviously the infant's spontaneous articulations ; these must be waited for by the instructor, who can only foster and maintain them when they come. The law of the will provides for the fostering part of the process. The child is, in all probability, gratified by the sound of its voice, when it gives forth any new sound, and so is stimulated to keep up the vocal exertion. Next in efficacy is the catching up and repeating of the sound by others, which is an addition to the pleasing stimulus. Under the two-fold agency, there is opportunity for an association to grow up between the vocal impulse and the sensation of the sound heard ; which association is ultimately the medium of bringing on the articulation whenever it is desired.

The other cases of Imitation describe the same routine. The movements are initiated by random spontaneity ; and when they arise, they are accompanied by a sensible impression on the eye, or on the ear ; the concurrences, being regular and uniform, are at length contiguously associated ; the muscular exertion of lifting the hand is connected with the visible pic-ture of a lifted hand. At a certain stage, the association may be brought to operate in the inverted order,—the sensation first,—the movement next,—which is the whole fact of Imitation.

A numerous class of voluntary links consists in obeying the word of command, or in following verbal directions. This, as will be admitted, can be nothing but association. It is an association that would not be attainable without the spontaneous commencement. A child, or an animal, must perform a certain action, *proprio motu*, in the first instance; the name is then uttered in company with it; this being done repeatedly, a connexion is made whereby the word can induce or single out the movement.

In the training of animals, a hastening process is resorted to, which well exemplifies the difficulties in the early education of the will. In breaking a horse, the whip and the curb form the earliest instrumentality. The animal must still commence moving of its own accord. The business is to guide the spontaneity into definite channels, in consistency with the law of the will, and to connect all the various desired movements with language and signs, by whose means they can always be brought into play. When the colt under discipline is moving in the desired pace, it is allowed to go on without molestation or hindrance; when it deviates in any way, it is made to feel the pain of the whip or other check; this, by the law of pain, abates the existing movements; and if the abatement is the thing sought, the end is gained. The application may, however, be such as to quicken the movements by the smarting stimulus; an effect both exceptional and uncertain, and of use as causing a diversion of pace, out of which may come the movement desired. The surest agency of control, however, in the early and crude stage of the will, is the abatement of an excessive or a wrong movement by a decidedly painful check, such as the operation of the curb, which by pressing severely on a sensitive surface, is a certain means of depression; whereas, the light, irritating smart of the whip operates by a spasmodic uncertain stimulation. It is by the tendency of pain to put an arrest upon the wrong movement, and of the relief from pain to indicate the right movement, that the trainer secures the obedience of the animal ; he, at the same time, familiarizing its ear with the sounds that are to signify the various paces and movements. The spontaneous commencement is essential under all circumstances ; according as this spontaneity is, from the first, ready, vigorous, and various, is the facility in attaining and cementing the initial links of voluntary command.

It will now be apparent that the immediate antecedent of a voluntary act is not solely the idea of the action to be performed. The successive upbuilding of the voluntary associations developes a series of phases, under which the direct antecedent is transformed into various shapes. The sensation of hunger may be the sole antecedent in prompting an animal to the search for food ; the painful sensation is coupled at a very early stage with the sight and the idea of food. When a child first attains the power of lifting a sweet morsel to its mouth, the antecedent of the voluntary act is the sight of the morsel coupled with the remembrance of the sweetness. A farther advance takes place by associating the ultimate object with intermediate actions, as when the child learns to entreat what it wants from other persons. The stage that first brings in an idea of the moving members themselves is Imitation ; in imitating by sight, the antecedent is the view of the parts moved. Through this medium, we pass to what is popularly considered the type of voluntary control, the moving from a wish to move. I will to raise the arm, and the act follows ; the antecedent is the idea of the raised arm (together with some feeling to be gratified by the act). In the highest developments of voluntary acquisition, there is another case, also of frequent occurrence ; namely, where the intellectual antecedent is the idea of the work to be done ; as, for example, in the act of washing the hands, where we do not think of the movements to be gone through, but of a certain appearance to be produced.

In Chapter X., on Memory, it is remarked:—'When we

are said to will, there must be in the mind what is willed.'
But the idea of what is immediately willed, with reference to
the same ultimate end, may assume all the variations above
described.   To gain a pleasure or free ourselves from a pain,
we may employ different instrumentalities; and the explanation of the will should comprehend them all.—*B*.

CHAPTER XXV.

INTENTION.

THE word "intend," the concrete, seems to be employed on two occasions. 1. We are said to intend, or not to intend, certain actions of our own. 2. And we are said to intend, or not to intend, certain consequences of our own actions.

We have to examine what is the state of mind which the word designates on each of those occasions.

1. We are said to intend only a *future* action. When the action is immediate, we are not said to INTEND, but to WILL it; an action intended, is an action of ours contemplated as *future*, or certainly to be.

We have minutely analysed, on a former occasion, the state of mind which exists, when events, other than actions of our own, are contemplated as future. An association, from prior habit, exists, between antecedent and consequent, in a series of events; an association, such, that we cannot think of one of the events as existing, without thinking of the others as existing; that is, without anticipating their existence.

That this process is involved in anticipating that peculiar event, called an action of our own, cannot be doubted. The only question is, what are the circumstances from which it derives its peculiar character.

Something peculiar is imparted to it, from the very circumstance of its being an action of our own. In anticipating an action of our own, we necessarily anticipate the mental processes, which are its antecedents. Among these we necessarily anticipate what is called the act of willing. In such anticipations, the association is of that intimate character, which constitutes belief. In anticipating an action of our own, therefore, we contemplate the act as certainly future : that is, we believe that we shall will it. But to look forward through a certain train of antecedents and consequents, the concluding part of which is a certain act, which we shall then will, and then do, is a process which apparently involves in it all that is meant by what, in this class of cases, we call Intention.

It may still, however, be objected, that the explanation thus presented, recognises, in the state of mind in question, only the ideas involved in the process called willing, with the idea of the action, and the belief that the action will take place ; but that there seems to be something more than the present existence of ideas and belief, in that state of mind which we call intending, which seems to partake of the nature of willing at the moment of its existence.

There is something here of the customary illusions of language. The word "intend" is an active verb. And, wherever we use an active verb, we have the association of activity and of willing, involved in it.

That there can be nothing of willing in the case, is abundantly certain; since the will relates only to immediate acts.

It may, however, be objected, that though there is nothing of willing in the case, there is nevertheless a determination or purpose to will. A man may say, I not only believe that I shall act so and so, but I am determined that I shall act so and so.

In this objection, the words "determine," and "determination," are still but substitutes for "intend," and "intention." At most, they only mark a degree of strength in the intention. There is another expression, however, which deserves notice. A man may not only resolve to do a thing, but he may promise to do it. And the promises of men form a very important class of their actions.

After all, a Promise is in its very essence merely the *Declaration* of an *Intention*. If it be asserted that it is not only the declaration of an intention, but the declaration that nothing shall occur to hinder that intention of its effect ; what is this but the declaration of another intention ; the intention not to frustrate an existing intention ? But this second intention is included in the first. The very existence of an intention implies the absence of any counter intention.

Why is it that a man intends ? For the same reason, of course, that he wills. In willing, a certain act is contemplated as a cause of pleasure ; an immediate act, and an immediate pleasure. In intending, a certain future act is contemplated as cause of a future pleasure. The idea of the pleasure and its cause, united by association, constitute the motive. In this act of anticipation, the sequence, consisting of motive as cause, action as effect, is indissoluble. In our supposed state of intention, the motive is presented to the mind as about to exist at the time in contemplation; the idea of the act as existing irresistibly follows. An act of our own anticipated by irresistible association, when the motive is immediate, is willed; when the motive is future, is intended. Intention is the strong anticipation of a future will. But every thing which strengthens the motive, that is, associates the idea of the act with that of a greater amount of good arising from it, increases the certainty of the act. A promise to perform the act strengthens the motive; in some cases exceedingly. As it is of great consequence to men in general, that promises should be performed, they take care to reward the performing of promises, to punish the non-performing of them, with their favour in the one case, their disfavour in the other. When the favour and disfavour of mankind are general, and strong, to a certain degree, they amount to the highest of all punishments, and all rewards. A promise, then, which is the *declaration* of an intention, greatly strengthens the certainty of the act, by greatly adding to the force of the motive.

2. The next case of the meaning of Intention is of easy explanation. When we will, or when we intend, an action, we either foresee, or do not foresee, certain of its consequences. In what associations the act of foreseeing or anticipating consists, we need not again explain. The question, whether a man did

or did not foresee certain consequents of his acts, is of great importance in certain cases of judicature, because upon this circumstance depends the propriety of a less or greater degree of punishment, perhaps the propriety or impropriety of punishing at all.

A person administers to another person a medicine. It turns out to be poison. The person whose act the administration was, believing the drug to be salubrious, not hurtful, anticipated good consequences; in other words, intended the benefit of the patient; intending, and anticipating, here, being only two names for the same thing. He did not foresee the evil consequences; and this we commonly express by saying he did not intend them. If the person who administered the drug, instead of believing it to be a proper medicine, and anticipating from it salutary effects, knew it to be poison, anticipating from it destructive effects, he would be said to intend those effects.

It thus appears, that when a man, having certain consequences of an act in view, proceeds to the performance of the act, the having in view, or anticipating, receives, in these circumstances, the name of intention. It is a case of anticipation, anticipation in peculiar circumstances, and is marked by a peculiar name.

The consequence of an act may be such, that the person had no reason to anticipate them, or could not possibly anticipate them; or they may be such, that, though actually not foreseen, they might, with more or less of care, have been foreseen. These are questions respecting the nature of one solitary act.

They are what in law are called questions of fact. The exact determination of them is essential to the right decision of the judge in the particular case; but any further consideration of them is not within the province of this inquiry.[69]

[69] This chapter is devoted to clearing up the confusion and disentangling the ambiguity connected with the word Intention. And it fully attains the purpose, save where the refusal to admit any difference between expectation and a strong association, throws a certain haze over an operation into which they both enter.

Intention, when the word is used in reference to our future conduct, is well characterized by the author as "the strong anticipation of a future will." It is an unfaltering present belief that we shall hereafter will a particular act, or a particular course of action. There may be, over and above this belief, an intention "that nothing shall occur to hinder that intention of its effect;" "the intention not to frustrate an existing intention." The author thinks that "this second intention is included in the first:" but it is not necessarily so. It is the first intention, fortified by some additional motive which creates a special desire that this particular desire and intention should continue. It is another case of what the author never recognizes, the desire of a desire.

Intention, when we are said to intend the consequences of our actions, means the foresight, or expectation of those consequences; which is a totally different thing from desiring them. The particular consequences in question, though foreseen may be disagreeable to us: the act may be done for the sake of other consequences. Intention, and motive, are two very different things. But it is the intention, that is, the foresight of consequences, which constitutes the moral rightness or wrongness of the act. Which among the many consequences of a crime, are those, foresight of which constitutes guilt, and non-foresight entitles to acquittal, depends on the par-

Thus, then, the Exposition of the Human Mind, as far as the imperfection of the execution may allow the accomplishment to be predicated of the attempt, may be regarded as brought to its close. The phenomena which characterize man as a thinking Being, have been brought forward, have been carefully resolved into their component elements, and traced to certain general and undisputed laws. I should call this the THEORY of the Human Mind, if I could hope that the word would be understood in its original and literal meaning, that is, VIEWING or OBSERVING, AND CORRECTLY RECORDING THE MATTERS OBSERVED. This is the task, the execution of which

---

ticular nature of the case. We may say generally, that it is the hurtful consequences. When the question arises judicially, we must say it is the consequences which the law intended to prevent. Reverting to the author's illustration; a person who gives a drug to a patient, who dies in consequence, is not guilty (at least of intentional crime) if he expected good consequences, or no consequences at all, from its administration. He is guilty, if he expected that the consequence would be death; because that was the consequence which the legislator intended to prevent. He is guilty, even if he thought that the death of the patient would be a good to the world: because, though the law did not intend to prevent good to the world, it did intend to prevent persons from killing one another. Judged by a moral instead of a legal standard, the man may be innocent; or guilty of a different offence, that of not using his thinking faculty with sufficient calmness and impartiality, to perceive that in such a case as that of taking life, the general presumption of pernicious consequences ought to outweigh a particular person's opinion that preponderant good consequences would be produced in the particular instance.—*Ed.*

has been endeavoured throughout the preceding pages. But, unhappily, the word Theory has been perverted to denote an operation very different from this, an operation by which VIEWING OBSERVING—is superseded; an operation which essentially consists in SUPPOSING, AND SETTING DOWN MATTERS SUPPOSED AS MATTERS OBSERVED. Theory, in fact, has been confounded with Hypothesis; and it is probably vain to think of restoring it to its proper signification.

If, however, the *Theoretical*, or Expository part of the Doctrine of the Human Mind were perfected; another great branch, the *Practical* (which, to be rationally founded, must be founded on the Theoretical) would still remain. This subject, it appears, might be conveniently treated in three Books:

I. The Book of Logic; containing the Practical Rules for conducting the mind in its search after Truth:

II. The Book of Ethics; or the Book of Rules for regulating the actions of human beings, so as to deduce from them the greatest amount of good, both to the actor himself, and to his fellow-creatures at large:

III. The Book of Education; or the Book of Rules, for training the Individual to the greatest excellence of his nature; that is, to the highest possible state of efficiency (ability and will included), as cause of good to himself, and to his species.

THE END.

LONDON:
SAVILL, EDWARDS AND CO., PRINTERS, CHANDOS STREET,
COVENT GARDEN.

39 PATERNOSTER ROW, E.C.

LONDON, *July* 1879.

GENERAL LIST OF WORKS

PUBLISHED BY

MESSRS. LONGMANS, GREEN & CO

———∘⦂⫶⦂∘•———

HISTORY, POLITICS, HISTORICAL MEMOIRS, &c.

A History of England
from the Conclusion of the Great War in 1815. By SPENCER WALPOLE, Author of 'Life of the Rt. Hon. Spencer Perceval.' VOLS. I. & II. 8vo. 36s.

History of England in
the 18th Century. By W. E. H. LECKY, M.A. VOLS. I. & II. 1700–1760. 2 vols. 8vo. 36s.

The History of England
from the Accession of James II. By the Right Hon. Lord MACAULAY.

STUDENT'S EDITION, 2 vols. cr. 8vo. 12s.
PEOPLE'S EDITION, 4 vols. cr. 8vo. 16s.
CABINET EDITION, 8 vols. post 8vo. 48s.
LIBRARY EDITION, 5 vols. 8vo. £4.

Critical and Historical
Essays contributed to the Edinburgh Review. By the Right Hon. Lord MACAULAY.

CHEAP EDITION, crown 8vo. 3s. 6d.
STUDENT'S EDITION, crown 8vo. 6s.
PEOPLE'S EDITION, 2 vols. crown 8vo. 8s.
CABINET EDITION, 4 vols. 24s.
LIBRARY EDITION, 3 vols. 8vo. 36s.

Lord Macaulay's Works.
Complete and uniform Library Edition. Edited by his Sister, Lady TREVELYAN. 8 vols. 8vo. with Portrait £5. 5s.

The History of England
from the Fall of Wolsey to the Defeat of the Spanish Armada. By J. A. FROUDE, M.A.

CABINET EDITION, 12 vols. cr. 8vo. £3. 12s.
LIBRARY EDITION, 12 vols. 8vo. £8. 18s.

The English in Ireland
in the Eighteenth Century. By J. A. FROUDE, M.A. 3 vols. 8vo. £2. 8s.

Journal of the Reigns of
King George IV. and King William IV. By the late C. C. F. GREVILLE, Esq. Edited by H. REEVE, Esq. Fifth Edition. 3 vols. 8vo. price 36s.

The Life of Napoleon III.
derived from State Records Unpublished Family Correspondence, and Personal Testimony. By BLANCHARD JERROLD. In Four Volumes, 8vo. with numerous Portraits and Facsimiles. VOLS. I. to III. price 18s. each.

The Constitutional History of England since the Accession
of George III. 1760–1870. By Sir THOMAS ERSKINE MAY, K.C.B. D.C.L. Fifth Edition. 3 vols. crown 8vo. 18s.

Democracy in Europe;
a History. By Sir THOMAS ERSKINE MAY, K.C.B. D.C.L. 2 vols. 8vo. 32s.

A

Introductory Lectures on

Modern History delivered in 1841 and 1842. By the late Rev. T. ARNOLD, D.D. 8vo. price 7s. 6d.

On Parliamentary Go-

vernment in England; its Origin, Development, and Practical Operation. By ALPHEUS TODD. 2 vols. 8vo. price £1. 17s.

History of Civilisation in

England and France, Spain and Scotland. By HENRY THOMAS BUCKLE. 3 vols. crown 8vo. 24s.

Lectures on the History

of England from the Earliest Times to the Death of King Edward II. By W. LONGMAN, F.S.A. Maps and Illustrations. 8vo. 15s.

History of the Life &

Times of Edward III. By W. LONG-MAN, F.S.A. With 9 Maps, 8 Plates, and 16 Woodcuts. 2 vols. 8vo. 28s.

History of the Life and

Reign of Richard III. To which is added the Story of PERKIN WARBECK, from Original Documents. By JAMES GAIRDNER. With Portrait and Map. Second Edition. Crown 8vo. 10s. 6d.

Memoirs of the Civil

War in Wales and the Marches, 1642-1649. By JOHN ROLAND PHILLIPS, of Lincoln's Inn, Barrister-at-Law. Second Edition, in One Volume. 8vo. 16s.

The Life of Simon de

Montfort, Earl of Leicester, with special reference to the Parliamentary History of his time. By G. W. PROTHERO. Crown 8vo. Maps, 9s.

History of England un-

der the Duke of Buckingham and Charles I. 1624-1628. By S. R. GARDINER. 2 vols. 8vo. Maps, 24s.

The Personal Govern-

ment of Charles I. from the Death of Buckingham to the Declaration in favour of Ship Money, 1628-1637. By S. R. GARDINER. 2 vols. 8vo. 24s.

Popular History of

France, from the Earliest Times to the Death of Louis XIV. By ELIZA-BETH M. SEWELL. With 8 Maps. Crown 8vo. 7s. 6d.

The Famine Campaign in

Southern India, (Madras, Bombay, and Mysore,) in 1876-78. By WIL-LIAM DIGBY, Secretary of the Madras Famine Committee. With Maps and many Illustrations. 2 vols. 8vo. 32s.

A Student's Manual of

the History of India from the Earliest Period to the Present. By Col. MEADOWS TAYLOR, M.R.A.S. Third Thousand. Crown 8vo. Maps, 7s. 6d.

Indian Polity; a View of

the System of Administration in India. By Lieut.-Col. G. CHESNEY. 8vo. 21s.

Waterloo Lectures; a

Study of the Campaign of 1815. By Colonel C. C. CHESNEY, R.E. 8vo. 10s. 6d.

The Oxford Reformers—

John Colet, Erasmus, and Thomas More; a History of their Fellow-Work. By F. SEEBOHM. 8vo. 14s.

General History of Rome

from B.C. 753 to A.D. 476. By Dean MERIVALE, D.D. Crown 8vo. Maps, price 7s. 6d.

The Fall of the Roman

Republic; a Short History of the Last Century of the Commonwealth. By Dean MERIVALE, D.D. 12mo. 7s. 6d.

Carthage and the Cartha-

ginians. By R. BOSWORTH SMITH, M.A. Second Edition. Maps, Plans, &c. Crown 8vo. 10s. 6d.

History of the Romans

under the Empire. By Dean MERI-VALE, D.D. 8 vols. post 8vo. 48s.

The History of Rome.

By WILHELM IHNE. VOLS. I. to III. 8vo. price 45s.

The Sixth Oriental Monarchy ; or, the Geography, History, and Antiquities of Parthia. By G. RAWLINSON, M.A. With Maps and Illustrations. 8vo. 16s.

The Seventh Great Oriental Monarchy ; or, a History of the Sassanians. By G. RAWLINSON, M.A. With Map and 95 Illustrations. 8vo. 28s.

The History of European Morals from Augustus to Charlemagne. By W. E. H. LECKY, M.A. 2 vols. crown 8vo. 16s.

History of the Rise and Influence of the Spirit of Rationalism in Europe. By W. E. H. LECKY, M.A. 2 vols. crown 8vo. 16s.

The History of Philosophy, from Thales to Comte. By GEORGE HENRY LEWES. Fourth Edition. 2 vols. 8vo. 32s.

Zeller's Stoics, Epicureans, and Sceptics. Translated by the Rev. O. J. REICHEL, M.A. Cr. 8vo. 14s.

Zeller's Socrates & the Socratic Schools. Translated by the Rev. O. J. REICHEL, M.A. Second Edition. Crown 8vo. 10s. 6d.

Zeller's Plato & the Older Academy. Translated by S. FRANCES ALLEYNE and ALFRED GOODWIN, B.A. Crown 8vo. 18s.

Epochs of Modern History. Edited by C. COLBECK, M.A.

Church's Beginning of the Middle Ages, 2s. 6d.

Cox's Crusades, 2s. 6d.

Creighton's Age of Elizabeth, 2s. 6d.

Gairdner's Houses of Lancaster and York, 2s. 6d.

Gardiner's Puritan Revolution, 2s. 6d.

———— Thirty Years' War, 2s. 6d.

Hale's Fall of the Stuarts, 2s. 6d.

Johnson's Normans in Europe, 2s. 6d.

Ludlow's War of American Independence, 2s. 6d.

Morris's Age of Anne, 2s. 6d.

Seebohm's Protestant Revolution, price 2s. 6d.

Stubbs's Early Plantagenets, 2s. 6d.

Warburton's Edward III. 2s. 6d.

Epochs of Ancient History. Edited by the Rev. Sir G. W. COX, Bart. M.A. & C. SANKEY, M.A.

Beesly's Gracchi, Marius & Sulla, 2s. 6d.

Capes's Age of the Antonines, 2s. 6d.

———— Early Roman Empire, 2s. 6d.

Cox's Athenian Empire, 2s. 6d.

———— Greeks & Persians, 2s. 6d.

Curteis's Macedonian Empire, 2s. 6d.

Ihne's Rome to its Capture by the Gauls, 2s. 6d.

Merivale's Roman Triumvirates, 2s. 6d.

Sankey's Spartan & Theban Supremacies, 2s. 6d.

Epochs of English History. Edited by the Rev. MANDELL CREIGHTON, M.A. Fcp. 8vo. 5s.

Browning's Modern England, 1820-1874, 9d.

Cordery's Struggle against Absolute Monarchy, 1603-1688, 9d.

Creighton's (Mrs.) England a Continental Power, 1066-1216, 9d.

Creighton's (Rev. M.) Tudors and the Reformation, 1485-1603, 9d.

Rowley's Rise of the People, 1215-1485, 9d.

Rowley's Settlement of the Constitution, 1688-1778, 9d.

Tancock's England during the American & European Wars, 1778-1820, 9d.

York-Powell's Early England to the Conquest, 1s.

Creighton's Shilling History of England, introductory to the above. Fcp. 8vo. 1s.

The Student's Manual of Modern History ; the Rise and Progress of the Principal European Nations. By W. COOKE TAYLOR, LL.D. Crown 8vo. 7s. 6d.

The Student's Manual of Ancient History; the Political History, Geography and Social State of the Principal Nations of Antiquity. By W. COOKE TAYLOR, LL.D. Cr. 8vo. 7s. 6d.

BIOGRAPHICAL WORKS.

Memoirs of the Life of
Anna Jameson, Author of 'Sacred and Legendary Art' &c. By her Niece, GERARDINE MACPHERSON. 8vo. with Portrait, price 12s. 6d.

Memorials of Charlotte
Williams-Wynn. Edited by her Sister. Crown 8vo. with Portrait, price 10s. 6d.

The Life and Letters of
Lord Macaulay. By his Nephew, G. OTTO TREVELYAN, M.P.

CABINET EDITION, 2 vols. crown 8vo. 12s.
LIBRARY EDITION, 2 vols. 8vo. 36s.

The Life of Sir Martin
Frobisher, Knt. containing a Narrative of the Spanish Armada. By the Rev. FRANK JONES, B.A. Portrait, Maps, and Facsimile. Crown 8vo. 6s.

Gotthold Ephraim Les-
sing, his Life and Works. By HELEN ZIMMERN. Crown 8vo. 10s. 6d.

The Life, Works, and
Opinions of Heinrich Heine. By WILLIAM STIGAND. 2 vols. 8vo. Portrait, 28s.

The Life of Mozart.
Translated from the German Work of Dr. LUDWIG NOHL by Lady WALLACE. 2 vols. crown 8vo. Portraits, 21s.

Life of Robert Frampton,
D.D. Bishop of Gloucester, deprived as a Non-Juror in 1689. Edited by T. S. EVANS, M.A. Crown 8vo. 10s. 6d.

The Life of Simon de
Montfort, Earl of Leicester, with special reference to the Parliamentary History of his time. By G. W. PROTHERO. Crown 8vo. Maps, 9s.

Maunder's Biographical
Treasury ; a Dictionary of Universal Biography. Latest Edition, thoroughly revised and for the most part re-written, with over Fifteen Hundred additional Memoirs, by WILLIAM L. R. CATES. Fcp. 8vo. 6s.

Felix Mendelssohn's Let-
ters, translated by Lady WALLACE. 2 vols. crown 8vo. 5s. each.

Autobiography. By JOHN
STUART MILL. 8vo. 7s. 6d.

Apologia pro Vitâ Suâ ;
Being a History of his Religious Opinions by JOHN HENRY NEWMAN, D.D. New Edition. Crown 8vo. 6s.

Isaac Casaubon, 1559-
1614. By MARK PATTISON, Rector of Lincoln College, Oxford. 8vo. 18s.

Leaders of Public Opi-
nion in Ireland ; Swift, Flood, Grattan, O'Connell. By W. E. H. LECKY, M.A. Crown 8vo. 7s. 6d.

Essays in Ecclesiastical
Biography. By the Right Hon. Sir J. STEPHEN, LL.D. Crown 8vo. 7s. 6d.

Cæsar ; a Sketch. By JAMES
ANTHONY FROUDE, M.A. formerly Fellow of Exeter College, Oxford. With Portrait and Map. 8vo. 16s.

Life of the Duke of Wel-
lington. By the Rev. G. R. GLEIG, M.A. Crown 8vo. Portrait, 6s.

Memoirs of Sir Henry
Havelock, K.C.B. By JOHN CLARK MARSHMAN. Crown 8vo. 3s. 6d.

Vicissitudes of Families.
By Sir BERNARD BURKE, C.B. Two vols. crown 8vo. 21s.

MENTAL and POLITICAL PHILOSOPHY.

Comte's System of Positive Polity,
or Treatise upon Sociology :—

VOL. I. General View of Positivism and Introductory Principles. Translated by J. H. BRIDGES, M.B. 8vo. 21*s.*

VOL. II. The Social Statics, or the Abstract Laws of Human Order. Translated by F. HARRISON, M.A. 8vo. 14*s.*

VOL. III. The Social Dynamics, or the General Laws of Human Progress (the Philosophy of History). Translated by E. S. BEESLY, M.A. 8vo. 21*s.*

VOL. IV. The Theory of the Future of Man ; with COMTE'S Early Essays on Social Philosophy. Translated by R. CONGREVE, M.D. and H. D. HUTTON, B.A. 8vo. 24*s.*

De Tocqueville's Democracy in America,
translated by H. REEVE. 2 vols. crown 8vo. 16*s.*

Analysis of the Phenomena of the Human Mind.
By JAMES MILL. With Notes, Illustrative and Critical. 2 vols. 8vo. 28*s.*

On Representative Government.
By JOHN STUART MILL. Crown 8vo. 2*s.*

On Liberty.
By JOHN STUART MILL. Post 8vo. 7*s.* 6*d.* crown 8vo. 1*s.* 4*d.*

Principles of Political Economy.
By JOHN STUART MILL. 2 vols. 8vo. 30*s.* or 1 vol. crown 8vo. 5*s.*

Essays on some Unsettled Questions of Political Economy.
By JOHN STUART MILL. 8vo. 6*s.* 6*d.*

Utilitarianism.
By JOHN STUART MILL. 8vo. 5*s.*

The Subjection of Women.
By JOHN STUART MILL. Fourth Edition. Crown 8vo. 6*s.*

Examination of Sir William Hamilton's Philosophy.
By JOHN STUART MILL. 8vo. 16*s.*

A System of Logic, Ratiocinative and Inductive.
By JOHN STUART MILL. 2 vol. 8vo. 25*s.*

Dissertations and Discussions.
By JOHN STUART MILL. 4 vols. 8vo. price £2. 6*s.* 6*d.*

Philosophical Fragments
written during intervals of Business. By J. D. MORELL, LL.D. Crown 8vo. 5*s.*

The Philosophy of Reflection.
By S. H. HODGSON, Hon. LL.D. Edin. 2 vols. 8vo. 21*s.*

The Law of Nations considered as Independent Political Communities.
By Sir TRAVERS TWISS, D.C.L. 2 vols. 8vo. £1. 13*s.*

A Systematic View of the Science of Jurisprudence.
By SHELDON AMOS, M.A. 8vo. 18*s.*

A Primer of the English Constitution and Government.
By S. AMOS, M.A. Crown 8vo. 6*s.*

A Sketch of the History of Taxes in England
from the Earliest Times to the Present Day. By STEPHEN DOWELL. VOL. I. to the Civil War 1642. 8vo. 10*s.* 6*d.*

Principles of Economical Philosophy.
By H. D. MACLEOD, M.A. Second Edition in 2 vols. VOL. I. 8vo. 15*s.* VOL. II. PART I. 12*s.*

The Institutes of Justinian ;
with English Introduction, Translation, and Notes. By T. C. SANDARS, M.A. 8vo. 18*s.*

Lord Bacon's Works,
collected & edited by R. L. ELLIS, M.A. J. SPEDDING, M:A. and D. D. HEATH. 7 vols. 8vo. £3. 13*s.* 6*d.*

Letters and Life of Francis Bacon,
including all his Occasional Works. Collected and edited, with a Commentary, by J. SPEDDING. 7 vols. 8vo. £4. 4*s.*

The Nicomachean Ethics

of **Aristotle,** translated into English by R. WILLIAMS, B.A. Crown 8vo. price 7s. 6d.

Aristotle's Politics, Books

I. III. IV. (VII.) Greek Text, with an English Translation by W. E. BOL-LAND, M.A. and Short Essays by A. LANG, M.A. Crown 8vo. 7s. 6d.

The Politics of Aristotle;

Greek Text, with English Notes. By RICHARD CONGREVE, M.A. 8vo. 18s.

The Ethics of Aristotle;

with Essays and Notes. By Sir A. GRANT, Bart. LL.D. 2 vols. 8vo. 32s.

Bacon's Essays, with An-

notations. By R. WHATELY, D.D. 8vo. 10s. 6d.

Picture Logic; an Attempt

to Popularise the Science of Reasoning. By A. SWINBOURNE, B.A. Post 8vo. 5s.

Elements of Logic. By

R. WHATELY, D.D. 8vo. 10s. 6d. Crown 8vo. 4s. 6d.

Elements of Rhetoric.

By R. WHATELY, D.D. 8vo. 10s. 6d Crown 8vo. 4s. 6d.

On the Influence of Au-

thority in Matters of Opinion. By the late Sir. G. C. LEWIS, Bart. 8vo. 14s.

The Senses and the In-

tellect. By A. BAIN, LL.D. 8vo. 15s.

The Emotions and the

Will. By A. BAIN, LL.D. 8vo. 15s.

Mental and Moral Sci-

ence; a Compendium of Psychology and Ethics. By A. BAIN, LL.D. Crown 8vo. 10s. 6d.

An Outline of the Neces-

sary Laws of Thought; a Treatise on Pure and Applied Logic. By W. THOMSON, D.D. Crown 8vo. 6s.

Essays in Political and

Moral Philosophy. By T. E. CLIFFE LESLIE, Hon. LL.D. Dubl. of Lincoln's Inn, Barrister-at-Law; late Examiner in Polit. Econ. in the Univ. of London; Prof. of Jurisp. and Polit. Econ. in the Queen's University. 8vo. price 10s. 6d.

Hume's   Philosophical

Works. Edited, with Notes, &c. by T. H. GREEN, M.A. and the Rev. T. H. GROSE, M.A. 4 vols. 8vo. 56s. Or separately, Essays, 2 vols. 28s. Treatise on Human Nature, 2 vols. 28s.

The Schools of Charles

the Great, and the Restoration of Education in the Ninth Century. By J. BASS MULLINGER, M.A. 8vo. price 7s. 6d.

MISCELLANEOUS & CRITICAL WORKS.

The London Series of

English Classics. Edited by JOHN W. Hales, M.A. and by CHARLES S. JERRAM, M.A. Fcp. 8vo.

Bacon's Essays, annotated by E. A. ABBOT, D.D. 2 vols. 6s. or in 1 vol. without Notes, 2s. 6d.

Ben Jonson's Every Man in His Humour, by H. B. WHEATLEY, F.S.A. Price 2s. 6d.

Macaulay's Clive, by H. C. BOWEN, M.A. 2s. 6d.

Marlowe's Doctor Faustus, by W. WAGNER, Ph.D. 2s.

Milton's Paradise Regained, by C. S. JERRAM, M.A. 2s. 6d.

Pope's Select Poems, by T. ARNOLD, M.A. 2s. 6d.

Miscellaneous Writings

of J. Conington, M.A. Edited by J. A. SYMONDS, M.A. 2 vols. 8vo. 28s.

Selected Essays, chiefly

from Contributions to the Edinburgh and Quarterly Reviews. By A. HAY-WARD, Q.C. 2 vols. crown 8vo. 12s.

Literary Studies. By the
late WALTER BAGEHOT, M.A. and
Fellow of University College, London.
With a Prefatory Memoir. Edited by
R. H. HUTTON. 2 vols. 8vo. with
Portrait, 28s.

Short Studies on Great
Subjects. By J. A. FROUDE, M.A.
3 vols. crown 8vo. 18s.

Manual of English Lite-
rature, Historical and Critical. By
T. ARNOLD, M.A. Crown 8vo. 7s. 6d.

Lord Macaulay's Miscel-
laneous Writings : -

LIBRARY EDITION, 2 vols. 8vo. 21s.
PEOPLE'S EDITION, 1 vol. cr. 8vo. 4s. 6d.

Lord Macaulay's Miscel-
laneous Writings and Speeches.
Student's Edition. Crown 8vo. 6s.

Speeches of the Right
Hon. Lord Macaulay, corrected by
Himself. Crown 8vo. 3s. 6d.

Selections from the Wri-
tings of Lord Macaulay. Edited,
with Notes, by G. O. TREVELYAN,
M.P. Crown. 8vo. 6s.

The Wit and Wisdom of
the Rev. Sydney Smith. Crown
8vo. 3s. 6d.

Miscellaneous and Post-
humous Works of the late Henry
Thomas Buckle. Edited by HELEN
TAYLOR. 3 vols. 8vo. 52s. 6d.

Miscellaneous Works of
Thomas Arnold, D.D. late Head
Master of Rugby School. 8vo. 7s. 6d.

German Home Life; a
Series of Essays on the Domestic Life
of Germany. Crown 8vo. 6s.

Realities of Irish Life.
By W. STEUART TRENCH. Crown
8vo. 2s. 6d. boards, or 3s. 6d. cloth.

Max Müller and the
Philosophy of Language. By
LUDWIG NOIRÉ. 8vo. 6s.

Lectures on the Science
of Language. By F. MAX MÜLLER,
M.A. 2 vols. crown 8vo. 16s.

Chips from a German
Workshop ; Essays on the Science of
Religion, and on Mythology, Traditions
& Customs. By F. MAX MÜLLER,
M.A. 4 vols. 8vo. £2. 18s.

Language & Languages.
A Revised Edition of Chapters on Language and Families of Speech. By
F. W. FARRAR, D.D. F.R.S. Crown
8vo. 6s.

The Essays and Contri-
butions of A. K. H. B. Uniform
Cabinet Editions in crown 8vo.

Recreations of a Country Parson, Three
Series, 3s. 6d. each.

Landscapes, Churches, and Moralities,
price 3s. 6d.

Seaside Musings, 3s. 6d.

Changed Aspects of Unchanged
Truths, 3s. 6d.

Counsel and Comfort from a City
Pulpit, 3s. 6d.

Lessons of Middle Age, 3s. 6d.

Leisure Hours in Town, 3s. 6d.

Autumn Holidays of a Country Parson,
price 3s. 6d.

Sunday Afternoons at the Parish
Church of a University City, 3s. 6d.

The Commonplace Philosopher in
Town and Country, 3s. 6d.

Present-Day Thoughts, 3s. 6d.

Critical Essays of a Country Parson,
price 3s. 6d.

The Graver Thoughts of a Country
Parson, Three Series, 3s. 6d. each.

DICTIONARIES and OTHER BOOKS of REFERENCE.

Dictionary of the English Language. By R. G. LATHAM, M.A. M.D. Abridged from Dr. Latham's Edition of Johnson's English Dictionary. Medium 8vo. 24s.

A Dictionary of the English Language. By R. G. LATHAM, M.A. M.D. Founded on Johnson's English Dictionary as edited by the Rev. H. J. TODD. 4 vols. 4to. £7.

Roget's Thesaurus of English Words and Phrases, classified and arranged so as to facilitate the expression of Ideas, and assist in Literary Composition. Revised and enlarged by the Author's Son, J. L. ROGET. Crown 8vo. 10s. 6d.

English Synonymes. By E. J. WHATELY. Edited by R. WHATELY, D.D. Fcp. 8vo. 3s.

Handbook of the English Language. By R. G. LATHAM, M.A. M.D. Crown 8vo. 6s.

Contanseau's Practical Dictionary of the French and English Languages. Post 8vo. price 7s. 6d.

Contanseau's Pocket Dictionary, French and English, abridged from the Practical Dictionary by the Author. Square 18mo. 3s. 6d.

A New Pocket Dictionary of the German and English Languages. By F. W. LONGMAN, Ball. Coll. Oxford. Square 18mo. 5s.

A Practical Dictionary of the German and English Languages. By Rev. W. L. BLACKLEY, M.A. & Dr. C. M. FRIEDLÄNDER. Post 8vo. 7s. 6d.

A Dictionary of Roman and Greek Antiquities. With 2,000 Woodcuts illustrative of the Arts and Life of the Greeks and Romans. By A. RICH, B.A. Crown 8vo. 7s. 6d.

The Critical Lexicon and Concordance to the English and Greek New Testament. By the Rev. E. W. BULLINGER. Medium 8vo. 30s.

A Greek-English Lexicon. By H. G. LIDDELL, D.D. Dean of Christchurch, and R. SCOTT, D.D. Dean of Rochester. Crown 4to. 36s.

Liddell & Scott's Lexicon, Greek and English, abridged for Schools. Square 12mo. 7s. 6d.

An English-Greek Lexicon, containing all the Greek Words used by Writers of good authority. By C. D. YONGE, M.A. 4to. 21s.

Mr. Yonge's Lexicon, English and Greek, abridged from his larger Lexicon. Square 12mo. 8s. 6d.

A Latin-English Dictionary. By JOHN T. WHITE, D.D. Oxon. and J. E. RIDDLE, M.A. Oxon. Sixth Edition, revised. 1 vol. 4to. 28s.

White's College Latin-English Dictionary, for the use of University Students. Medium 8vo. 15s.

A Latin-English Dictionary for the use of Middle-Class Schools. By JOHN T. WHITE, D.D. Oxon. Square fcp. 8vo. 3s.

White's Junior Student's Latin-English and English-Latin Dictionary. Square 12mo.
ENGLISH-LATIN DICTIONARY, 5s. 6d.
LATIN-ENGLISH DICTIONARY, 7s. 6d.
COMPLETE, 12s.

M'Culloch's Dictionary of Commerce and Commercial Navigation. Re-edited by HUGH G. REID. With 11 Maps and 30 Charts. 8vo. 63s.

Keith Johnston's General Dictionary of Geography, Descriptive, Physical, Statistical, and Historical; a complete Gazetteer of the World. Medium 8vo. 42s.

The Public Schools Atlas of Ancient Geography, in 28 entirely new Coloured Maps. Edited by the Rev. G. BUTLER, M.A. Imperial 8vo. or imperial 4to. 7s. 6d.

The Public Schools Atlas of Modern Geography, in 31 entirely new Coloured Maps. Edited by the Rev. G. BUTLER, M.A. Uniform, 5s.

ASTRONOMY and METEOROLOGY.

Outlines of Astronomy.
By Sir J. F. W. Herschel, Bart. M.A. Latest Edition, with Plates and Diagrams. Square crown 8vo. 12s.

Essays on Astronomy.
A Series of Papers on Planets and Meteors, the Sun and Sun-surrounding Space, Star and Star Cloudlets. By R. A. Proctor, B.A. With 10 Plates and 24 Woodcuts. 8vo. 12s.

The Moon ; her Motions,
Aspects, Scenery, and Physical Condition. By R. A. Proctor, B.A. With Plates, Charts, Woodcuts, and Lunar Photographs. Crown 8vo. 10s.6d.

The Sun ; Ruler, Light, Fire,
and Life of the Planetary System. By R. A. Proctor, B.A. With Plates & Woodcuts. Crown 8vo. 14s.

The Orbs Around Us ;
a Series of Essays on the Moon & Planets, Meteors & Comets, the Sun & Coloured Pairs of Suns. By R. A. Proctor, B.A. With Chart and Diagrams. Crown 8vo. 7s. 6d.

Other Worlds than Ours ;
The Plurality of Worlds Studied under the Light of Recent Scientific Researches. By R. A. Proctor, B.A. With 14 Illustrations. Cr. 8vo. 10s. 6d.

The Universe of Stars ;
Presenting Researches into and New Views respecting the Constitution of the Heavens. By R. A. Proctor, B.A. Second Edition, with 22 Charts (4 Coloured) and 22 Diagrams. 8vo. price 10s. 6d.

The Transits of Venus ;
A Popular Account of Past and Coming Transits. By R. A. Proctor, B.A. 20 Plates (12 Coloured) and 27 Woodcuts. Crown 8vo. 8s. 6d.

Saturn and its System.
By R. A. Proctor, B.A. 8vo. with 14 Plate , 14s.

The Moon, and the Con-
dition and Configurations of it Surface. By E. Neison, F.R.A.S. With 26 Maps & 5 Plates. Medium 8vo. 31s. 6d.

A New Star Atlas, for the
Library, the School, and the Observatory, in 12 Circular Maps (with 2 Index Plates). By R. A. Proctor, B.A. Crown 8vo. 5s.

Larger Star Atlas, for the
Library, in Twelve Circular Maps, with Introduction and 2 Index Plates. By R. A. Proctor, B.A. Folio, 15s. or Maps only, 12s. 6d.

A Treatise on the Cy-
cloid, and on all forms of Cycloidal Curves, and on the use of Cycloidal Curves in dealing with the Motions of Planets, Comets, &c. and of Matter projected from the Sun. By R. A. Proctor, B.A. With 161 Diagrams. Crown 8vo. 10s. 6d.

Dove's Law of Storms,
considered in connexion with the Ordinary Movements of the Atmosphere. Translated by R. H. Scott, M.A. 8vo. 10s. 6d.

Air and Rain ; the Begin-
nings of a Chemical Climatology. By R. A. Smith, F.R.S. 8vo. 24s.

Schellen's Spectrum
Analysis, in its Application to Terrestrial Substances and the Physical Constitution of the Heavenly Bodies. Translated by Jane and C. Lassell, with Notes by W. Huggins, LL.D. F.R.S. 8vo. Plates and Woodcuts, 28s.

B

NATURAL HISTORY and PHYSICAL SCIENCE.

Professor Helmholtz' Popular Lectures on Scientific Subjects. Translated by E. ATKINSON, F.C.S. With numerous Wood Engravings. 8vo. 12s. 6d.

Professor Helmholtz on the Sensations of Tone, as a Physiological Basis for the Theory of Music. Translated by A. J. ELLIS, F.R.S. 8vo. 36s.

Ganot's Natural Philosophy for General Readers and Young Persons; a Course of Physics divested of Mathematical Formulæ and expressed in the language of daily life. Translated by E. ATKINSON, F.C.S. Third Edition. Plates and Woodcuts. Crown 8vo. 7s. 6d.

Ganot's Elementary Treatise on Physics, Experimental and Applied, for the use of Colleges and Schools. Translated and edited by E. ATKINSON, F.C.S. Eighth Edition. Plates and Woodcuts. Post 8vo. 15s.

Arnott's Elements of Physics or Natural Philosophy. Seventh Edition, edited by A. BAIN, LL.D. and A. S. TAYLOR, M.D. F.R.S. Crown 8vo. Woodcuts, 12s. 6d.

The Correlation of Physical Forces. By the Hon. Sir W. R. GROVE, F.R.S. &c. Sixth Edition, revised and augmented. 8vo. 15s.

Weinhold's Introduction to Experimental Physics; including Directions for Constructing Physical Apparatus and for Making Experiments. Translated by B. LOEWY, F.R.A.S. With a Preface by G. C. FOSTER, F.R.S. 8vo. Plates & Woodcuts 31s. 6d.

A Treatise on Magnetism, General and Terrestrial. By H. LLOYD, D.D. D.C.L. 8vo. 10s. 6d.

Elementary Treatise on the Wave-Theory of Light. By H. LLOYD, D.D. D.C.L. 8vo. 10s. 6d.

Fragments of Science. By JOHN TYNDALL, F.R.S. Sixth Edition, revised and augmented. 2 vols. crown 8vo. 16s.

Heat a Mode of Motion. By JOHN TYNDALL, F.R.S. Fifth Edition in preparation.

Sound. By JOHN TYNDALL, F.R.S. Third Edition, including Recent Researches on Fog-Signalling. Crown 8vo. price 10s. 6d.

Researches on Diamagnetism and Magne-Crystallic Action; including Diamagnetic Polarity. By JOHN TYNDALL, F.R.S. New Edition in preparation.

Contributions to Molecular Physics in the domain of Radiant Heat. By JOHN TYNDALL, F.R.S. Plates and Woodcuts. 8vo. 16s.

Six Lectures on Light, delivered in America in 1872 and 1873. By JOHN TYNDALL, F.R.S. Second Edition. Portrait, Plate, and Diagrams. Crown 8vo. 7s. 6d.

Lessons in Electricity at the Royal Institution, 1875-6. By JOHN TYNDALL, F.R.S. With 58 Woodcuts. Crown 8vo. 2s. 6d.

Notes of a Course of Seven Lectures on Electrical Phenomena and Theories, delivered at the Royal Institution. By JOHN TYNDALL, F.R.S. Crown 8vo. 1s. sewed, or 1s. 6d. cloth.

Notes of a Course of Nine Lectures on Light, delivered at the Royal Institution. By JOHN TYNDALL, F.R.S. Crown 8vo. 1s. sewed, or 1s. 6d. cloth.

Principles of Animal Mechanics. By the Rev. S. HAUGHTON F.R.S. Second Edition. 8vo. 21s.

Text-Books of Science,

Mechanical and Physical, adapted for the use of Artisans and of Students in Public and Science Schools. Small 8vo. with Woodcuts, &c.

Abney's Photography, 3s. 6d.

Anderson's (Sir John) Strength of Materials, 3s. 6d.

Armstrong's Organic Chemistry, 3s. 6d.

Barry's Railway Appliances, 3s. 6d.

Bloxam's Metals, 3s. 6d.

Goodeve's Mechanics, 3s. 6d.

—— —— Mechanism, 3s. 6d.

Gore's Electro-Metallurgy, 6s.

Griffin's Algebra & Trigonometry, 3/6.

Jenkin's Electricity & Magnetism, 3/6.

Maxwell's Theory of Heat, 3s. 6d.

Merrifield's Technical Arithmetic, 3s. 6d.

Miller's Inorganic Chemistry, 3s. 6d.

Preece & Sivewright's Telegraphy, 3/6.

Rutley's Study of Rocks, 4s. 6d.

Shelley's Workshop Appliances, 3s 6d.

Thomé's Structural and Physiological Botany, 6s.

Thorpe's Quantitative Analysis, 4s. 6d.

Thorpe & Muir's Qualitative Analysis, price 3s. 6d.

Tilden's Systematic Chemistry, 3s. 6d.

Unwin's Machine Design, 3s. 6d.

Watson's Plane & Solid Geometry, 3/6.

Light Science for Leisure

Hours; Familiar Essays on Scientific Subjects, Natural Phenomena, &c. By R. A. PROCTOR, B.A. 2 vols. crown 8vo. 7s. 6d. each.

An Introduction to the

Systematic Zoology and Morphology of Vertebrate Animals. By A. MACALISTER, M.D. Professor of Comparative Anatomy and Zoology, University of Dublin. With 28 Diagrams. 8vo. 10s. 6d.

The Comparative Anatomy

and Physiology of the Vertebrate Animals. By RICHARD OWEN, F.R.S. With 1,472 Woodcuts. 3 vols. 8vo. £3. 13s. 6d.

Homes without Hands;

a Description of the Habitations of Animals, classed according to their Principle of Construction. By the Rev. J. G. WOOD, M.A. With about 140 Vignettes on Wood. 8vo. 14s.

Wood's Strange Dwell-

ings; a Description of the Habitations of Animals, abridged from 'Homes without Hands.' With Frontispiece and 60 Woodcuts. Crown 8vo. 7s. 6d.

Wood's Insects at Home;

a Popular Account of British Insects, their Structure, Habits, and Transformations. With 700 Woodcuts. 8vo. 14s.

Wood's Insects Abroad;

a Popular Account of Foreign Insects, their Structure, Habits, and Transformations. With 700 Woodcuts. 8vo. 14s.

Wood's Out of Doors; a

Selection of Original Articles on Practical Natural History. With 6 Illustrations. Crown 8vo. 7s. 6d.

Wood's Bible Animals; a

description of every Living Creature mentioned in the Scriptures, from the Ape to the Coral. With 112 Vignettes. 8vo. 14s.

The Sea and its Living

Wonders. By Dr. G. HARTWIG. 8vo. with numerous Illustrations, price 10s. 6d.

Hartwig's Tropical

World. With about 200 Illustrations. 8vo. 10s. 6d.

Hartwig's Polar World;

a Description of Man and Nature in the Arctic and Antarctic Regions of the Globe. Chromoxylographs, Maps, and Woodcuts. 8vo. 10s. 6d.

Hartwig's Subterranean

World. With Maps and Woodcuts. 8vo. 10s. 6d.

Hartwig's Aerial World;

a Popular Account of the Phenomena and Life of the Atmosphere. Map, Chromoxylographs, Woodcuts. 8vo. price 10s. 6d.

Kirby and Spence's Introduction to Entomology, or Elements of the Natural History of Insects. Crown 8vo. 5s.

A Familiar History of Birds. By E. STANLEY, D.D. Fcp. 8vo. with Woodcuts, 3s. 6d.

Rocks Classified and Described. By BERNHARD VON COTTA. An English Translation, by P. H. LAWRENCE (with English, German, and French Synonymes), revised by the Author. Post 8vo. 14s.

The Geology of England and Wales; a Concise Account of the Lithological Characters, Leading Fossils, and Economic Products of the Rocks. By H. B. WOODWARD, F.G.S. Crown 8vo. Map & Woodcuts, 14s.

Keller's Lake Dwellings of Switzerland, and other Parts of Europe. Translated by JOHN E. LEE, F.S.A. F.G.S. New Edition, enlarged, with 206 Illustrations. 2 vols. royal 8vo. 42s.

The Primæval World of Switzerland. By Professor OSWAL HEER, of the University of Zurich. Edited by JAMES HEYWOOD, M.A. F.R.S. With Map, 19 Plates, & 372 Woodcuts. 2 vols. 8vo. 16s.

The Puzzle of Life and How it Has Been Put Together; a Short History of Praehistoric Vegetable and Animal Life on the Earth. By A. NICOLS, F.R.G S. With 12 Illustrations. Crown 8vo. 3s. 6d.

The Origin of Civilisation, and the Primitive Condition of Man; Mental and Social Condition of Savages. By Sir J. LUBBOCK, Bart. M.P. F.R.S. 8vo. Woodcuts, 18s.

A Dictionary of Science, Literature, and Art. Re-edited by the late W. T. BRANDE (the Author) and the Rev. Sir G. W. COX, Bart., M.A. 3 vols. medium 8vo. 63s.

The History of Modern Music, a Course of Lectures delivered at the Royal Institution. By JOHN HULLAH, LL.D. 8vo. 8s. 6d.

The Transition Period of Musical History, from the Beginning of the 17th to the Middle of the 18th Century. A Second Series of Lectures. By the same Author. 8vo. 10s. 6d.

Loudon's Encyclopædia of Plants; comprising the Specific Character, Description, Culture, History, &c. of all the Plants found in Great Britain. With upwards of 12,000 Woodcuts. 8vo. 42s.

De Caisne & Le Maout's System of Descriptive and Analytical Botany. Translated by Mrs. HOOKER; edited and arranged according to the English Botanical System, by J. D. HOOKER, M.D. With 5,500 Woodcuts. Imperial 8vo. 31s. 6d.

The Treasury of Botany, or Popular Dictionary of the Vegetable Kingdom; with which is incorporated a Glossary of Botanical Terms. Edited by J. LINDLEY, F.R.S., and T. MOORE, F.L.S. With 274 Woodcuts and 20 Steel Plates. Two Parts, fcp. 8vo. 12s.

Rivers's Orchard-House; or, the Cultivation of Fruit Trees under Glass. Sixteenth Edition, re-edited by T. F. RIVERS. Crown 8vo. with 25 Woodcuts, price 5s.

The Rose Amateur's Guide. By THOMAS RIVERS. Latest Edition. Fcp. 8vo. 4s. 6d.

Town and Window Gardening, including the Structure, Habits and Uses of Plants; a Course of Sixteen Lectures given out of School-Hours to Pupil Teachers and Children attending the Leeds Board Schools. By Mrs. BUCKTON, Member of the Leeds School Board. With 127 Woodcuts. Crown 8vo. 2s.

CHEMISTRY and PHYSIOLOGY.

Miller's Elements of Chemistry, Theoretical and Practical. Re-edited, with Additions, by H. MACLEOD, F.C.S. 3 vols. 8vo.

PART I. CHEMICAL PHYSICS. 16s.
PART II. INORGANIC CHEMISTRY, 24s.
PART III. ORGANIC CHEMISTRY, New Edition in the press.

Animal Chemistry, or the Relations of Chemistry to Physiology and Pathology : a Manual for Medical Men and Scientific Chemists. By CHARLES T. KINGZETT, F.C.S. 8vo. price 18s.

Health in the House : Twenty-five Lectures on Elementary Physiology in its Application to the Daily Wants of Man and Animals. By Mrs. BUCKTON. Crown 8vo. Woodcuts, 2s.

A Dictionary of Chemistry and the Allied Branches of other Sciences. By HENRY WATT, F.C.S. assisted by eminent Scientific and Practical Chemists. 7 vols. medium 8vo. £10. 16s. 6d.

Third Supplement, completing the Record of Chemical Discovery to the year 1877. PART I. 8vo. 36s. PART II. completion, in the press.

Select Methods in Chemical Analysis, chiefly Inorganic. By WM. CROOKES, F.R.S. With 22 Woodcuts. Crown 8vo. 12s. 6d.

The History, Products, and Processes of the Alkali Trade, including the most recent Improvements. By CHARLES T. KINGZETT, F.C.S. With 32 Woodcuts. 8vo. 12s.

The FINE ARTS and ILLUSTRATED EDITIONS.

In Fairyland ; Pictures from the Elf-World. By RICHARD DOYLE. With a Poem by W. ALLINGHAM. With 16 coloured Plates, containing 36 Designs. Folio, 15s.

Lord Macaulay's Lays of Ancient Rome. With Ninety Illustrations on Wood from Drawings by G. SCHARF. Fcp. 4to. 21s.

Miniature Edition of Macaulay's Lays of Ancient Rome, with Scharf's 90 Illustrations reduced in Lithography. Imp. 16mo. 10s. 6d.

Moore's Lalla Rookh. TENNIEL's Edition, with 68 Woodcut Illustrations. Fcp. 4to. 21s.

Moore's Irish Melodies, MACLISE's Edition, with 161 Steel Plates. Super-royal 8vo. 21s.

Lectures on Harmony, delivered at the Royal Institution. By G. A. MACFARREN. 8vo. 12s.

Sacred and Legendary Art. By Mrs. JAMESON. 6 vols. square crown 8vo. price £5. 15s. 6d.

Jameson's Legends of the Saints and Martyrs. With 19 Etchings and 187 Woodcuts. 2 vols. 31s. 6d.

Jameson's Legends of the Monastic Orders. With 11 Etchings and 88 Woodcuts. 1 vol. 21s.

Jameson's Legends of the Madonna. With 27 Etchings and 165 Woodcuts. 1 vol. 21s.

Jameson's History of the Saviour, His Types and Precursors. Completed by Lady EASTLAKE. With 13 Etchings and 281 Woodcuts. 2 vols. 42s.

The Three Cathedrals dedicated to St. Paul in London. By W. LONGMAN, F.S.A. With numerous Illustrations. Square crown 8vo. 21s.

The USEFUL ARTS, MANUFACTURES, &c.

The Art of Scientific
Discovery. By G. GORE, LL.D. F.R.S. Author of ' The Art of Electro-Metallurgy.' Crown 8vo. 15s.

The Amateur Mechanics'
Practical Handbook ; describing the different Tools required in the Workshop. By A. H. G. HOBSON. With 33 Woodcuts. Crown 8vo. 2s. 6d.

The Engineer's Valuing
Assistant. By H. D. HOSKOLD, Civil and Mining Engineer, 16 years Mining Engineer to the Dean Forest Iron Company. 8vo. 31s. 6d.

Industrial Chemistry ; a
Manual for Manufacturers and for Colleges or Technical Schools ; a Translation (by Dr. T. H. BARRY) of Stohmann and Engler's German Edition of PAYEN's ' Précis de Chimie Industrielle;' with Chapters on the Chemistry of the Metals, &c. by B. H. PAUL, Ph.D. With 698 Woodcuts. Medium 8vo. 42s.

Gwilt's Encyclopædia of
Architecture, with above 1,600 Woodcuts. Revised and extended by W. PAPWORTH. 8vo. 52s. 6d.

Lathes and Turning, Sim-
ple, Mechanical, and Ornamental. By W. H. NORTHCOTT. Second Edition, with 338 Illustrations. 8vo. 18s.

The Theory of Strains in
Girders and similar Structures, with Observations on the application of Theory to Practice, and Tables of the Strength and other Properties of Materials. By B. B. STONEY, M.A. M. Inst. C.E. Royal 8vo. with 5 Plates and 123 Woodcuts, 36s.

A Treatise on Mills and
Millwork. By the late Sir W. FAIRBAIRN, Bart. C.E. Fourth Edition, with 18 Plates and 333 Woodcuts. 1 vol. 8vo. 25s.

Useful Information for
Engineers. By the late Sir W. FAIRBAIRN, Bart. C.E. With many Plates and Woodcuts. 3 vols. crown 8vo. 31s. 6d.

The Application of Cast
and Wrought Iron to Building Purposes. By the late Sir W. FAIRBAIRN, Bart. C.E. With 6 Plates and 118 Woodcuts. 8vo. 16s.

Hints on Household
Taste in Furniture, Upholstery, and other Details. By C. L. EASTLAKE. Fourth Edition, with 100 Illustrations. Square crown 8vo. 14s.

Handbook of Practical
Telegraphy. By R. S. CULLEY, Memb. Inst. C.E. Seventh Edition. Plates & Woodcuts. 8vo. price 16s.

A Treatise on the Steam
Engine, in its various applications to Mines, Mills, Steam Navigation, Railways and Agriculture. By J. BOURNE, C.E. With Portrait, 37 Plates, and 546 Woodcuts. 4to. 42s.

Recent Improvements in
the Steam Engine. By J. BOURNE, C.E. Fcp. 8vo. Woodcuts, 6s.

Catechism of the Steam
Engine, in its various Applications. By JOHN BOURNE, C.E. Fcp. 8vo. Woodcuts, 6s.

Handbook of the Steam
Engine, a Key to the Author's Catechism of the Steam Engine. By J. BOURNE, C.E. Fcp. 8vo. Woodcuts, 9s.

Examples of Steam and
Gas Engines of the most recent Approved Types as employed in Mines, Factories, Steam Navigation, Railways and Agriculture, practically described. By JOHN BOURNE, C.E. With 54 Plates and 356 Woodcuts. 4to. 70s.

Encyclopædia of Civil
Engineering, Historical, Theoretical, and Practical. By E. CRESY, C.E. With above 3,000 Woodcuts. 8vo. 42s.

Ure's Dictionary of Arts,
Manufactures, and Mines. Seventh Edition, re-written and enlarged by R. HUNT, F.R.S. assisted by numerous contributors. With 2,604 Woodcuts. 4 vols. medium 8vo. £7. 7s.

Practical Treatise on Metallurgy.
Adapted from the last German Edition of Professor KERL'S Metallurgy by W. CROOKES, F.R.S. &c. and E. RÖHRIG, Ph.D. 3 vols. 8vo. with 625 Woodcuts. £4. 19s.

Anthracen; its Constitution,
Properties, Manufacture, and Derivatives, including Artificial Alizarin, Anthrapurpurin, &c. with their Applications in Dyeing and Printing. By G. AUERBACH. Translated by W. CROOKES, F.R.S 8vo. 12s.

On Artificial Manures,
their Chemical Selection and Scientific Application to Agriculture ; a Series of Lectures given at the Experimental Farm at Vincennes in 1867 and 1874–75. By M. GEORGES VILLE. Translated and edited by W. CROOKES, F.R.S. With 31 Plates. 8vo. 21s.

Practical Handbook of
Dyeing and Calico Printing. By W. CROOKES, F.R.S. &c. With numerous Illustration- and -pecimens of Dyed Textile Fabric . 8vo. 42s.

Mitchell's Manual of
Practical Assaying. Fourth Edition, revised, with the Recent Di-coveries incorporated, by W. CROOKES, F.R.S. Crown 8vo. Woodcuts, 31s. 6d.

Loudon's Encyclopædia
of Gardening ; the Theory and Practice of Horticulture, Floriculture, Arboriculture & Landscape Gardening. With 1,000 Woodcuts. 8vo. 21s.

Loudon's Encyclopædia
of Agriculture ; the Laying-out, Improvement, and Management of Landed Property ; the Cultivation and Economy of the Productions of Agriculture. With 1,100 Woodcuts. 8vo. 21s.

RELIGIOUS and MORAL WORKS.

Four Lectures on some
Epochs of Early Church History. By the Very Rev. C. MERIVALE, D.D. Dean of Ely. Crown 8vo. 5s.

A History of the Church
of England ; Pre-Reformation Period. By the Rev. T. P. BOULTBEE, LL.D. late Fellow of St. John's College, Cambridge. 8vo. 15s.

Sketch of the History of
the Church of England to the Revolution of 1688. By T. V. SHORT, D.D. Crown 8vo. 7s. 6d.

The English Church in
the Eighteenth Century. By CHARLES J. ABBEY, late Fellow of University College, Oxford ; and JOHN H. OVERTON, late Scholar of Lincoln College, Oxford. 2 vols. 8vo. 36s.

The Human Life of Christ
revealing the Order of the Universe, being the Hulsean Lectures for 1877 ; with an APPENDIX. By G. S. DREW, M.A. Vicar of Holy Trinity, Lambeth, 8vo. 8s.

An Exposition of the 39
Articles, Historical and Doctrinal. By E. H. BROWNE, D.D. Bishop of Winchester. Eleventh Edition. 8vo. 16s.

A Commentary on the
39 Articles, forming an Introduction to the Theology of the Church of England. By the Rev. T. P. BOULTBEE, LL.D. New Edition. Crown 8vo. 6s.

Historical Lectures on
the Life of Our Lord Jesus Christ. By C. J. ELLICOTT, D.D. 8vo. 12s.

Sermons preached most-
ly in the Chapel of Rugby School by the late T. ARNOLD, D.D. Collective Edition, revised by the Author's Daughter, Mrs.W. E. FORSTER. 6 vols. crown 8vo. 30s. or separately, 5s. each.

The Eclipse of Faith ; or
a Visit to a Religious Sceptic. By HENRY ROGERS. Fcp. 8vo. 5s.

Defence of the Eclipse of
Faith. By H. ROGERS. Fcp. 8vo. 3s. 6d.

Nature, the Utility of

Religion and Theism. Three Essays by JOHN STUART MILL. 8vo. 10s. 6d.

A Critical and Grammatical Commentary on St. Paul's

Epistles. By C. J. ELLICOTT, D.D. 8vo. Galatians, 8s. 6d. Ephesians, 8s. 6d. Pastoral Epistles, 10s. 6d. Philippians, Colossians, & Philemon, 10s. 6d. Thessalonians, 7s. 6d.

Conybeare & Howson's Life and Epistles of St. Paul.

Three Editions, copiously illustrated.

Library Edition, with all the Original Illustrations, Maps, Landscapes on Steel, Woodcuts, &c. 2 vols. 4to. 42s.

Intermediate Edition, with a Selection of Maps, Plates, and Woodcuts. 2 vols. square crown 8vo. 21s.

Student's Edition, revised and condensed, with 46 Illustrations and Maps. 1 vol. crown 8vo. 9s.

The Jewish Messiah;

Critical History of the Messianic Idea among the Jews, from the Rise of the Maccabees to the Closing of the Talmud. By JAMES DRUMMOND, B.A. 8vo. 15s.

The Prophets and Prophecy in Israel;

an Historical and Critical Inquiry. By Prof. A. KUENEN, Translated from the Dutch by the Rev. A. MILROY, M.A. with an Introduction by J. MUIR, D.C.L. 8vo. 21s.

Mythology among the Hebrews

and its Historical Development. By IGNAZ GOLDZIHER, Ph.D. Translated by RUSSELL MARTINEAU, M.A. 8vo. 16s.

Bible Studies. By M. M.

KALISCH, Ph.D. PART I. *The Prophecies of Balaam.* 8vo. 10s. 6d. PART II. *The Book of Jonah.* 8vo. 10s. 6d.

Historical and Critical Commentary on the Old Testament;

with a New Translation. By M. M. KALISCH, Ph.D. Vol. I. Genesis, 8vo. 18s. or adapted for the General Reader, 12s. Vol. II. Exodus, 15s. or adapted for the General Reader, 12s. Vol. III. Leviticus, Part I. 15s. or adapted for the General Reader, 8s. Vol. IV. Leviticus, Part II. 15s. or adapted for the General Reader, 8s.

Ewald's History of Israel.

Translated from the German by J. E. CARPENTER, M.A. with Preface by R. MARTINEAU, M.A. 5 vols. 8vo. 63s.

Ewald's Antiquities of

Israel. Translated from the German by H. S. SOLLY, M.A. 8vo. 12s. 6d.

The Types of Genesis,

briefly considered as revealing the Development of Human Nature. By A. JUKES. Crown 8vo. 7s. 6d.

The Second Death and

the Restitution of all Things; with some Preliminary Remarks on the Nature and Inspiration of Holy Scripture. By A. JUKES. Crown 8vo. 3s. 6d.

Commentaries, by the Rev.

W. A. O'CONOR, B.A. Rector of St. Simon and St. Jude, Manchester.

Epistle to the Romans, crown 8vo. 3s. 6d. Epistle to the Hebrews, 4s. 6d. St. John's Gospel, 10s. 6d.

Supernatural Religion;

an Inquiry into the Reality of Divine Revelation. Complete Edition, thoroughly revised, with New Preface and Conclusions. 3 vols. 8vo. 36s.

Lectures on the Origin

and Growth of Religion, as illustrated by the Religions of India; being the Hibbert Lectures for 1878, delivered at the Chapter House, Westminster Abbey, in 1878, by F. MAX MÜLLER, M.A. Second Edition. 8vo. price 10s. 6d.

Introduction to the Science

of Religion, Four Lectures delivered at the Royal Institution; with Two Essays on False Analogies and the Philosophy of Mythology. By MAX MÜLLER, M.A. Crown 8vo. price 10s. 6d.

The Four Gospels in

Greek, with Greek-English Lexicon. By JOHN T. WHITE, D.D. Oxon. Square 32mo. 5s.

Passing Thoughts on

Religion. By ELIZABETH M. SEWELL. Fcp. 8vo. 3s. 6d.

Thoughts for the Age.
by ELIZABETH M. SEWELL. New Edition. Fcp. 8vo. 3s. 6d.

Preparation for the Holy
Communion; the Devotions chiefly from the works of Jeremy Taylor. By ELIZABETH M. SEWELL. 32mo. 3s.

Bishop Jeremy Taylor's
Entire Works; with Life by Bishop Heber. Revised and corrected by the Rev. C. P. EDEN. 10 vols. £5. 5s.

Hymns of Praise and
Prayer. Corrected and edited by Rev. JOHN MARTINEAU, LL.D. Crown 8vo. 4s. 6d. 32mo. 1s. 6d.

Spiritual Songs for the
Sundays and Holidays throughout the Year. By J. S. B. MONSELL, LL.D. Fcp. 8vo. 5s. 18mo. 2s.

Christ the Consoler; a
Book of Comfort for the Sick. By ELLICE HOPKINS. With a Preface by the Bishop of Carlisle. Second Edition. Fcp. 8vo. 2s. 6d.

Lyra Germanica; Hymns
translated from the German by Miss C. WINKWORTH. Fcp. 8vo. 5s.

The Temporal Mission
of the Holy Ghost; or, Reason and Revelation. By HENRY EDWARD MANNING, D.D. Crown 8vo. 8s. 6d.

Hours of Thought on
Sacred Things; a Volume of Sermons. By JAMES MARTINEAU, D.D. LL.D. Crown 8vo. Price 7s. 6d.

Endeavours after the
Christian Life; Discourses. By JAMES MARTINEAU, D.D. LL.D. Fifth Edition. Crown 8vo. 7s. 6d.

The Pentateuch & Book
of Joshua Critically Examined. By J. W. COLENSO, D.D. Bishop of Natal. Crown 8vo. 6s.

Lectures on the Penta-
teuch and the Moabite Stone; with Appendices. By J. W. COLENSO, D.D. Bishop of Natal. 8vo. 12s.

TRAVELS, VOYAGES, &c.

A Voyage in the 'Sun-
beam,' our Home on the Ocean for Eleven Months. By Mrs. BRASSEY. Cheaper Edition, with Map and 65 Wood Engravings. Crown 8vo. 7s. 6d.

A Freak of Freedom;
or, the Republic of San Marino. By J. THEODORE BENT, Honorary Citizen of the same. With a Map and 15 Woodcuts. Crown 8vo. 7s. 6d.

One Thousand Miles up
the Nile; a Journey through Egypt and Nubia to the Second Cataract. By AMELIA B. EDWARDS. With Plans, Maps & Illustrations. Imperial 8vo. 42s.

The Indian Alps, and How
we Crossed them; Two Years' Residence in the Eastern Himalayas, and Two Months' Tour into the Interior. By a LADY PIONEER. With Illustrations. Imperial 8vo. 42s.

Discoveries at Ephesus,
Including the Site and Remains of the Great Temple of Diana. By J. T. WOOD, F.S.A. With 27 Lithographic Plates and 42 Wood Engravings. Medium 8vo. 63s.

Memorials of the Dis-
covery and Early Settlement of the Bermudas or Somers Islands, from 1615 to 1685. By Major-General Sir J. H. LEFROY, R.A. With Maps, &c. 2 vols. Imp. 8vo. 60s.

Eight Years in Ceylon.
By Sir SAMUEL W. BAKER, M.A. Crown 8vo. Woodcuts, 7s. 6d.

The Rifle and the Hound
in Ceylon. By Sir SAMUEL W. BAKER, M.A. Crown 8vo. Woodcuts, 7s. 6d.

Guide to the Pyrenees,

for the use of Mountaineers.   By CHARLES PACKE.   Crown 8vo. 7s. 6d.

The Alpine Club Map of

Switzerland, with parts of the Neighbouring Countries, on the scale of Four Miles to an Inch.   Edited by R. C. NICHOLS, F.R.G.S.   4 Sheets in Portfolio, 42s. coloured, or 34s. uncoloured.

The Alpine Guide.   By

JOHN BALL, M.R.I.A.   Post 8vo. with Maps and other Illustrations.

The Eastern Alps, 10s. 6d.

Central Alps, including all

the Oberland District, 7s. 6d.

Western Alps, including

Mont Blanc, Monte Rosa, Zermatt, &c. Price 6s. 6d.

On Alpine Travelling and

the Geology of the Alps.   Price 1s. Either of the 3 Volumes or Parts of the 'Alpine Guide' may be had with this Introduction prefixed, 1s. extra.

The Fenland Past and

Present.   By S. H. MILLER, F.R.A.S. F.M.S.; and S. B. J. SKERTCHLEY, F.G.S. of H.M. Geological Survey. With numerous Illustrations and Maps. Royal 8vo. 31s. 6d.   Large Paper, fcp. folio, 50s. half-morocco.

WORKS of FICTION.

Novels and Tales.   By the

Right Hon. the EARL of BEACONSFIELD, K.G.   Cabinet Editions, complete in Ten Volumes, crown 8vo. 6s. each.

Lothair, 6s.	Venetia, 6s.
Coningsby, 6s.	Alroy, Ixion, &c. 6s.
Sybil, 6s.	Young Duke &c. 6s.
Tancred, 6s.	Vivian Grey, 6s.

Henrietta Temple, 6s.

Contarini Fleming, &c. 6s.

Tales from Euripides;

Iphigenia, Alcestis, Hecuba, Helen, Medea.   By VINCENT K. COOPER, M.A. late Scholar of Brasenose College, Oxford.   Fcp. 8vo. 3s. 6d.

Whispers from Fairyland.   By the Right Hon. E. H. KNATCHBULL-HUGESSEN, M.P.   With 9 Illustrations.   Crown 8vo. 3s. 6d.

Higgledy-Piggledy; or,

Stories for Everybody and Everybody's Children.   By the Right Hon. E. H. KNATCHBULL-HUGESSEN, M.P. With 9 Illustrations.   Cr. 8vo. 3s. 6d.

Stories and Tales.   By

ELIZABETH M. SEWELL.   Cabinet Edition, in Ten Volumes, each containing a complete Tale or Story:—

Amy Herbert, 2s. 6d.   Gertrude, 2s. 6d. The Earl's Daughter, 2s. 6d.   The Experience of Life, 2s. 6d.   Cleve Hall, 2s. 6d.   Ivors, 2s. 6d.   Katharine Ashton, 2s. 6d.   Margaret Percival, 3s. 6d.   Laneton Parsonage, 3s. 6d. Ursula, 3s. 6d.

The Modern Novelist's

Library.   Each work complete in itself, price 2s. boards, or 2s. 6d. cloth.

By Lord BEACONSFIELD.

> Lothair.
> Coningsby.
> Sybil.
> Tancred.
> Venetia.
> Henrietta Temple.
> Contarini Fleming.
> Alroy, Ixion, &c.
> The Young Duke, &c.
> Vivian Grey.

THE MODERN NOVELIST'S LIBRARY *continued.*

By ANTHONY TROLLOPE.
Barchester Towers.
The Warden.

By Major WHYTE-MELVILLE.
Digby Grand.
General Bounce.
Kate Coventry.
The Gladiators.
Good for Nothing.
Holmby House.
The Interpreter.
The Queen's Maries.

By the Author of 'The Rose Garden.'
Unawares.

By the Author of ' Mlle. Mori.'
The Atelier du Lys.
Mademoiselle Mori.

By Various Writers.
Atherstone Priory.
The Burgomaster's Family.
Elsa and her Vulture.
The Six Sisters of the Valleys.

The Novels and Tales of the Right Honourable

the Earl of Beaconsfield, K.G. Complete in Ten Volumes, crown 8vo. cloth extra, gilt edges, price 30s.

POETRY and THE DRAMA.

Lays of Ancient Rome;
with Ivry and the Armada. By LORD MACAULAY. 16mo. 3s. 6d.

Horatii Opera. Library
Edition, with English Notes, Marginal References & various Readings. Edited by Rev. J. E. YONGE, M.A. 8vo. 21s.

Poems by Jean Ingelow.
2 vols. fcp. 8vo. 10s.

FIRST SERIES, containing ' Divided,' ' The Star's Monument,' &c. Fcp. 8vo. 5s.

SECOND SERIES, ' A Story of Doom,' ' Gladys and her Island,' &c. 5s.

Poems by Jean Ingelow.
First Series, with nearly 100 Woodcut Illustrations. Fcp. 4to. 21s.

Brian Boru, a Tragedy.
By J. T. B. Crown 8vo. 6s.

Festus, a Poem. By
PHILIP JAMES BAILEY. 10th Edition, enlarged & revised. Crown 8vo. 12s. 6d.

The Iliad of Homer, Ho-
mometrically translated by C. B. CAYLEY, Translator of Dante's Comedy, &c. 8vo. 12s. 6d.

The Æneid of Virgil.
Translated into English Verse. By J. CONINGTON, M.A. Crown 8vo. 9s.

Bowdler's Family Shak-
speare. Genuine Edition, in 1 vol. medium 8vo. large type, with 36 Woodcuts, 14s. or in 6 vols. fcp. 8vo. 21s.

Southey's Poetical
Works, with the Author's last Corrections and Additions. Medium 8vo. with Portrait, 14s.

RURAL SPORTS, HORSE and CATTLE MANAGEMENT, &c.

Annals of the Road; or,
Notes on Mail and Stage-Coaching in Great Britain. By Captain MALET. With 3 Woodcuts and 10 Coloured Illustrations. Medium 8vo. 21s.

Down the Road; or, Re-
miniscences of a Gentleman Coachman. By C. T. S. BIRCH REYNARDSON. Second Edition, with 12 Coloured Illustrations. Medium 8vo. 21s.

Blaine's Encyclopædia of

Rural Sports; Complete Accounts, Historical, Practical, and Descriptive, of Hunting, Shooting, Fishing, Racing, &c. With 600 Woodcuts. 8vo. 21s.

A Book on Angling ; or,

Treatise on the Art of Fishing in every branch ; including full Illustrated Lists of Salmon Flies. By FRANCIS FRANCIS. Post 8vo. Portrait and Plates, 15s.

Wilcocks's Sea-Fisher-

man : comprising the Chief Methods of Hook and Line Fishing, a glance at Nets, and remarks on Boats and Boating. Post 8vo. Woodcuts, 12s. 6d.

The Fly-Fisher's Ento-

mology. By ALFRED RONALDS. With 20 Coloured Plates. 8vo. 14s.

Horses and Riding. By

GEORGE NEVILE, M.A. With 31 Illustrations. Crown 8vo. 6s.

Horses and Stables. By

Colonel F. FITZWYGRAM, XV. the King's Hussars. With 24 Plates of Illustrations. 8vo. 10s. 6d.

Youatt on the Horse.

Revised and enlarged by W. WATSON, M.R.C.V.S. 8vo. Woodcuts, 12s. 6d.

Youatt's Work on the

Dog. Revised and enlarged. 8vo. Woodcuts, 6s.

The Dog in Health and

Disease. By STONEHENGE. With 78 Wood Engravings. Square crown 8vo. 7s. 6d.

The Greyhound. By

STONEHENGE. Revised Edition, with 25 Portraits of Greyhounds, &c. Square crown 8vo. 15s.

Stables and Stable Fit-

tings. By W. MILES. Imp. 8vo. with 13 Plates, 15s.

The Horse's Foot, and

How to keep it Sound. By W. MILES. Imp. 8vo. Woodcuts, 12s. 6d.

A Plain Treatise on

Horse-shoeing. By W. MILES. Post 8vo. Woodcuts, 2s. 6d.

Remarks on Horses'

Teeth, addressed to Purchasers. By W. MILES. Post 8vo, 1s. 6d.

The Ox, his Diseases and

their Treatment ; with an Essay on Parturition in the Cow. By J. R. DOBSON, M.R.C.V.S. Crown 8vo. Illustrations, 7s. 6d.

WORKS of UTILITY and GENERAL INFORMATION.

Maunder's Treasury of

Knowledge and Library of Reference ; comprising an English Dictionary and Grammar, Universal Gazetteer, Classical Dictionary, Chronology, Law Dictionary, Synopsis of the Peerage, Useful Tables, &c. Fcp. 8vo. 6s.

Maunder's Biographical

Treasury. Latest Edition, reconstructed and partly re-written, with above 1,600 additional Memoirs, by W. L. R. CATES. Fcp. 8vo. 6s.

Maunder's Treasury of

Natural History ; or, Popular Dictionary of Zoology. Revised and corrected Edition. Fcp. 8vo. with 900 Woodcuts, 6s.

Maunder's Scientific and

Literary Treasury ; a Popular Encyclopædia of Science, Literature, and Art. Latest Edition, partly re-written, with above 1,000 New Articles, by J. Y. JOHNSON. Fcp. 8vo. 6s.

Maunder's Treasury of

Geography, Physical, Historical, Descriptive, and Political. Edited by W. HUGHES, F.R.G.S. With 7 Maps and 16 Plates. Fcp. 8vo. 6s.

Maunder's Historical

Treasury ; Introductory Outlines of Universal History, and Separate Histories of all Nations. Revised by the Rev. Sir G. W. COX, Bart. M.A. Fcp. 8vo. 6s.

INDEX.

Spottiswoode & Co., Printers, New-street Square, London.